Bureaucrats in Business

A World Bank Policy Research Report

Bureaucrats in Business

The Economics and Politics
of Government Ownership

Published for the World Bank
OXFORD UNIVERSITY PRESS

Oxford University Press

OXFORD   NEW YORK   TORONTO
DELHI   BOMBAY   CALCUTTA   MADRAS   KARACHI
KUALA LUMPUR   SINGAPORE   HONG KONG   TOKYO
NAIROBI   DAR ES SALAAM   CAPE TOWN
MELBOURNE   AUCKLAND

and associated companies in

BERLIN   IBADAN

Published by Oxford University Press, Inc.
200 Madison Avenue, New York, N.Y. 10016

Manufactured in the United States of America
First printing September 1995

Cover photographs: At the top, a coal-fired power station; Hilary Wilkes (International
Stock). At the bottom, a labor demonstration; Peter S. Heller.

The World Bank does not guarantee the accuracy of the data included in this publication and
accepts no responsibility whatsoever for any consequence of their use.

Library of Congress Cataloging-in-Publication Data

Bureaucrats in business : the economics and politics of government ownership
    p. cm. — (World Bank policy research report, ISSN 1020-0851)
    "Published for the World Bank."
    Includes bibliographical references and index.
    ISBN 0-19-521106-5
    1. Government ownership—Developing countries. 2. Government
    business enterprises—Developing countries. 3. Industrial
    efficiency—Developing countries. 4. Socialism—Developing
    countries. 5. Developing countries—Economic conditions.
    I. International Bank for Reconstruction and Development.
    II. Series.
    HD4420.8.B87 1995
    338.6'2'091724—dc20   95-33961
                                               CIP

ISSN 1020-0851

♾ Text printed on paper that conforms to the American National Standards for Permanence
of Paper for Printed Library Materials. Z39.48-1984

Contents

Boxes

Tables

Appendix tables

Figures

Box Figures

Foreword

PUBLICATION OF THIS REPORT COMES AT A PROPITIOUS TIME. Throughout the developing world and in the transition countries, governments are striving to reform their economies. Yet in many countries, particularly the poorest, some parts of the economy have remained stubbornly resistant to reform. This report deals with one of the more important of these: the inefficient, loss-making state-owned enterprises that are a significant burden on government budgets and scarce resources in many countries. These enterprises hinder growth, impede market liberalization, and thus both directly and indirectly limit efforts to reduce poverty.

Drawing on a unique data base and detailed case studies, the report analyzes which types of state enterprise reform measures have worked best. It describes the formidable obstacles governments face when attempting to divest state-owned enterprises or otherwise improve their performance, and how successful reformers have overcome these barriers. It looks at company experience in depth and creatively applies institutional analysis to determine how contracts between management and government can serve as tools to reform enterprises. Finally, it suggests policy courses to be pursued under different country and enterprise conditions.

One central finding of the report is encouraging: some governments have indeed overcome the obstacles. Following a comprehesive reform strategy, they have divested when possible, and improved performance incentives for firms remaining in government hands. Trade and investment have usually followed, bringing more rapid growth and enhanced opportunities for society at large.

But why haven't more governments privatized or otherwise reformed state-owned enterprises? Reform entails political costs. Because politics is integral to reform, a study of reforms in public ownership cannot exclude political analysis. A key finding of the report is that political obstacles are the main reason that state enterprise reform has made so little headway in the last decade. The report makes an innovative attempt to objectively disentangle and measure the elements that constitute the political constraints on reform. While this is a significant contribution, we should also bear in mind that our analytical knowledge of political processes, though arguably older, is less complete than that of economic forces and motives. It is an area in which additional analytical work and more data will no doubt enhance our knowledge in the years to come. However, it is our belief that the thrust of the main findings of this study will hold true even with further scrutiny and more observations.

We hope that the research presented in this book will give political leaders, policymakers, and the broader development community a clearer picture of the substantial benefits that could result from state-owned enterprise reform and, just as important, a better understanding of how the obstacles to reform can be overcome.

Bureaucrats in Business is the fourth in a series of Policy Research Reports designed to bring to a wide audience the results of World Bank research on development policy issues. While accessible to nonspecialists, books in the series also seek to move forward the discussion among academics and policymakers of the appropriate public policy objectives and instruments for developing economies. Like previous Policy Research Reports, this report is a product of the staff of the World Bank; the judgments made herein do not necessarily reflect the views of its Board of Directors or the governments that they represent.

Michael Bruno
Vice President, Development
   Economics, and Chief Economist
The World Bank

September 1995

The Report Team

THE REPORT TEAM WAS LED BY MARY SHIRLEY. THE PRINCIPAL co-authors were Ahmed Galal and Mary Shirley; Philip Keefer was the principal author of chapter 4. Sections draw heavily on work by Asli Demirgüç-Kunt and Ross Levine (finance), Alan Gelb and I. J. Singh (transition economies), and Hafeez Shaikh (management contracts). Bharat Nauriyal compiled the statistical appendix and provided research assistance; Luke Haggarty wrote many of the boxes and provided research assistance. Other assistance was provided by Abdalla Gergis, Rebecca Hife, and Clemencia Torres. Herbert Baer wrote box 2.9, Gerald Caprio wrote box 5.3, and David Wheeler wrote box 1.3. The report was produced under the direction of Lyn Squire and Michael Bruno.

Lawrence MacDonald was the principal editor. The editorial-production team for the report was led by Jenepher Moseley, with additional help from Luke Haggarty, Audrey Heiligman, and Bill Moore. Polly Means produced the graphics. Alfred Imhoff provided additional editorial advice. The support staff team was led by Zeny Kranzer and included Daniele Evans, Bill Moore, and Paulina Sintim-Aboagye.

Acknowledgments

MANY INDIVIDUALS INSIDE AND OUTSIDE THE WORLD BANK provided valuable contributions and comments. Special thanks are due to the Fiscal Affairs Department of the International Monetary Fund for help on the data base and to our external Advisory Board—Robert Bates, Heba Handoussa, Moises Naim, David Newbery, Lawrence H. Summers, Vito Tanzi, John Vickers, John Waterbury, and Oliver Williamson—for its guidance and comments. Particular thanks are also due to Robert Klitgaard, Douglass North, and Raymond Vernon for their comments. Many Bank staff provided valuable comments. Special thanks to Luca Barbone, Harry Broadman, Eliana Cardoso, Maureen Cropper, Marinela Dado, Shanta Deveragan, William Easterly, Jeffrey Hammer, Ulrich Hewer, Ishrat Husain, Magdi Iskander, Emmanuel Jimenez, Hyung-Ki Kim, Robert Lacey, Muthukumara Mani, Martha de Melo, John Nellis, Robert Picciotto, Lant Pritchett, Enrique Rueda-Sabater, Joanne Salop, Luis Servin, Ulrich Thumm, Paulo Vieira Da Cunha, and Douglas Webb.

A good deal of invaluable background work was done for this report by Arup Banerji (labor), Ed Campos (political economy), Nichola Dyer Cissé (performance contracts), Robert Cordón (case studies), Hadi Esfahani (political economy), Gunnar Fors (trade), E. Gyimah-Boadi (case studies), Song Dae Hee (case studies), William Heller (political economy), Rolf Lüders (case studies), Mathew McCubbins (political economy), Vedot Milor (case studies), Richard Sabot (labor), Luis Servin (macroeconomy), Andrés Solimano (macroeconomy), Raimundo Soto (macroeconomy), Pankaj Tandon (product markets), and Bruce Tolentino (case studies).

Definitions

LOW-INCOME AND MIDDLE-INCOME ECONOMIES ARE SOMEtimes referred to in this report as "developing economies." The use of the term is convenient; it is not intended to imply that all economies in the group are experiencing the same kind of development or that other economies have reached a preferred or final stage of development. Classification by income does not necessarily reflect development status. Similarly, the term "industrial economies" has been used for high-income economies and is not intended to imply that countries in other groupings are unindustrialized nor that industry is the sole determinant of economic development.

Economy Groups

- *Low-income economies* are those that had a 1992 per capita income of $675 or less
- *Middle-income economies* are those that had a 1992 per capita income of $676 to $8,355
- *Developing economies* are those that had a 1992 per capita income of $8,355 or less
- *Industrial economies* are those that had a 1992 per capita income of $8,356 or more

Geographic Groups

THE FOLLOWING ARE GENERAL GUIDELINES TO THE GEOgraphic analytical groupings used in this report. Some calculations, graphs, and tables use varying geographical definitions because they are based on different data sets. Sources should be consulted for the exact group composition.

Africa	Generally includes all of Africa. *Sub-Saharan Africa* excludes the North African countries of Morocco, Algeria, Tunisia, Libya, and Egypt.
Asia	Includes South Asia, Southeast Asia and the Pacific, and nontransitional economies in Central Asia.
Latin America	Short for *Latin America and the Caribbean*; refers to all American and Caribbean economies south of the United States.
Transition economies	Refers to the former socialist economies in Central and Eastern Europe, Central Asia, and China.

Complete coverage may not be available for all countries in each group. See the technical notes in the statistical appendix for specific countries in the different groupings.

Data Notes

HISTORICAL DATA IN THIS BOOK MAY DIFFER FROM THOSE IN other World Bank publications if more reliable data have become available, if a different base year has been used for constant price data, or if countries have been classified differently.

- *Billion* is 1,000 million.
- *Dollars* ($) are current U.S. dollars unless otherwise specified.
- *Net aid flows* are disbursements net of principal payments + interest

Acronyms and Abbreviations

ADB	Asian Development Bank
ADI	African Development Indicators (World Bank)
AfDB	African Development Bank
CFA	Refers to the CFA franc, a currency known in West Africa as the "franc de la Communauté financière d'Afrique" and known in Central Africa as the "franc de la Coopération financière en Afrique centrale"

CPI	Consumer price index
DFI	Direct foreign investment
ECU	European currency unit
EU	European Union
GATT	General Agreement on Tariffs and Trade
GDP	Gross domestic product
GNP	Gross national product
IBRD/IDA	International Bank for Reconstruction and Development/ International Development Association (the World Bank)
IDB	Inter-American Development Bank
IMF	International Monetary Fund
NAFTA	North American Free Trade Agreement
OECD	Organisation for Economic Co-operation and Development
ROA	Return on assets
UNDP	United Nations Development Programme
TFP	Total factor productivity
TVE	Township and village enterprise (China)
S-I	Savings minus investment
SOE	State-owned enterprise
WTO	World Trade Organization (successor to GATT)

Introduction and Overview

BUREAUCRATS ARE STILL IN BUSINESS. DESPITE MORE than a decade of divestiture efforts and the growing consensus that governments perform less well than the private sector in a host of activities, state-owned enterprises (SOEs) account for nearly as large a share of developing economies today as twenty years ago. Indeed, as data compiled for this study show, the size of the state-owned enterprise sector has significantly diminished only in the former socialist economies and a few middle-income countries. In most developing countries, particularly the poorest, bureaucrats run as large a share of the economy as ever. Government employees operate a casino in Ghana, bake cookies in Egypt, assemble watches in India, mine salt in Mexico, make matches in Mali, and bottle cooking oil in Senegal. In many developing countries that continue to support large SOE sectors, inefficient state-owned firms generate deficits that hinder economic growth, making it more difficult for people to lift themselves out of poverty.

Consider these facts:

- In many developing economies, SOEs absorb a large amount of funds that could be better spent on basic social services. In Tanzania, central government subsidies to SOEs equal 72 percent of central government spending on education and 150 percent of central government spending on health.
- SOEs often capture a disproportionate share of credit, squeezing out private sector borrowing. In Bangladesh, SOEs take about one-fifth of domestic credit, although SOE output accounts for less than 3 percent of gross domestic product (GDP).

- State-owned factories often pollute more than privately owned factories. In Indonesia, for example, government factories discharge about five times as much water pollution per unit of output as private factories of the same size and age engaged in the same activity.
- A modest improvement in state-owned enterprise efficiency would substantially reduce and in some cases eliminate the fiscal deficit in most developing countries. In Egypt, Peru, Senegal, and Turkey a mere 5 percent reduction in SOE operating costs would reduce the fiscal deficit by about one-third.

Many governments have announced plans to sell state-owned enterprises and to improve the performance of firms that remain in government hands, but only a few developing countries have made measurable progress. Our study found that

- Developing countries, excluding the transition economies, are divesting an average of just three enterprises per year, although most governments own hundreds of firms.
- Although SOE deficits have declined, they continue to be a significant burden to government finances and to banking systems in developing economies.
- Notwithstanding the sale of some very large firms, the state-owned enterprise share of developing market economies has remained stubbornly high since 1980, at about 11 percent of GDP, even as it fell in the industrial countries from about 9 percent to less than 7 percent.
- The state-owned enterprise sector is larger and the problems associated with it are more severe in the world's poorest countries, where SOEs account for 14 percent of GDP.

In sum, although the potential gains from privatization and other reforms are substantial, only a few countries have reformed their state-owned enterprises successfully. Why haven't more countries reformed their SOEs? What distinguishes the few that have from the many that have not? What are the political obstacles to reform, and how have these been overcome? How can leaders and policymakers in developing economies hasten reform and increase the likelihood of success? And finally, what is the role of foreign aid? These are the questions this book sets out to answer.

To do so, we examine the economic problems that arise when bureaucrats are in business—that is, when governments own and operate enterprises that could be run as private firms—and the political obstacles to change. We do not suggest that bureaucrats are to blame for these ills. To the contrary, we find that divestiture and other state-owned enterprise reforms cannot succeed without a sound bureaucracy. Requiring bureaucrats to oversee businesses better handled by private entrepreneurs places a heavy toll on bureaucracies in developing economies, diverting attention from problems that only governments can address. Bureaucrats typically perform poorly in business, not because they are incompetent (they aren't), but because they face contradictory goals and perverse incentives that can distract and discourage even very able and dedicated public servants. The problem is not the people but the system, not bureaucrats per se but the situations they find themselves in as bureaucrats in business.

We begin our study by measuring the size and economic impact of the SOE sector in developing economies. As noted above, we find that SOE sectors remain large in many developing countries and that large SOE sectors have a negative effect on growth (chapter 1). To understand the differences between the few countries that reformed successfully and the many that have not, we next investigate SOE reform efforts in twelve countries representing a broad cross-section of regions and experiences. Our sample includes nine developing market economies (Chile, Egypt, Ghana, India, Mexico, the Philippines, Republic of Korea, Senegal, and Turkey) and three transition economies (China, the Czech Republic, and Poland). We find that the countries that improved the performance of their SOEs made the most of divestiture, competition, hard budgets, and financial sector reforms. In addition, all twelve countries tried to improve the incentive structure by changing the relationship between government and state-owned enterprises, but this last measure rarely worked alone (chapter 2). To discover why, we go a level deeper and explore changes at the enterprise level. We find that improving the performance of SOEs or privatized monopolies requires a better incentive structure. In other words, the contract between government and SOE management, or between government and private management, or between government and the owners of a privatized, regulated monopoly must be rewritten to motivate both sides to improve performance (chapter 3).

Taken together, this analysis shows that divestiture and other reforms can indeed improve SOE performance but that only a few governments have adopted the policies necessary to reform successfully. Why haven't more governments attempted these policies? To answer this question, we investigated the politics of SOE reform in our twelve-country sample, identifying political obstacles and the ways that successful reformers overcame them (chapter 4). What can policymakers and the development community do to speed the reform process? Our final chapter draws on the findings of the previous work to construct a decision tree that reform advocates can use in deciding whether or not a country is ready for reform and how to proceed in each instance (chapter 5). We conclude with a note outlining ways foreign assistance can help to encourage reform. The remainder of this introduction and overview highlights the central arguments and findings of the book from chapter 2 onward.

What Makes for Success in State Enterprise Reform?

TO UNDERSTAND THE DIFFERENCES BETWEEN SUCCESSFUL and unsuccessful SOE reform, we first need an objective measure of success. We establish three objective indicators: state-owned enterprise financial returns, state-owned enterprise productivity, and the state-owned enterprise savings-investment deficit (for a detailed discussion of these measures, see chapter 2). Using these indicators, we find that Chile, Korea, and Mexico achieved the best results; their SOE sectors performed better than the other countries and they were able to improve on already good performance. Egypt, Ghana, and the Philippines had mixed results; and India, Senegal, and Turkey had the poorest results. Although we lacked comparable data for ranking the three transition economies, partial indicators suggest that China, the Czech Republic, and Poland show mixed to good results.

What explains these differences? To find out, we considered the extent to which each country in our sample used the five components of reform that economic theorists and reform practitioners widely recommend. These components are divestiture, competition, hard budgets, financial sector reform, and changes in the institutional relationship between SOEs and governments. *We found that the more successful reformers made the most of all five components.* Indeed, they used them not as separate options but as mutually supportive components of an overall strategy. Other countries in our sample achieved less in individual reform elements and followed a less comprehensive strategy overall.

Key findings about the ways that successful reformers, on one hand, and the mixed performers and least successful performers, on the other, approached each of these five components of SOE reform include the following:

- *Successful SOE reformers divested more, especially where the initial size of the state enterprise sector was large.*
- *Successful SOE reformers introduced more competition. They liberalized trade, eased restrictions on entry, and unbundled large enterprises .*
- *Successful SOE reformers hardened SOE budgets. They reduced or eliminated direct subsidies, put access to credit on a more commercial basis, improved regulation of SOE monopoly prices, and reduced or eliminated hidden subsidies.*
- *Successful SOE reformers reformed the financial sector. They strengthened supervision and regulation, relaxed controls over interest rates, and reduced directed credit. They also relaxed entry restrictions and privatized banks once SOE reform and supervisory and regulatory reform were well under way.*
- *Surprisingly, successful and unsuccessful reformers alike tried to improve the incentive structure by changing the relationship between SOE managers and the government. Countries at the top and bottom of our performance ratings introduced new oversight bodies, increased managerial autonomy, and signed explicit performance agreements.*

Why did the apparently similar efforts to change relationships between SOE managers and governments produce different results? Partly, such institutional reforms only work in conjunction with the other reforms just described. In addition, there may be differences in the ways that countries designed and implemented these changes that would show up only in detailed company-level analysis. To find out, we analyzed the ways that governments rewrote their contracts with managers of state-owned enterprises, with private managers contracted to run government firms, and with the owners of privatized, regulated monopolies.

Contracting: What Works, What Doesn't, and Why

EACH RELATIONSHIP BETWEEN A GOVERNMENT AND the manager of a state-owned enterprise, or between a government and private managers of a state's assets, or between a government and the owner of a regulated, private monopoly can be seen as a contract, that is, an agreement between the government and the other party based on shared expectations. Written contracts have been established for only a small proportion of state enterprises worldwide, but their use is growing. Countries often use written contracts for their most important and problematic activities, such as infrastructure monopolies (electricity, water, and telecoms), and major exporters and revenue earners (tea in Sri Lanka, gold in Ghana, and hotels in Egypt). Yet little is known about whether such contracts work, what distinguishes the successful contracts, or which type of contract works best in which circumstances. Our study (chapter 3) focused on three types of contracts:

- *Performance contracts,* which define the relationship between the government and *government employees* managing a state-owned enterprise
- *Management contracts,* which define the relationship between the government and a *private firm* contracted to manage a state-owned enterprise
- *Regulatory contracts,* which consist of the regulations and legislation that define the relationship between the government and the owner of a private, regulated monopoly.

For each type of contract, we first examined a sample of firms to determine whether the contract improved performance. To understand differences in outcomes, we then analyzed how each contract resolved, or failed to resolve, problems in three areas: information, rewards and penalties, and commitment.

We found that performance contracts worked least well. Management contracts worked better, but only in circumstances identified below. Regulatory contracts, when properly designed and implemented, worked well for enterprises in monopoly markets. Overall, then, the greater the participation of private agents in ownership and management, the better enterprise performance. Our analysis suggests that this was because private managers and owners, unlike their government counterparts, could readily capture the benefits if performance improved; responding to these incentives, they worked harder than government managers and obtained better results. We summarize the main findings for each type of contract below.

Performance Contracts Rarely Improve Incentives and May Do More Harm than Good

Performance contracts are currently used in thirty-three developing economies. Our analysis of a sample of twelve companies in six countries gives little support to the premise that these contracts help improve SOE performance. Only three of the twelve case study companies showed a turnaround in total factor productivity (TFP) after contracts were introduced (Ghana Water, Mexico Electricity, and Senegal Telecoms), six continued their past trends, and three performed substantially worse under contracts than before. The rate of return on assets deteriorated for three firms; the rest show little change.

Why did performance contracts work so badly? We found that these contracts did not improve, and in some cases exacerbated, the poor incentive structures facing government managers. Indeed, performance contracts failed to address all three contracting problems. They did not reduce the managers' information advantage; instead managers were able to use their knowledge of the firm to negotiate multiple soft targets that were easy for them to reach. Similarly, performance contracts rarely included rewards and penalties that could motivate managers and staff to exert more effort. When cash bonuses were offered they had little effect because they were not linked to better performance; other promised incentives, such as greater managerial autonomy, were often not delivered; and penalties for poor performance, such as firing or demotion, were seldom applied. Finally, governments demonstrated little commitment to the terms of the contracts, frequently reneging on key promises. This increased managers' incentive to use their information advantage to negotiate soft targets.

Each of these problems can be seen with the performance contract governing Senegal Electricity. The contract included twenty-two criteria for judging performance, but no rewards if managers attained them; moreover, government regulators lacked the power to enforce penalties reliably. Finally, although the government promised to take actions that would make it possible for the firm to meet its targets, such as forcing other state-owned enterprises to pay their electricity bills, these promises were often broken. The company suffered declining productivity. Indeed, as with several other enterprises in our sample, it appears that the contract may have actually worsened incentives and performance.

Management Contracts Work but Are Not Widely Used

Management contracts are not widely used but have generally been successful where they were attempted. Our worldwide search using a relatively broad definition (see chapter 3) found only 150 management contracts: forty-four involved hotels managed by major international chains; the rest were concentrated in agriculture and water. Our analysis of management contracts governing twenty firms in eleven countries found that profitability and productivity improved in two out of three cases.

What were the characteristics of the successful management contracts? And, since they are often successful, why aren't they used more often? Analysis of the ways that the successful contracts addressed the problems of information, rewards and penalties, and commitment answers both questions.

Where management contracts succeeded, governments used competition to reduce management's information advantage. Of the thirteen successful contracts, ten involved SOEs in competitive markets; the other three involved competitive bidding for monopoly enterprises (two water companies and a container port). Successful contracts also established meaningful rewards and penalties, usually by linking the contractor's fee to the firm's performance. Finally, successful contracts were set up in ways that elicited a strong commitment from both parties. For example, they covered longer periods, included the possibility of renewal, and provided for arbitration of disputes.

If management contracts work, why are they not used more often? We concluded that the costs to the government of obtaining the information needed to negotiate, monitor, and enforce a management contract are one reason that they are largely confined to hotels, agriculture, and water. Information is more easily available, and contract transaction costs thus lower, in sectors where technology is not changing rapidly and output is a single, homogeneous product (as with water or sugar); or where the private contractor has an international reputation to protect, the market is competitive, and quality is easily compared (as with hotels). Moreover, under the conditions where management contracts can work, privatization will often offer governments higher benefits (revenue from the sale) and lower costs (no need to monitor, enforce, and renegotiate the contract).

Regulatory Contracts Work but Require Careful Design

Nearly all privatized firms providing infrastructure services operate in monopoly markets where government regulation is needed to prevent firms from abusing their market power. These regulations and other divestiture provisions constitute a regulatory contract, that is, an agreement between the government and the firm's owners about the conditions under which the firm should operate.

To evaluate these contracts, we analyzed the experience in the seven developing countries where the basic telephone network is privately owned and government regulated (Argentina, Chile, Jamaica, Malaysia, Mexico, the Philippines, and Venezuela). We found that regulatory contracts improved performance in most cases; investment and labor productivity increased significantly in five countries, and the quality and quantity of service usually improved rapidly. Not all regulatory contracts are successful, however, as we can see from a comparison of their successful use in Chile and the problems encountered in the Philippines.

Again countries with successful contracts addressed all three contracting issues. In Chile, for example, the government reduced its information disadvantage by selling the franchise for local telephone service through competitive bidding and by injecting other elements of competition into the contract wherever possible. Price regulations were designed to reward improved performance and penalize failure to improve. Finally, the Chilean government demonstrated its commitment to abide by the contract to investors in many ways; for example, the legislature passed laws defining procedures for arbitration and appeal of disputes.

The overall evidence from our sample suggests that divestiture of state-owned enterprises in noncompetitive markets, accompanied by appropriate regulation, usually does result in greater efficiency, expanded service, and overall improved welfare. But only a small proportion of the countries with large government monopolies in noncompetitive sectors have attempted regulatory contracts. Indeed, as we have seen, despite the potentially large economic benefits of divestiture and other types of SOE reform, relatively few countries have made a systematic, determined attempt to reform their SOEs. To find out why, we studied the politics of state-owned enterprise reform.

The Politics of Reforming State-Owned Enterprises

THE REFORM OF SOES CAN COST A GOVERNMENT ITS SUPPORT base, because reforms almost invariably involve eliminating jobs and cutting long-established subsidies. Not surprisingly, politicians carefully weigh any change in SOE policies, naturally preferring policies that benefit their constituents and help them remain in power over policies that undermine support and may cause them to be turned out of office. While some exceptional leaders may be able to change their support base and mobilize new constituents for reform, most are inherently responsive to the supporters who put them in office. How have the countries that reformed successfully overcome the political obstacles to reform? What can other countries learn from their example to hasten the reform process? In considering these questions, we found that there are three necessary conditions for successful reform:

- Reform must be politically *desirable* to the leadership and its constituencies. Reform becomes desirable to the leadership and its supporters when the political benefits outweigh the political costs. This usually happens with a change in regime or coalition shift in which those favoring the status quo lose power. It may also happen when an economic crisis makes SOE subsidies so costly that reform becomes preferable to the status quo.
- Reform must be politically *feasible*. Leaders must have the means to implement change and to withstand opposition to reform.
- Promises central to state-owned enterprise reform must be *credible*. Investors must believe that the government will not renationalize privatized firms; SOE employees and others who fear that they may lose out in reform must believe that the government will deliver on any promises of future compensation.

Chapter 4 describes these conditions in detail, using as examples the twelve successful and unsuccessful reformers we present in chapter 2. The analysis does not support the widely held view that SOE reform is more likely in authoritarian regimes. In our sample, among authoritarian governments there were both successful and unsuccessful reformers, while reform was slow in some democracies and rapid in others. Below we illustrate the three conditions with brief examples, then present possible predictors of reform readiness.

Condition I: Political Desirability

Reforms become desirable to the leadership in two complementary ways. The first involves a change in government: either an outright regime shift (as in Chile in 1973 or the Velvet Revolution in Czechoslovakia in 1989) or a shift in the governing coalition (as in Mexico in 1988) that alters the leadership's constituencies in such a way that those who might lose from SOE reform are no longer a significant part of the leadership's support base. The second involves an economic crisis—for example, a significant drop in GDP (Czechoslovakia, Ghana, Mexico) or a sharp fall in net foreign assistance (Senegal, Egypt)—that makes it increasingly difficult for the government to continue subsidizing SOEs. The size of the economic crisis needed to make reform desirable depends on how much the leadership relies on the support of those who benefit from the status quo.

All the more successful reformers in our sample met the political desirability test, while most of the countries with mixed or poor reform records did not. Even though most of the latter group experienced either a significant regime shift or economic problems that could have created an opening for reform, the continued importance of the SOE sector in the government's support base meant reform did not become politically desirable. In Turkey, for example, a regime change in 1983 resulted in numerous economic reforms. However, these efforts stopped short of privatizing or otherwise reforming state-owned enterprises because SOE employees were crucial to the new government's support base.

Condition II: Political Feasibility

Reform is politically feasible when the leadership can secure the approval and support of other government entities whose cooperation is critical to success. These include legislatures, bureaucracies, and the state or provincial governments that are responsible for formulating policy or carrying out the reform. In addition, the leadership must be able to withstand opposition to reform from potential losers; these may be SOE employees, especially when such groups are organized, numerous, and ready to engage in demonstrations, work stoppages in strategic industries, and other actions that might be costly to the government. The likelihood of opposition is greatest when the enterprise has many extra employees—in some SOEs up to 90 percent of employees may not be needed. In such instances, workers, rightly worried that reform might lead to layoffs, have a strong incentive to resist.

In all the successfully reforming countries in our sample, the leadership controlled policymaking and implementation when reform began; moreover, in each country the leadership offered compensation and sometimes used compulsion sufficient to overcome resistance outside normal political channels. Compulsion can have high social costs and reforms enacted through coercion are often not sustainable. No government relied solely on compulsion to overcome opposition. In Chile, for example, the military government in the 1970s employed often harsh measures to curb union powers but also offered high severance pay to port employees who might otherwise have disrupted the economy. In the 1980s, the government sold some SOE shares to the general public and SOE employees under various generous financing alternatives. Neither Poland nor the Czech Republic used compulsion but instead satisfied reform opponents with different distributions of enteprise shares.

Ghana, which we rank as partially meeting Condition II, illustrates the difficulties that less successful reformers faced in overcoming opposition to reform. Throughout most of the 1980s and into the 1990s, the executive controlled policymaking. In 1985, to overcome substantial resistance to SOE reform, the government tried a mix of compulsion and compensation. On the one hand, it reduced the power of the state-owned enterprise union, detaining labor leaders critical of the reform; on the other, it began to give fired state-owned enterprise workers more generous severance payments. With the approach of district elections in 1988, however, the government became increasingly reluctant to compel compliance with decisions about layoffs. Severance payments became so expensive that the government had to abandon efforts to cut SOE employment.

Condition III: Credibility

The third and final condition for successful state-owned enterprise reform is government credibility. We identified three ways to judge a government's credibility. First, credible governments have a reputation for keeping promises; for example, because they announced and implemented overall economic reforms or have not previously expropriated private firms. Second, they face domestic restraints on policy reversal, such as constitutional restrictions that make it hard to overturn legislation or wide ownership of shares in privatized SOEs that creates a large, pro-reform constituency. Third, they submit to international restraints, such as trade treaties or loan covenants, which make it costly to reverse reforms. Some mechanisms are more powerful than others. A government with a solid reputation, or strong domestic restraints, may enjoy sufficient credibility whether or not it accedes to international treaties. The reverse is not true, however: international restraints are usually too weak to confer credibility where other conditions are absent.

The range of abilities that countries exhibit to credibly commit to reform can be seen by looking at two less successful reformers, India and Egypt, and two more successful reformers, the Czech Republic and Poland. Although India did not meet the first two conditions of reform, any reforms that it might have undertaken would have enjoyed substantial credibility. India had significant domestic restraints on policy reversal and was regarded by investor risk services as a relatively safe place to commit resources. In contrast, Egypt in the 1980s had a low confidence score with foreign investors and few domestic restraints to protect reforms from being overturned. The experience of the Czech Republic and Poland illustrates how decisive moves to implement macroeconomic reform while at the same time putting in place domestic restraints that make policy reversal difficult can enable a country to build credibility in remarkably little time.

Predicting Reform Readiness

Knowing how countries meet the conditions of desirability, feasibility, and credibility helps predict reform outcomes. Political behavior is inherently complex and dynamic, making prediction difficult. Nevertheless, the methodology developed in the report allows us to formulate objective and transparent indicators for prediction that can be tested for accuracy and consistency and applied systematically to our entire sample. Table 1 shows which countries in our sample failed to meet the three necessary conditions according to objective measures. Countries that met all three conditions reformed successfully. Countries that failed to meet any one of the three conditions were less successful re-

Table 1 Unmet Conditions in Less Than Successful SOE Reformers

Country	Condition I Desirability	Condition II Feasibility	Condition III Credibility
Egypt	●		●
Ghana			●
Philippines		●	
India	●	●	
Senegal 1983–88	●		
1988–	●	●	●
Turkey 1983–91	●	●	
1991–92	●	●	

● Does not meet the condition.

Condition I: Met if coalition change *or* exogenous crisis *and* PE reform losers outside government's support base; not met if reform losers in the government's support base.

Condition II: Met if reformers can secure approval *and* design sufficient compensation packages to defuse opposition; not met otherwise.

Condition III: Met if government known for keeping promises, faces domestic international restraint on policy reversal. Note that by OECD standards, in which countries score much higher in ICRG (Switzerland with thirty, for example), and receive scores of seven on constraints on the executive, none of the sample countries would be judged to fully meet Condition III. For the purposes of this table, Chile, Korea, and the Czech Republic were used as benchmarks against which the remaining countries in the sample were compared. In general, countries that did worse on two dimensions and no better than on others were judged not to meet the condition.

Source: See text.

formers. Thus, unready countries privatized less and failed to implement nondivestiture reforms effectively. *This illustrates a key finding of our analysis: reform cannot succeed until countries fulfill each of the three conditions of readiness.*

What Can Be Done to Spur Reforms and Improve Outcomes?

THE EVIDENCE MAKES IT CLEAR THAT REDUCING THE ROLE OF bureaucrats in business and improving the performance of the remaining SOEs can bring a country substantial economic gains. Yet reform has been slow and seldom successful. Chapter 5 concludes our study by suggesting ways that leaders and policymakers in developing countries can foster more rapid and successful state-owned enterprise reform, and ways foreign aid can assist them more effectively.

A Decision Tree for Reform of State-Owned Enterprises

State-owned enterprise reform involves a multitude of choices, each with its own set of problems and opportunities. The choices made will inevitably vary from country to country; but to lead to successful outcomes, they must be made in a logical order. It might seem obvious, for example, that countries will not reform successfully until the leadership perceives reform as desirable. Yet, perhaps precisely because the economic gains of reform are substantial, well-intentioned outsiders, including the World Bank, have sometimes attempted to prod developing countries that are not ready for reform into acting. Similarly, developing country leaders and policymakers, persuaded of the benefits of reforming SOEs, have sometimes attempted to do so, only to choose an option that meets with failure. How can those who rightly favor reform organize the multitude of choices they face in a way that will increase the likelihood of success?

In thinking about the prerequisites of reform and the conditions that are necessary for the success of various reform options, we have found it useful to draw a decision tree (figure 1). At each juncture we ask a question, the answer to which sends us in one of two directions, where we encounter another juncture and another question. Chapter 5 describes that decision tree, offering checklists that reform advocates can use in deciding how to proceed in a particular country or with a particular enterprise in order to avoid the potential pitfalls along the way. We conclude this overview with a brief summary of the main decision points.

The essential first question is whether or not the country is ready for reform. The answer will be determined by whether or not a country meets each of the three conditions for readiness described above. In the borderline cases, of which there may be many, upfront actions, such as trimming an oversized SOE workforce or selling or liquidating a large firm, can be a good signal of readiness to proceed with a broader program of SOE reform. Depending on the answer, the course of action is radically different. *If the country is not ready, then SOE reforms are unlikely to succeed.* Instead, policymakers should pursue reforms in other areas that are desirable in their own right and at the same time lay the groundwork for future SOE reform. Because foreign aid can have an important influence on the timing of SOE reform and how it is pursued, we suggest ways to enhance its effectiveness in supporting SOE reform at the end of the book, summarized here in box 1.

Figure 1 A Decision Tree for State-Owned Enterprise Reform

```
                                                              Introduce competition in markets
                                                    yes    →  Ensure transparency and competitive bidding
                                                              Other implementation details in text


                                                                      Management contracts preferable where
                         yes    →  Is divestiture possible?    yes  →  technology and taste do not change rapidly
                                                                       - auction the contract
                                                                       - use performance-based fees
                                                                       - provide commitment mechanisms

                 Are SOEs potentially      no
                 competitive?                    →  Are contractual arrangements
                                          no        with the private sector possible?
    yes

Is country ready
for SOE reform?          no                                              Unbundle large firms, increase competition in markets
                                  →  Are natural monopolies      no   →  Restrict soft credit, end subsidies and transfers
                                     to be divested?                     Ensure managerial autonomy to respond to competition
                                                                         Use performance contracts selectively

    no           Enhance readiness          yes
                 for SOE reform                  →  Ensure adequate regulations are in place
                 - implement other reforms          - unbundle large firms
                 - reduce worker opposition          - auction the franchise
                 - improve reputation, boost credibility  - establish appropriate pricing regimes
                                                     - provide commitment mechanisms
```

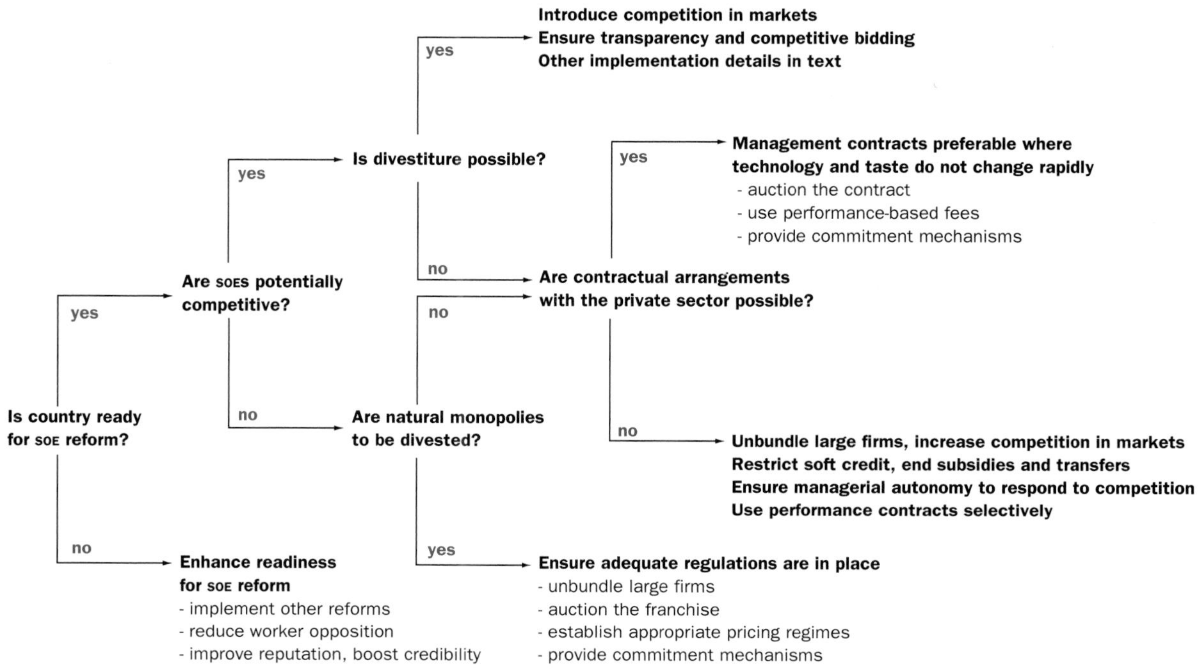

Source: See chapter 5 text.

The decision tree helps to organize the multitude of choices facing reformers.

What to Do in Countries Not Ready to Reform State-Owned Enterprises

Failed reform attempts can be very costly. For example, money spent to restructure state enterprises and pay off their bad debts is wasted if the enterprises fail to improve. More difficult to quantify, but no less important, are the costs in wasted human and political capital. *Reform of state-owned enterprises, both privatization and reforms short of divestiture, should therefore not be attempted in countries that do not meet the three conditions of readiness.*

Are we suggesting that nothing can be done in such situations? Certainly not. Rather, policymakers can take actions that are beneficial in their own right, and also make state-owned enterprise reform more desirable, feasible, and credible. Such reforms are often possible in environments where SOE reforms are not, because they affect different constituencies. Macroeconomic reforms, for example, can increase the pressure and support for SOE reform, thus making it politically more desirable. Specific steps include:

Box 1 How Foreign Aid Can Better Assist State-Owned Enterprise Reform

THE FINDINGS OF THIS REPORT, PARTICULARLY the three conditions of reform readiness, have important implications for foreign assistance. External support for SOE reform is often highly beneficial, but the evidence suggests that it can sometimes do harm as well as good. This box summarizes the implications of the report's findings for such support; a more detailed discussion is presented in "Implications for Foreign Assistance" at the end of the book.

We found that aid intended to promote SOE reform can be counterproductive in several situations. First, financial assistance to unready countries may make it easier for interests that oppose reform to sustain the status quo. For example, in at least two of our case study countries, Egypt and Senegal, foreign assistance that ameliorated a fiscal crisis may have reduced pressure to reform. Second, going through the motions of reform without making real changes can cause a deterioration in SOE performance. For example, we found that signing a performance contract without changing incentives gives SOE managers an opportunity to negotiate multiple soft targets at odds with the goals of improved performance. Third, we found that governments that ended overt state enterprise subsidies to meet aid conditions sometimes then expanded covert subsidies and bank credits, which are harder to identify and curb and which spread SOE problems to the financial system. Fourth, some reluctant governments were slow to privatize, then rushed into bad bargains to meet deadlines set by external assistance agreements. And finally, although this is harder to document, support for reforms that are not implemented and, therefore, don't show results can tarnish the reputation of reform advocates in developing countries, and of foreign assistance, undermining the credibility of SOE and other types of reform. This suggests:

- Foreign assistance is more effective when it differentiates between countries that are ready to reform their state-owned enterprises successfully and those that are not.

- Countries that clearly meet the three conditions of reform readiness are most likely to benefit from foreign assistance for SOE reform. Much foreign assistance is already predicated on government commitment to recommended policy actions; our suggestion is to assess commitment more reliably by focusing systematically on the conditions of SOE reform readiness that underlie success.

- For borderline cases (which may well be the majority), up-front government actions are the most reliable way to determine which countries meet the three conditions for successful reform. Actions that signal that reform has become politically desirable and politically feasible include, for example, laying off unnecessary workers or selling a very large firm; actions that increase credibility include establishing restraints to prevent policy reversal (such as constitutional prohibitions on renationalization) or widely distributing shares in privatized firms (thus enlarging the constituency with a stake in reform success).

- The design of foreign assistance needs to take account of the possibility that reform readiness was overestimated or that circumstances have changed in such a way that a country no longer meets the readiness criteria. These include moves to protect SOEs from competition, writing off state-owned enterprise debt without addressing the underlying causes of over-indebtedness, or failing to pay state-owned enterprises for goods or services delivered.

- Foreign aid can help governments of unready countries lay the groundwork for SOE reform by encouraging and assisting policy reform in other areas. As we discuss in the text, this leaves a large agenda, including the reduction of fiscal deficits and trade restrictions and the removal of barriers to entry. Although similar tests of readiness may well apply to reforms in

(Box continues on the following page.)

Box 1 *(continued)*

other areas, the constituencies for and against reform differ depending on the policy and sector involved; thus, some non-SOE reforms are possible in countries where the conditions for SOE reform do not yet exist. External assistance can also help prepare the way for SOE reform by providing information about the net costs of maintaining the status quo and the net benefits from reform and by informing political leaders, policymakers, opinion leaders, and others about SOE reform experiences in other countries.

■ Foreign assistance can help reform-ready governments attract private investors. A government that is otherwise ready to reform but is just beginning to establish its credibility may find it hard to attract private buyers for large, asset-specific investments in regulated monopolies. In such instances, guarantees by international agencies could be investigated as a way to help attract initial private investment while the government is building up its credibility. Such guarantees are not without risk and should be approached cautiously, taking into account the pros and cons, which we discuss in box 5.3. Even without guarantees, foreign assistance can signal to investors which countries appear ready to reform their state-owned enterprises by clearly distinguishing those that are ready from those that are not.

■ *Reducing fiscal deficits.* Fiscal and monetary reforms that bring revenues and expenditures into line also increase pressure for SOE reform by making the burden of SOE deficits explicit.

■ *Easing trade restrictions.* Liberalizing trade restrictions gives exporters a stronger position in the economy, and exporters can become an important constituency for SOE reform, demanding more efficient provision of the goods and services that SOEs supply.

■ *Removing barriers to entry.* Removing barriers to entry increases the number of voices calling for SOE reform. New entrants who must rely on state-owned enterprise services or compete with subsidized SOE products help enlarge the constituency for reform.

■ *Initiating financial sector reform.* Governments not ready to reform SOEs may still be prepared to develop their financial system by improving supervisory and regulatory capacity, reducing directed credit and direct government control over financial intermediaries, and easing some interest rate controls.

Similarly, governments can make SOE reform more feasible by reducing the opposition to reform by workers and others dependent on state-owned enterprises. Possible actions include:

- *Eliminating obstacles to private job creation.* One reason state-owned enterprise workers typically oppose reform is that while overstaffing makes layoffs likely, appealing alternative employment is often lacking. Policymakers can thus ease the way for SOE reform by improving private employment opportunities. Steps include eliminating interest rate subsidies (these encourage employers to substitute capital for labor) and complex employment regulations (which have been shown to inhibit private job growth).

- *Uncoupling SOE jobs and social services.* State workers who receive many goods and social services through their jobs are especially fearful of being fired. In socialist economies, for example, state firms traditionally provided housing, health care, transport, educational assistance, and other benefits. Transition economies need alternatives to enterprise benefits—a commercial housing market or public health care, for example—so that SOEs can stop providing these services and offer offsetting higher pay instead. This gives workers greater mobility and reduces their resistance to reforms that may threaten their jobs.

Finally, to enhance their credibility, governments can:

- *Improve their reputation.* By announcing in advance programs such as the macroeconomic reforms mentioned above, and adhering to the program scrupulously, governments can enhance their reputation with potential reform supporters.

- *Establish domestic and international constraints.* Enacting and adhering to constitutional provisions guaranteeing the right to property can help reassure investors that the government will honor its commitments. Trade treaties and multilateral agreements raise the cost of reversing future SOE reforms and help enhance credibility.

Policymakers who pursue this agenda will eventually find themselves on the opposite branch of the decision tree, among countries that are ready for SOE reform.

What to Do in Countries Ready to Reform State-Owned Enterprises

A country that meets the political conditions for successful SOE reform faces a multitude of choices about how to handle each enterprise.

The decisions will depend on the nature of the market, the firm, and the country's capacity to divest and, in the case of monopoly markets, to regulate. Returning to our decision tree, we see that it asks policymakers in countries ready to reform to classify SOEs into two types:

- Those operating in competitive or potentially competitive markets (all manufacturing and most services) and
- Those operating in natural monopoly markets where regulation is necessary to protect consumers (some utilities and most infrastructure).

Enterprises in competitive or potentially competitive markets can be divested in such a way that competition is enhanced and arrangements for the sale are transparent and competitive or at least open to the possibility of competitive bidding. Enterprises in natural monopoly markets can also be divested, provided that the sale is transparent and open to competitive bidding *and* that a credible regulatory structure can be put in place. These two outcomes correspond to the two outermost branches of our decision tree.

For both types of enterprises, policymakers undertaking divestiture face many questions that have different answers depending on country conditions and, in some instances, on the size and condition of the enterprise being sold. Questions that policymakers will want to consider when designing a divestiture strategy include the following:

- *Is it better to begin with small enterprises or big enterprises?* Selling big firms first produces bigger welfare gains: the bigger the firm, the bigger the potential benefits. It also signals that the government is serious about reform and, properly done, can create new proreform constituencies. On the other hand, starting with small firms and gaining experience before tackling the large firms makes sense if bureaucratic capacity is the limiting factor.
- *Should the government financially restructure firms before selling them?* Although some financial restructuring may be necessary, new investments are seldom recovered in the sale price. Even so, government assumption of SOE debt is sometimes the only feasible way to unload a company whose debt exceeds the sales value of its assets.
- *Should the government lay off workers before selling an enterprise?* Countries as diverse as Argentina, Japan, Mexico, and Tunisia have sometimes had to fire state-owned enterprise employees prior

to privatization. This is sometimes necessary because investors will not buy a firm where acrimonious labor disputes seem likely. Moreover, governments are usually better able than private investors to alleviate adverse social effects of mass layoffs. Severance pay can reduce the risks facing SOE workers.

Selling monopolies is more complex than selling firms in competitive or potentially competitive markets. Even so, as long as the sale is competitive and transparent and a credible regulatory contract can be devised and implemented, divesting monopolies can produce major welfare gains. Policymakers who decide their country is ready to divest state-owned monopolies will want to incorporate the following findings in their divestiture plans:

- *Regulatory contracts work better when government reduces the firm's information advantage through competition.* In addition to competitive bidding for the contract itself, postsale competition can be increased by splitting competitive activities from natural monopolies and breaking national monopolies into regional monopolies. In markets that still remain monopolies, the government could require the winning bidder to meet specified targets or lose the concession.
- *Price regulation is more effective when it allows firms to retain some of the benefits of improved performance while passing part to consumers in the form of lower prices.* Where possible, basing prices on information from sources other than the firm can eliminate the firm's incentive to inflate costs. Infrequently revising prices gives firms an incentive to cut costs between adjustments.
- *Credible regulatory contracts lower costs to the consumer.* Governments that credibly commit to meeting their end of the regulatory contract can drive a harder bargain with investors. When the regulatory contract is based only on a presidential decree or lacks provisions for impartial adjudication of conflicts, investors demand higher returns or greater monopoly powers to compensate for higher risk. When such costs are very high, policymakers may wish to improve credibility before divesting. Alternatively, they may seek external guarantees. (See box 5.3.)

Even in countries where the leadership is committed to rapid and extensive privatization, some SOEs are likely to remain in government hands for a long time, for political if not for economic reasons. What to do with these enterprises is the final question on the decision tree; it asks: are contractual arrangements with the private sector possible? Management contracts with the private sector are the preferred course; however, as we have shown above, these are useful only in a limited number of circumstances where the enterprise's technology changes slowly and output is primarily a single, homogeneous product (such as water and sugar) or where quality is easily monitored (such as hotels).

For firms that cannot be divested but are unsuitable for management contracts, policymakers have no choice but to attempt improvements within the existing ownership and management arrangements. Specific measures that must be implemented include introducing competition, cutting government subsidies, reforming financial arrangements to eliminate soft credits, and holding managers responsible for results while giving them the freedom to make necessary changes. The performance of SOEs that are not divested can be improved through these actions; but getting the details right is tough, because each reform relies on the successful implementation of others. Policymakers will want to keep in mind the following:

- *Foster competition wherever possible to create incentives for improved performance.* State-owned enterprise managers will only exert the effort needed to improve performance if pushed by competition.
- *End subsidies and transfers.* Fostering competition is fundamental to improving the performance of SOEs in potentially competitive markets. But competition can only be effective if government transfers and subsidies are eliminated.
- *Eliminate access to soft credit.* Cutting subsidies and transfers only results in hard budgets if access to soft credit is also eliminated.
- *Give managers the autonomy to respond to competition and hold them accountable for results.* Managers must have the power to lay off workers, seek lower-cost suppliers, end unprofitable activities, and pursue new markets. And they must be held accountable for results. Lacking autonomy and responsibility, managers may respond to the increasing number of constraints in ways that hurt the enterprise, such as cutting spending on maintenance, marketing, and even supplies.
- *Only use performance contracts when they address underlying problems.* Performance contracts should only be used if they convey

clear signals for reform, provide rewards for improved performance, and curb governments' tendency to renege. Writing a sound performance contract can seem simple; however, they have usually failed to address the problems of information, rewards and penalties, and commitment. In general, the effort that goes into such contracts could be better spent pursuing the measures described above, in particular, putting in place the conditions for divestiture.

■■■

In sum, this study shows that large and inefficient state-owned enterprise sectors are costing developing economies dearly, especially the poorest among them. Yet reform is possible and offers potentially large benefits, including more goods and services of better quality at lower prices; increased availability of resources for health, education, and other social spending; and improved fiscal stability—all of which could contribute to more rapid economic growth. Reforming SOEs isn't easy, however, and reforms often entail political costs. Indeed, we found that political obstacles are the main reason that state-owned enterprise reform has made so little headway in the last decade. Nevertheless, this study documents that countries in very different economic and political circumstances have overcome these barriers and successfully reformed.

CHAPTER 1

Bureaucrats Are Still in Business

ARE STATE-OWNED ENTERPRISES A PROBLEM? TOO often the answer varies depending on where a person sits on the ideological spectrum. To minimize such subjectivity, we set out to determine empirically whether and how state-owned enterprises (SOEs) influence the economies of developing countries. Our first step was to define SOEs (see box 1.1). We then assembled the best available evidence to estimate the size of the SOE sector in developing countries and to assess whether this has changed over time.

State-Owned Enterprise Sector Remains Large Despite Increasing Divestiture

WE FOUND THAT ALTHOUGH GOVERNMENTS ARE SELLING more and bigger enterprises, outside Eastern Europe and the former Soviet Union and a handful of countries in other regions, the SOE sector has remained stubbornly large. We concluded that large SOE sectors can hinder growth for a variety of reasons, in part because individual SOEs are usually less efficient than private firms and in part because the resulting aggregate SOE deficits are typically financed in ways that undermine macroeconomic stability. In addition, subsidies to SOEs often divert scarce funds from growth-enhancing public spending, such as education and health. Finally, we found that because SOE sectors tend to be larger in low-income countries, SOEs are likely to be most costly in the countries that can least afford them. This chapter presents the evidence for these findings.

Box 1.1 What Is a State-Owned Enterprise?

THERE ARE MANY POSSIBLE DEFINITIONS OF WHAT CONSTITUTES an SOE. In this report, we define SOEs as government owned or government controlled economic entities that generate the bulk of their revenues from selling goods and services.* This definition limits the enterprises we consider to commercial activities in which the government controls management by virtue of its ownership stake. It encompasses enterprises directly operated by a government department or those in which the government holds a majority of the shares directly or indirectly through other SOEs. It also encompasses enterprises in which the state holds a minority of the shares, if the distribution of the remaining shares leaves the government with effective control. It excludes much state-owned sector activity, such as education, health services, and road construction and maintenance, that are financed in other ways, usually from the government's general revenue. We have focused on nonfinancial SOEs, since to include financial SOEs we would need to consider many issues about the management of the financial system that would lengthen our already substantial report.

*This definition was first developed by Jones (1975) for the case of the Republic of Korea and has since been used to analyze SOEs as unique units of observation. See the statistical appendix for more on definitional issues.

Some Governments Are Selling More—and More Important—Enterprises

The number of countries selling SOEs increased in the 1980s, as divestiture spread from the industrial economies, notably the United Kingdom, to developing economies throughout the world. In the 1990s, many governments intensified their efforts, selling more enterprises and shifting their attention from small firms operating in competitive markets to large monopolies. Mass privatization efforts were begun in Eastern Europe and the republics of the former Soviet Union.

The growing number of countries undertaking divestitures and the shifting regional focus is shown in table 1.1. There were more than five times as many transactions in the six years from 1988–93 as in the previous eight years (1980–87).[1] Although most of the increase was due to the explosion of privatization activity in the transition economies of

Table 1.1 Divestiture in Developing Countries, 1980–93

	1980–87		1988–93[a]		1988–93[a]	
Region	Number of transactions	Percentage of total	Number of transactions	Percentage of total	Value of transactions ($ billions)	Percentage of worldwide value
Africa	210	46	254	11	3.2	3
Asia	108	24	367	16	19.7	21
Latin America	136	30	561	25	55.1	57
Eastern Europe and Central Asia	2	0[b]	1,097	48	17.9	19
Total developing countries	456	100	2,279	100	96.0	100
Industrial countries	240		376		174.9	
Divestitures worldwide	696		2,655		270.9	

a. Figures are from Sader (1994) who excludes privatizations with a sales value less than $50,000, any divestitures where state-owned enterprises were simply shut down and the assets mothballed, and all mass voucher divestitures. The latter comprises an especially significant form of divestiture in some Eastern European and Central Asian economies such as Russia and the Czech Republic.

b. Less than one percent.

Source: Derived from Candoy-Sekse (1988), Sader (1993), and Gelb and Singh (1994).

Eastern Europe and Central Asia, the number of divestitures increased more than fourfold in Latin America and more than threefold in the rest of Asia. Even Sub-Saharan Africa experienced an increase in divestitures, albeit a much more modest one that left the continent with fewer privatizations than any developing region. As a result of these increases, developing countries accounted for 86 percent of transactions in the second period, up from 66 percent during the first.

The available information on the size and nature of divested enterprises supports the view that divestiture was not only more common, but also more significant during the second period. Data on the value of firms sold during the first period are not available, but country evidence and a sectoral breakdown indicate that early sales involved relatively small SOEs, primarily in agribusiness, services, and light manufacturing. In 1988–93, by contrast, divestiture included the sale of large SOEs in such important sectors as electric and water utilities, transportation, and telecommunications, as well as major firms in the financial and industrial sectors (table 1.2). Of the $96 billion in public revenue generated by divestiture in developing economies during this period, the largest share ($32 billion) came from infrastructure. Even the $12.1 billion in sales revenue from the primary sector during this period is largely attributable to the sale of petroleum-related activities, which tend to be large scale; mines and agribusinesses account for most of the remainder.

Table 1.2 Revenue from Divestiture in Developing Countries by Region and Sector, 1988–93
(dollars, billion)

Country	Primary	Industrial	Finance	Infrastructure	Others	Total revenue
Africa	0.7	0.5	0.3	0.1	1.6	3.2
Asia	1.8	6.4	2.6	7.4	1.5	19.7
Latin America	8.2	9.9	13.3	22.5	1.2	55.1
Eastern Europe and Central Asia	1.4	8.9	3.7	2.0	1.9	17.9
Total	12.1	25.7	19.9	32.0	6.2	95.9
Total number of divestitures	392	1,036	146	267	438	2,279
Total divestitures for 1980–87	126	92	35	51	152	456

Note: Figures exclude privatizations with a sales value less than $50,000, divestitures where state-owned enterprises were simply shut down and assets mothballed, and all mass voucher divestitures.
Source: Derived from Candoy-Sekse (1988) and Sader (1993).

Further analysis of the data on the number and value of transactions in table 1.1 reveals wide regional divergence in the average size of firms. Latin America, with just one-fourth of the transactions, accounts for almost 60 percent of the value, while Central and Eastern Europe, with almost half of the transactions, account for only 19 percent of the value. This may reflect the fact that the Latin American countries, having greater experience with divestiture, were selling larger enterprises, while Central and Eastern European governments, new to the process, were selling smaller enterprises, as well as giving away shares through mass privatization schemes. Asia, with 16 percent of the transactions and 21 percent of the value, is second only to Latin America in average revenue per sale. By contrast, Africa, with a slim 11 percent of transactions, accounts for an even slimmer 3 percent of the enterprise value. This may reflect a smaller average size of African enterprises, as well as a greater reluctance by governments in the region to sell off large state monopolies.

Governments Are Also Investing Less in State-Owned Enterprises

Consistent with the perception that governments have reduced the role of SOEs in the economy is the decline in their share in investment over the period 1978–91 (figure 1.1).

Although they still absorb a larger percentage of investment in developing countries than in industrial countries, the share of SOEs in investment in developing countries has fallen from 22 percent in the early

Figure 1.1 Share of State-Owned Enterprise Investment in Gross Domestic Investment, by Region

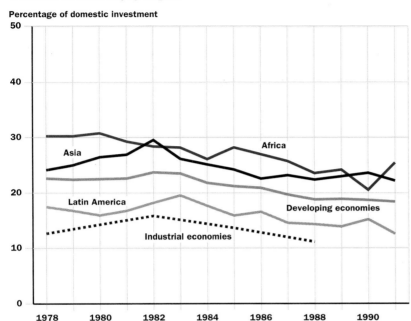

Percentage of domestic investment

Source: Statistical appendix.

The state-owned enterprise share of gross domestic investment has been slowly declining everywhere.

1980s to 19 percent in the early 1990s. A similar observation holds for the share of SOE investment relative to GDP, which declined from 5 percent in the early 1980s to 4 percent in the early 1990s. Again, we see wide regional variations. In Africa, the SOE sector averaged 27 percent of total investment over the period 1978–91, declining from 30 percent in the early 1980s to 25 percent in the early 1990s. In contrast, SOEs in Latin America accounted on average for 16 percent of total investment in the period 1978–91, declining from 17 percent in the early 1980s to 13 percent in the early 1990s. SOE investment in Asia (excluding China, for which comparable data were not available) has held steadier, at an average of 24.6 percent.

But the Importance of the SOE Sector Worldwide Has Not Declined

Sales of more, and more important, enterprises as well as the declining share of SOE investment would tend to suggest that the importance of SOEs has diminished in recent years. Neither trend, however, appears to have made a significant dent. First, although divestiture has grown, it is still small relative to the stock of SOEs. Dividing total transactions worldwide (3,351) by the number of divesting countries (ninety-five) over thirteen years (1980–93) yields an annual average of less than three divestitures per country per year, against hundreds of SOEs that could have been divested in almost all countries.[2] In fact, most countries fell well short of the average, because transactions have been concentrated in only a few countries. In 1980–87, eight countries accounted for 45 percent of divestiture transactions in developing countries. In 1988–93, just five countries (Argentina, Brazil, Hungary, Mexico, and Poland) accounted for about 30 percent of developing-country transactions and 60 percent of the value of enterprises sold. Second, the declining share of SOE investment may not have affected the size of the SOE sector in the period we examined, because investment typically represents a small proportion of capital stock. To the extent that this trend continues, the relative role of the SOE sector in the economy will diminish in the future. But for now, the small number of divestitures relative to the total number of SOEs, the concentration of sales in only a few countries, and the fact that the decline in the SOE share of investment will only gradually reduce the size of SOE capital stock relative to the rest of the economy all suggest that the importance of the SOE sector on average has remained substantially unchanged in developing countries.

The share of SOEs in developing-country GDP supports this view. Excluding the transition economies, SOE value added as a percentage of developing-country GDP has not decreased over time (figure 1.2). In the late 1980s it was about 11 percent, little changed from the beginning of the decade and higher than in the late 1970s. In contrast, SOEs' share of GDP in industrial countries fell from about 9 percent in 1982 to less than 7 percent by 1988. During the 1986–91 period as a whole, setting aside the transition economies, SOEs played the biggest role in Africa, where they accounted for an average of 14 percent of GDP, followed by Latin America with 10 percent and Asia with 9 percent (figure 1.2).

Is SOE value added as a proportion of GDP a meaningful measure of the relative importance of the SOE sector? It is possible, of course, that SOE price increases in the 1980s offset the effects of divestiture and lower investment; in that case, an SOE sector smaller by other measures would nonetheless remain constant in terms of value added. This argument would be valid if SOE selling prices rose faster than prices in the rest of

Figure 1.2 Share of State-Owned Enterprises in Gross Domestic Product, by Region

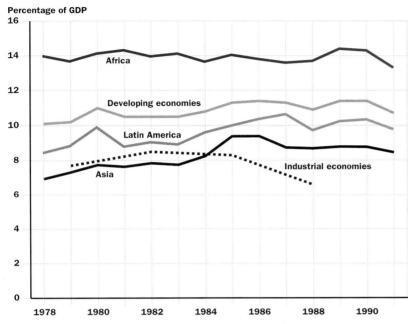

Percentage of GDP

Source: Statistical appendix.

But the state-owned enterprise share of gross domestic product has remained about constant, except in the industrial countries.

the economy. As we will see in chapters 2 and 3, however, it is unlikely that this is the case. While some SOEs did indeed raise prices during this period, company-level evidence suggests that SOE price increases often failed to keep pace with inflation. In other cases, SOEs cut prices in response to increased competition due to trade liberalization and generally reduced protection. Thus, it is unlikely that SOE price increases would account for the relatively constant share of SOE value added in GDP. A more likely explanation is that divestiture and declining investment have yet to reduce significantly the size of the SOE sector.

This premise is also supported by the lack of change in the SOE share of total employment (figure 1.3). As with several other measures, however, important variations exist at the regional level. SOEs in Africa accounted for 23 percent of employment in 1991, up from 19 percent in the early 1980s (figure 1.3). In contrast, SOEs accounted for only about 2

Figure 1.3 Share of State-Owned Enterprise Employment in Total Employment, by Region

Percentage (unweighted averages)

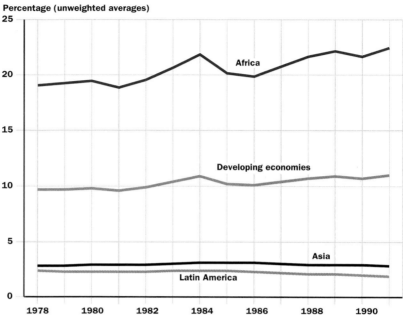

The state-owned enterprise share in total employment has shown little change over time.

Source: Statistical appendix.

percent of employment in Latin America in 1990–91, a share that has declined slightly. The SOE share of employment has remained steady in Asia, at a modest 3 percent.

Taken together, then, the evidence suggests that, notwithstanding the extensive privatization efforts of the past two decades, divestiture has yet to change substantially the balance between the state-owned and private sectors in the majority of developing countries.

State-Owned Enterprises Are Most Important in the Poorest Countries

Generally, the evidence suggests that the poorer the country, the larger the relative size of its SOE sector. During the 1980s, SOEs accounted for a substantially larger share of the economy in low-income countries (14 percent of GDP, 18 percent of nonagricultural GDP, and 28 percent of investment) than in middle-income countries (9 percent of GDP, 10 percent of nonagricultural GDP, and 17 percent of investment); while the SOE share of the economy in high-income (industrial) countries was the lowest of all (8 percent of GDP and 13 percent of investment).[3]

Moreover, in contrast to the high- and middle-income economies, where the average share of SOEs in the economy has declined, the share of SOEs in the least developed economies—higher to begin with—has held nearly constant (figure 1.4). In middle-income economies, the importance of SOEs in GDP, gross domestic investment, and employment peaked in the mid-1980s and has fallen since. In the low-income economies, the average share of SOEs in GDP climbed until 1989 before dropping to mid-1980s levels; the SOE share of employment has remained nearly constant since the late 1970s. Of the three measures of SOE importance in the low-income economies, only investment shares have fallen, erratically, since the mid-1980s.

These measures clearly indicate that, despite divestiture efforts, SOEs continue to play an important role in developing economies, especially in the poorest countries. Whether or not this is a problem depends upon the effect of SOEs on the economy. If that effect is negative, then reform is vital, especially in least developed economies. We turn, therefore, to an evaluation of the effect of SOEs on economic performance.

How SOEs Affect Economic Performance

WHILE A HANDFUL OF SOES UNDOUBTEDLY PERFORM VERY well, there is a wealth of anecdotal evidence suggesting that many more do not. Consider the following examples:

- In Turkey, Turkiye Taskorumu Kurmu, a state-owned coal mining company, lost the equivalent of about $6.4 billion between 1986 and 1990. Losses in 1992 worked out to about $12,000 per worker, six times the average national income. Yet health and safety conditions in the mine were so poor that a miners' life expectancy was forty-six years, eleven years below the national average. In short, the miners and the government would have been better off if the government had imported coal and paid the miners to stay home.

Figure 1.4 Three Measures of SOE Importance in Low-Income Economies

A. State-Owned Enterprise Share in Gross Domestic Product

Percentage (unweighted averages)

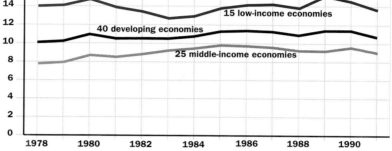

B. State-Owned Enterprise Share in Gross Domestic Investment

Percentage (unweighted averages)

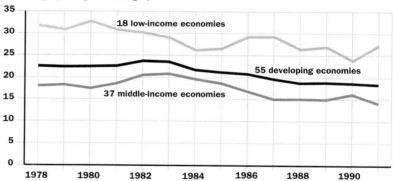

C. State-Owned Enterprise Share in Employment

Percentage (unweighted averages)

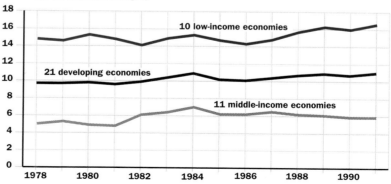

These figures show that, despite divestiture efforts, SOEs continue to play an important role in developing economies, especially the poorest.

Source: Statistical appendix.

- In the Philippines, the performance of the National Power Corporation steadily deteriorated from 1985 until the early 1990s. In 1990 the capital region alone lost an estimated $2.4 billion in economic output due to power outages. By 1992–93, electricity was shut off about seven hours a day in many parts of the country.

- In Bangladesh, in 1992 the state sugar milling monopoly had twice as many office workers as it needed, or about 8,000 extra employees. Farmers near the outmoded state mills were required to sell their sugar cane to the government at below-market prices, with the result that many planted other crops, causing a shortage of cane. Meanwhile, sugar cost twice as much on the open market in Bangladesh as it did internationally.

- In Tanzania, the state-owned Morogoro shoe factory, built in the 1970s with a World Bank loan, never manufactured more than about 4 percent of its supposed annual capacity. Designed to turn out four million pairs of shoes a year, four times the international norm, the factory planned to export three-quarters of its production to Europe, even though Tanzania lacked high-quality leather, experienced designers, and shoe assembly-line workers. Ill-suited to Tanzania's tropical heat, with steel pillars, aluminum walls, and no ventilation system, the plant deteriorated quickly after it was commissioned. Production ceased in 1990.

Of course such anecdotal evidence, no matter how disturbing, does not in itself constitute a convincing argument for or against state ownership; nor does it enable us to quantify the effect on the economy and welfare of large SOE sectors. In this, the final section of this chapter, we attempt such an assessment. We begin by presenting arguments and empirical evidence at the microeconomic level that, on balance, private firms are more efficient than SOEs in markets that are competitive or potentially competitive and that, under certain circumstances, the same is true in monopoly markets as well. We include in this analysis an assessment of the welfare consequences of privatizing SOEs and recent findings about the negative effect of SOEs on the environment. We then turn to the way SOE sectors in the aggregate finance their operation and expansion, given that their finances may undermine fiscal stability and fuel inflation. Finally, we draw on our microeconomic and finance discussions to consider the impact of large SOE sectors on growth.

The Impact of State Ownership at the Company Level

The argument for government ownership rests primarily on the assumption that governments can use SOEs to correct for various types of market failure. Markets may fail where there are public goods (e.g., clean air or water, which no individual or group will fund for everyone), lumpy investments (e.g., large outlays such as roads or harbors that the private sector is unwilling or unable to take on), failures in coordination (e.g., no market for steel unless there is a steel mill, and no steel mill unless there is a market), or underdeveloped capital markets. These conditions, arguably more prevalent in developing economies, have often been cited to justify the creation and support of SOEs in developing countries. (Arguments that SOEs can help achieve social objectives are also made; we address this issue in chapter 2.)

The argument against SOEs recognizes market failure but asserts that the risk of government failure is often greater. Government is not a monolithic entity; rather it answers to many constituencies and lacks a unified chain of command. Because no individual or group owns a state enterprise, no one has a clear stake in SOE returns, hence no one has the responsibility and motivation to set clear performance goals and assure they are attained.[4] Instead, politicians, bureaucrats, employees, and other interest groups thrust upon SOEs multiple and often conflicting goals (e.g., profit maximization, employment maximization, and a host of other social objectives) while simultaneously imposing a bewildering and sometimes contradictory collection of constraints (e.g., restricting layoffs, price increases, and the choice of suppliers or markets). Multiple objectives and multiple constraints increase transaction costs, distort the incentives facing SOE managers, and reduce managerial effort.[5] If SOEs have access to subsidies, transfers, or government guaranteed loans, as they often do, then there is, in addition, no threat of bankruptcy to act as a check on inefficiency.[6]

Both arguments accept that SOEs are less efficient than private firms when markets work and when governments are able to provide credible commitment to the private sector not to expropriate its assets. Where markets fail, the choice of private versus state ownership is less clear cut and will depend, case by case, on the tradeoffs between market failure on one hand and government failure on the other. In monopoly or oligopoly markets, private firms may be more efficient than SOEs, but they may exploit consumers and set prices so high that their products are available only to a wealthy few. For example, a poorly regulated private water monopoly might price clean water out of reach of many households. But a poorly managed and supervised water SOE may not do any better. That is, it may also provide service only to a small proportion of the population, not because of overpricing, but because its revenues have been so eroded by underpricing, overstaffing, or mismanagement that it has underinvested in expansion and maintenance. Both these undesirable outcomes have remedies: better regulation for the private enterprise, better pricing and incentive policies for the state-owned enterprise. These tradeoffs and the conditions under which the balance tips toward state or private ownership are a subject for further empirical investigation, which we undertake in chapter 3. As we shall see, although the outcome varies according to sector and country circumstances, the evidence suggests it more often tilts toward privatization, especially in middle-income countries. In the remainder of this section, we consider the available empirical evidence about the advantages of state versus private ownership in competitive and monopoly markets.

The empirical literature that deals with the issue of private versus public efficiency is of two types. Early studies compared the performance of state-owned and private enterprises in the same sector, across sectors, and over time. (For surveys, see Borcherding, Pommerehne, and Schneider 1982; Millward 1982).[7] A general problem with most of this literature is that it necessarily compares enterprises that, aside from the obvious differences in ownership, have other differing characteristics. Although some studies attempted to adjust for the size of firms, market structure, or enterprise objectives, it is almost impossible to eliminate all interfirm differences. Indeed, Millward and Parker (1983) assert the impossibility of reaching an unambiguous conclusion on the basis of such comparisons. This problem is particularly acute in developing countries, where most SOEs, even those in potentially competitive markets, have few comparable firms.

More recent work compares the performance of SOEs before and after divestiture, divested with undivested SOEs, or divested firms with a hypothetical counterfactual in which the same firm is assumed to continue under state ownership. (For partial surveys of this literature, see Galal and others 1994; Kikeri, Nellis, and Shirley 1992; Vickers and Yarrow 1988).[8] In competitive markets this literature gives the edge to the private sector. Thus, Vickers and Yarrow (1988, 426) conclude, "theoretical analysis and empirical evidence support the view that private ownership is most efficient—and hence privatization is most suitable—in markets where effective (actual and potential) competition prevails." Where SOEs operate in noncompetitive markets, the results and interpretations are less clear. However, one study (Galal and others 1994) analyzed twelve divestiture cases from Chile, Malaysia, Mexico, and the United Kingdom (three telecommunications firms, four airlines, two electricity companies, a container terminal, a truck transport, and a lottery). The study finds that divestiture improved world and domestic welfare in eleven of the twelve cases, as the figure in box 1.2 shows. The gains came primarily from improved productivity, increased investment, and better pricing; they occurred in both competitive and monopoly markets, in part because the regulatory framework for the monopolies was sound enough to allow private firms to function efficiently and to protect consumers. The sample is small, but the methodology is especially careful. The study measures the effects of divestiture on the producers, consumers, workers, government, and competitors and measures them over enough time to capture dynamic effects. It isolates the effects of ownership from other factors by asking: what would have happened in the absence of divestiture?

Although privatization can fail if not carried out properly, as we discuss in chapters 2 and 5, the potential benefits from successful privatization are not confined to the measured gains to buyers, sellers, workers, and consumers. Divestiture can, in addition, stimulate new private sector activities, help develop the capital market, and induce more competitive behavior in general, none of which is readily measurable. Similarly, although the economic effect is difficult to quantify, recent World Bank research indicates that divesting SOEs, especially older ones, helps the environment, since state-owned plants tend to be more polluting than their private sector counterparts.

Figure 1.5 illustrates the large gap in abatement activity between state and private pulp and paper plants in four countries (Bangladesh, India, Indonesia, and Thailand). In the study, private plants, whether foreign or domestically owned, control pollution much better than state-owned plants operating at similar scale and efficiency (Hettige and others 1995).[9] Of course, part of the problem is that state-owned plants tend to be old, inefficient, and unprofitable. But even these factors don't explain why state-owned plants pollute more. Figure 1.6 illustrates the public-private gap in water pollution per unit of output that remained even after size, efficiency, and age were accounted for in

Box 1.2 Welfare Consequences of Selling State-Owned Enterprises

DOES DIVESTITURE IMPROVE DOMESTIC AND world welfare? Who wins, who loses, and how much? One study evaluated these questions in a sample of twelve divestiture case studies in four countries (Chile, Malaysia, Mexico, and the United Kingdom). The cases cover nine monopolies (in telecommunications, energy, airlines, and ports) and three firms in competitive markets (in trucking, gambling, and electricity generation). They find that in eleven of the twelve cases divestiture made the world a better place by fostering more efficient operation and new investment. The gains in some cases were significant or unexpected. For example, productivity improved in nine of the twelve cases, most dramatically in Aéromexico, the Mexican airline, where it rose by 48 percent. In others, the gains did not necessarily follow from productivity improvement but from increased investment. This occurred in four of the twelve cases, doubling the number of telephone lines in the case of the Chilean phone company in four years after divestiture. Moreover, the gains were shared by most of the actors involved, including buyers, government, workers, consumers, and even competitors. This success did not follow from divestiture alone. Countries in the sample also did a host of other things right. These varied from case to case but included increasing competition in the product market where possible, regulating monopolies where required, and, in most cases, a competitive sale of enterprises. Moreover, divesting countries enjoyed sound macroeconomic policy at the time of divestiture.

Source: Galal and others (1994).

Box Figure 1.2 Welfare Effects of Selling State-Owned Enterprises

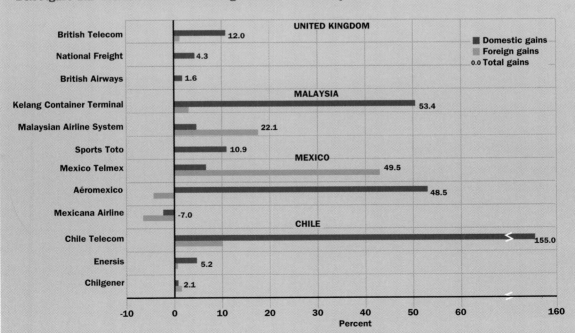

Note: Welfare gains are presented as a percentage of annual sales in the last year before privatization.

Figure 1.5 Pollution Abatement Efforts

Index of abatement effort

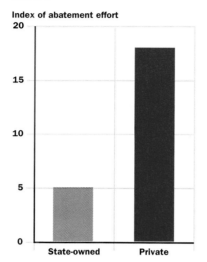

State-owned plants tend to be more polluting than private plants.

Note: This data covers Bangladesh, India, Indonesia, and Thailand.
Source: Hemamala and others (1995).

Figure 1.6 Water Pollution Levels, by Age and Ownership of Firm, Indonesia

Water pollution per unit of output (kg/million rupiah)

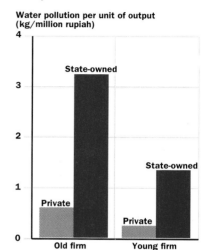

Source: Pargal and Wheeler (1995).

a study of Indonesian factories. State-owned factories polluted over five times as much per unit of output as comparable plants in the private sector. Research into these dramatic differences continues, but the main explanation seems to be that SOEs are better placed to evade pollution regulators than their private counterparts (see box 1.3).

On balance, then, theory and the available microeconomic evidence suggests that, in competitive or potentially competitive markets, private firms are more efficient than state-owned firms. In monopoly markets, the potential gains from privatization can be very large, but their attainment depends on a set of preconditions (most notably on the regulatory framework), as we detail in chapter 3. Finally, private ownership can lead to better compliance with pollution regulations, improving welfare in ways that are not readily captured in measures of efficiency. We now turn to a consideration of the aggregate finances of the SOE sector, analyzing how SOE deficits can undermine fiscal stability and fuel inflation.

Box 1.3 Privatization and Pollution

CUBATAO, BRAZIL, USED TO BE KNOWN AS "THE Valley of Death" because of its extreme pollution problem. It is much cleaner these days, thanks to the dedicated work of CETESB (Companhia de Technologia de Saneamento Ambiental), the pollution control agency of São Paulo State. But even CETESB has found a few nuts too tough to crack—large, highly polluting state-owned factories that have failed to comply with pollution control regulations for over a decade. The figure below shows the proportion of air and water pollution in the valley contributed by COSIPA (steel) and PETROBRAS (petroleum), two state-owned plants that have been the valley's biggest sources of pollution and CETESB's biggest regulatory headaches. The situation in Cubatão may be unusually dramatic, but it is not unique. World Bank research in Asia has also found that state-owned firms are much less aggressive in reducing pollution than their private sector counterparts.

Why should this be so? As SOEs, state-owned plants should theoretically do more, not less, to assure public health and safety by complying with en-

vironmental regulations. In addition, state-owned factories with soft budget constraints should find it easier to absorb the costs of pollution control equipment. They also tend to be large facilities, which can control pollution more cheaply than small plants. Although part of the problem may be that SOEs have older, less efficient plants, state-owned plants tend to be dirtier than privately owned plants even after size and age are taken into account.

The main problem seems to be that SOEs use their bureaucratic connections to escape pollution regulation. In Cubatão, a veteran pollution inspector summarized it this way: "To a public enterprise, we are just another government bureau. They feel that we have no right to tell them what to do, and they have enough clout in the government to keep us away." Officials of the state pollution control agency are eagerly anticipating the privatization of COSIPA, since they have far fewer problems with private firms. For the people of Cubatão, privatization of COSIPA will literally bring a breath of fresh air.

Source: CETESB (1994).

Box Figure 1.3 SOE and Private Contribution to Pollution in Brazil

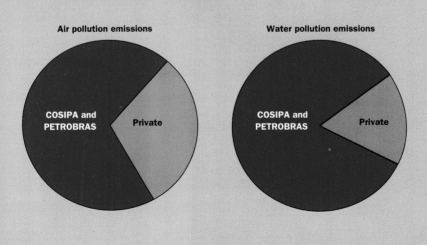

Air pollution emissions · Water pollution emissions

COSIPA and PETROBRAS · Private

The Impact of Financing Aggregate State-Owned Enterprise Deficits

SOE sectors are often unable to generate the resources to finance their operation and expansion and to service their debt. This is the SOE savings-investment deficit (or SOE S-I deficit), defined as the difference between the SOE sector's current surplus and investment, which is filled by government transfers, domestic private savings, foreign borrowing, or a mix of all three.[10] Of course, a temporary SOE S-I deficit is not necessarily bad; private firms, too, borrow to finance their operations and to expand. S-I deficits *are* a waste of a country's scarce resources, however, when SOEs run these deficits because their productivity is low or because their prices are set below an economically efficient level. How often is this the case? We have seen above that SOEs are often less efficient than private companies. Moreover, as we shall see from the country evidence in chapter 2, the SOE S-I deficit tends to be larger in countries where SOEs have been less productive and less profitable (for example, in the Philippines, Senegal, and Turkey). Taken together, this evidence suggests that a large and continuous S-I deficit indicates poor SOE performance. As we discuss below, this deficit hurts economic growth in a variety of ways.

Our data suggest that the SOE S-I deficit has narrowed somewhat in developing countries overall; however, improvements are concentrated in middle-income economies while in the poorer countries the problem remains acute. Figure 1.7 shows trends in SOE savings minus investment as a percentage of GDP for the forty-six developing countries for which data were available. For the entire group, the annual average S-I deficit went from 2.2 percent of GDP during 1978–85 to 0.8 percent during 1986–91, thanks to a combination of rising SOE savings and the decline in SOE investment noted above.[11] As a result, the SOE resource requirements also diminished, as reflected in lower SOE shares of total external and domestic credit: the share of SOEs in external debt declined from an average of 14.8 percent in 1978–85 to 12.0 percent in 1986–91, while their share in domestic credit in relation to GDP declined from 5.2 to 4.1 percent. Their contribution to the government budget on a net basis went from a drain of 0.2 percent of GDP (1978–85) to a positive contribution of 0.9 percent of GDP (1986–91).[12] However, the figure also reveals a worrying divergence of trends in the SOE S-I deficit in middle-income economies on the one hand and the low-income economies on the other. From 1978 until the mid-1980s, the average ratio of the S-I deficit to GDP narrowed for both groups. After 1985, the SOE S-I deficit in the twenty-nine middle-in-

Figure 1.7 State-Owned Enterprise Savings Minus Investment

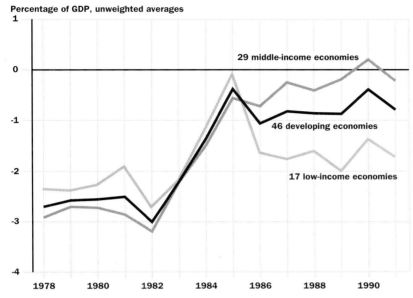

Percentage of GDP, unweighted averages

Source: Statistical appendix.

The SOE savings-investment deficit improved in most countries until the mid-1980s. Since then it has deteriorated in the poorest countries.

come economies in the sample continued to narrow to the point where SOEs in these countries showed a surplus in 1990. But the seventeen poor countries in the overall sample lost ground, so that their SOE S-I deficit fell back to an average of 1.7 percent of GDP during 1986–91; moreover, the deficit widened even though, as we saw in figure 1.4, SOE investments were declining in low-income as well as middle-income economies.

Our data also suggest that there are significant differences in the ways that poor economies and middle-income economies finance their SOE deficits. Perhaps because they lack ready access to foreign credit, low-income economies are more likely than middle-income economies to finance their SOE deficits from the government budget and through domestic credit, rather than foreign borrowing (figures 1.8, 1.9). In contrast, middle-income economies, having greater access to foreign credit and, perhaps, more bankable SOEs, have tended to finance their SOE deficits through foreign borrowing, as can be seen in the larger, albeit declining, SOE share of middle-income country total external debt (figure 1.10). Thus, even though SOEs in middle-income economies on

Figure 1.8 Net Financial Transfers to State-Owned Enterprises as a Share of Gross Domestic Product

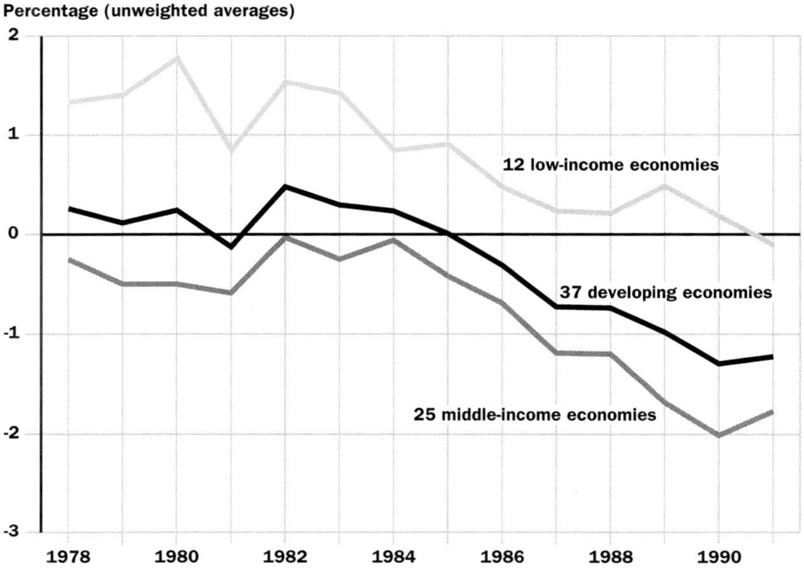

Percentage (unweighted averages)

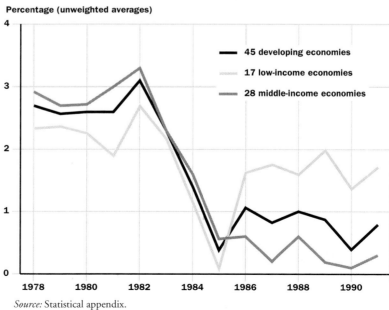

Financial transfers to state-owned enterprises in low-income economies have improved, but middle-income countries are still doing better.

Source: Statistical appendix.

Figure 1.9 State-Owned Enterprise Share in Gross Domestic Credit

Percentage (unweighted averages)

Since the mid-1980s, state-owned enterprises have taken a larger share of credit in poorer countries.

Source: Statistical appendix.

Figure 1.10 State-Owned Enterprise Share in Total External Debt

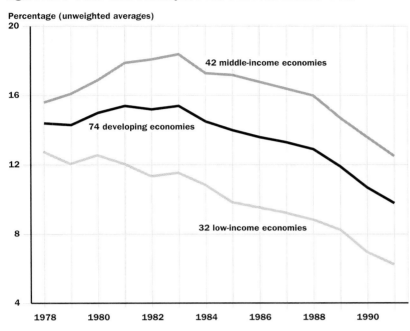

Percentage (unweighted averages)

42 middle-income economies

74 developing economies

32 low-income economies

The SOE share of total external debt has been falling, but middle-income countries still use foreign borrowing more than poorer countries.

Source: Statistical appendix.

average ran an overall deficit during the 1980s, they were nonetheless able to make net transfers to the government (figure 1.8). In lower income economies, on the other hand, state enterprise deficits have fallen more heavily on the government budget and domestic credit.

Assessing the Impact of State Ownership on Growth

The generally poor performance of SOEs at the microeconomic level, together with the SOE S-I deficit at the aggregate level, suggest that a large SOE sector is likely to have a negative effect on growth in a variety of ways. The inefficiency of individual SOEs would be expected, in the aggregate, to exert a drag on growth, so that, other things being equal, the larger a country's SOE sector, the lower its growth rates. Moreover, the more extensive government ownership in an economy, the greater the likelihood that bureaucrats facing perverse incentives and contradictory demands are running businesses in which private entrepreneurs facing clear-cut incentives for profit maximization in competitive markets would be more efficient. Financially, the burden of SOE deficits can hinder growth by crowding out expenditure on health and education, by increasing fiscal deficits, and by contributing to inflation. Although data limitations preclude a full assessment of the effect of SOEs on growth, we conclude this chapter by exploring first the effect of the efficiency differential at the level of the firm and then the aggregate effect of SOE deficits on growth.[13]

One obvious piece of evidence of the impact of state ownership is the dramatic collapse of the former centrally planned economies of Eastern and Central Europe. This massive political, economic, and social transformation is, of course, due to a host of factors, including some, such as distorted incentives, central planning, and excessive regulation, that could, theoretically at least, be divorced from state ownership. But the fact remains that these economies were nearly fully state-owned. To be sure, these economies were able to grow rapidly in the postwar period, thanks to high investment rates. However, the relative inefficiency of the use of this investment ultimately meant that SOEs were unable to deliver the goods and services, and, eventually, the economic growth, taken for granted by people in market-oriented countries with similar resource and population endowments. In the 1970s and 1980s, growth in Eastern Europe slowed markedly to, for example, an annual rate of only 1.0 percent in Poland during 1980–88. Since the late 1980s, these economies have been engaged in a major transformation in which the private sector is playing a much more important role. The story for China, which is also undergoing a plan-to-market transition, is more complex but in keeping with the premise that extensive state ownership is an impediment to growth.[14]

The evidence on the impact of state ownership in mixed economies, is less dramatic than in the former centrally planned economies because the size of the SOE sector was less significant; but it also supports the premise that large SOE sectors are bad for growth. The study of 12 divestitures reported in Box 1.2 suggests that, if the experience of this small sample holds more broadly, then divesting half the SOE sector in a country where SOEs account for 10 percent of GDP—about typical for a developing country—would increase GDP by 1 percent; and gains of a similar magnitude in absolute terms would follow year after year (Galal and others 1994).[15] In a country like Egypt, where the SOE sector accounts for one-third of the economy, the gains could be even higher.

As for large SOE S-I deficits, which we have shown above to be particularly acute and persistent in the poorest countries, these have a negative effect on growth in two specific ways. At the simplest level, money spent to support a money-losing enterprise is then unavailable for growth-promoting social services, such as education and health. In a somewhat more complex way, SOE deficits undermine fiscal stability and contribute to inflation, making it more difficult for governments to provide a macroeconomic environment conducive to rapid, sustained growth.

Subsidies to SOEs are sometimes justified on social grounds, that they provide jobs or inexpensive goods and services that would otherwise be unavailable to the poor. Setting aside the question of whether or not SOEs actually attain these goals (see chapter 2), our data suggest that in many countries the explicit operating subsidies that SOEs absorb would provide a very significant boost to government efforts to provide basic health and education, which previous studies have shown to be closely correlated to long-term growth. Diverting SOE operating subsidies to basic education, for example, would increase central government education expenditures by 50 percent in Mexico, 74 percent in Tanzania, 160 percent in Tunisia, and 550 percent in India. Alternatively, diverting SOE subsidies to health care would have allowed central governments to more than double health expenditures in Senegal and increase them by threefold in Turkey, about fourfold in Mexico and Tunisia, and fivefold in India.[16] Of course, in countries where the SOE sector is smaller and/or SOEs are better run, very little money is diverted to cover SOE operating subsidies. In Thailand, for example, SOE subsidies are equivalent to only one-tenth of 1 percent of government expenditures on education. Figure 1.11 shows the percentage by which central governments could increase spending on education and health if they eliminated direct SOE subsidies.

The other cost to growth of SOE deficits, the impact on fiscal stability and inflation, is harder to quantify but perhaps ultimately more significant, given the abundant evidence of the importance of macroeconomic stability to long-term growth.[17] A large SOE S-I deficit can be financed in a variety of ways, all of which have a potentially negative effect on growth. For example, a government may resort to central bank financing, effectively printing money to pay SOE debts, with the attendant inflationary pressures. Alternatively, the government may direct the banking system to loan money to financially strapped SOEs, diverting credit that would otherwise have gone to the private sector. Finally, governments may borrow abroad to finance SOE deficits, thereby contributing to a balance of payments deficit and hence the current account deficit, and so exerting downward pressures on the real exchange rate.

Figure 1.11 Explicit Operating Subsidies to State-Owned Enterprises

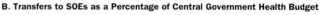

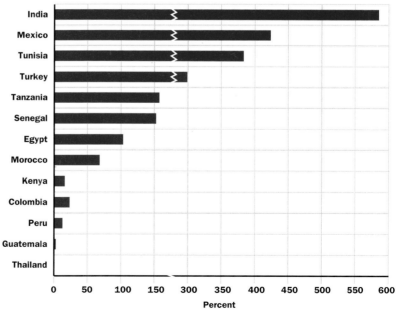

Subsidies to SOEs consume scarce government funds that could better be spent on education and health.

Source: IMF; statistical appendix.

Our data strongly support the premise that the larger the SOE sector's overall deficit, the larger the fiscal and current account deficits. The average annual SOE S-I deficit for thirty-eight developing countries from 1978 to 1991 moves closely in tandem with their fiscal and current account deficits (figure 1.12), and the SOE deficit is also correlated with both deficits. That the SOE S-I deficit is important for fiscal stability is further evidenced by the fact that it averaged 35 percent of the fiscal deficit in the same thirty-eight countries (measured by the ratio of the means of both variables). The general improvement in the SOE deficit that we discussed earlier has helped reduce the fiscal and current account deficits. The picture is less sanguine for lower income countries whose SOE S-I deficits have remained stubbornly large (Figure 1.7).

In sum, then, the microeconomic evidence, the experience of formerly centrally planned economies, and the strong negative effect SOEs have on fiscal deficits all collectively support the premise that large SOE sectors can

Figure 1.12 Indicators of State-Owned Enterprise Performance in Developing Countries

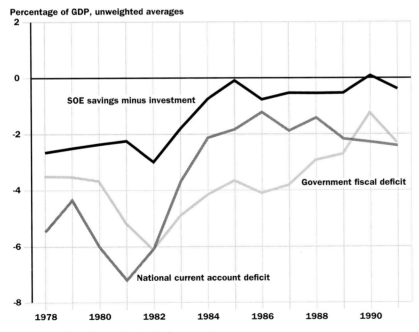

Percentage of GDP, unweighted averages

SOE savings minus investment

Government fiscal deficit

National current account deficit

The SOE savings-investment deficit moves closely in tandem with fiscal and current account deficits.

Note: Sample is thirty-eight developing countries.
Source: Statistical appendix.

49

hinder growth. Moreover, because SOE sectors tend to be larger in low-income countries, SOEs are likely to be most costly in the countries that can least afford them.

Conclusion

WE HAVE SHOWN THAT DESPITE A DECADE OF DIVESTI-ture, SOEs continue to dominate an important share of the economy in a large number of developing-market economies. The relative size of the SOE sector is much larger in the poorest economies than in industrial and middle-income countries. Of course, the relative size of the SOE sector would not matter if SOEs were efficient. However, we have presented evidence that SOEs are less efficient than the private sector in competitive markets and, with effective regulation of private firms, in monopoly markets as well. Finally, we have shown that large SOE sectors can be a drag on the economy because of the aggregate impact of inefficient operation at the microeconomic level and because large SOE sectors are typically associated with large fiscal and current account deficits, which in turn have negative repercussions on growth.

In sum, although much has been written about the potential benefits of reforming SOEs, and leaders in nearly all developing countries have said that they intend to reform, these efforts have not significantly reduced the economic role of SOEs nor have they measurably improved SOE performance. What explains this gap between rhetoric and results? Given the high cost of preserving the SOE status quo, and the very significant benefits of reform, why have so few countries reformed successfully? To answer these questions, we need first to understand how the policies affecting SOEs have differed between countries that reformed successfully and those that did not. We turn to this inquiry in our next chapter.

Notes

1. The two periods come from different data sets and may not be strictly comparable. No data are available on value of transactions for the earlier period. Data for the later period exclude East Germany and the voucher sales and privatization of small-scale enterprises in Eastern Europe.

2. If we had included the recent voucher privatization in Eastern Europe and former Soviet Union, it would have increased our total number of privatizations several-fold, but it would also have added many thousands of SOEs to the stock of enterprises that could have been divested.

3. There are fifteen low-income and twenty-five middle-income countries in our sample for SOE value added (eighteen low-income and thirty-seven middle-income economies for SOE investment) using the 1994 *World Development Report*'s definitions of per capita income of $675 or less for lower-income and $676 to $8,355 for middle-income economies. Periods cited vary according to data availability: figures for low-income and middle-income economies are for 1978–91; figures for industrial economies are for 1979–88 (for SOE share of GDP) and 1978–88 (for SOE share of investment). See the statistical appendix for details.

4. This argument also applies to large private corporations where ownership is divorced from management, leading managers to try to maximize their utility at the expense of profit. For further elaboration, see Williamson (1975).

5. In the language of the principal-agent literature, the agent (SOE management in this case) has more information than the principal (government) and can choose how much effort to expend. The principal can only observe outcomes and cannot measure accurately the effort expended by the agent and sort it out from other factors affecting productivity. The challenge, then, is to design an efficient contract that motivates the agent to be productive, including a premium paid to the agent to compensate him or her for the added risk. The problem is that SOEs have multiple principals who may have neither the

authority, capacity, or motivation to monitor the SOE. At the same time, measuring performance is especially difficult because SOEs are typically expected to pursue a number of commercial and noncommercial objectives. (For a review of the theoretical arguments, see, for example, Ross 1991; Stiglitz 1974; Sappington 1991).

6. Jones and Mason (1982) go further, arguing that activities that require decentralized decisionmaking and rapid response to changes in markets and technology are especially ill-suited for state ownership. Such activities are typically small relative to the product and factor markets (restaurants or chocolate factories), produce differentiated products (women's clothing), and use rapidly changing technologies (computers) or labor-intensive techniques (textiles).

7. A number of studies from the earlier, comparative literature concludes that private enterprises perform better than SOEs (for example, Boardman and Vining 1989; Bennett and Johnson 1979; Boycko, Shleifer, and Vishny 1993). Others (for example, Caves and Christensen 1980; Aharoni 1986) argue that SOE inefficiency can be traced to the lack of competition or to the social and political demands imposed on them. Surveys of these studies reach different conclusions. For example, on the one hand, Milward (1982) finds "no evidence of a statistically satisfactory kind to suggest that SOEs in developing economies have a lower level of technical efficiency than private firms operating at the same scale of operation." On the other hand, an extensive review of studies comparing unit cost structures in public and private firms found that forty of the more than fifty studies surveyed attributed superior results to the private firms (Borcherding, Pommerehne, and Schneider 1982).

8. Bishop and Kay (1988) compare the performance of divested and undivested firms in the United Kingdom in different sectors over the same period of time. Although they find that divested as well as undivested firms improved their performance, they hypothesize that the reasons for this improvement could have been the business cycle or the threat of divestiture to the remaining SOEs. Vickers and Yarrow (1988) also analyze the United King-

dom's divestiture experience, but their conclusion attributes improved performance to improved competition and regulation. Megginson, Nash, and Randenborgh (1994) analyze the effect of divestiture on performance, using a panel of forty-one divested firms from fifteen countries. They find that divestiture correlates significantly with higher profitability, better utilization of human and physical resources, company growth, and greater employment.

9. Submitted for publication, available in mimeo from the World Bank's Environment, Infrastructure, and Agriculture Department.

10. Thus, the identity of the SOE S-I deficit can be stated as follows:

$$(I-S)_{SOE} = (S-I)_g + (S-I)_{pr} + CA$$

where

$(I-S)_{SOE}$ = SOE investment − SOE savings

$(S-I)_g$ = government savings − government investment

$(S-I)_{pr}$ = private savings − private investment

CA = foreign borrowing (the counterpart of the current account deficit).

11. Savings are defined as the difference between SOE operating and nonoperating revenues (excluding all transfers, be it from the treasury or any other source) and all operating and nonoperating expenses (excluding all distribution of profit, such as dividends). Capital expenditures are total investments, including stock changes. The net budgetary transfers represent the flow of funds from the treasury to SOEs (e.g., subsidies, equity, loans) minus the flow of funds from SOEs to treasury (e.g., royalties, dividends, loan repayment). (This leaves out implicit transfers—for example, tax and import duty exemptions and cheap credit—which can be important in some cases.) Thus, a negative figure for transfers means the SOEs have transferred to the treasury more resources than they have received from it.

12. Although the averages for the SOE savings-investment deficit and for external and domestic credit cover more or less the same countries, the number of countries included in each variable varies. As shown in the statistical appendix, the averages for the SOE savings-investment deficit cover forty-five countries, those for external borrowing

cover seventy-four countries, and those for domestic credit cover thirty-seven countries. These variations in coverage were dictated by data availability.

13. We attempted to test the effect of state ownership on growth by adding a measure of the size of the SOE sector relative to GDP to Barro's (1991) growth variables. Although the results showed a significant negative correlation between the level of state ownership and growth, limited data meant that the results were not robust. In particular, there was insufficient time-series data on SOE sector size for enough countries over a sufficiently long time to conduct satisfactory growth regression analysis. Indeed, the data were not even sufficient to identify the standard determinants of growth.

14. SOEs have been less important in China than in transition economies in Europe, mostly because agriculture is so much more important. Even so there is little to suggest that the dominant role of state ownership in the industrial and service sectors contributed to growth, and there is mounting evidence to the contrary. Although China averaged a seemingly respectable 5 percent annual GDP growth rate from 1955 to 1978, the average masks erratic swings; moreover, the growth that was achieved was due almost entirely to massive investment programs that at times, such as the 1958 Great Leap Forward, led to widespread deprivation. Significantly, the estimated growth in industrial total factor productivity during this period was close to zero (Gelb and Singh 1994). After 1978, China's growth rate spurted, due largely to agricultural reforms that restored family based farming and improved production incentives, particularly for smaller firms owned by townships and villages (see chapter 2). This growth appears to have occurred despite, rather than because of, the continued dominance of large-scale SOEs. For example, SOEs absorbed 61.5 percent of investment in industry and employed 43 percent of the industrial labor force but produced only 43 percent of industrial output in 1993. In the same year, the state-owned sector generated losses equivalent to 2.4 percent of GDP (Broadman 1995).

15. Galal and others (1994) estimated the average annual gains in welfare from divestiture to be in the vicinity of 8 percent of predivestiture annual sales. Given that SOEs typically generate 10 percent of GDP and given that

sales are typically 2.5 times value added, the divestiture of half the sector would translate into a gain equivalent of about 1 percent of GDP, other things being equal. The estimated welfare gains themselves were derived as the difference between the net present value of the divested firm (to the producers and consumers) and the net present value of the firm (also to the producers and consumers) under the counterfactual scenario of continued state ownership. The annual component of the net gains to society was related to the sales of the respective enterprise to allow comparisons across firms.

16. Data periods vary by country within the overall period 1978–1991.

17. Several studies have shown that large fiscal deficits negatively correlate with growth (see, for example, Fischer 1993; Easterly, Rodriguez, and Schmidt-Hebbel 1995). It has also been shown that large fiscal deficits are a leading cause of high inflation, which in turn undermines economic growth (see, for example, Wijnbergen 1991; Bruno and others 1991; Edwards and Tabellini 1991). A negative relationship between inflation and growth has also been documented by de Gregorio (1993), Gylfason (1991), and Fischer (1993). More recently, Bruno and Easterly (1994) report a significant negative association between high inflation episodes and growth, more specifically where inflation exceeds 40 percent. Accordingly, to the extent that SOE savings-investment deficits are strongly correlated with fiscal imbalance, we can conclude that SOEs adversely affect economic growth.

CHAPTER 2

Success and Failure in SOE Reform

MOST DEVELOPING COUNTRIES FACE THE state-owned enterprise problems described in chapter 1, and many have announced their intention to reform. A smaller but still significant number have actually attempted reform programs. A detailed assessment of all of these efforts would be a gargantuan task, but the available information, analyzed at length in this book, suggests that only a few of these countries have been truly successful, a somewhat larger number have achieved mixed results, and a still larger number, perhaps the majority, have made very limited progress or none at all. What differences in policy distinguish the few successful countries from the many that have failed?

This chapter addresses this question by examining the experience of twelve countries—nine developing-market countries and three former socialist economies in transition. First, we assess the performance of state-owned enterprises in these countries; then, having established measures for success and failure, we analyze how the approach followed by the successful countries differed from that of the unsuccessful countries. In particular, we consider the extent to which each country used five components of reform that economic theorists and reform practitioners widely endorse: divestiture, competition, hard budgets, financial sector reform, and changes in the relationship between SOEs and government. As we shall see, these five components are so closely interlinked that the success of one often depends on doing another successfully. Moreover, although it is difficult to attach specific weights to the relative importance of these components, divestiture appears to be critical to success, especially where the initial size of the SOE sector is much larger than the world average of about 10 percent of GDP.

Table 2.1 shows the per capita GDP of the countries in our sample, as well as the relative size of the SOE sector and the approximate year that state-owned enterprise reform began. The sample is small and nonrandom, selected to provide a mix of regions, income levels, and reform strategies. Moreover, as we shall see, to produce rankings for the nine developing economies, we have aggregated across different types of enterprises. For all these reasons, our results should be treated with caution. Nonetheless, although neither our sample nor any of our indicators are perfect, we demonstrate that, taken together, they reveal patterns that can help us to understand what differences in policy distinguish the few countries that have successfully reformed their SOEs from the many that have failed; they also suggest ways that countries that have done poorly might improve their chances of success.

Table 2.1 Twelve Countries Undertaking State-Owned Enterprise Reform

Country	Country characteristics		Public enterprise characteristics	
	Average per capita GNP[a] (dollars, 1978–91)	Rank[b]	Average size of SOEs to GDP[c] (percent, 1978–91)	Beginning of SOE reform (year, approximately)
Chile	1,784	85	13.8	1974, 1985
China	315	28	53.0[c]	1984
Czech Republic	2,254	83	95.9	1991
Egypt	594	46	34.1	1991
Ghana	384	36	7.0	1983
India	286	18	12.1	1985
Republic of Korea	2,872	106	9.9	1983
Mexico	2,324	99	11.6	1983, 1988
Philippines	639	27	1.9	1986
Poland	1,967	76	71.4	1990
Senegal	519	48	7.7	1986
Turkey	1,324	80	7.5	1983

a. For the transition economies, average per capita GNP is for year 1991; average size of SOEs to GDP is for 1989 except for China, which is for industrial state enterprises in 1990. For definition of SOEs in China, see box 2.1.

b. Rank is relative to 132 countries.

c. Share of industrial GDP.

Source: World Development Report (1994); table A1 in statistical appendix; Gelb and Singh (1994).

Measuring Success and Failure

W E ASSESS SUCCESS OR FAILURE OF REFORM EFFORTS IN our sample on the basis of three types of results: SOE financial performance, productivity, and the savings-investment deficit.[1]

- *Financial performance.* We gauge financial performance in two ways: operating surplus to sales in current prices, which measures the returns to all investors, owners, and creditors; and before-tax profits in current prices, which measure the government's return on its investment as if it were a private owner.[2]
- *Productivity.* To neutralize the effect of prices, we also estimate two productivity measures: real variable unit costs and total factor productivity (TFP). Productivity improves when the real cost per unit goes down or TFP goes up (i.e., the quantity of outputs increases by more than the inputs used to produce them).[3]
- *Savings-investment deficit.* As in chapter 1, we define this as the extent to which SOEs rely on outside sources to finance their operations, expansion, and debt service. While an occasional deficit for a single enterprise, or for an entire sector over a relatively short period, is not necessarily evidence of poor performance, a large savings-investment deficit for the entire SOE sector over many years exacerbates fiscal deficits, and ultimately long-term growth, as we discussed in chapter 1. Moreover, a persistent deficit may also reflect poor investment decisions, price controls, or inefficient operations. As we see later in the country and company cases, we find that a large S-I deficit is generally associated with poorer performance on the other measures. For the purposes of this exercise, the larger the savings-investment deficit, the lower the rating.

The remainder of this section looks at the sample countries' performance for each of these indicators from 1978 to 1991 and compares changes in performance over the period. Since reforms cover many years (Chile, for example, underwent major reforms starting in 1975 and again in 1985), we could not simply compare before and after. We selected 1985 as an arbitrary midpoint. Nine of our sample of twelve countries did reform their SOEs within two years of our midpoint.

Where the start of reform is more than two years from the midpoint (as it was in the Czech Republic, Egypt, and Poland), we explain the effects in the discussion. Because we only measure the performance of enterprises that remain in the state sector, divestiture, the first of the five reform components we discuss, could, in theory, affect performance negatively or positively. If a country sells or liquidates its worst state-owned enterprises, the performance for the sector would be expected to improve; if, on the other hand, a country sells its best-performing enterprises, keeping only the poor performers, then the SOE sector's performance would be expected to deteriorate. In practice, as we shall see, countries that divested the most also tended to improve SOE performance the most. We will consider possible reasons for this seeming anomaly in our discussion of divestiture. First, however, we assess the SOE performance of the countries in our sample using the three measures we set forth: finance, productivity, and the savings-investment deficit.

Assessing Financial Performance

The state-owned enterprise sectors in Chile, Mexico, and the Republic of Korea outperformed the rest of the sample in both net operating surplus and profits before taxes (figures 2.1A and 2.1B), while India, Turkey, and Senegal did least well. The performance of the SOE sector in Ghana, Egypt, and the Philippines falls in between these two groups, although the Philippines falls into last place by the profitability measure (figure 2.1B).

If we take 1985 as an arbitrary midpoint, net operating surplus improved in all countries except Mexico and Senegal. Profitability improved in all but Turkey, Senegal, and the Philipines. Although the three top performers were doing better than the rest of the sample to begin with, they still managed to improve further. The deterioration in Mexico's operating surplus is due to the effects of oil prices on its large oil company, PEMEX. If PEMEX is excluded Mexico's SOEs went from a 19 percent deficit in 1978–85 to a 10 percent surplus in 1986–91.[4]

The financial performance of SOEs in our sample improved for a variety of reasons. In Mexico, low prices for SOE products and services were increased; for example, the Mexican electricity firm, Comisión Federal de Electricidad, received real increases of 7.7 percent in 1990. In Ghana, enterprises reduced overstaffing through layoffs; for example, the Ghana Cocoa Board shed about 30,000 workers between 1985

Figure 2.1 Financial Performance of State-Owned Enterprises

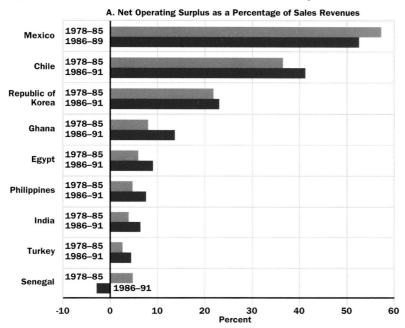

A. Net Operating Surplus as a Percentage of Sales Revenues

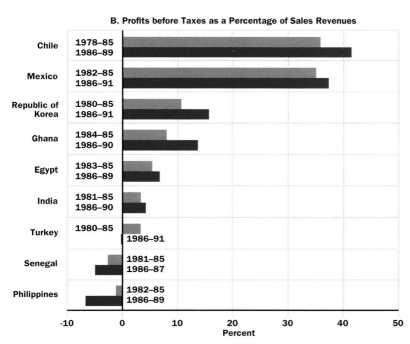

B. Profits before Taxes as a Percentage of Sales Revenues

State-owned enterprises in Chile, Korea, and Mexico ranked higher on both measures of financial performance and in most cases improved.

Source: World Bank estimates.

and 1987. Although reform in Egypt only began in 1991, performance improved in the 1980s thanks to increases in the prices of some SOE products and declines in real SOE wages. Finally, several countries, most notably Chile, Korea, and Mexico, improved productivity (see productivity discussion below).

Are these financial measures an appropriate indicator of SOE performance? Advocates of state ownership sometimes argue that some SOEs show poor financial performance because they were created to achieve noncommercial goals such as poverty reduction, job creation, or regional development. This being the case, a comprehensive calculation of their returns should include any net benefits from pursuit of these objectives. This argument has not been analyzed sufficiently to draw robust conclusions, but its importance may be overstated for several reasons. First, some noncommercial objectives are achieved when the investment is made (for example, locating an enterprise in a remote area to promote regional development) so that subsequent *trends* in financial performance would be largely unaffected (even though the *level* of performance may be lower than in some other locale). Second, it is doubtful that these noncommercial objectives are often achieved. Holding selling prices below marginal cost or market-clearing values to help the poor, a common rationale for SOE price controls, may help poor people very little, if at all. For example, one study has shown that low electricity prices intended to help the poor actually benefit the affluent more, since they own larger homes and appliances and therefore use more electricity; moreover, electricity is often unavailable in rural areas, where the poorest people live (Jones 1985). Third, SOEs whose social contribution is questionable may divert funds from programs with broader benefits that also more directly assist the poor. For example, Pedro Aspe, Mexico's former minister of finance, has asserted that part of the funding provided by the government to keep SIDERMEX (a state steel conglomerate) afloat would have been sufficient to bring drinkable water, sewerage, hospitals, and education to all the poor communities in southeastern Mexico (Aspe 1991). Finally, even if we assume that SOEs do achieve their noncommercial objectives, we would still need to assess whether the cost of using SOEs to achieve these goals is less or more than the cost of using alternative instruments, for example, taxes or direct subsidies. For these reasons, we regard the financial measures to be useful indicators of SOE performance, even though they do not include a calculation of net social benefits.

Assessing Productivity

Low financial rates of return do not necessarily mean low productivity, especially where price controls hold down SOE revenue or inflate input costs. An extensive study of the performance of the Egyptian SOEs (Handoussa, Nishimizu, and Page 1986) found that productivity and financial performance often moved in opposite directions. In our sample, however, the three countries where the SOEs had the strongest financial performance also did best by our two productivity measures; the rankings of the other countries were also broadly consistent with the financial rankings, although they varied somewhat depending on the measure used.

Figures 2.2A and 2.2B show productivity rankings as measured by average real variable costs per unit and TFP. In both instances, Mexico, Chile, and Korea come out on top, while Egypt and Turkey rank among the bottom three.[5] Our TFP calculations show nearly the same country pattern as the variable cost per unit rankings; the only difference is the Philippines, which ranks in the middle according to the unit price measure but drops to last place in the TFP ranking.[6]

Comparing productivity trends, we see that average real variable costs per unit of output improved in the second half of the 1980s in five of our sample countries; the largest gains were in two of the countries that were already doing better: Mexico and Korea. Real variable costs per unit of output worsened in Chile, Egypt, Ghana, and Senegal. TFP improved in four countries. Again the largest gains were in Mexico and Korea. TFP worsened in Chile, Egypt, the Philippines, and Senegal.[7] The deterioration in productivity in Chile can be attributed in part to the divestiture of some of its largest and best-performing SOEs in the second half of the decade in a privatization of utilities unmatched in the rest of the sample during this period (see discussion of divestiture below).[8] In Egypt, SOE reform is too recent to be reflected in the data. In Senegal and Ghana, the only explanation seems to be that reform efforts have so far been ineffective in improving productivity.

Assessing Savings-Investment Deficits

An SOE savings-investment deficit is cause for concern when it results from low rates of return on SOE capital and low SOE productivity. This is the case for all countries in our sample with large SOE savings-investment deficits except for Korea, where the SOEs had higher than

Figure 2.2 Productivity of State-Owned Enterprises

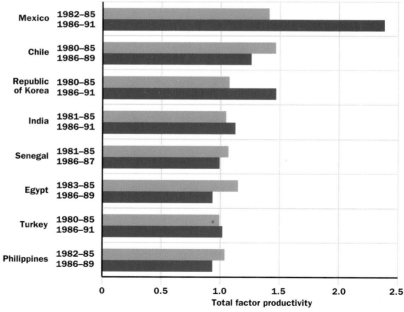

A. Real Variable Costs per Unit (Annual Averages)

Country	Period
Mexico	1982–85 / 1986–91
Chile	1978–85 / 1986–89
Republic of Korea	1981–85 / 1986–91
Philippines	1982–85 / 1986–89
India	1981–85 / 1986–90
Senegal	1982–85 / 1986–87
Ghana	1984–85 / 1986–90
Egypt	1984–85 / 1986–89
Turkey	1980–85 / 1986–92

Real variable costs per unit

B. Total Factor Productivity[a] (Annual Averages)

Country	Period
Mexico	1982–85 / 1986–91
Chile	1980–85 / 1986–89
Republic of Korea	1980–85 / 1986–91
India	1981–85 / 1986–91
Senegal	1981–85 / 1986–87
Egypt	1983–85 / 1986–89
Turkey	1980–85 / 1986–91
Philippines	1982–85 / 1986–89

Total factor productivity

State enterprises in Mexico, Chile, and Korea also ranked better on both measures of productivity, and improved performance in most cases.

a. Data did not permit calculation of TFP in Ghana.
Source: World Bank estimates.

average rates of return on capital and productivity. As figure 2.3 shows, Chile and Mexico are again among the three top performers; indeed, they are the only two countries where state-owned enterprises consistently showed savings-investment surpluses. Chile managed to improve its already large surplus over the period, while Korea recorded the most dramatic improvement, going from an annual average deficit of 3.1 percent of GDP during the first period to a surplus of 0.7 percent of GDP during the second. Among the remainder, average deficits as a percentage of GDP for the entire period were largest in Turkey (6.1 percent), the Philippines (3.6 percent), and Senegal (3.0 percent). The most significant deterioration was in Egypt, where the average deficit grew from 1.6 percent of GDP during the earlier period to 3.4 percent during 1985–91 (the period does not include the reform effort begun in 1991).

Some readers may be struck by the fact that the three best performers in our sample of market economies are middle-income countries. There are many middle- and upper-income countries that have not reformed,

Figure 2.3 Savings Minus Investment as a Percentage of Gross Domestic Product

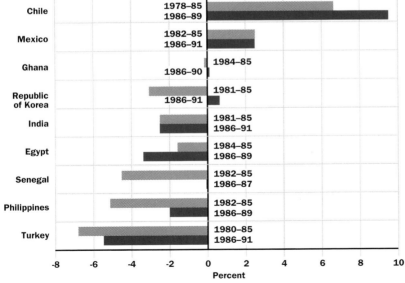

Note: Negative number equals deficit.
Source: Statistical appendix.

State enterprises in Chile, Korea, and Mexico had a savings-investment surplus from the mid-1980s.

however, including Turkey, which is part of our sample, and a number of OECD and more developed market countries, which are not. The evidence presented in chapter 1 suggests that worldwide, most countries are not reforming, regardless of income level, but that the problem caused by unreformed SOEs is more acute in lower-income economies. In sum, although none of the indicators is perfect and the ranking of the SOE sector's performance varies slightly depending on which of the indicators we consider, a consistent pattern emerges:

- *State-owned enterprises performed better in Chile, Korea, and Mexico and showed substantial improvement in already good performance. SOEs performed worse in India, Senegal, and Turkey, although there was slight improvement on some measures.*
- *The performance of SOEs in Ghana, the Philippines, and Egypt either falls somewhere in between or, by certain measures, in the bottom third of the sample, with improvements in some measures offset by deteriorations in others.*

We shall rely on these rankings to help us determine the associated characteristics of success and failure in SOE reform.[9] First, however, we consider briefly reform outcomes in the three transition economies in our sample.

Transition Economies

Transforming SOEs in the transition economies is obviously a much larger undertaking than in the developing-market economies. In the transition economies, state-owned enterprises until recently dwarfed all other forms of ownership, whereas in the developing-market economies, SOEs rarely account for more than 15 percent of GDP and frequently less. Moreover, precisely because the transition economies are involved in broad, systemic reforms, and because their SOE data are often not comparable over time, we did not try to rank the three transition economies in our sample against the nine developing-market economies. Thus, our evaluation of their success or failure is based on broad indicators, partial evidence, and the reform process itself. In this section, as elsewhere in this book, we consider the two Central European countries in our sample first, then China.

Evaluating reform in Poland and the Czech Republic is especially difficult. Reforms are relatively recent (launched in Poland in 1990 and in the Czech Republic in 1991), and it is hard to separate their impact from wrenching changes in trade (the collapse of the Eastern and Central European trading block) and systemic transformation (devaluation and currency convertibility, severe tightening of credit and increases in interest rates to real positive levels, the shift from state profit retention to taxation, etc.).[10] Both countries suffered large declines in industrial output following these reforms and shocks: in Poland industrial output fell by 24 percent in 1990 and 12 percent in 1991 but has since begun to recover; in the Czech Republic it fell by 3.5 percent in 1990, almost 25 precent in 1991, and 15 percent in 1992.

Microeconomic evidence indicates that reform is leading to industrial transformation, which would eventually lead to better performance.[11] SOEs have been shedding workers (SOE industrial employment fell by 20 percent in four years in Poland and by slightly less in the Czech Republic), with the largest firms (those with more than 5,000 workers) shrinking the most (Gelb and Singh 1994). Firms in both countries have responded to increased competition with internal restructuring designed to improve marketing, control costs, and improve management of finances.[12] Thus, while we cannot rank these countries systematically, early impressions are that, despite the very rough start, reform is resulting in significant improvements in state-owned enterprises.

China's approach to economywide reform has been slower and less wrenching than the upheavals in Eastern Europe. Reform began in the countryside in 1978 with a reversion to household farming and the "open door" policy. This was extended in 1984 to the industrial sector and included the liberalization of prices and markets and an easing of restrictions on private businesses and the nonstate, collective enterprises known as Township and Village Enterprises (TVEs). These reforms allowed market forces to emerge in many sectors of the economy; as a result, economic growth has been very rapid. Against this backdrop and bolstered by generous credit from China's state-owned banking system, real industrial production of state enterprises, which are roughly analogous to state-owned enterprises in other countries (see box 2.1), expanded by an impressive 7.8 percent a year on average during 1980–91; however, this was lower than the industrial growth of any other form of ownership in China.[13]

What of our three measures of SOE performance: financial performance, productivity, and the savings-investment deficit? Available data permit only very rough estimations. State enterprise losses, although decreasing, were still almost 2.5 percent of GDP in 1993 (Broadman

Box 2.1 China's Ownership Patterns: Not State but Not Private

BESIDES THE 104,700 STATE ENTERPRISES (GUOJIA qiye) that accounted for 43 percent of industrial output in 1993, and that we treat as SOEs in the text, there are a number of nonstate firms, most of which are not privately owned, but still differ in important ways from SOEs. These nonstate industrial enterprises can be grouped into four categories:

(i) *Urban collectives* (including urban cooperatives) affiliated with municipalities, counties, or a district. In 1993, about 240,000 such enterprises accounted for about 12 percent of total industrial output. Many are subsidiaries of SOEs, which provide their start-up capital and employees, and most suffer from the same problems as the SOEs (bureaucratic inertia, interference, inefficiencies, and lack of clear autonomy).

(ii) *Township and village enterprises (TVEs)* (including rural cooperatives), most of which are effectively owned by township or village governments. In 1993,

the 1.8 million collectively owned enterprises (over 1.5 million of which were TVEs) accounted for 26 percent of total industrial output.

(iii) *Individual or family businesses* with seven or less employees. They account for about 8 percent of industrial output. In 1993, 92 percent of the nearly 6.3 million individual businesses in China were in rural areas. (The number of individual businesses is closer to 17 million if one includes household and private ventures in agriculture and in the tertiary sectors.)

(iv) *Other types,* private enterprises with more than seven employees, foreign firms and joint ventures with foreigners or other partners (e.g., between state and nonstate and foreign partners), and joint stock companies. Some 32,000 such enterprises account for about 10 percent of industrial output.

Source: Based on Singh and Jefferson (1993); numbers updated using State Statistical Bureau (1994) and Broadman (1995).

1995).[14] An accurate assessment of productivity growth is similarly difficult; estimates of state enterprise TFP growth range from 2.4 to 4 percent a year, high by international standards but again low compared to other forms of ownership in China.[15] Overall, although some of the productivity measures for China's state enterprises are impressive, their apparently poor financial performance suggests that China ranks with the mixed performers in our sample.

What Reform Characteristics Distinguish Successful Reformers?

THE PRECEDING SECTION RANKED THE OUTCOME OF STATE-owned enterprise reform for nine countries using three types of quantitative indicators (financial performance, productivity, and the state-owned enterprise savings-investment deficit). For three transition economies whose data are insufficient for cross-country comparisons of performance, the section described broadly the reform approach and outcomes. The remainder of this chapter analyzes the reform process in all twelve countries to discover how success and failure are related to policymakers' reliance on the five components of state-owned enterprise reform—divestiture, competition, hard budgets, financial reforms, and changes in the relationship between the government and SOE managers. Although these reforms are intended to improve the incentive structure facing firms, their ultimate impact on performance depends on how the firm's managers and workers respond to these new incentives with changes in corporate governance (box 2.2).

Divestiture and SOE Reform

CHAPTER 1 SUMMARIZED EVIDENCE THAT DIVESTITURE—selling, liquidating, or giving away a state-owned enterprise—improves the performance of the divested firms in competitive or potentially competitive markets and perhaps in monopoly markets as

---

Box 2.2 External Incentives and Corporate Behavior: The Case of Shepheard's Hotel

A FIRM'S EXTERNAL ENVIRONMENT—THE COMpetition it faces, the nature of its budget constraint, the discipline imposed on it by the financial sector, its relationship with the government—determines the incentives that pressure its management to adapt. Ultimately, the success or failure of that adaptation will depend critically on changes within the enterprise, in particular, changes in internal management, corporate culture, and worker motivation. There is a large and growing literature on these issues, which time and space limitations do not allow us to cover in this study. However, our neglect of these issues should not be misinterpreted; these are important issues deserving of a study in their own right.

To illustrate the link between the changes in the incentive structure and internal adjustments, consider the case of Shepheard's Hotel in Cairo. For-

merly one of the leading five star hotels in Egypt, the hotel was nationalized in 1961, and management was given to the state-owned Egyptian Hotel Company (EHC). The poorer quality of this management caused Shepheard's performance and reputation to fall. Despite a major renovation in 1977, the decline could not be reversed. Finally in 1987, the EHC signed a management contract with the Helnan Company of Denmark, which manages hotels in Florida, Yemen, and Saudi Arabia, as well as four other hotels in Egypt.

The contract specified a four-year turnaround period, during which Helnan was paid a set fee; from the fifth year on, the contract stipulated that the company receive 20 percent of gross operating profits. This arrangement very explicitly gave the new

(Box continues on the following page.)

Box 2.2 *(continued)*

managers a strong interest in seeing the firm's profits improve, as the entire management fee would be dependent on profits after the fourth year. Management clearly recognized that success depended on restoring the hotel's reputation for quality service and that this, in turn, necessitated a change in the hotel's corporate culture. Management responded to these pressures by recruiting an almost entirely new staff to be trained to meet international standards of hotel service. The new managers also changed Shepheard's marketing strategy, actively targeting tour groups, and invested heavily in refurbishment to restore the hotel to its former state. This strategy has dramatically raised occupancy rates and average room rates and substantially improved the Shepheard's gross operating profit.

Since the early 1980s, the Egyptian Ministry of Tourism has relied increasingly on management contracts with private hotel companies in order to encourage the sort of changes in corporate behavior that occurred at Shepheard's. These hotel chains bring sophisticated marketing and cost accounting techniques, modern training systems, and incentives to motivate workers and managers. In interviews government officials stated that it would be difficult for a public manager to cut through the bureaucratic procedures and red tape to make the hard operational decisions necessary to run a hotel at a profit. As a result, almost all publicly owned hotels in Egypt operate under private management contracts.

Source: Shaikh and Minovi (1994).

well. In this section we assess the role of divestiture in the reform process in our sample. Because it is also possible to reduce the share of SOEs in the economy by encouraging faster private sector growth, and because this is sometimes put forward as an alternative to divestiture, we consider this strategy as well.

Sales, Liquidations, and Giveaways

The more successful reformers in our sample reduced state ownership, especially where it accounted for a large share of the economy. The magnitude of divestiture is measured by the changes in the share of SOEs relative to GDP as well as the ratio of revenue from the sale of enterprises to GDP and SOEs' sales (table 2.2). Of the three better performers, Korea divested least, but the magnitude of state ownership in Korea was the smallest at the outset. In contrast, the least successful reformers did not reduce the size of the SOE sector, even when it was initially very large during the period under consideration.

The better-performing countries in our sample reduced state ownership by divesting SOEs in a wide variety of competitive and potentially competitive markets and in some cases in monopoly markets. The ex-

Table 2.2 Successful Reformers Divested More

| Country | SOE value added as percentage of GDP | | | | Revenue from sale as percentage of 1990 GDP |
| | Before divestiture | | After divestiture | | |
	Year	Size (percent)	Year	Size (percent)	
Better performers					
Chile	1973	39.0	1991	8.0	9.4
Republic of Korea	1980	10.4	1990	10.2	1.0
Mexico	1983	17.2	1991	8.4	8.7
Mixed performers					
Egypt	1982	38.9	1991	32.8	0.0
Ghana	1986	10.6	1991	10.7	1.2
Philippines	1983	1.7	1989	3.0	0.9
Poor performers					
India	1983	11.1	1989	13.8	0.1
Senegal	1984	10.3	1989	—	0.9
Turkey	1983	7.3	1991	7.2	1.1
Transition economies[a]					
China	1978	80.0[b]	1991	53.0[b]	0.9
Czech Republic	1989	95.9	1992	80.0	8.1
Poland	1989	71.4	1992	52.5	2.2

— Not available.

a. Estimated.

b. Share of industrial GDP.

Source: Privatization Yearbook (1992); Hachette and Lüders (1993); Sader (1994); Tandon (1992); Morin (1993); European Bank for Reconstruction and Development (1993); State Statistical Bureau (1992, 365); Gelb and Singh (1994).

tent to which countries curbed SOEs in competitive markets is illustrated by the SOE share of manufacturing shown in table 2.3. Chile and Korea reduced SOE shares sharply (and more recent data for Mexico would show a more dramatic reduction than evident in the table). But manufacturing is only part of the story. The more successful reformers also reduced state ownership in banking and services such as transport and construction. Moreover, Chile and, to a lesser extent, Mexico unbundled monopolies and sold them in such sectors as petrochemicals, telecommunications, and power.

Why did these countries curb state ownership in competitive sectors? Commitment to efficiency may hold part of the answer: policymakers may have recognized that private firms would be more efficient than state-owned firms. There could also be a political explanation: as markets liberalize, privatizing SOEs in competitive sectors may be the only

Table 2.3 Privatization in Manufacturing

| | SOEs in manufacturing | | | |
| | Prereform | | Postreform | |
Country	Year	Percent	Year	Percent
Better performers				
Chile	1973	40.0	1991	0.0
Republic of Korea	1980	15.5	1990	8.1
Mexico	1979–82	5.8	1983–87	5.0
Mixed performers				
Egypt[a]	1982	72.2	1992	57.8
Ghana	1978–80	27.1	—	—
Philippines	1984	0.3	1989	0.6
Poor performers				
India	1981	13.3	1989	18.2
Senegal	1980	1.6	1986	2.6
Turkey	1985	18.8	1990	14.3

— Not available.
a. Includes mining.
Source: Various country sources; World Bank data; International Monetary Fund data.

way to avoid protecting or subsidizing them. If SOEs in competitive markets are not privatized, the political pressure to assist those that cannot compete may lead governments to subsidize them rather than let them go out of business (see the discussion under competition below for an example of this policy reversal).

Why should countries that divested the most improve the performance of their remaining state-owned enterprises the most? As we noted above in the discussion of the changes in SOE productivity in Chile, selling the best-performing state-owned enterprises can indeed result in a lower performance for those that remain. Overall, however, this has not been the case. Our cases suggest that the countries that divested the most also reformed the remaining SOEs the most. By reducing the size of the state-owned enterprise sector, they may have been able to concentrate scarce managerial skills on those that remain, thus improving their performance. Further, former SOEs that have been privatized may have induced greater competitive pressure on remaining SOEs (as suppliers or customers), thereby improving SOE performance. Although difficult to establish concretely, it appears that a reduction in the SOE share in our sample is strongly correlated with improved performance for the enterprises that continue to be state owned.

Two of the transitional economies in our sample, the Czech Republic and Poland, have also divested, the Czech Republic extensively. In just four years, the Czech Republic sold or gave away almost all of its competitive SOEs in one of the most extensive privatization programs ever undertaken. Among the divested enterprises were 120,000 retail shops, restaurants, and service business and 13,000 small manufacturing enterprises auctioned in 1991–92; 80,000 to 100,000 businesses were returned to former owners; and close to 5,000 medium to large state-owned enterprises were privatized in 1993–94 partly by exchanging shares for vouchers distributed to all adult citizens for a small fee and partly through trade sales and other transactions. Poland has also divested nearly all retail services but has made slower progress on large firms. Of more than 8,000 medium to large enterprises owned by the government in 1990, less than one-third were in the process of privatization or liquidation in 1993, and fewer than 100 had been turned into corporations and sold; 852 smaller firms had been privatized through liquidation; and 1,013 firms had been bankrupted and their assets sold.[16] As for China, bankruptcies and privatization of SOEs have been virtually nonexistent.[17] The increase in the proportion of the nonstate sector in China's economy, shown in table 2.2, is almost entirely due to its rapid growth rather than to a reduction in the size of the state sector, which, as we have seen, has continued to grow.

Judging from our sample, divestiture is a useful tool for reducing the size of the state-owned enterprise sector, especially when the sector is large. Moreover, evidence at the company level from other sources suggests that efficiency and welfare gains from divestiture can be substantial. (See, for example, box 1.2.) These gains are not automatic, however. Surveys of privatization experience have identified several elements of successful divestiture efforts. These are noted in box 2.3.

Outgrowing State-Owned Enterprises: An Alternative to Divestiture?

SEVERAL COUNTRIES HAVE MANAGED TO REDUCE THE RELATIVE size of their state-owned enterprise sector by outgrowing it—that is, achieving very rapid growth of the private sector—rather than through divestiture. Korea, which relied less on divestiture than either

Box 2.3 Getting the Most from Privatization

EVIDENCE PRESENTED IN THIS CHAPTER SHOWS that successful privatization can bring many benefits, including reduced state sector deficits, increased investment in the privatized enterprise, and, for consumers, better quality goods and services, often at lower prices. In addition, governments sometimes reap substantial one-time revenue from privatization proceeds. None of these benefits are automatic, however. Surveys of privatization experience show that different approaches to privatization bring different results. The following are some of the lessons from these surveys about how to get the most from privatization:

- Efficiency gains are usually higher when the transaction is transparent, competitive, and fair and undertaken as part of a wider program of reforms to open markets and remove price and other distortions.
- Once markets are open and function reasonably well, many potentially competitive firms can be divested without complex regulation. Financial SOEs are an exception. Breaking up firms to reduce their market power can enhance competition. If the SOE is a natural monopoly, then a well-designed regulatory contract, setting forth the obligations of the government and the buyer is critical to positive results (see chapter 3).
- Although governments have sometimes had to cut the size of a firm's labor force and absorb some debt in order to make a firm attractive to potential buyers, more extensive investments in restructuring have usually not paid off in terms of higher privatization proceeds.
- With a strong centralized body in place to

oversee sales, actual implementation can be decentralized.
- Prequalifying bidders and requiring buyers to put up sufficient equity are important in preventing later defaults; but restrictions on types of bidders (excluding foreigners, for example) or on changes that the new owners can make after privatization reduce the competitiveness of the bidding and the sales price.

Several of these lessons can be seen in an analysis of the privatization of 346 state-owned enterprises in Mexico. The study, which controlled for company and industry effects, found that the government generally reaped more when sales were more competitive (e.g., there were more bidders), when the state-owned sector manager was removed prior to the sale (most lacked specific experience in the firm's business), and when the labor force was cut. The analysis found that prior investments by government in the company and other programs designed to raise efficiency did not improve the sales prices, nor did government absorption of debt owed to outsiders. This last finding runs counter to the experience of other countries, where governments have had to absorb some debt to privatize firms so heavily indebted that they would otherwise have had a negative market value. Interestingly for countries trying to decide how quickly to privatize, delays generally caused a deterioration in performance and lowered sales proceeds. Setting minimum periods before a buyer could resell the company (usually for three to five years) and limiting the pool of prospective bidders to Mexican nationals also reduced the price.

Source: Galal and others (1994); Kikeri, Nellis, and Shirley (1994); and López-de-Salinas (1994).

Chile or Mexico, nevertheless reduced the share of SOEs in manufacturing GDP from about 20 percent in 1969 to around 10 percent in the mid-1980s largely by encouraging faster private sector growth. Similarly, in China, fast growth of the nonstate sector, especially the TVEs, has substantially reduced the state enterprise share of the economy (figure 2.4). Between 1980 and 1990, total real industrial output grew by an average of 12.6 percent a year; this included annual SOE growth of 7.7 percent, annual urban collective growth of 10.7 percent, and annual TVE growth of an astonishing 18.7 percent. See box 2.4 for an explanation of why the TVEs, although publicly owned, are different from state enterprises (Gelb and Singh 1994, 26).[18] Thus, despite respectable SOE output growth, the *share* of SOEs in industrial output fell from 80 percent at the start of the reforms to barely half by 1991 and to only 43 percent in 1993. Such rapid TVE growth was possible in part because rural reforms encouraged the use of underutilized resources; for example, many TVEs hired under-employed farm laborers to work in new food processing ventures set up

Figure 2.4 China: Growth Rates by Ownership Type

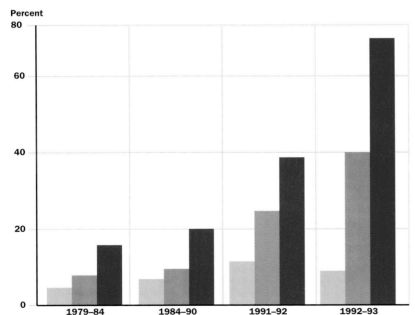

Percent

SOEs   Collectives   TVEs

Of the three main types of group ownership in China, the township and village enterprises have grown most rapidly.

Note: Data for 1991–92 and 1992–93 are provisional and in nominal terms.
Source: State Statistical Bureau (various years); Singh and Jefferson (1993).

Box 2.4 How China's Township and Village Enterprises Differ from State Enterprises

CHINA'S TOWNSHIP AND VILLAGE ENTERPRISES (TVEs) are an anomaly. Publicly owned, usually by a township or village government, they are nonetheless similar in some ways to private enterprises. China's state enterprises, on the other hand, more closely resemble the state-owned enterprises of other countries in that they are run by central bureaus and ministries. For these reasons, the term state-owned enterprise (SOE), as generally understood and as defined in this book, includes China's state enterprises but not the TVEs. The following differences between TVEs and state enterprises help to explain why TVEs perform better.

- *Better governance.* TVEs are locally owned, supervised, and managed instead of being supervised by far-off central bureaus and ministries. As much as 90 to 95 percent of local revenues as well as the incomes, perks, and de facto pay of local officials come from TVE earnings. As a result local governments, which themselves face a hard budget constraint, have a direct stake in their performance. TVEs' goals are clear: maximize posttax returns to capital investments and employ the local labor force (as distinct from migrant casual labor).
- *Hard budget constraint:* TVEs do not receive subsidized bank credits or centrally allocated materials; they buy and sell inputs and outputs at market prices. TVEs must rely mostly on cap-

ital generated from their own earnings or local and household resources. (Only 8 percent of all banking loans go to TVEs, while SOEs capture at least 80 percent).

- *Greater autonomy with fewer social obligations:* Compared to SOEs, TVEs are more free to hire and fire labor, link wages to performance, rent and buy land locally, construct, and transact business with buyers and sellers of their own choice. Unlike state enterprises, TVEs are not obligated to provide such services as housing, health care, education, and lifetime employment and pensions to their employees and their dependents.
- *Greater competition:* The number and smaller average size of TVEs, coupled with the growth of domestic demand and reduction of barriers to internal trade, ensure growing and ever fiercer domestic competition. Each year thousands of new TVEs enter the market, while thousands of old and failing ones exit from it. The greater concentration of TVEs in coastal provinces (though by no means confined to them) and the strong links to investors from Hong Kong and Taiwan (China) increase competitive pressures by bringing new technologies, new management methods, export markets, and a kindred model to emulate.

Source: Singh and Jefferson (1993).

in little-used buildings owned by town or village governments. In Poland, rapid private sector growth also played a role in creating a mixed economy. There, however, liquidations and privatizations were crucial in releasing assets and labor from SOEs to fuel private sector growth.[19]

Despite these apparent successes, the strategy of achieving relative SOE shrinkage by having the private sector outgrow the SOE sector has clear limits. In some market economies with very extensive state sectors and in some transitional economies where there are significant nonstate assets, this strategy could reduce the state share. But in most developing economies, businesses where new private entry is easy (trade, construction, small manufacturing) have long been open to the private sector so that, barring divestiture, the potential for sudden rapid growth is not large. As for the transition economies, the private sector must grow very rapidly indeed to begin to overshadow the huge SOE sector, but there are limits to how fast and how much the private sector can grow when a much larger state-owned sector absorbs substantial amounts of resources and performs at lower efficiency. As one study points out, as long as subsidies to SOEs are large enough to offset the productivity difference with the non-state sector, resources remain in the state sector rather than flow to the nonstate sector (Sachs and Woo 1993, 16–17). This traps a large amount of resources in the least productive sector of the economy. Moreover, many new private businesses in the transition economies are too small to compete with or take over large-scale activities of the SOEs. For example, despite the impressive performance of China's TVEs, one study found that these enterprises were only one-tenth the size of their SOE competitors (Jefferson 1993). Thus, even though China's nonstate enterprises have been able to grow rapidly for over fifteen years without privatization or liquidation of SOEs, the limits of this strategy may be approaching. Indeed, state subsidies to money-losing SOEs have recently created inflationary pressures that threaten to undermine nonstate as well as state expansion.

Divestiture Alone Is Seldom Enough

EVEN COUNTRIES THAT HAVE EXTENSIVELY SOLD, LIQUIDATED, and shrunk the relative share of SOEs are often left with a substantial proportion of the economy under state ownership, as can be seen for our sample in table 2.2. As we discussed in chapter 1, widespread attention to divestiture has yet to have a major effect on the SOE share in many countries. Moreover, even if the SOE share in an economy is brought down significantly, this is no guarantee that the country's remaining SOEs will perform well, or that their burden on the economy and government finances will be light. Indeed, several countries in our sample with relatively small SOE sectors at times devoted a disproportionate share of resources to state-owned enterprises. For example, in the Philippines during the first half of the 1980s, the SOE savings-investment deficit was greater than 5 percent of GDP, even though the state-owned enterprises themselves accounted for only 2 percent of GDP. Similarly, in Turkey during the 1980s, the SOE savings-investment deficit averaged about 6 percent of GDP, only slightly less than the 7.5 percent of GDP that the SOEs produced. For these reasons, measures to improve the performance of SOEs that are not divested have an important role to play in the overall reform strategy. The remainder of this chapter considers four—competition, hard budgets, financial reforms, and changes in the relationship between SOE managers and government—to see what role each played in the reform process of the countries in our sample.

Improving SOE Performance through Competition

COMPETITION IMPROVES THE PERFORMANCE OF SOES, NOT only because competitors push state-owned (and private) firms to do better, but also because competition makes explicit the costs of allowing SOEs to operate inefficiently or of using SOEs to pursue social and political goals. Competition also provides information about managerial performance; governments can assess the level of managerial effort by comparing an SOE's efficiency with that of its competitors (Vickers and Yarrow 1988).[20] Competition's beneficial effects can be seen clearly in analysis of provincial data for China: the larger the nonstate share of a province's industrial output, the higher the TFP of its state enterprises (figure 2.5).

If governments used SOEs primarily to correct market failures, then the prospects for competition improving performance would be quite limited. In practice, however, SOEs are found in many potentially competitive activities. To name just a few especially egregious examples from our sample: a glue factory, a casino, and a shipping line (in Ghana); pharmaceuticals, glass, vegetable oil, and earth-moving equipment (in India); hotels, building materials, baked goods, and electric motors (in Egypt); housing and chemicals (in Korea); a coal mine, sugar, tobacco, and alcohol (in Turkey); edible oils, phosphate, and the import and distribution of films (in Senegal); and poultry, dairy products, and furniture (in the Philippines). In each of these instances, there would seem to be no economic justification for government ownership. Divestiture,

Figure 2.5 China: Response of State Sector to Competition from Nonstate Enterprises

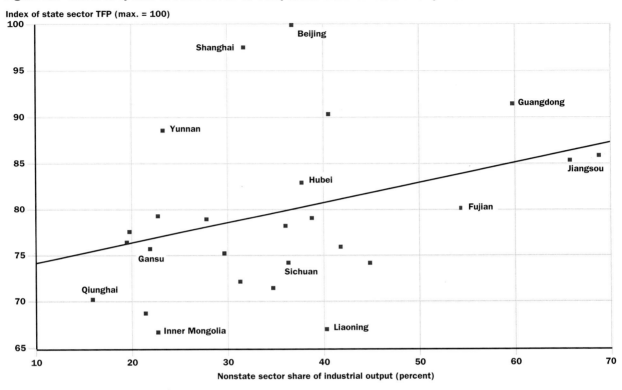

Source: Singh, Xiao, and Ratha (1994).

therefore, makes the most sense economically, but exposing these enterprises to competition and thus making explicit any inefficiencies would be a good first step.

This is, in fact, what the successful reformers have done: they increased domestic competition by removing price controls and barriers to entry, and they increased international competition by liberalizing foreign trade. Tables 2.4a and b illustrate changes in the degree of domestic competition as revealed by the extent of price controls and government-imposed monopolies in eleven activities frequently reserved for SOEs. Comparison of the two tables shows the striking extent to which all the countries in our sample reduced price controls and eased entry. Not surprisingly, the three countries that had the best overall SOE performance ratings (Chile, Korea, and Mexico) are among those that eased barriers to internal com-

Among China's provinces, the larger the nonstate share of industrial output, the higher the total factor productivity of the state enterprise sector.

Table 2.4a Prereform Status of Domestic Competition, Selected Industries

Sector	Chile (1974)	Korea (1984)	Mexico (1983)	Philippines (1986)	Egypt (1973)	Ghana (1983)	India (1985)	Senegal (1985)	Turkey (1980)
Products									
Petroleum									
Production/import	●	●	●	●	●	●	●	✪	●
Price	●	●	●	●	●	●	●	●	●
Fertilizer									
Production	●	●	●	●	●	●	○	●	●
Price	●	●	●	○	●	●	●	●	●
Mining	●	●	●	○	●	●	●	●	●
Sugar									
Production	●	●	●	●	●	●	○	✪	●
Price	●	○	●	●	●	●	●	●	●
Textiles	●	●	○	○	●	○	○	✪	○
Cement									
Production	●	●	○	○	●	●	○	✪	○
Price	●	○	—	⊛	●	●	●	●	○
Steel									
Production	●	●	●	●	●	●	●	n.a.	○
Price	●	○	●	●	●	●	●	●	●
Services									
Airlines									
Provision	●	✪	●	●	●	●	●	●	●
Price	●	●	●	●	●	●	●	●	●
Urban transport									
Provision	●	●	○	⊛	●	○	●a	●	○
Price	●	●	●	●	●	●	●	●	○
Telecoms	●	●	●	✪	●	●	●	●	●
Ports	●	●	●	⊛	●	●	●	●	●

— Not available.
n.a. Not applicable.

Production/provision		*Price*
SOE monopoly	●	Controlled prices
Private monopoly	✪	
No monopoly, heavy regulation	⊛	Heavily regulated
No monopoly	○	Free prices

petition the most. The Philippines, which scored poorly in our SOE performance ratings, nonetheless scores high for increasing internal competition. As we shall see, this seeming anomaly can be explained by the Philippines' less satisfactory performance on other aspects of SOE reform. Changes in the degree of international competition are shown in

Table 2.4b Postreform (1994) Status of Domestic Competition, Selected Industries

Sector	Better performers			Mixed performers			Poorer performers		
	Chile	Korea	Mexico	Philippines	Egypt	Ghana	India	Senegal	Turkey
Products									
Petroleum									
Production/import	●	✪	●	●	●	●	●	✪	○
Price	○	○	●	●	●	●	●	●	●
Fertilizer									
Production	○	✪	○	○	●	○	○	○	○
Price	○	○	○	○	○	○	○b	○	○
Mining	●c	●c	○	○	●	○	●	○	●
Sugar									
Production	○	✪	○	○	●	○	○	✪	○
Price	○	○	○	○	○d	○	●	●	○
Textiles	○	○	○	○	○	○	○	✪e	○
Cement									
Production	○	✪	○	○	●	✪	○	✪	○
Price	○	○	○	○	●	○	○	●	○
Steel									
Production	○	○	○	○	○	○	○	n.a.	○
Price	○	○	○	○	●	○	○	n.a.	○
Services									
Airlines (domestic)									
Provision	○	○	○	○	●	●	○	●	○
Price	○	●	○	○	●	●	○	●	○
Urban transport									
Provision	○	●	○	○	○	○	●a	●	○
Price	○	●	●	●	✪	○	●	●/○f	○
Telecoms	○	●	✪	✪	●	●	○	●	●
Ports	○	○	○	○	●	●	●	●	●

Note: Any ● may represent an activity with a single SOE monopoly, a partial SOE monopoly, or be reserved for SOEs.
a. Depends on city. SOE monopolies in Bombay and Madras, but open in Calcutta.
b. Phosphatic and potassic fertilizers only; urea and nitrogenous are still controlled.
c. Coal mining is an SOE monopoly. Other mining is open.
d. Free pricing exists for nonrationed sugar.
e. Private duopoly.
f. The sector is partial monopoly; nonmonopolistic segment is free pricing, monopolistic is controlled.
Source: World Bank data.

table 2.5. Once again, the top three SOE performers were most open to competition; thus they had lower than average import charges and non-tariff restrictions. Foreign competition need not only be from imports; Korea also used export rivalry—rewarding firms that exported more—to push its SOEs to perform better.

Table 2.5 Measures of Foreign Competition

Country	Intensity of foreign competition	
	Overall import charges (percent)[a]	Nontariff charges (percent)[b]
Better performers		
Chile	20.2	16.1
Korea	22.7	14.2
Mexico	13.4	24.1
Mixed performers		
Egypt	41.4	38.6
Ghana	31.0	38.4
Philippines	29.8	63.6
Poor performers		
India	140.0	87.4
Senegal	29.9	14.9
Turkey	44.8	90.6

a. Unweighted average of all imports in 1991.

b. Based on unweighted frequency of applications by tariff line as percent of discretionary licensing, quotas, and import prohibitions in 1988.

Source: UNCTAD (1989); GATT (various years).

As mentioned above in the discussion of divestiture, the better-performing countries in our sample not only liberalized markets, they also divested most of their SOEs in competitive or potentially competitive sectors. In the case of Mexico and Chile, they broke up monopolies and sold the competitive parts. Chile's large electricity producer, CHILECTRA, was broken into three separate companies—two regional electricity distribution companies and one generating company. The sale of such activities reduces the risk that the government, under political pressure, subsidizes SOEs unable to cope with private competition. Ghana, for example, is in this position, with two government-owned bus companies and several private bus companies competing on the same routes. Although the government-owned companies have chronically lost money, thanks to government subsidies, they have been able to lure passengers from the private lines by charging lower fares.

The differences in what our sample countries did in introducing competition are summarized in appendix 2.1. (The appendix also summarizes their measures to harden SOE budgets, which we discuss in the next section.) We can illustrate the difference in these measures by contrasting the approaches in Chile and Turkey. Chile began liberalizing trade in 1974, removing all quantitative restrictions and slashing average nominal tariffs from 94 percent to 10 percent in five years. This exposed all enterprises producing tradable goods, state-owned or private, to intense foreign competition. Product markets were largely deregulated by 1978, by which time Chile had already privatized its entire manufacturing sector. Today, virtually all firms in competitive sectors (among them construction, finance, and trade) are private. The only substantial sector not privatized was mining.[21]

In contrast, Turkey removed some formal barriers to competition in the 1980s but failed to follow through by eliminating informal barriers and privatizing firms in competitive sectors. The government liberalized trade starting in 1980, reducing the number of quantitative restrictions and drastically cutting tariffs. In 1984 the government lifted official price controls on all but six commodities (coal, electricity, fertilizer, grains, cargo transport, and sugar) and abolished the legal monopolies in sugar, tea, tobacco, alcohol, and the distribution of fertilizer. In 1990, import licenses were abolished. However, as some barriers to competition fell, others rose in their place. When SOEs ran into trouble coping with foreign competition, the government came to their rescue: in the mid-1980s it introduced import levies that effectively raised the average tariff from 7.4 percent in 1984 to 12.5 percent in 1988, offsetting much of the effect of the earlier tariff reductions; it also allowed SOEs to increase debt to sustain operations (World Bank 1992, 36–39; World Bank 1993). Import levies, plus nontariff barriers (such as quality controls) and measures forcing SOEs to purchase goods from one another, explain why in 1990 the average price of goods produced by Turkish SOEs was 44 percent higher than the import CIF prices.[22] Although Turkey has since sold some SOEs in competitive markets, it still owns textile, paper and printing, fertilizer, and electronics firms.

Among transitional economies, Poland moved quickly to open markets to domestic and foreign competition, introducing low average tariffs (18 percent) and removing most quantitative restrictions on trade. The Czech Republic continued to apply the already low tariffs inherited from the previous system. China, which began earlier, gradually removed restrictions on domestic competition so that by 1993 only about 6 percent of state industrial production was still sold at controlled prices. China has also gradually liberalized trade. As with the restraints on domestic competition, however, openness seems not to have reached the levels of the Czech Republic and Poland. Imports remain controlled, and tariff levels, although lower, remain high for many key SOE products.

Hard Budgets

COMPETITION ONLY PRESSURES STATE-OWNED ENTERPRISES to improve performance if they face a hard budget constraint, that is, if they do not have access to subsidies, privileges, or other forms of soft capital that enable them to compete without improving efficiency.[23] Hard budgets, therefore, are crucial to reforming SOEs in competitive markets. They are also key to reforming monopolies: only when soft finance is curbed can regulators judge a monopoly's performance and require that it perform up to commercial standards. An SOE could be said to have a hard budget when:

- It gets no subsidies, transfers, or special privileges, such as tax exemptions, procurement set-asides, or favorable access to foreign exchange, and must pay its bills or debts on time.

- Its access to credit is decided by independent banks on the basis of commercial principles, without government guarantee, and on market-determined terms.
- Its prices are set by the market or, for monopolies, through regulations that approximate economic prices so that the firm does not earn monopoly rents.

But hard budgets are difficult to measure, which in turn makes them difficult to implement—and to evaluate. This section first describes the difficulties in measuring hard budgets, then provides an estimate of this measure for SOEs in the countries in our sample to see whether the imposition of hard budgets is, as we expect, associated with improved performance.

Whether a state-owned enterprise faces a hard budget or not depends on any direct or indirect subsidies it receives from the government. But subsidies are often hidden and cannot be uncovered without detailed investigation of the individual firm (box 2.5). Moreover, capital transfers

Box 2.5 Uncovering Hidden Subsidies

GOVERNMENT SUBSIDIES TO STATE-OWNED ENterprises are difficult to quantify, in part because they are often hidden. Many hidden subsidies involve loans from governments to SOEs at below market interest rates; often principal and interest payments are repeatedly rolled over or even wiped off the books, converting a loan into a direct transfer. Similarly, state-owned enterprises may be in arrears on their taxes or on payments to other state-owned enterprises, and these arrears are sometimes forgiven. In addition, state-owned enterprises may have special privileges to bid on government contracts, to purchase goods or services from the government or other SOEs at below market prices, or to use government land or buildings rent-free. Finally, a state-owned enterprise may benefit from requirements that government agencies or other SOEs buy its output.

Untangling these hidden subsidies to discover the true cost to the government of an inefficient state-owned enterprise is especially difficult when several exist simultaneously, which is very often the case. In Turkey, for example, subsidized electricity prices from the state power company helped the state aluminum company survive competition from imported aluminum. Turkish SOEs received many other implicit subsidies including lower interest rates on loans than their private counterparts; and if they defaulted on debt service payments for international loans received via the government, the government would make the payment to preserve its credit with international investors. Although SOEs were fined for such behavior, the penalty interest rate was only 30 percent until 1990 compared with a 50 percent rate for commercial loans.

Table 2.6 Government Transfers to State-Owned Enterprises (1978–91) and Price Regulation

| Country | Government transfers to SOEs | | | Price regulation[a] |
| | Total | Capital | Operating | |
	(as percentage of transfers/SOE sales)			
Better performers				
Chile	2.1	0.0	2.1	Benchmark regulation (early 1980s)
Republic of Korea	14.3	13.7	0.6	Fair ROR, keeping up with inflation
Mexico	13.9	4.8	9.2	RPI-X regulation in the late 1980s
Mixed performers				
Egypt	7.7	5.8	1.9	Erratic cost plus formulation
Ghana	2.6	1.6	1.0	Erratic cost plus formulation
Philippines	27.7	21.4	6.3	ROR
Poor performers				
India	16.5	10.8	5.7	ROR, set by local governments
Senegal	17.0	10.4	6.6	Erratic cost plus formulation
Turkey	12.7	6.4	6.3	Erratic cost plus formulation

a. ROR = rate of return; RPI-X = price cap regulation.
Note: Years for tranfers: Chile 1978–89; Egypt 1984–90; India 1980–91; Korea 1980–91; Mexico 1982–91; Philippines 1980–89; Senegal 1981–87; Turkey 1980–91.
Source: Statistical appendix; World Bank data.

(both equity infusions and allowing an SOE to retain its surplus) are difficult to assess. On the one hand, such transfers may make commercial sense if they support the firm's investments in activities with high rates of return. On the other, they may be a subsidy in disguise if they support projects with low returns, service the firm's debt, or disappear into other accounts. Price controls can also provide a subsidy, if prices are set to cover the SOEs' costs regardless of its efficiency. Finally, there are other forms of soft finance, such as privileged access to credit, via government guarantees or directives to banks, and government bailouts of debts or forgiveness of arrears on taxes or debts. These, too, are difficult to identify using aggregate data. Yet investigating the budget of every SOE in each of our twelve sample countries was impractical for this report.

For these reasons, the explicit operating subsidies and capital transfers, in table 2.6 are not very satisfactory measures of hard budgets since low explicit transfers tell us nothing about hidden subsidies. Pricing rules (table 2.6) give a better indication and we also assessed the way countries acted on general financing and pricing policies. As it turns out, although these indicators are less than comprehensive, they add up to a pretty clear picture of whether budgets tend to be hard or soft.

Some of the more successful reformers in our group had lower subsidies and transfers, particularly operating subsidies, but the picture is mixed; Ghana also kept transfers low. More important, successful reformers also improved price regulation, introducing pricing mechanisms, such as benchmark pricing (discussed in chapter 3), that motivated SOE managers to reduce costs more than the widely used cost-plus or rate of return regulation. Improved pricing mechanisms helped regulators set prices closer to scarcity values and gave monopoly SOEs an incentive to improve their performance. They also curbed hidden subsidies and easy access to credit (see the next section). Chile went the farthest of the three, ending virtually all SOE subsidies and privileges, overt and covert, soon after reforms began in 1974. SOE borrowing no longer received a state guarantee, and SOEs were required to pay dividends (in most cases equivalent to 100 percent of profits). Companies that could not break even were denied subsidies but encouraged to improve efficiency and allowed to sell assets; for example, Chile's railroad reacted to the phasing out of subsidies by reducing overstaffing from 27,000 in 1971 to 7,000 in 1984, selling off its real estate and other assets unrelated to railways, and by closing down some uneconomic services. Thus, Chile's railroad reduced, and in some years eliminated, its operating loss.

The mixed performers have begun to phase out overt transfers, but pricing regulations fail to encourage efficiency, remaining fixed for long periods, then moving up erratically. They have made little progress in curbing hidden subsidies and privileged SOE access to soft financing. This has reduced the effectiveness of their efforts to increase competition. Egypt, for example, began to phase out budgeted payments to SOEs in 1991 but by the mid-1990s continued to allow money-losing SOEs to exist on overdrafts and foreign loans, periodically writing off their domestic debts. In some instances, even such support isn't enough to make a firm competitive. Egypt's Public Battery Company, which lost money even when it had a monopoly, has fared poorly since its market was opened to competition in 1984. Technically insolvent since 1986, the state company has lost 91 percent of its market and continues to exist only because of overdrafts and the government's assumption of all outstanding liabilities (Sherif 1992; Sherif and Soos 1993).

The countries with poor-performing SOEs had little success in hardening SOE budgets. Transfers and subsidies were large, and efforts to reduce them produced a "waterbed effect"; that is, the reduction of overt soft financing led to a corresponding buildup in covert forms of subsidy and credits (Galal 1992). Erratic changes in regulated prices left state monopolies starved for cash much of the time, facing an unpredictable pricing regime. Privileges such as tax exemptions or procurement preferences gave SOEs an advantage over private competitors (box 2.6). For example, Senegal began to end direct operating subsidies in 1985, stopped guaranteeing SOE borrowing, and abolished SOEs' preferential interest rates in 1990; but SOEs still have access to indirect subsidies, such as cheap overdrafts and arrears. Cross debts between SOEs and the government build up and are then periodically written off. As in Egypt, the effects of competition are offset through soft budgets. For example, the state-owned transport company, SOTRAC, loses money while the heavily regulated private sector is profitable, despite government restrictions on private fleet expansion and replacement. Part of the subsidies are intended to make up for the requirement that SOTRAC serve unprofitable routes and offer discounts to students, government workers, and military and police personnel, which together account for more than half its riders. But the pre-

---

Box 2.6 Procurement Favors SOEs over Private Manufacturers in India

UNTIL THE EARLY 1990s, SOES IN INDIA THAT called for competitive bids from suppliers were required to give other state-owned enterprises a 10 percent price preference; that is, a private supplier could only win if it bid at least 10 percent lower than the lowest SOE bid. In some cases, state-owned enterprises were allowed to adjust their bids until the price preference assured success. When Cochin Refineries, a central government owned petroleum refinery in southern India, expanded, the company called for bids for instrumentation. A private firm bid 25 percent lower than the competing state-owned enterprise, Instrumentation Ltd. Kota (ILK); a technical review by consultants recommended that the private firm be awarded the contract. At the board meeting to finalize the contract, however, a representative of the Ministry of Petroleum produced a letter from ILK, offering to reduce its bid to a level where the price preference would give it the advantage. The board agreed, and ILK submitted a new offer that was *still* more than 10 percent above the private bid. Under ministry pressure, ILK was allowed a third bid. This bid was 8 percent above the private bid, but within the preference range. At this point the private firm asked to be allowed to rebid. Its request was denied, and the contract was awarded to ILK. The 10 percent price preference was eliminated in 1992, but SOEs still win the contracts if their bids are the same as those of the private bidders (this preference was set to be abolished in 1995).

Source: A. Ranganathan (1988).

cise link between the costs of these requirements and the subsidies is not made clear. Moreover, in addition to direct subsidies, SOTRAC receives low interest loans to purchase new vehicles and parts, tax exemptions for some imports, and tax deferments. The deferred liability is usually canceled after it accumulates. Between 1989 and 1991 SOTRAC received an estimated 32.1 billion CFA ($113.8 million at 1991 exchange rates) in subsidies, loans, and advances from the state, yet in 1993 the company was insolvent, with negative working capital (Etievent 1993).

Among the transition economies, the Central European countries have taken important steps toward hard budgets. Budgetary subsidies were almost eliminated in Poland after 1990 and in the Czech Republic after 1991, and both have moved to curb access to soft credits (Poland has gone even farther; see box 2.9 below). In contrast, China has not yet hardened its budgets for its SOEs, as we discussed above. Instead, their large losses are financed through budget subsidies, although increasingly the burden has shifted to the banking system. (Subsidies financed 78 percent of losses in 1986 and only 55 percent by 1993.) This has contributed to a rising stock of bad debt, estimated in the mid-1990s at 10 to 20 percent of outstanding bank loans (Hwa 1992). Another sign of soft budgets in China is the fact that SOEs continue to receive the lion's share of bank credit (most of which is subsidized), even though their productivity is lower than that of other forms of ownership.[24]

Financial Sector Reform

AS WE HAVE SEEN, HARD BUDGETS CANNOT BE FULLY IMPLEmented without a sound financial sector to prevent well-connected SOEs from simply replacing government transfers with soft credits. Of course, a sound financial sector is important in its own right, and there is a valuable and growing literature on the importance of financial sector reforms to development. It is not our intention to review that literature here. Rather, we examine the ways that financial sector reforms—or the absence of them—influence SOEs. These reforms include improving supervision and regulation, reducing directed credit programs and direct government control over financial intermediaries, and reducing interest rate controls and similar measures designed to strengthen the capacity of the financial system to allocate capital on a commercial basis. Such reforms are key to competition and hard budgets, because they make loans to SOEs subject to independent, commercially driven decisions. They also make privatization easier by enhancing the ability of banks to mobilize savings, assess entrepreneurs, finance sales of SOEs, and oversee new management; all of which, in turn, help expand the number of investors that can participate in the privatization process, ensure that SOEs go to qualified owners, and compel new owners to act appropriately. Finally, by strengthening the capacity and incentive of the financial system to serve new borrowers, reforms ease entry and enhance competitive pressure on SOEs. Box 2.7 summarizes the ways in which a well-developed financial system operates in three roles important to SOE reform.

Box 2.7 Roles of a Well Developed Financial System in SOE Reform

A WELL DEVELOPED FINANCIAL SYSTEM PLAYS three important roles that contribute to successful state-owned enterprise reform:

It allocates resources to enterprises with high expected returns. Participants in the financial market evaluate firms, managers, sectors, and business trends in order to choose the most promising and credit worthy ventures. These participants include not only large intermediaries, such as banks, mutual funds, pension funds, and insurance companies, but also small venture capital institutions and individual entrepreneurs. The better the financial system is at obtaining and processing information, the better the allocation of capital.

It mobilizes capital from disparate savers through banks, insurance companies, pension funds, investment companies, and capital markets. By agglomerating savings from many individuals, these intermediaries enlarge the set of projects available to society, including projects that require large capital inputs and enjoy economies of scale. Furthermore, financial systems that both effectively mobilize savings and select promising firms intensify competition. Domi-

nant firms will face more competition if sound financial systems are able to identify and fund competing enterprises.

It helps compel managers to act in the interests of those who hold claims against the firm (stock, bond, and debt holders). In large enterprises with dispersed claimants, small bond and equity holders may be unable (or unwilling to invest the large effort required) to obtain information, process that information, and effectively oversee the management of large, complex corporations. Managers may, therefore, funnel enterprise resources to themselves or make decisions based on personal, as opposed to corporate, criteria. A well developed financial system can help improve corporate governance, because large financial intermediaries have the incentives and the staff to undertake the difficult tasks of monitoring managers and obliging them to act more in the interests of claim holders. In addition to improving resource allocation, good corporate governance encourages more investment, since investors and lenders feel more confident that firms will maximize owner profits and service debt obligations.

Source: Demirgüç-Kunt and Levine (1994).

Although conventional wisdom about SOE reform has not generally stressed the importance of establishing a sound financial sector, analysis of our sample suggests that successful financial reform greatly enhances the chances for success in SOE reform. A comparison of financial reforms in our sample (appendix 2.2) shows that the better performers strengthened their financial systems' ability to allocate capital on a commercial basis, to mobilize savings for investment, and to assess which entrepreneurs would repay loans. Reforms often proceeded in a two-track manner. Initially, governments took steps to enhance supervisory and regulatory capacity, cut back on directed credit programs, and reduced direct government control of financial intermediaries. They varied in how well they matched deregulation with better supervision and regulation. Chile in the early 1980s and Mexico in the mid-1990s liberalized before a strong enough supervisory structure was in place, contributing to a financial crisis, but both moved promptly to correct the problem. They also varied in their treatment of interest rates, but when real rates were negative, all moved toward positive real rates. These reforms were followed by a reduction in the importance of state banks, bank privatization, and the strengthening of private financial intermediaries. Thanks to these efforts, the better performers in our sample have more developed financial systems with greater depth, a larger role for nonbank financial intermediaries, a higher level of stock market capitalization relative to GDP, and more private banks. We illustrate this graphically with a composite indicator of financial sector development for the sample countries in figure 2.6; box 2.8 explains how these indicators were derived.

To understand what the better performers did to improve their financial sectors, consider the example of Korea. In the early 1980s, Korea liberalized interest rates, reduced directed credits, lowered barriers to entry, and formalized the curb market into an important private nonbank financial intermediary sector. It also strengthened supervision of both banks and nonbanks. Liberalization and improvements in the regulatory systems set the stage for privatization of banks in 1983. Although the government still retains some control over bank lending decisions, bank lending stagnated as a share of GDP in the 1980s, while nonbank credit boomed, rising as a share of GDP from around 10 percent in 1976 to close to 40 percent by the end of the 1980s. By the mid-1990s these programs had laid the basis for a more developed financial system.

In contrast, in most of the mixed and all of the poor performers, promising recent reforms have not yet overcome a history of underde-

Figure 2.6 Indicators of Financial Sector Development, 1991

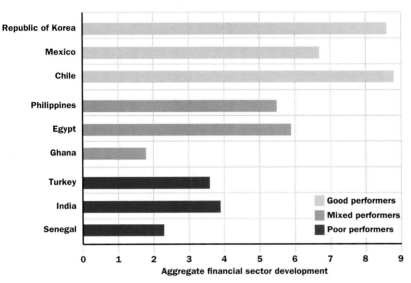

The most successful state enterprise reformers in our sample had the highest levels of financial sector development.

a. Aggregate measures of bank, nonbank, and stock market development. See box 2.7.
Source: Demirgüç-Kunt and Levine (1994).

veloped financial systems, subservient to state direction. For example, beginning in 1992, Egypt eased interest rate controls, strengthened prudential regulation and supervision, relaxed entry barriers, capitalized some weak state-owned banks, and, in 1993, privatized a public-private joint venture bank. Nevertheless, by the mid-1990s state-owned banks still held more than 50 percent of the country's financial assets. In India, one of the poor SOE performers, reforms begun in 1992, while promising, have yet to have a significant impact: state banks, which held more than 90 percent of total banking assets in the mid-1990s, continued to play key roles in financing government expenditures and providing subsidized credit to state-owned firms.

Among transitional economies, Poland and the Czech Republic have gone farthest in reforming their financial systems, introducing real positive interest rates and stricter commercial criteria for lending. Poland not only hardened SOE's access to credit, it has introduced legislation that gives the banks the responsibility and the incentives to decide whether poor-performing firms should be bankrupted (box 2.9), while the Czech Republic privatized minority shares in most of the commer-

Box 2.8 Measuring Financial Sector Development

TO ASSESS THE LEVEL OF DEVELOPMENT OF THE financial systems in our sample countries, we used four indicators:

Financial depth measures the size of the formal financial intermediary sector relative to economic activity. This indicator, DEPTH, is defined as the ratio of liquid liabilities of the financial system to GDP. Since it measures the degree to which the formal financial sector mobilizes domestic savings, larger DEPTH should in most cases reflect greater financial development.

The *level of stock market development* (the ratio of market capitalization to GDP, or MCAP/GDP) augments the information in DEPTH. The size of the financial system does not fully capture how well it provides key financial services such as risk management, information processing, and corporate governance. Better developed stock markets make it easier for individuals to price and diversify risks, to raise capital, and to take over poorly managed firms. Higher values of MCAP/GDP should reflect greater financial development.

The share of total financial assets in *private, nonbank financial institutions* is important, because nonbanks complement commercial banks and, more important, they often function as effective substitutes for the commercial banking sector when that sector is suppressed by government regulations or taxation. Since nonbanks are less likely to funnel credit to the government or SOEs, larger shares of nonbank financial intermediaries reflect a broadening and deepening of the financial system.

Commercial bank ownership is an indicator of the banking sector's degree of independence from the government and the extent of competition in the credit markets. Public banks are the usual tool for providing financing to SOEs at nonmarket terms. If the banking sector is mostly private, this may be a signal that SOEs are less likely to have access to subsidized financing.

To test these measures we calculated the first three for industrial countries and developing countries in

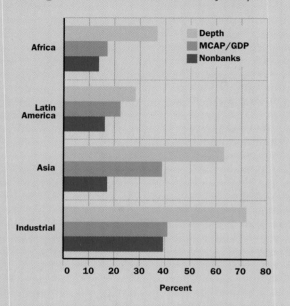

Box Figure 2.8 Financial Sector Development, 1991

Note: "Nonbanks" are nonbank financial intermediary assets as a percentage of total financial assets. Depth is M3 as a percentage of GDP. MCAP/GDP is stock market capitalization as a percentage of GDP.

three regions, Sub-Saharan Africa (Africa), Latin America, and Asia, for 1991, as shown in the above figure. As we would expect, the level of financial development as measured by our indicators is closely aligned with per capita GDP; that is, middle-income countries have a higher level of financial development than poor countries, and rich countries have the highest level of financial development of all. None of the indicators is perfect; for example, DEPTH would be misleading in transition economies. Moreover, they do not measure the quality of financial supervision and regulation, and they measure directed credit only indirectly. Nevertheless taken together, they do provide a useful tool for measuring the level of a country's financial development.

Source: Demirgüç-Kunt and Levine (1994).

Box 2.9 The Financial Sector and SOE Reform: The Case of Poland

IN MARKET ECONOMIES WITH A DEVELOPED financial sector and legal framework, creditors are often in a strong position to decide the fate of poor-performing firms. In transition economies with hundreds of state-owned enterprises, many of which are poor performers, the financial sector and legal framework are often too weak to enable creditors to play this role. Moreover, the main creditors, the banks, are often state-owned enterprises themselves, subject to the same distorted incentive structures as the enterprises to which they lend.

In Poland the government has attempted to address this problem by restructuring and ultimately privatizing state-owned banks, while giving the banks incentives to play an increasingly assertive role in selling or liquidating poor-performing firms. The process got under way in 1992, when the government ordered the nine state-owned banks to stop lending to poorly performing firms. In 1993, the banks were required to wrap up their oldest nonperforming loans by having the loans fully repaid or the payments brought up to date; by working out a new, feasible repayment schedule with the firm; or, where this was not possible, by liquidating the firm to collect on the loan. With bank balance sheets thus in the process of being cleaned up, the government moved to privatize the banks themselves. Three had been privatized by mid-1995, and a fourth was scheduled for sale by the end of the year. Bank employees, who have preferential access to bank shares during privatization, have a strong stake in seeing that the banks do not lend again to poor performers, especially since the government will recapitalize the banks prior to sale only on the basis of what their condition was in 1991. The banks' more stringent lending criteria are forcing changes in poorly performing SOEs, which can no longer expect easy credit

from the banks or elsewhere. (Ready loans from nonbank trade creditors have also dried up, since the trade creditors no longer receive subsidies or easy credit themselves.)

From the creditors' standpoint, Poland's legal framework is far from ideal. Bank claims on collateral have low priority, foreclosure is slow and cumbersome, and liquidation is inefficient and leaves bank and trade creditors in an unfavorable position. To overcome these problems, the Polish government gave banks the right to negotiate workout agreements with debtor firms on behalf of all creditors, if creditors holding at least 50 percent of the debt agree. Under this process, the claims of nongovernment creditors get higher priority than before: nongovernment creditors can terminate the agreement if the SOE fails to implement the promised reorganization, and creditors can acquire shares in the firm by swapping their debt for equity.

Although it is too early to judge the success of Poland's approach, early signs are promising. By mid-1994, of the 775 state-owned enterprises that had bank loans classified as nonperforming in 1991, about 16 percent had been liquidated, 27 percent had fully repaid their loans, and another 13 percent had brought their payments up to date. Most of the remaining firms had been reorganized, and in about a quarter of these cases the creditors received shares through debt-equity swaps. There have been some notable successes. For example, the Szczin shipyard, reorganized in 1992, is now profitable, has full order books, and is in the process of being privatized. By giving creditors the right incentives and control, Poland seems to have found a decentralized way to propel troubled firms to restructure and privatize more rapidly and to push inviable firms to liquidate.

Source: Baer and Gray (1994).

cial banks and transferred management control to the new private owners. In contrast, financial sector reform lags in China, where credit is administratively allocated with no clear link to performance, and there is a plethora of nonmarket and negative interest rates.

The sequencing of financial reforms and their coordination with state-owned enterprise reform is a complex issue, in part because it raises questions about how quickly financial markets should be liberalized and state-owned banks should be privatized. Decontrolling interest rates, freeing entry, and privatizing banks before there are strong supervisory and regulatory institutions and procedures to deal with bad SOE debts could create perverse incentives and so are risky measures. For example, banks with large exposure to troubled SOEs might imprudently bid up deposit interest rates to attract funds to prop up weak SOEs so that the SOEs would not immediately default and cause the bank to fail. The banks would make the loans, hoping either that the SOEs would become profitable or, more likely, that the government would ultimately pay SOE debts. Another risk is that undercapitalized banks facing increased competition will have both the incentives and means to attract resources for excessively risky projects. Thus, overly aggressive privatization and interest rate liberalization without sufficiently strong supervision and regulation and without a policy for coping with bad SOE debts may stymie SOE reform and set the stage for financial crisis.

Korea and, on its second try, Chile substantially improved the financial infrastructure—legal codes, regulations, supervision, and enforcement—early in the reform process. Once these measures and SOE reform were under way, policymakers began fostering the development of private financial intermediaries. They did this by reducing the funds directed from state-owned banks to SOEs on less than market terms under less than market conditions, by gradually removing impediments to the expansion of private financial institutions, and by ultimately privatizing state-owned banks. The costs of moving too quickly with bank privatizations are evident from Chile's first attempt at financial and SOE reform, when undercapitalized banks were quickly privatized despite shortcomings in the regulatory and supervisory system. Box 2.10 describes this attempt during the late 1970s and early 1980s and the financial crisis that resulted, as well as Chile's recovery to a second, much more successful effort. The financial problems in Mexico in early 1995 may indicate that it, too, liberalized interest rates and privatized its financial system before a sufficiently strong supervisory and regulatory system was in place.

Box 2.10 Weak Financial Regulation Can Undermine Privatization: The Case of Chile

CHILE TWICE PRIVATIZED A LARGE NUMBER OF state-owned enterprises. Problems encountered during the first attempt (1974–82) illustrate the importance of establishing adequate financial sector regulation and supervision. Chile began the first period with deregulation: the government abolished interest rate ceilings, eliminated credit allocation controls, reduced banks' reserve requirements, freed capital controls, and allowed new entry. The authorities also privatized state banks. Many were purchased by business conglomerates, with a mere 20 percent down payment. The conglomerates then used loans from the banks to finance the purchase of nonfinancial firms with down payments of only 10 to 40 percent. These highly leveraged purchases concentrated financial and industrial power in the same hands. Under such circumstances, the ineffective, understaffed, and underfunded bank supervisory system was unable to prevent insider lending. When domestic economic problems, external shocks, and an overvalued exchange rate caused a depression in 1992, the con-

glomerates used their banks to prop up their failing firms, so that banks and firms alike were quickly in serious trouble. During the resulting financial crisis, the government took back control of some fifty previously privatized enterprises, including banks that accounted for 60 percent of total bank deposits.

Following the 1982 crisis, Chile strengthened the role, staffing, and funding of its bank supervisory system; it then recapitalized and reprivatized the banks and sold off the nonfinancial enterprises for a second time. Regulations prohibited the sort of highly concentrated, highly leveraged purchases and insider lending that had characterized the first reform effort. Today, Chile's private financial system is well developed, with a large number of nonbank intermediaries, and supports a booming private industrial sector. Chile's experience suggests that countries undertaking bank privatization and liberalization of interest rates and credit controls should make sure that sound supervision and regulation mechanisms are in place first.

Changing the Relationship between Governments and SOE Managers

D IVESTITURE WHEREVER POSSIBLE, COMBINED WITH INcreased competition, hard budgets, and financial sector reforms create substantial pressures for SOEs to improve performance. How SOEs respond depends on whether SOE managers have the freedom and incentives to improve performance. Many governments do not give SOE managers the power to react to competition with appropriate measures, such as laying off excess workers, seeking cheaper suppliers, stopping money-losing services, or searching for new markets.

Even if managers have the autonomy to make changes, they will have no incentive to act unless the government systematically evaluates their performance and delivers fitting rewards and punishments. Both problems—freedom and incentives—are evident in the National Textile Corporation of India (NTC), a money loser since its creation in 1974. Since 1991 the company has come under increasing pressure to improve its performance, but to do that it needs to close fourteen mills, shed 59,000 workers, and sell off an estimated Rs.1.2 billion ($36.8 million in 1995) worth of unused land and other idle assets. Not only has the authority to undertake such changes been lacking, but rapid management turnover would appear to have greatly reduced any incentive to act: from 1974 to 1987, NTC chief executives lasted an average of eleven months. Clearly, in such instances the reforms we have discussed above can only be effective if there are substantial changes in the relationship between the government and SOE management.

Table 2.7 Institutional Reforms of State-Owned Enterprises in the 1980s

Country	Changes in supervision		Changes in decisionmaking pattern		Explicit performance agreements	
	Yes/no	Year	Yes/no	Year	Yes/no	Year
Better performers						
Chile	no	n.a.	yes	1974	no	n.a.
Republic of Korea	yes	1984	yes	1984	yes	1984
Mexico	yes	1986	yes	1986	yes	1986
Mixed performers						
Egypt	yes	1991	yes	1991	yes	*
Ghana	yes	1986	yes	1986	yes	1989
Philippines	yes	1987	yes	1989	yes	1989
Poor performers						
India	no	n.a.	yes	1988	yes	1987
Senegal	yes	1987	yes	1987	yes	1986
Turkey	yes	1984	yes	1984	no	n.a.

n.a. Not applicable.
* Not yet implemented.
Note: Changes in supervision = placing SOEs under a new ministry, holding company, or board of directors. *Decisionmaking pattern* = giving managers more autonomy in personnel, production, and finance decisions. *Performance agreements* = agreements between SOE managers and bureaucrats on performance targets.
Source: Galal (1992); Shirley (1989); Song (1993); various World Bank reports.

Strikingly, all the countries in our sample, successful and unsuccessful, attempted to change government-SOE management relations (table 2.7). These reforms included introducing new oversight bodies, increasing managerial autonomy, and signing explicit performance agreements. New supervisory bodies were created in Egypt (the Public Investment Office headed by the prime minister), the Philippines (Government Corporation Monitoring Coordinating Committee), Ghana (the State Enterprise Commission), and Senegal (the Delegation for the Parapublic Sector Reform). The composition of SOE boards of directors was changed to include representatives of consumers or professionals in, for example, Korea, Mexico, the Philippines, and Turkey. All the countries expanded the power of SOE managers (formally, if not always in practice) over such matters as pricing, procurement, production, and personnel. Most adopted explicit, performance-based agreements with SOE managers.

Since all countries made broadly similar attempts to alter the relationship between the government and SOE managers, what accounts for the differences in outcome? We have argued throughout this chapter that the five components of state-owned enterprise reform are closely interdependent. It would therefore be reasonable to conclude that the differences in achievement in the first four components go a long way to explaining why some countries had better-performing SOE sectors than others. Yet theory and common sense suggest that changes in the relationship between the government and SOE managers are probably important in their own right, and that differences in such changes may not show up in country-level data. To understand why institutional reforms seem to have worked in some countries and not in others, we need to distinguish between reforms that are mere formalities and those that genuinely alter the incentives for government and management, thus changing behavior and outcomes. To do so we need to go beyond country-level analysis and consider the relationship between managers and governments in individual firms. This is the subject of the next chapter.

Conclusion

THIS CHAPTER HAS ARGUED THAT FIVE ELEMENTS OF STATE-owned enterprise reform—divestiture, competition, hard budgets, financial sector reform, and changes in the relationship between government and SOE managers—are closely interdependent. *Countries with the best performing SOE sectors not only tended to do better on each of the first four elements (and perhaps the fifth); they also followed a more comprehensive approach, in which success in one area supported success in the others. Countries with SOE sectors that performed less well frequently undertook broadly similar reform efforts; but these differed from those of the successful countries in degree and in design. Not only did the less successful countries achieve less in each individual reform element, they also followed less comprehensive strategies overall.*

Appendix 2.1 Reforms to Open SOE Markets to Competition and Introduce Hard Budget Constraints

This matrix defines the measures taken for market reform in our sample countries. Reforms are ranked by country in relation to the degree of hardness in their budgets, and success is defined by the degree to which competition is encouraged.

Better Performers

Chile—Year of Reform, 1974.

Market reforms: Removed all quantitative restrictions on imports and reduced average nominal tariffs from 94 percent to 10 percent in five years. (Tariffs have subsequently risen slightly.) SOE product markets almost totally deregulated by 1978. Privatized all competitive SOEs except in mining.

Hard budget: Ended virtually all subsidies, transfers, privileges, guarantees on lending. SOEs required to pay dividends, in most cases 100 percent of profits.

Mexico—Year of Reform, 1983.

Market reforms: Reduced tariffs from a maximum 100 percent to a maximum 20 percent and import licensing requirements, which covered 83 percent of imports in mid-1985, to 20 percent by 1988 and 9 percent by 1991. Price controls in most SOE sectors reduced or abolished. Private entry allowed into sectors that were previously the preserve of state-owned enterprises, such as petrochemicals, fertilizer, ports, rail transport, and power. All but a few SOEs in competitive sectors were sold; exceptions are petroleum, paper, and salt.

Increasingly hard budget: Reduced operating subsidies to about 4 percent of sales in 1991.

Republic of Korea—Year of Reform, 1982.

Market reforms: By 1985 had liberalized imports for 90 percent of its manufactured goods. However, has relied more on export rivalry (requiring that SOEs compete abroad) than on import competition to spur SOE performance. Share of SOEs in manufacturing and other competitive sectors reduced, partly through sales and partly by restraining the growth of SOEs in the face of rapidly expanding private enterprises.

Somewhat hard budget: Low operating subsidies, but SOEs allowed to retain sizable earnings to reinvest and government guaranteed loans.

Mixed Performers

Egypt—Year of Reform, 1990.

Market reforms: Reduced nontariff barriers from 25 percent in March 1990 to 9 percent by June 1991 (nontariff barriers for the private sector fell to 1 percent). Tariffs reduced from a maximum 120 percent in 1990 to 70 percent by 1994, and SOE quotas on foreign exchange ended in 1991. Price controls being phased out, as are SOE monopolies over distribution of products such as cement and fertilizer. In 1992 Egypt had SOEs in such potentially competitive sectors as hotels, food products, textiles, tourism, building materials, electric motors, and transport; SOEs were responsible for close to 60 percent of manufacturing value added in 1992. Privatization has recently begun to accelerate.

Not yet a hard budget: Subsidies and transfers being phased out, but SOEs have had easy access to overdrafts and foreign credits and government has periodically written off arrears. Past policies of allowing money-losing SOEs to subsist on bank debt have weakened the impact of competition on SOEs; it is too early to tell how the recent reforms will play out.

Ghana—Year of Reform, 1983.

Market reforms: Tariffs harmonized at 25 to 30 percent, but imports face higher sales taxes than domestic goods. Price controls still exist for some products (e.g., textiles and wheat flour). Sold, leased, or liquidated forty-four SOEs by mid-1994 in competitive sectors but has retained some competitive firms, especially in transport.

Not a hard budget: Has curbed operating subsidies, but SOEs have had preferences in bidding, reduced taxes, and priority access to credit from government owned financial institutions. Little to no systematic monitoring of credit to SOEs, and nonpayment has been a serious problem.

Philippines—Year of Reform, 1986.

Market reforms: Removed quantitative restrictions on trade and began to ease restrictions on entry. Average nominal tariffs have declined from about 43 percent in 1980 to just over 5 percent in 1991, but foreign exchange controls were liberalized only in 1992. Has few SOEs in competitive markets and has sold, or plans to sell, all manufacturing SOEs except a petroleum refinery.

Not a hard budget: Transfers and subsidies have been large, averaging almost 25 percent of SOE sales in the second half of the 1980s.

Poor Performers

Senegal—Year of Reform, 1986.

Market reforms: Reduced and rationalized tariffs and removed most quantitative restrictions between

Not a hard budget: Began to end direct operating subsidies in mid-1980s, stopped guaranteeing SOE

1986 and 1988 and removed price controls on most products in 1987; but some of these reforms were subsequently reversed in the late 1980s. As a result, average effective rate of protection fell from 165 percent in 1985 to 90 percent in 1988 but rose again to 98 percent in 1990. Has relatively few manufacturing SOEs; most of its SOEs in competitive markets are in services, such as transport or tourism. Between 1980 and 1991 divested about four dozen small SOEs in banking, hotels and tourism, and agriculture, privatizing twenty-six and liquidating twenty-one. But state-owned enterprises remain active in several potentially competitive sectors, including edible oils, textiles, tourism, and transport.

India—Year of Reform, 1985.

Market reforms: Allowed private investment in previously restricted sectors and delicensed some imports. However, although reduction in coverage of open general licenses raised import penetration rates in 1980s in intermediate materials and capital equipment, products mainly produced by SOEs, subsequent analysis showed that only about 5 percent of imported products were in direct competition with domestic production. Reforms deepened with devaluations of the exchange rate in mid-1980s and 1991, reduction of quantitative restrictions, and adoption of a liberalized system for managing the exchange rate in 1991. Price controls and restrictions on private investments are being phased out (for example, a list of industries reserved for SOEs has been reduced to six: armaments, atomic energy, coal, mineral oils, other minerals of use in atomic energy, and rail transport). Many SOEs in competitive sectors; SOEs responsible for over 18 percent of manufacturing in 1989.

Turkey—Year of Reform, 1980.

Market reforms: Quantitative restrictions reduced and import tariffs cut, further cuts in 1984. In 1990, import licenses abolished. However, import levies borrowing, and abolished SOE preferential interest rates in 1990. However, SOEs have had many indirect subsidies, such as overdrafts and arrears, tax exemptions, and deferments. Cross debts with government and other SOEs periodically written off.

Not a hard budget: Loss-making SOEs subsidized—as are loss-making private firms—although subsidies are declining. Government equity support and loans are scheduled to decline. SOEs have enjoyed privileges that private firms did not. For example, until 1992 SOEs enjoyed a 10 percent price preference over their private competitors in government procurement; since 1992 SOEs get preference if their bid is equal to a private bidder (this scheme to be abolished in 1995). SOEs rely heavily on subsidized borrowing from state-owned banks with government guarantees to cover S-I deficit.

Not a hard budget: SOEs that have trouble competing subsidized. SOEs received equity injections, payments for losses from noncommercial objectives, on goods competing with SOEs raised from 7.4 percent in 1984 to 12.5 percent in 1988, offsetting much of effect of earlier tariff reductions. Nontariff barriers also introduced, such as quality control on steel. In 1984 lifted official price controls on all but six commodities; abolished legal monopolies in sugar, tea, tobacco, alcohol, and fertilizer distribution. Sold some competitive SOEs but continues to own SOEs in such activities as textiles, paper and printing, fertilizer, and electronics.

and "aid" to cover losses that equaled 3 percent of GDP in 1993. SOEs also receive government guarantees for foreign borrowing and loans and rediscounts from central bank. SOEs run up arrears to the treasury, social security administration, commercial banks, and suppliers.

Transition Economies

Czech Republic—Year of Reform, 1991.

Market reforms: Liberalized most prices by 1992, made currency convertible and pegged to a basket, reduced average tariff to 5 percent, and eliminated all but a few quantitative restrictions. Domestic entry controls relaxed.

Increasingly hard budget: Most budgetary subsidies eliminated by 1991 and privatized enterprises now have to seek credit on commercial terms.

Poland—Year of Reform, 1989.

Market reforms: Ninety percent of all prices decontrolled by January 1990, made currency convertible (crawling peg), and reduced average tariffs to 18 percent. (They have subsequently risen somewhat.) Eliminated quantitative restrictions on imports. Removed most restrictions on entry.

Increasingly hard budget: Budgetary subsidies eliminated after 1990. Moved to positive real rates; introduced incentives to subject SOE credit decisions to commercial criteria and motivate banks to push SOEs to restructure. (See box 2.9 in text.)

China—Year of Reform, 1979.

Market reforms: Gradually liberalized trade, decentralizing from twelve or so foreign trade corporations to over 3,500 state-owned companies. Two-tier foreign exchange market developed, and devaluations have shrunk the parallel premium (to a low of 10 percent by 1991). Import controls remain and tariff rates still high for many SOE products. Prices liberalized; market prices now play central role in allocating resources. Competition high in activities where nonstate sector active.

Not a hard budget: Losses, at 2.4 percent of GDP, are financed through budget subsidies and the banking system.

Appendix 2.2 Financial Sector Reform

This comparison of financial reforms in our sample shows that the better performers strengthened their financial systems' ability to allocate capital on a commercial basis, to mobilize savings for investment, and to assess which entrepreneurs would repay loans.

Better Performers

Chile—Period of Reform, from 1974. Financial liberalization started in 1974 with interest rate liberalization. Banks were privatized (1975–77). Entry restrictions were relaxed, credit ceilings were eliminated, permitted scope of activities expanded. Pension funds were privatized in 1980. Restrictions on foreign capital inflows were gradually lifted in 1977, and capital account was completely liberalized in 1980. Financial crisis came in 1982, and the government had to clean up and bail out the banks. After the crisis, prudential regulation and supervision were strengthened, culminating in the passage of a new banking law in 1986.

Mexico—Period of Reform, from 1988. Financial sector reform started in 1988 with liberalization of interest rates. Exchange controls were abolished, forced investment in government securities was eliminated, and most of the restrictions on commercial bank activity were lifted during 1989. Regulation and supervision were strengthened during 1989–90. Banks' privatization started in 1991 and was completed in 1992.

Republic of Korea—Period of Reform, from 1980. A gradual reform started in 1980. Deposit rates were partially liberalized to establish positive real rates. Preferential lending rates were abolished in 1982. Privatization of the state-owned city banks started in 1982 and was completed by 1983. Restrictions on nonbank financial institutions were relaxed.

New domestic entry into the financial system was allowed. A gradual opening up to international competition started. Capital markets were also gradually opened to foreign participation. Lending rates were officially deregulated in 1988. In 1991 government announced a plan to completely deregulate money market and deposit rates by 1997.

Mixed Performers

Egypt—Period of Reform, from 1992. Financial sector reform only started in 1992. Interest rates were liberalized, and prudential regulation and supervision were strengthened. Banks were recapitalized, and entry barriers were relaxed. In 1993, one private/state-owned joint-venture bank was privatized.

Ghana—Period of Reform, from 1987. The financial reform initiated in 1987 included a strengthening of the regulatory framework, liberalization of government controls, and bank restructuring. Interest rates were liberalized in 1988. 1989 banking law strengthened bank regulation and supervision. In 1990, banks were restructured, and government announced plans to privatize banks in 1993.

Philippines—Period of Reform, from 1980. Financial sector reform focused on strengthening the banking system, reducing taxation, and increasing competition. Banks were allowed to expand into new areas of activity, and loan and deposit rates were freed. The share of state-owned banks in total banking assets was reduced from 28 percent in 1980 to 1.4 percent in 1990.

Poor Performers

Senegal—Period of Reform, from 1989. Financial reform program started in 1989 and included restructuring of state-owned banks, increasing capital requirements, and improving banking supervision. Government ownership in each bank was decreased to less than 25 percent.

India—Period of Reform, from 1992. Financial sector reform started quite late, in 1992. Entry and expansion conditions have been made less restrictive. Interest rates on term loans and most debt instruments were recently decontrolled and increased. Reform efforts to improve prudential and regulatory environment, to recapitalize weak institutions, and to promote greater private sector participation and further financial policy liberalization are continuing.

Turkey—Period of Reform, from 1980. Financial sector reform started with interest liberalization on deposit and loan rates in 1980. Commercial banks were deregulated, and foreign bank entry was allowed. Financial crisis came in 1982. Interest ceilings were reimposed, and a deposit insurance system was established. Later reforms emphasized prudential regulation and improved supervision, leading to a new banking law in 1985. Interest rates were partially liberalized in 1988. Recently several state-owned banks were slated for privatization.

Notes

1. Even though SOE reform also has macroeconomic effects, we chose to focus on its microeconomic results since these are more clearly outcomes of the reform measures.

2. Specifically we used the ratio of operating surplus (or quasi rents) and before-tax profit to sales for 1980–91. Sales are used in the denominator as a proxy for revalued capital because consolidated capital stock for SOEs was not available for all countries. Not all countries have data for all indicators for all years in the period; see footnotes to graphs for specifics. Operating surplus is defined as operating revenues (principally sales) minus operating expenditures (wages, intermediate inputs, and other costs of operation) and is gross (i.e., depreciation is not included as an operating expenditure). Profits before taxes is defined as the operating surplus net of depreciation and interest expenses, plus nonoperating revenue minus nonoperating expenses.

3. Real variable unit costs are estimated as the ratio of total real variable costs (i.e., the cost of labor and intermediate inputs) to real output, expressed in constant 1985 prices. A decline in the real variable cost per unit of output over time implies improved productivity, other things being equal. Also, lower real variable cost per unit of output in country A compared with country B implies that SOEs perform better in country A than in country B.

TFP is estimated as

$$TFP = Q/V$$

where Q is a quantity index of all outputs and V is a quantity index of all inputs (including labor, intermediate inputs, and capital). In the absence of information on capital stock in all countries, the cost of capital was measured by the sum of interest and depreciation. A TFP ratio greater than one means that more real output is produced than real outputs used. An increase in TFP over time means that more real output is produced with the same level of real inputs (or the same level of output is produced with fewer inputs). And, a higher level of TFP in absolute terms in country A compared with country B means that SOEs are more productive in country A than in country B.

Outputs and inputs were disaggregated into major items and deflated by specific price indexes wherever possible, or by relevant general price indexes where specific indexes were unavailable. For example, wages were deflated by wage indexes where available; otherwise by the CPI.

As calculated, unit variable cost and TFP have to be interpreted with caution. Because they are derived in part using general price indexes, the deflators may or may not coincide with the changes in the prices of SOE outputs and inputs. To the extent that SOEs selling prices fall behind these general indexes, real variable unit costs and TFP will underestimate productivity and vice versa.

4. If we exclude Chile's large copper company, CODELCO, from the analysis, Chile's ranking does not change. If we exclude Ghana's Cocoa Marketing Board, however, Ghana falls into the poor-performing group. PEMEX, CODELCO, and the Cocoa Marketing Board were included in the calculations for figures 2.1 to 2.3.

5. The ranking for real variable costs per unit changes when we exclude these large SOEs where savings in international prices might skew results. Excluding Mexico's oil company PEMEX and Ghana's Cocoa Marketing Board causes Mexico to become a mixed performer and Ghana to fall into the lowest performing category. Excluding Chile's state-owned copper industry, CODELCO, does not change Chile's rank.

6. These findings are consistent with other studies analyzing changes in SOE productivity in the sample countries over time or in comparison with the private sector. See, for example, Dekle and Sokoloff (1990) for Korea, and Martin del Campo and Winkler (1991) for Chile and Mexico. The ranking does not change if we exclude the large exporting SOEs such as CODELCO.

7. Data limitations precluded the calculation of TFP in Ghana.

8. For example, Chile divested its phone and power companies during this period . When the phone company and two of the power companies (CHILGENER and ENDESA) are excluded from the analysis, TFP increases rather than falls. (Mexico's sale of its phone company occurred too late to affect the period under consideration.)

9. Countries within each subgroup are ranked alphabetically because data are not detailed enough to permit more specific rankings. Egypt is classified as a mixed performer despite its poor and deteriorating performance on three of the five indicators because of improvements resulting from reforms in 1991 that are too recent to be captured by our data.

10. One study estimates the negative impact of the collapse of Soviet and CMEA trade alone was in the range of 8.5 percent of GDP in the Czech Republic and 6.3 percent in Poland (Rosati 1993). See also Brada and King (1991).

11. See Gelb and Singh (1994) for a detailed analysis of the increasing differentiation between more and less successful firms in these countries. Microeconomic evidence is largely for Poland and is taken from Gelb, Jorgensen, and Singh (1992); Estrin, Schaffer, and Singh (1993); Pinto, Belka, and Krajewski (1992 and 1993); Dabrowski, Federowicz, and Szomberg (1992); Gora (1993); Schaffer (1993); Gomulka (1993); Dittus (1993); Estrin, Gelb, and Singh (1993); and Brada, King, and Ma (1993).

12. SOEs responded to the opening of markets by creating sales departments, setting up distributorships, and searching for foreign partners with marketing expertise (Gelb, Jorgensen, and Singh 1992; Estrin, Gelb, and Singh 1993). They introduced cost accounting, profit centers, management information systems, and improved financial management in general. In Poland a number of managers have been replaced and are earning higher salaries linked to company performance (Gelb, Jorgensen, and Singh 1992).

13. See Sachs and Woo (1993), 22, table 6. See also box 2.1 in this chapter for ownership types in China.

14. Losses may be underreported due to accounting practices; some estimates place actual losses almost twice as high as those reported (Gelb and Singh 1994, 24–25).

15. Jefferson, Rawski, and Zheng (1992) found that TFP for the state sector grew by 2.4 percent a year from 1980 to 1988, while for the collective sector (of which TVEs are the largest part) it rose at an annual rate of 4.6

percent. Xiao, using a smaller sample for 1980–85, found TFP growth was 4 percent for SOEs and 8.8 percent for TVEs. Even when allowances are made for differences in starting point, size, type of industry, and institutional factors, TVE had a significantly higher productivity growth (Jefferson and Rawski 1992; Jefferson 1993). TFP levels comparable to the rest of the sample countries were not available.

16. Much of the actual privatizations in transitional economies have been spontaneous or unofficial; for example, SOE assets are sometimes leased to private businesses owned by SOE managers.

17. By mid-1993 some 100 SOEs had issued shares on the stock markets in Shanghai and Shenzhen, and sixteen were listed on foreign exchanges; a few SOEs have become limited liability companies whose shares are held by employees, local residents, or (much rarer) the general public. An estimated 10 percent of SOEs have been leased to individuals, collectives, and local governments. Mergers and takeovers are an allowed form of exit, but the number of mergers is very small compared to the total number of SOEs (Gelb and Singh 1994, 23; Bank staff estimates).

18. See box 2.4 for a description of ownership types.

19. From 1989 to 1991 the number of sole proprietorships grew from by 78 percent to 1.42 million, private firms quadrupled (to 45,000), joint ventures grew tenfold (to almost 5,000), and cooperatives went from 15,000 to 17,000. While many new private enterprises are small trading firms, the number of industrial companies is also expanding (by 35 percent in 1992). These manufacturing firms are small: 60 percent had fewer than twenty employees in 1991 (Webster 1993).

20. We only consider competition in product markets. Competition for corporate control (through takeovers, for example) can also have incentive effects on firms.

21. Chile privatized most of its state-owned enterprises between 1974 and 1978, but many of these firms were acquired by banks when they defaulted on their loans. When the banking crisis hit in 1981–83, the gov-

ernment "intervened" in the banks and resold both the enterprises and the banks from 1985 to 1989. The few SOEs that remain are in water and sewage, copper and coal mining, petroleum, railways, the Santiago metro, and shipping.

22. Products include paper, cement, iron, coal, fertilizer, sugar, meat, tea, and copper (World Bank 1993).

23. The phrase "hardening the budget constraint" was coined by Janos Kornai (1980).

24. In the first half of 1993, industrial investments grew by 71 percent and SOEs accounted for 62 percent of these investments—a clear case of industrial credits not going to the most productive sectors of the economy.

CHAPTER 3

Contracting: What Works, What Doesn't, and Why

I N CHAPTER 2 WE FOUND THAT COUNTRIES THAT REFORMED their state-owned enterprises successfully and those that did not both attempted to change the relationship between the government and SOE managers. Successful and unsuccessful reformers alike introduced new oversight bodies and, on paper at least, expanded managers' power over pricing, procurement, production, and personnel. Most also adopted explicit, performance-based agreements with SOE managers. Many countries have attempted such reforms, but only a few have improved SOE performance. Do differences in the design and implementation—in particular, the ways that reforms affected incentives of the government and firm managers—help explain the differences in outcome?

To find out, we analyzed relationships between governments and SOE managers, between government and private managers of state enterprises, and between governments and the owners of regulated monopolies. Each of these relationships is founded on a contract, that is, an agreement between the government and another party based on shared expectations about obligations and outcomes. These contracts are often written, although they need not be, and in fact we found that even when contracts are written, crucial provisions affecting incentives are frequently only implicit. We identified three types of contracts important to state-owned enterprise reform:

- *Performance contracts* define the relationship between government and *public* managers; we found over 550 such contracts in thirty-two developing countries, and more than 100,000 in China.

- *Management contracts* define the relationship when government contracts management of the firm to *private* managers; we found 202 management contracts in forty-nine developing countries.
- *Regulatory contracts* define the relationship between a government and a regulated monopoly. Such contracts may include explicit agreements about pricing or performance and implicit expectations about, for example, the powers of regulators. Regulatory contracts are being increasingly used as monopolies in telecoms, electricity, and transport are privatized; we found seven such contracts for basic telecoms service, the sector we investigated.

It will be immediately apparent that formal contract arrangements have been established for only a small proportion of the SOEs worldwide; however, countries often use contracts for important and problematic activities, such as infrastructure monopolies (electricity, water, and telecoms) and major exporters and revenue earners (tea in Sri Lanka, gold in Ghana, and hotels in Egypt). Moreover, the use of contracts has been increasing and is likely to continue to grow as governments, recognizing the costs of poor SOE performance, attempt various remedies. Yet little is known empirically about what distinguishes successful from unsuccessful contracts or what type of contract works best in which circumstances. As we shall see, the findings of this chapter, the first systematic, empirical evaluation of the three main forms of SOE contracting worldwide, form a crucial component of our recommendations in chapter 5 about the design and implementation of a successful SOE reform strategy.

We begin by surveying three factors that determine the incentives that contracting parties face: information, rewards and penalties, and commitment.[1] Next we analyze available data for the three types of contracts, moving from contracts with the greatest degree of government involvement to the least. We find that, in general, the greater the involvement of the private sector, the better enterprise performance. We argue that this is because private managers and owners, unlike public managers, can readily capture the returns when enterprise performance improves. They therefore have greater incentives than public managers to exert effort to improve performance and to enter into contracts only when government manifests credible commitment to keeping its side of the bargain.

How Incentive Factors Interact to Influence Outcomes

BEFORE INDIVIDUALLY CONSIDERING THE THREE INCENTIVE factors—information, rewards and penalties, and commitment—it is useful to sketch the relationship between them. *Information* problems arise because contracting agents (government on one hand and public or private managers or owners of a monopoly on the other) have different sets of information; thus, each side can use the information it holds exclusively to improve its position at the expense of the other. At the same time, neither side knows everything, so it is impossible to design a contract that will cover all eventualities. To alleviate the information problems, contracts usually include promises of *rewards and penalties* to induce the contracting parties to reveal information and comply with contract provisions. But promises of rewards and penalties alone are not enough. Each party needs to be convinced of the *commitment* of the other to deliver.

Thus, like a chain with three strong links, contracts that include effective mechanisms to handle problems arising from information, rewards and penalties, and commitment are more effective than those with one or more weak links in attaining the desired outcome—improved enterprise performance.

Addressing Information Problems

How do information problems arise, and how can they be addressed? Enterprises have a great deal of information—for example, about input costs, demand, and productivity—that the government supervisory or regulatory body lacks. Moreover, these government bodies cannot know everything about how a firm performs. These two problems—information asymmetry and imperfect observability of performance—give company managers the leeway to pursue interests that are at odds with the government's interests.

Of the various mechanisms to reveal information, competition is the most effective and least expensive. Competition can uncover information in a variety of ways, as we discussed in chapter 2, thus strengthening the government's hand. Competition also helps to align the incentives of the contracting parties with the desired outcome—more efficient performance. If technology or other factors do not permit direct competition in product markets, governments can adopt other mechanisms to introduce competitive pressures. These include the following:

- *Yardstick competition.* Comparing the performance of two or more regional monopolies operating in similar environments gives governments a way to assess the performance of firms. For example, the Argentine government broke its telecom monopoly into two regional monopolies, north and south, that can now be compared.
- *Auctions.* When competing interests bid for the right to provide goods or services, the government obtains information that can be incorporated into the contract. For example, the management contract for water supply in Guyana was awarded to the bidder offering the lowest prices for each new water connection and cubic meter of forecast water sales.
- *Threat of competition.* After the contract is awarded, the threat of competition can help induce the contractor to operate efficiently. For example, the monopoly on basic phone service enjoyed by the privatized Mexico telephone company will end in 2026, but it could be ended sooner if the company fails to meet its performance targets under the contract.

Designing Rewards and Penalties

For a contract to improve performance, it must include rewards and penalties that persuade management *and* government not to use information opportunistically, but rather to strive toward the contract goal of improving firm performance.

The importance of rewards and penalties for managers is obvious and widely understood. These may take the form of bonus schemes (for public managers), contracting fees (for private managers), or price adjustments (for private owners of regulated monopolies). They work best when improvements in performance are clearly linked to higher rewards, while failure to improve, or a deterioration in performance, is punished by cutting or withholding rewards. Some contracts incorporate more effective rewards and penalties than others. For example, the contract for the Cairo Sheraton promises management success fees that are paid only when the hotel makes a profit. In contrast, the contract for Nzoia Sugar mill in Kenya provides the contractor a fixed fee that covers all costs; there are no penalties for poor performance and no rewards for good performance.

The need for rewards and penalties to motivate government compliance with contracts is often overlooked, but governments, responding to diverse and contradictory demands, behave in ways that reduce firm efficiency; for example, governments often prohibit SOEs from shedding excess workers or require that they purchase inputs from other SOEs, even when these are not priced competitively. As we explain below, lack of effective rewards and penalties to ensure government support for the goal of improved firm performance leads to problems of commitment. For example, governments may be less motivated to adhere to the contract if they are not risking their reputation with important constituents or risking adverse press reports.

Ensuring Commitment

The third factor, commitment, arises because it is impossible to include all possible contingencies in the contract. The rewards may look good, but what assurances do contracting parties have that they will be forthcoming? Commitment problems are particularly acute with contracts governing SOEs and regulated monopolies, because it may be difficult or impossible to find a neutral third party with the power to compel the government (or its successor) to meet its promises. Faced with such a situation, management may protect its interests by taking actions that work against the contract's objectives. Thus, a public manager who doubts that government will pay its bills may run up arrears on government guaranteed debt or withhold payment from public suppliers.[2] For example, the government of Senegal failed to keep its promise to pay Senegal Electricity for power and to force state-owned electricity users to do the same; Senegal Electricity, in turn, ran up arrears with its suppliers and on taxes and government loans. In the case of privatized, regulated monopolies, new buyers who doubt government commitment may withhold needed investments because they fear that their assets will be expropriated. Such problems are difficult to overcome and are, therefore, common in the contracts we examined.

One way to overcome these problems is to specify a neutral conflict resolution mechanism, clarifying when and how it can be invoked and how it will be enforced. Enforcing agencies may include the courts (where they are strong and independent of politics), a new oversight or regulatory commission, the executive branch, or outside arbitration. International tribunals or arbitrators and donors who may withhold funds if a government reneges can sometimes partly substitute for domestic mechanisms if the courts and other government bodies are perceived as biased or weak. Less formally, the press and informed public opinion may exert pressure on governments to comply with their promises. The appropriate mix of conflict resolution and enforcement mechanisms will vary depending on country conditions.[3]

In the sections that follow, we analyze how these contracting issues affected enterprise performance in the three kinds of contracts central to SOE reform—performance contracts, management contracts, and regulatory contracts. For each, we first measure performance before and after implementation of contracts in a sample of firms; we then assess how the contracts dealt with the problems of information, rewards and penalties, and commitment and how this led to the outcomes we observed.

Performance Contracts: With Public Managers

ALL GOVERNMENTS HAVE AN IMPLICIT CONTRACTUAL RELAtionship with managers of their SOEs. In recent years, many reforming countries made these contracts explicit, spelling out the obligations of management, and sometimes government, in written performance contracts.[4] Performance contracts were in use in twenty-eight developing countries, largely in Asia and Africa, in the mid-1990s (table 3.1). Substantial resources have been sunk into the design and enforcement of these contracts, yet the few assessments to date show mixed results. (Shirley,

Table 3.1 Number of Performance Contracts in Developing Countries, by Sector

Sector	Africa	Asia	Latin America	Middle East and North Africa	Central Europe[a]	Total
Transport	26	8	4	6	2	46
Telecom and post	15	2	1	1	0	19
Extractive industries	6	26	2	2	3	39
Agriculture	13	3	2	0	0	18
Water	4	4	0	1	0	9
Electricity	11	8	6	1	1	27
Other	61	160	1	1	4	227
Total	136	211	16	12	10	385[b]

a. Data for Romania only. Contracts are also being used in Bulgaria, but no details are available.

b. Total figures cover thirty-one countries. In addition, Indonesia reports 180 firms, and China 103,000; no breakdown by industry was available. Data reflects situation as of June 1994. Based on a worldwide search using World Bank and other sources. In some countries additional contracts may have been awarded.

Source: Survey of World Bank reports and staff.

1989, 1991; Nellis 1989; Trivedi 1990). We set out to assess whether explicit performance contracts improve economic performance and the reasons for success or failure. First we examined the evidence from twelve case studies on how performance contracts affect outcomes. As we shall see, the empirical results suggest that explicit performance contracts have frequently been a waste of time and effort. When we considered why these contracts so often failed to improve performance, we found that they generally did not significantly improve incentives in the three crucial areas of information, rewards and penalties, and commitment.

How Performance Contracts Perform

Did enterprise performance change in ways that can be attributed to the contract (or, more weakly, did enterprise performance change in ways that mean the contract cannot be ruled out as an explanatory factor)? We address this question by investigating performance before and after implementation of contracts in twelve companies in six countries, as shown in table 3.2 (Dyer Cissé 1994). (For ease of reading we have used simplified enterprise names; see table 3.2.)

The available sample is small and not random, so care must be used in generalizing from the results.[5] Also there are weaknesses in the data: we relied on the firm's own audited accounts, which are weak in Ghana and Senegal. In some cases our precontract period is short and the length of the postcontract period varies, which makes it hard to measure trends.[6] Even so, the sample does include countries at very different levels of income that employed varying approaches to performance contracting. An improvement in postcontract performance across such differing country and contract experiences would suggest that contracts can work (unless some other factor was at work, something we also investigated).[7]

To assess the companies' economic performance, we compared trends in profitability (return on assets, or ROA), labor productivity (LP), and total factor productivity (TFP) before and after the introduction of the contract.[8] To explore the underlying factors, we used a questionnaire and interviews with people in the country and World Bank staff knowledgeable about the enterprises. Box 3.1 addresses concerns about the validity of these measures.

Some readers may ask: "Why didn't you simply judge each firm's performance by its attainment of the economic targets specified in the con-

Table 3.2 Case Study Enterprises

Country (contract type)	Enterprise name: NAME USED IN TEXT	Contract duration	First contract year
Ghana (performance contract)	Electricity Corporation of Ghana (ECG): GHANA ELECTRICITY	Yearly	1989
	Ghana Water and Sewerage Corporation (GWSC): GHANA WATER		1989
	Ghana Posts and Telecommunications (GP&T): GHANA TELECOMS		1990
India (memorandum of understanding)	National Thermal Power Corporation (NTPC): INDIA ELECTRICITY	Yearly (published)	1987
	Oil and Natural Gas Commission (ONGC): INDIA OIL		
Korea (performance evaluation and measurement system)	Korea Electric Power Corporation (KEPCO): KOREA ELECTRICITY	List of yearly targets	1984
	Korea Telecommunications Authority (KTA): KOREA TELECOMS		
Mexico (convenio de rehabilitación financiera)	Comisión Federal de Electricidad (CFE): MEXICO ELECTRICITY	3 years	1986
Philippines (performance monitoring and evaluation system)	Metropolitan Water and Sewerage System (MWSS): PHILIPPINES WATER	List of yearly targets	1989
	National Power Corporation (NPC): PHILIPPINES ELECTRICITY		
Senegal (contrat plan)	Société Nationale d'Electricité (SENELEC): SENEGAL ELECTRICITY	3 years	1987
	Société Nationale des Télécommunications du Sénégal (SONATEL): SENEGAL TELECOMS		1986

Source: World Bank data.

tract, especially since these presumably indicate what the firm is striving to achieve?" It is true that all of the sample SOEs achieved at least satisfactory ratings where some sort of score was assigned (Senegal has no such scoring), and all of the contracts assign a high weight to economic goals (two-thirds on average). The problem, as we discuss in detail below, is that many of the targets are soft or flawed measures of economic performance. Thus, a firm attaining its contracted economic targets is not necessarily operating more profitably or productively.

An examination of the contract targets for India Electricity illustrates how flawed measures can easily lead to an overly rosy picture of perfor-

> ## Box 3.1 Measuring SOE Performance: What about Social Goals?
>
> SOME ARGUE THAT STATE-OWNED ENTERPRISES WERE CREATED to serve social goals rather than make profits and that they should be judged accordingly. Even by this standard, the three indicators we use—return on assets, labor productivity, and total factor productivity—provide a useful measure of changes in firm performance, since we do not compare them to an absolute standard but to the firm's own past performance. Provided that the incentives are appropriate, managers of a state-owned enterprise who face constraints related to social goals should nonetheless be able to improve company performance within these constraints. For example, if the prices for its output charged by a state-owned enterprise are held low to benefit the poor, we would expect this to affect the trend in return on assets but not trends in labor productivity or total factor productivity. Moreover, managers of a firm that is required to maintain low prices could nonetheless try to improve the return on assets by minimizing costs or expanding sales. Similarly, even if a firm is not allowed to lay off redundant labor, it should still be able to improve labor productivity and TFP by stopping the waste of raw materials or using its capital to full capacity. Thus taken together, our three indicators implicitly allow for social goals and are therefore well suited to our purpose in this section: determining whether performance contracts altered incentives in ways that in fact resulted in improved performance.

mance improvements. In 1991–92, 30 percent of India Electricity's score depended on the volume of electricity generated; output indeed went up, but the use of material inputs rose even faster. The target was flawed: it could be achieved by increasing inputs without any increase—indeed, even with a decrease—in the firm's efficiency. Thus, although India Electricity achieved its target under the contract and received a rating of excellent, total factor productivity actually fell below precontract levels. To varying degrees, all of the contracts in our sample included similarly flawed targets. Since our goal is to test whether the contracts improved SOE performance, we have therefore preferred the three performance measures below.

Profitability. The profitability trends in our sample do not support the notion that contracts improve performance. None of the twelve companies improved the trend in their ROA after the contract, and nine continued to improve or deteriorate without a significant change in their trends. On the negative side, three showed worse ROA trends after contracts than before (Philippines Electricity, Senegal Electricity, and Senegal Telecoms, see figure 3.1). For state-owned enterprises, ROA trends tend to reflect government behavior rather than managerial behavior, because an SOE's wages, input and output prices, and the like, may all be controlled by government. For example, to raise revenues, government set prices for Senegal Electricity's petroleum inputs at about twice world market prices in the 1980s without always allowing it to raise its price to the consumer.[9] Judging from the profitability trends in the sample, the contracts had little effect on government behavior. Only one company did better because of government mandated price increases (Philippines Water), and these gains were not enough to change its almost flat trend in ROA. As for the deteriorating

Figure 3.1 Pre- and Postcontract Performance: Net Rate of Return on Revalued Assets

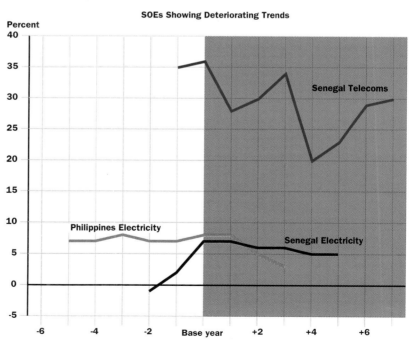

Source: Company data and World Bank estimates.

Performance contracts did not improve the trend in the rate of return on assets (ROA) for any of the firms in the sample. Three firms deteriorated.

firms, only one shows worse ROA because of government tariff decisions: Senegal Telecoms' very high ROA goes down after the contract (from an average of 25 percent to a still high 20 percent) mainly because the government reduced the firm's very high base tariffs. Senegal Telecoms has some of the highest phone charges in the world; according to Siemens AG, its charges were fourth highest in a sample of seventy countries in 1993.[10]

Labor Productivity. Labor productivity growth was positive in all twelve cases, but again the data suggest that the contracts had little effect on this trend. Only two companies show a kink in their labor productivity trends (declining labor productivity began to increase in Senegal Telecoms, and the rate of increase in labor productivity more than quadrupled after the contract in Ghana Water; see figure 3.2); in the rest, labor productivity continued its precontract trend upward. In four of the twelve cases, labor productivity growth was primarily due to the shedding of excess workers (plus the removal from the rolls of "ghost

Figure 3.2 Pre- and Postcontract Performance: Labor Productivity
(indexed to base year)

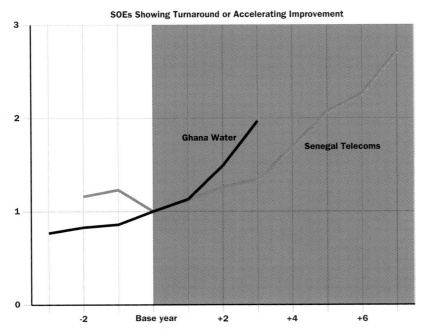

The contracts coincided with improving trends in labor productivity in only two of the twelve performance contracts studied.

Source: Company data and World Bank estimates.

workers"). In the rest, production gains outstripped employment increases. These data suggest that there had been a change in government's labor practices in SOEs, but in most cases it preceded the contract.

Total Factor Productivity. Partial measures such as labor productivity can be misleading: if labor productivity improved because the company increased output by using more material inputs, then the overall efficiency of the firm has not improved. Total factor productivity measures the efficiency with which all factors are used and is our most reliable indicator of whether the contracts were associated with performance improvements.

Performance on TFP is mixed: in three of the twelve companies (Ghana Water, Mexico Electricity, and Senegal Telecoms) declining TFP began to increase after the contracts were introduced, while in six others precontract trends continued upward. The three remaining firms (India Electricity, Philippines Water, and Senegal Electricity; see figure 3.3) suffered a downturn in what had been an improving TFP trend, suggesting that, in these cases, the contracts may actually have contributed to a deterioration in performance.

Performance Contracts Had Little Positive Impact

Our performance measures show that contracts had little positive impact on most of our sample (see figure 3.4). Total factor productivity is the most reliable performance indicator we used; by that measure the contracts seem to be doing as much harm as good. We assessed whether the mixed and generally negative outcomes we measured could have been determined by factors other than the contracts by checking for major changes in markets, prices, natural or man-made disasters, and the like during the period under investigation. In each case we concluded that exogenous factors did not rule out the contracts as a possible source of performance changes. For example, we compared trends in company TFP with trends in GDP growth and found no acceleration or deceleration in growth (and thus demand) that could explain changes in firm performance. Nor could we find any exceptional developments in the companies' markets or major work stoppages that could fully account for the results. In fact, exogenous factors seemed important in only two cases—Philippines Electricity and Senegal Telecoms. Even for these, however, their magnitude was not so large as to rule out the contracts as a significant explanatory factor.[11]

Figure 3.3 Pre- and Postcontract Performance: Total Factor Productivity
(indexed to base year)

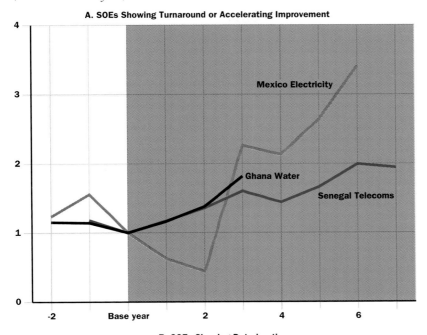

A. SOEs Showing Turnaround or Accelerating Improvement

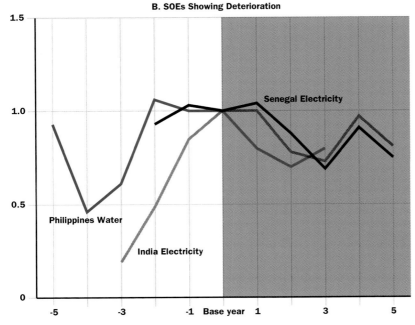

B. SOEs Showing Deterioration

Performance contracts were followed by improved trends in total factor productivity (TFP) in three of the seven cases. TFP trends in three cases deteriorated.

Source: Company data and World Bank estimates.

Figure 3.4 Performance Changes after the Introduction of Performance Contracts

Number of state-owned enterprises

In most of the twelve cases studied, performance contracts did not improve return on assets, labor productivity, or total factor productivity.

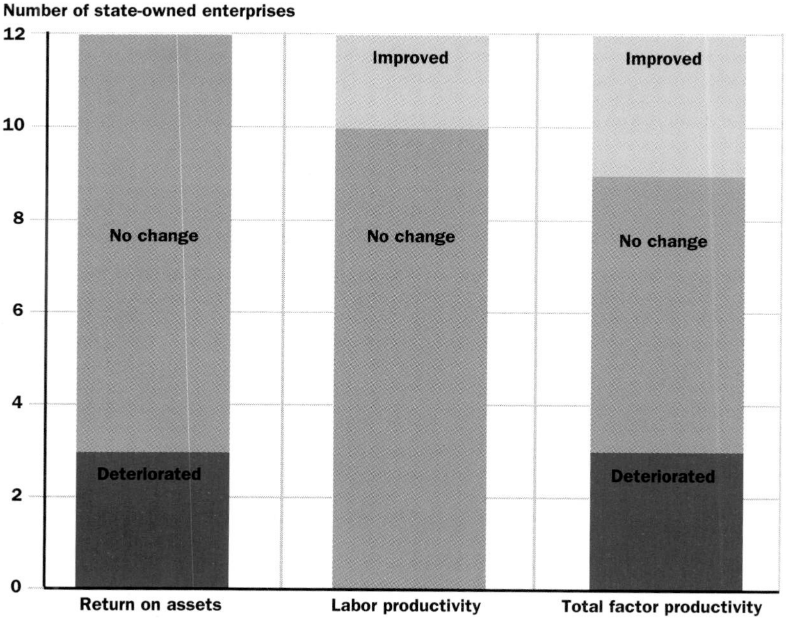

Source: Company data and World Bank estimates.

Why Contracts Failed to Improve Performance Substantially

To understand why the contracts in our sample generated so little improvement in performance we analyze their impact on each of the three contracting variables—information, rewards and penalties, and commitment.

Information. A closer examination of the incentives faced by SOE managers during and after contract negotiations reveals several reasons why improvements in information that could have resulted from a written performance did not in fact materialize. Like any manager negotiating with outsiders, SOE managers have an information advantage. SOE managers may have incentives to use their information advantage to negotiate easily achievable targets. This will be especially true if the agents negotiating the targets and monitoring and evaluating the results are weak and depend entirely on the enterprise for information on its performance. Under such circumstances, managers have an incentive to negotiate easily attained targets; they may also seek numerous and changing targets, since this maximizes their information advantage by forcing government monitors to learn many new and different indicators. Each time a new criterion is added, monitors must decide on the criterion value—what constitutes a good, fair, or poor performance. Learning which values are hard and which are soft is more difficult when the criteria are constantly changing.[12]

The government agents in our sample often operated at a disadvantage. They were usually middle- or low-level civil servants while the SOE's representatives tended to be better paid and have higher status. One expert who advised Ghana on SOE contracts observed that the SOEs were often represented by a managing director with status similar to a cabinet minister (and even better pay), while the government supervisory agency was usually represented by a low-level functionary.[13]

Asymmetry in the status of the negotiators was aggravated in some of our sample contracts, because the agencies responsible for negotiating targets and monitoring and evaluating results were weakened by frequent changes in responsibilities and authority. For example, the agency negotiating, monitoring, and evaluating contracts in Senegal has moved twice since contracting began (from the president's office to the prime minister's office to the ministry of finance). According to field interviews, these moves diluted its authority vis-à-vis the enterprises; respondents to our survey (in both the SOEs and the government) said that the evaluations in Senegal are largely done by the firms themselves. Similar changes undermined the authority of monitoring agencies in the Philippines (where the agency also has a high rate of staff turnover) and Ghana.[14] Poor data further disadvantaged the government actors. For example, the monitors in Ghana rely on evaluations by the firms themselves, and the information they receive from the firms is usually late and unreliable. In 1991, twelve of the seventeen SOEs that the State Enterprise Commission (SEC) monitored were seven weeks late in delivering their 1990 fourth-quarter results. Only five of the firms had current audited accounts; the most recent audited accounts for the others ranged from one to three years old (State Enterprises Commission 1991). In contrast, the contracts in India, Mexico, and Korea were monitored by stronger, more stable agencies. In Korea the strength of monitoring was enhanced by the use of outsiders, something we explore below under commitment.

Under these circumstances, it is not surprising that the contracts in our sample have numerous targets—half the firms have more than twenty (table 3.3). Large numbers of targets yield many small goals of similar and low priority (most of Korea Telecoms' targets have weights of 1 percent or less), which are hard to translate into overarching objectives against which performance can be judged. This makes it more likely that bad performance goes unpunished and good performance unrewarded. Such contracts are even harder to monitor when the targets change every year. For example, between 1990 and 1991 the targets in Ghana Electricity's contract jumped from seventeen to twenty-nine when nineteen new criteria were added and seven were dropped. One way to make it easier to judge performance is to assign a weight to each target so they add up to 100 percent and the monitor can calculate an aggregate score. Although most of our sample used weighted targets (the exceptions are in Senegal and Mexico), fluctuations in the weights frequently offset this advantage, adding another layer of complexity and uncertainty. For example, the weight as-

Table 3.3 Comparison of Target Characteristics

TFP performance	Average number	Average yearly change (percent)[b]	Economic targets as a percentage of total[a]
Improving (average)			
Ghana Water	14	35	73
Mexico Electricity	11	23	84
Senegal Telecoms	37	9	68
Unchanged (average)			
Ghana Electricity	20	36	73
Ghana Telecoms	31	30	80
India Oil	20	9	58
Korea Electricity	41	8	48
Korea Telecoms	42	18	47
Philippines Electricity	11	6	74
Deteriorated (average)			
India Electricity	12	19	47
Philippines Water	10	18	68
Senegal Electricity	23	0	77

a. Where weights were assigned we used those; otherwise we used the number of financial, efficiency, and production targets as a percentage of the total.

b. May not equal the average of the average yearly change.

Source: World Bank data.

signed to India Oil's financial targets went from 20 percent in 1989 to 12 percent in 1990, then climbed to 40 percent by 1992.

There is also evidence that targets are soft. As we mentioned, all the firms in our sample were rated at least satisfactory (scores were not assigned for the two firms in Senegal), yet very few show marked improvement in their trends in profitability or productivity. Company evidence supports the view that some managers were able to negotiate targets that were easy to achieve.[15] Indeed, in some instances, even when a firm substantially exceeded a target in one year, the target was *reduced* the following year.[16] The following examples drawn from our case studies illustrate some of the ways in which performance contracts may be flawed:

- In Senegal, survey respondents described Senegal Telecoms as an effective negotiator of targets it could easily achieve. One important target, call completion rates, was lower in the 1986 performance contract than in the company's business plan of ten years before. In 1992 the call completion rate was a mere 55 percent in Dakar and less than 40 percent for inter-urban calls, about half the international industry standard.
- In India, negotiations on targets have sometimes dragged on so long that the targets were set to be the same as actual performance.[17]
- In Ghana, contract targets are set by the companies themselves; the monitoring and evaluating agency (the SEC) considers many targets too low and has established a penalty for under-targeting (State Enterprises Commission 1991).
- In the Philippines, one of Philippines Electricity's most important and difficult challenges is to improve its reliability, but its reliability indicator (the percentage of electricity its customers have contracted for but the company never supplied) has become less important in its performance score, falling from 30 percent of total targets in 1990 to 10 percent in 1991 and 15 percent in 1992. This is not because the firm became more reliable; on the contrary, by 1992–93 outages of seven hours per day were common in many parts of the country.
- In Korea there are indications that managers seek to soften their most meaningful target; Korea uses one of the best comprehensive targets for assessing performance of the sample: public profitability in constant prices.[18] This measure follows a trend very close to TFP, is easier for accountants and managers to understand than

TFP, and can be calculated using shadow prices to account for price distortions. Yet the share of public profitability in Korean targets has been falling: for telecoms and electricity it fell from 20 percent in 1985 to 12 percent in 1992. Field interviews suggest that SOE managers have successfully negotiated the addition of other targets at the expense of public profitability.

Targets are flawed in all the contracts, but contrary to what we might expect, firms with improving TFP have less stable targets and a lower rate of economic target achievement than firms where TFP deteriorated.[19] This could imply that some managers successfully negotiated such soft targets that their performance deteriorated or that some targets were at odds with improved performance and that the firms receiving the clearest signals were most likely to pursue these wrong targets. There is some evidence of targets with perverse effects. For example, Philippines Electricity, a company that badly needs to upgrade its infrastructure, achieved two 1991 targets by *cutting* capital expenditures by more than one-fifth.[20] India Oil can achieve its target of number of meters drilled regardless of whether it strikes oil or not. This might encourage riskier drilling and, in fact, the number of nonproducing wells has been increasing since 1990.[21] Thus, it could be that the clearer the targets, the worse the performance.

In sum, the contracts largely failed to solve the information problem, as evidenced by the flaws in the targets and the fact that the only association between the achievement of contract targets and performance is a negative one.

Rewards and Penalties. One reason managers use their information advantage to act opportunistically is that the rewards and penalties in the contract do not motivate them to try to improve performance. Managers (and staff) could get pecuniary bonuses as a reward for good achievement in only five of the twelve sample companies (three in Ghana and two in Korea); the two Indian firms could get an award in a public ceremony. Moreover, because bonuses are based on the achievement of the contract targets, if the targets are soft or poor measures of performance, bonuses will not motivate efficiency. This may explain why bonuses are not necessarily associated with improvements in TFP (although none of the firms that received a bonus showed a deterioration; table 3.4). As for explicit management penalties, only in the Korean contracts is there any evidence that management achievements under contracts have

Table 3.4 Comparison of Contract Incentives

(Companies ranked by TFP performance)

Company	Bonus/award	Contract has government promises	Government reneging?
Improving			
Ghana Water	Bonus/award	Yes	Some
Mexico Electricity	None	Yes	Little
Senegal Telecoms	None	Yes	Much
Unchanged			
Ghana Electricity	Bonus/award	Yes	Some
Ghana Telecoms	Bonus/award	Yes	Some
India Oil	Award	Yes	Much
Korea Electricity	Bonus/award	No	None[a]
Korea Telecoms	Bonus/award	No	None[a]
Philippines Electricity	None	No	Implicit[a]
Deteriorated			
India Electricity	Award	Yes	Much
Philippines Water	None	No	Implicit[a]
Senegal Electricity	None	Yes	Much

a. Although government actions are not specified in the contracts in Korea and the Philippines, the fact that targets are set in the Philippines that were not achieved because of government actions is taken as a form of implicit reneging, while the opposite situation is treated as no reneging in Korea.

Source: World Bank data and company reports.

some effect on managerial careers; survey respondents in the other countries said that managers' job assignments were largely politically determined and not driven by the contract results.[22] Unable to penalize managers' poor performance with firing or demotion, bureaucrats could only threaten to withhold promised rewards such as bonuses, increases in managerial autonomy, or government support to the enterprise, such as tariff increases or financial assistance. As we show below, however, in most countries such promises had little credibility to begin with, since they were often broken regardless of a manager's performance.

Besides facing few rewards or penalties directly linked to improved performance, all managers in our sample operated under government-imposed constraints that seriously limited their autonomy. Governments not only controlled prices of factors and products, decisions about wages and layoffs, procurement above minimal levels, and all senior appointments, they also strongly influenced whether the SOE was paid by its customers and had to pay its suppliers or creditors. Reductions in this type of government interference were explicitly promised in all but four of the contracts (the exceptions are the two Korean and two Philippines contracts). But these promises often were broken. Although in theory a contract can be written to motivate and measure managerial behavior in isolation, in practice it proved impossible to isolate SOE performance from the impact of these government actions. In any event, broken government promises were so frequent—and such a significant disincentive—that it seems likely they contributed to the deterioration in total factor productivity (table 3.4).

Although significant reneging was evident in all cases except Mexico Electricity, in two of the four cases where the government kept at least some important promises, TFP improved (see table 3.4).[23] For example, although the government of Ghana did not always approve Ghana Water's tariff increases promptly and required the company to serve some nonpaying customers, it did increase tariffs in real terms and support management in reducing the work force. Furthermore, all three contracts in Ghana provide for recalculation of targets if government reneges on its contractual obligations. Although this betrays a disconcerting expectation that government will renege, it also means that SOEs were not penalized for government misbehavior. Reneging was more apparent in the two contracts in Senegal, where the government's failure to honor its obligations to Senegal Telecoms evoked this comment in a 1989 company report: "It must be remembered that the contract plan was never considered a binding contract by the public powers." Even so, Senegal Telecoms did benefit from the contract, which was part of the process that separated it from the post office, thus enabling it to focus more on commercial operations. This may account for the firm's TFP improvement.

Companies that faced more extensive government reneging did not improve TFP. The two Indian SOEs in our sample were required to serve nonpaying customers and were not given promised tariff increases or all promised reductions in cumbersome and slow processes for approval of procurement, investment, and other expenditures (table 3.5). For example, every year the contract for India Electricity promised government help in enforcing prompt payment from its customers, the State Electricity Boards, yet circumstances have not improved. (Accounts receivable went from 149 days in 1986, the year before the contract was introduced, to 207 in 1990; in 1991 they fell to 150 days when a power plant was turned over to the SOE in partial payment of arrears.) Senegal

Table 3.5 Instances of Government Reneging in Whole or in Part

Company	Promises where government reneged
Ghana Electricity	Support collection revenues and arrears; timely approval of tariffs
Ghana Telecoms	Timely approval of tariffs
Ghana Water	Prompt payment of water bills by government and state-owned enterprises
	Release investment funds on schedule
	Reimburse for noncommercial obligations
India Electricity	Support collection of arrears; increase autonomy to invest
	Streamline red tape, prompt approvals; increase tariffs
India Oil	Increase autonomy to invest; streamline red tape, prompt approvals
Mexico Electricity	Delay in some promised support
Senegal Electricity	Prompt payment of bills by government and state-owned enterprises
	Contribute to investment program; increase tariffs
Senegal Telecoms	Prompt payment of bills by government and state-owned enterprises
	Increase tariffs; abolish subsidy to post by 1989
	Limit investment in rural areas

Source: World Bank data and company reports.

Electricity not only did not benefit from the contract, it lost access to funds when the World Bank suspended disbursements on a power loan because government reneged on its pledge to make other SOEs pay their bills. The contract expired in 1989; until now the government and Senegal Electricity management have yet to agree on a new contract.

The four contracts in Korea and the Philippines do not specify government obligations, but the different ways these governments handled management autonomy created different incentives that help explain the better performance in Korea. (TFP in Korea Electricity and Telecoms continued their upward trends after the contract, while postcontract TFP declined slightly in Philippines Electricity and sharply in Philippines Water.) When performance contracts were introduced in Korea in 1983–84, managerial autonomy of the two SOEs in our sample (and all other so-called Government Invested Enterprises) increased dramatically.[24] This boosted the contracts' credibility with managers and employees.[25] In contrast, the autonomy of the two sample SOEs in the Philippines has not changed much with the introduction of the contracts. Moreover, some of the Philippine SOE targets (such as return on assets) are directly dependent on government decisions. By setting targets that can only be achieved through government actions, the government makes an implicit commitment, which, if violated, reduces the contract's credibility. In contrast, almost all of the Korean SOEs' targets—transmission losses, thermal efficiency, minutes of outages per household, and profitability in constant prices—are independent of government pricing decisions.

Commitment. As the problems with rewards and penalties described above suggest, the failure of contracts in our sample adequately to address the commitment problem may be the most important explanation for the evident failure to improve performance. None of the contracts specify an enforcement mechanism in the sense of a neutral third party, insulated from politics, with the power and information to compel both parties to comply. In several cases government obligations were potentially enforceable by an outside party. The World Bank included government contractual obligations as covenants in its loans for SOEs in Ghana, Mexico, and Senegal, although these covenants were drawn up on the basis of project or sector needs rather than because they were part of the contracts. Although this outside involvement may have helped reduce reneging in Ghana and Mexico, its does not appear to have enhanced, and may even have reduced, the system's credibility in Senegal. Survey respondents and other observers agree that the contracts in Senegal were viewed by the signatories as donor driven and not as serious obligations. The suspension of disbursement of a World Bank loan to Senegal Electricity after government reneged on its contract obligations to settle arrears did not change government behavior and penalized the company as much as, if not more than, the government.

For the two Korean contracts, the participation of private individuals (nongovernment accountants, lawyers, and academics) and a prestigious government think tank, the autonomous Korea Development Institute, may have improved monitoring and evaluation. Knowledgeable outsiders not only bring additional skills, they may informally supervise the government monitors and act as a check on government actions that violate the contract. According to Korean SOE managers, public opinion was also an important incentive to improve performance: performance ratings are widely reported in the Korean press (Shirley 1991).

More commonly, contracts' vulnerability to the political process undermined government commitment and increased reneging, thus hurting performance. To make the contracts work, governments would need to meet numerous obligations to the firms, both explicit and implicit. Governments reneged on these obligations because it was politically too costly to meet them. These obligations include relinquishing control over the company labor force, diverting revenues from other uses to pay government bills to the firm and help fund government mandated investments, allowing the firm to pursue its creditors and apply legal penalties if they do not pay, and regulating monopoly prices according to clear and fair rules. Without setting prices excessively high in order to generate rents for the government, the rules would allow enough revenue for the firm to maintain and improve service, to upgrade its technology, and to expand to meet growing demand.

As this list suggests, a good contracting system is as demanding as a good system to regulate private monopolies; it requires impartial and informed regulators who have some discretion but also face checks on arbitrary actions, and it requires mechanisms to enforce rules and resolve disputes. Few of the governments in our sample were willing or able to pay the political price.

For those that were, the picture is mixed. Some examples:

- Ghana, which has had contracts only since 1989, showed spotty government compliance with the three contracts we studied, and the decision to suspend the awards ceremony because of the 1992 elections is worrying for the future credibility of performance contracts there.
- Korea has the oldest (ten years) and by far the best system we analyzed, but the two contracts don't seem to have changed the companies' already good performance trends. Furthermore, some of those interviewed cited waning government commitment to performance contracting in Korea, raising doubts about the contracts' sustainability even under very favorable circumstances.[26]
- Mexico has shown promising commitment to its electricity contract for eight years with good results. But Mexico Electricity's experience under the contract differs from that of other SOEs in Mexico in that the government followed through on its commitments under the contract.[27] A World Bank assessment of Mexico's standard performance contracts with five other SOEs concluded that the results were disappointing. The study attributed the poor outcomes to a lack of adequate consultation between government and

SOE, government attempts to treat the contracts as one more instrument of control among many, and targets that lack coherence, simultaneously overlapping and leaving gaps (World Bank 1992).

The mixed results from contracts in these market economies were also found in one of the transition economies we investigated (see box 3.2 on performance contracts in China). Indeed, during Communist rule in Central and Eastern Europe, most enterprises were governed by performance contracts; these suffered from problems similar to those we found in market economies, but much larger.

Performance Contract Findings

Only three of the twelve case study companies showed a turnaround in TFP after contracts were introduced, six continued their past trends, and three performed substantially worse under contracts than before. Labor productivity improved at a faster pace in four cases and deteriorated in none, but for most SOEs, the improvement long predates the contracts. ROA deteriorated for three firms; the rest showed little change. *Thus, the evidence from this sample gives little support to the premise that explicit contracts help improve SOE performance.*

Most of the contracts fell victim to information asymmetries that were not overcome by mechanisms to persuade managers to comply; instead weak rewards and penalties and lack of credible mechanisms for enforcement compounded the information problems (see table 3.6). Gains in productivity occurred only when government offered managers credible incentives (performance bonuses and increased autonomy or removal of constraints) and signaled their own commitment by following through on at least some government promises.

The deteriorating performers faced extensive government reneging on written promises, sometimes every year. The annual or triennial evaluation and negotiation exercises drew attention to governments' consistent noncompliance and may have resulted in worse morale and performance than before. Such repeated government reneging may well have increased managers' incentives to use their information advantage to negotiate targets they could easily achieve, even if they perform less well than before. Although we do not have enough information to say with confidence that contracts contributed to deteriorating trends in TFP, the results suggest that this possibility cannot be excluded.

Box 3.2 Performance Contracts in China

CHINA IS THE ONLY TRANSITIONAL ECONOMY IN our sample that used performance contracts during the period we studied. Beginning in 1987 a variety of contracts were introduced under the Contract Responsibility System. These gave managers of industrial SOEs greater control over enterprise operations (e.g., volume of output, technology, exports) in return for meeting profit remittance targets. Many of the contracts also gave the SOEs greater autonomy over sales outside the state plan and permitted managers to grant employee bonuses and hire contract workers if the firm met its profit remittance targets. Initially these were three- to five-year contracts but were renegotiated as one-year contracts in 1991. In 1992, a government directive stipulated that contracts could grant managers additional autonomy, including the rights to make production decisions, determine prices for outputs and inputs, purchase goods and materials, make investment decisions, hire workers, and determine wages and bonuses.

Assessing the extent to which these contracts have improved performance is difficult. Some studies have found that the greater autonomy allowed under the contracts contributed to an improvement in TFP: in particular, greater autonomy led to more use of worker incentives, which resulted in higher productivity (Groves, Hong, McMillan, and Naughton 1993). However, increasing competition from the nonstate sector over this period (see chapter 2) has also been cited as a factor in improved state enterprise performance (Singh, Xiao, and Ratha 1994; Jefferson 1993), and it is impossible to disentangle this effect from the possible effect of the contracts themselves.

Although the Chinese SOEs under contract operate under different circumstances from the firms in our sample (in particular, they face increasingly competitive markets), there are some striking parallels. These suggest that the contracts probably do not provide an incentive structure adequate to cause significant improvements in performance. As with our sample, the contracts in China have become increasingly and often confusingly complex. Also similar to our sample, the contracts in China provide incentives for good performance but fail to penalize bad performance (Gelb and Singh 1994). Finally and most important, real changes in government actions—whether or not specified in a contract—appear to be the most important incentive to managers in China, as with the managers of our sample firms.

Another indication that China's performance contracts may be less effective than their proponents hope is that TFP grew much faster in nonstate enterprises—including the so-called Township and Village Enterprises (TVEs), which are technically public but not state-owned—than in the state enterprises of the central government ministries (box 2.4). One explanation is that the TVEs, although not privately owned, are monitored by stakeholders with a kind of property right that gives them a clear interest in performance. Thus, although there are important differences between the situation in China and the situation faced by the enterprises in our sample, both point to the same broad conclusion: performance contracts are a less effective incentive to improved performance than clarifying and strengthening property rights.

Even if the contracts did not cause deterioration in performance, the lack of a clear link between performance contracts and improved productivity and efficiency makes it hard to justify the investment of time and effort they required. Other observers point to the fact that most firms achieved the targets they were set under the contract as a sign of

Table 3.6 Comparison of Performance with Selected Contract Characteristics
(SOEs grouped by TFP performance)

Country	Targets	Rewards	Reneging	Monitoring	Enforcement
Improving TFP					
Ghana Water	◐	●	◐	○	◐
Mexico Electricity	●	○	●	●	◐
Senegal Telecoms	◐	○	○	○	◐
No change					
Ghana Electricity	○	●	◐	○	◐
Ghana Telecoms	○	●	◐	○	◐
India Oil	○	◐	○	●	○
Korea Electricity	◐	●	●	●	◐
Korea Telecoms	○	●	●	●	●
Philippines Electricity	●	○	○	○	○
Deteriorating TFP					
India Electricity	●	◐	○	●	○
Philippines Water	◐	○	○	○	○
Senegal Electricity	◐	○	○	○	◐

Targets	Rewards	Reneging	Monitoring	Enforcement
● Few, stable	● Bonus	● Most contract promises kept (or targets adjusted to account for government action in countries without government commitments in the contract)	● Agency is stable and has authority to get necessary information	● Has external, objective enforcement mechanisms with authority to resolve disputes and force compliance (no cases of this)
◐ Either few or stable	◐ Award	◐ Some contract promises kept	○ Agency's authority weak because of shifts in power or role or lack of skilled staff	◐ Has external, objective enforcement mechanism with partial coercive authority or influence (e.g., the World Bank or local press)
○ Many, fluctuating	○ None	○ Most contract promises not kept (or targets not adjusted)		○ No external, objective enforcement mechanism

Source: World Bank data.

success. However, if a company achieves a contract target of doubling its production by trebling inputs, then the cost of such inefficiency must be assessed against the contracts. Some survey respondents said that the contracts helped improve the dialogue with government or the corporate culture in the firm, but again, if these qualitative judgments are not supported by performance improvements, it is hard to count them in favor of contracting.

Analysis of the outcomes and incentive problems associated with the performance contracts in our sample suggests some lessons:

- Performance contracts should be used sparingly and only when government commitment is manifest, since the mere formality of a performance contract wastes time and effort and could possibly even harm performance. The idea that SOE performance can be improved without any change in government behavior by designing a contract that provides targets and incentives directed at managers alone proved ephemeral. Managers' incentives depend on government actions, whether or not these actions are specified in a performance contract.
- Bonuses are associated with better performance, but they are only as good as the targets. And bonuses mean little in the face of government reneging on promises, especially when these promises directly affect the manager's opportunity to attain the bonus.
- Contract outcomes depend not only on management incentives, but also on the incentives of government negotiators, as well as their power and the quality of information they command. Large differences in status, income, and influence between government and SOE negotiators contributed to weak and incoherent targets. Frequent shifts in locale, staff, and responsibilities further weakened the position of government actors.
- The involvement of informed individuals outside government and politics may help prevent reneging and improve the caliber of monitoring. The involvement of donors as enforcement agents had mixed results, working best when the agency was viewed as helping rather than imposing the contract. But the role of outside pressure in performance contracts is necessarily a limited one, since outsiders are not party to the contract and have, at best, only an indirect stake in the outcome.

Management Contracts: With Private Managers

CONTRACTING OUT SOE MANAGEMENT TO THE PRIVATE sector is often recommended as a way to improve SOE performance and, where outright privatization is desirable, prepare an enterprise for sale. (Hegstad and Newport 1987; Kikeri, Nellis, and Shirley 1992; Roth 1987; World Bank 1994b; Berg 1993). Do management contracts work? Experience with these contracts has not been systematically analyzed to determine whether, and under what circumstances, they might improve SOE performance. This section aims to begin to fill that gap, analyzing where management contracts are found, how they have performed and why, and the factors that explain their thus far limited use. As before, in explaining outcomes we look at how the contracts affected the incentives in terms of information, rewards and penalties, and commitment.

We define a management contract as an agreement between the government and a private party to operate the firm for a fee (usually a success fee, but sometimes for a fixed fee as well). Under this definition, the government does not receive a fixed rent (as it would with a lease), it is responsible for fixed investments (which it would not be with a concession), and it holds majority ownership, ceding control only via an explicit contract (as distinct from a joint venture in which the government owns only a minority). Our definition does encompass contracts in which the private contractor provides working capital or owns a minority equity share. A few of the contracts are called leases in the country of signing, but we consider them management contracts when they do not involve fixed payments to government.

How widely used are management contracts? Even employing our broad definition, a worldwide search indicated that they are only commonly used in the hotel industry. Of the more than 200 management contracts we found in developing countries, 44 involved hotels managed by one of the five major chains (see table 3.7);[28] and it seems likely that other hotel management contracts not involving these chains also exist.[29] Although some transition economies, notably Poland and Romania, are taking steps to introduce management contracts for a large number of SOEs, so far no country has been relying on them extensively. Sri Lanka has the most, with 24 contracts, 22 of which involve tea and rubber plantations. Of the forty-nine other countries where contracts were found, if the hotel industry is excluded, we found that only five countries had more than 5 contracts and one country had more than 10.

Comparing regions, we found that management contracts are concentrated in Africa. Aside from the hotel contracts, which exist in all regions, and the Sri Lankan plantations, Africa accounts for two-thirds of the remaining management contracts in our sample (91 out of 136).

Table 3.7 Management Contracts by Country

Country	Number[a]	Country	Number[a]
Zambia	16	Pakistan	2
Tanzania	10	Sri Lanka[c]	2
Kenya	8	Trinidad and Tobago	2
Papua New Guinea	7	Angola	1
Guinea	6	Bangladesh	1
Poland[b]	5	Barbados	1
Burkina Faso	4	Congo	1
Cameroon	4	Czech Republic	1
Chad	4	Dominican Republic	1
India	4	Jamaica	1
Iran	4	Mali	1
Botswana	3	Niger	1
Gabon	3	Sierra Leone	1
Ghana	3	Senegal	1
Guyana	3	Solomon Islands	1
Nigeria	3	Somalia	1
Philippines	3	St. Kitts and Nevis	1
Uganda	3	Sudan	1
Malawi	2	Swaziland	1
Benin	2	Togo	1
Central African Republic	2	Venezuela	1
Colombia	2	Zimbabwe	1
Côte d'Ivoire	2		
Gambia, The	2	Total	136
Indonesia	2		
Madagascar	2	Sri Lanka (plantations)	22
Oman	2		
		Grand total	158

Note: Management contracts appear to have not been used in these countries: Argentina, Bolivia, Chile, Costa Rica, Ecuador, Egypt, El Salvador, Fiji, Guatemala, Honduras, Malaysia, Mexico, Panama, Peru, Uruguay, Ethiopia, Zaire, Tunisia, Turkey, Yemen, Korea, Thailand, and Vietnam.

a. Number excludes hotels.

b. These enterprises were part of a list of twenty-seven firms in the Privatization Through Restructuring Program.

c. Excluding the twenty-two plantations contracted out to domestic private firms.

Source: Based on a worldwide search using World Bank, UNDP, and other sources. In some countries additional contracts may have been awarded.

Many of the enterprises under management contract in Africa were formerly owned by multinational companies, were nationalized, and then contracted out, sometimes to the former owner. Thus, the high number of management contracts in Africa could stem from a sense that these formerly private firms would operate best under private management, as

Table 3.8 Management Contracts, by Sector

Industry	Number
Hotels[a]	44
Nonhotels	
Sugar	24
Food processing and beverages	13
Electricity[b]	12
Water[b]	7
Mining	6
Oil and gas	6
Cement	5
Telecommunications	4
Automotive	4
Airline and airport service	4
Other	48
Unknown	3
Total nonhotels	136
Sri Lanka (plantations)	22
Grand total	202

a. Mainly based on information from Marriott, Intercontinental, Sheraton, Hyatt, plus case studies; not a comprehensive survey of all management contracts in state-owned hotels.

b. Some contracts could be concessions.

Source: Based on a worldwide search using World Bank, UNDP, and other sources. In some countries additional contracts may have been awarded.

well the relative paucity of government technical expertise. It may also reflect a ready supply of private management services; in addition to the frequent involvement of former owners, two prominent private contractors have focused their marketing efforts on the region: Booker Tate in agroindustry and African Management Services Company (AMSCO) in mining, industry and other sectors.

Contracts were also concentrated by sector. Of the 158 contracts we found, 45 percent were in one of only two sectors: hotels (44 contracts) and agriculture (24 in sugar and 22 in the Sri Lankan plantations). If we add agroindustry (12), infrastructure (12 in electricity, 7 in water, and 4 in telecoms), and extractive sectors (6 in mining and 6 in oil and gas), we have accounted for 68 percent of the world's management contracts (see table 3.8). Judging from these data, management contracts are not widely used in other sectors, such as manufacturing, finance, trade, transport, and so on. There is a reason for this, as we explain below.

Do Management Contracts Improve SOE Performance?

To assess how management contracts affected management and government incentives—and hence the performance of the firm—we studied the experience with twenty contracts in a range of countries and sectors (table 3.9).[30] We looked for changes in performance using two sets of indicators—profitability and productivity. For each set of indicators, we attempted two types of comparison: performance before and after the contract and performance of firms under management contracts against similar firms managed under other arrangements. In five cases we had data sufficient for both types of comparison with both sets of indicators; for the remainder we could only compare performance (both profitability and productivity) before and after the contract (see table 3.10 below).

Profitability is, of course, an imperfect measure of performance, since profits may increase for many reasons that are unrelated to management. Nevertheless, because most of our sample not only sells its output in competitive markets, but also buys inputs from competitive markets, profitability is a more meaningful measure of performance for the management contracts sample than for the monopoly SOEs under performance contracts that we examined in the previous section.

Productivity measures are also problematical since, as we noted in the discussion of performance contracts, one or more productivity indica-

Table 3.9 Sample of Management Contracts

Enterprise	Country	Contractor	Sector
Successful			
Manila Terminal	Philippines	ISTSI (domestic)	Ports
Mumias Sugar	Kenya	Booker Tate (UK)	Sugar
Hino-Pak	Pakistan	Consortium (UAE, Japan)	Auto/truck assembly
Domestic Appliances	Pakistan	Al-Futtain (UAS)	Electrical appliance assembly
Guyana Sugar Corp.	Guyana	Booker Tate (UK)	Sugar
SONEG	Guinea	SEEG (Guinea and France)	Water
SNE	Central African Republic	SAUR (France)	Hotel
Shepheard Hotel	Egypt	Helnan (Denmark)	Hotel
Cairo Sheraton	Egypt	Sheraton (USA)	Hotel
Nile Hilton	Egypt	Hilton (USA)	Hotel
Sofia Sheraton	Bulgaria	Sheraton (USA)	Hotel
Hotel Stadt	Germany	InterContinental (USA)	Hotel
Sri Lanka plantations	Sri Lanka	Domestic contractors	Tea, rubber
Borderline			
Linmine Guyana	Guyana	Minprod (Australia)	Bauxite mining
Mount Kenya Textiles	Kenya	AMSCO (Netherlands)	Textiles
Naga Power Plant	Philippines	Ontario Hydro (Canada)	Electricity
State Gold Mining Co.	Ghana	Canada-Guyana Mining (Canada)	Gold mining
Light Rail (LRTA)	Philippines	Meralco (domestic)	Transport
Failures			
Nzoia Sugar	Kenya	Arkel (USA)	Sugar
Sanata Textile Limited	Guyana	SOE (China)	Textiles

Note: Ranked according to indicators in table 3.10, which are explained in text.
Source: Shaikh and Minovi (1994).

tors may rise even though overall efficiency has deteriorated. To minimize this problem, we used several productivity measures for each contract, including industry-specific measures (such as room occupancy rates in hotels, rejects and product defects in textiles, and recovery rates in sugar), and targets specified in the contracts (such as improvement in quality, export market penetration, diversification, and rehabilitation of plant and equipment). For each contract, we required an overall improvement in several productivity indicators (although not necessarily all) to rank a firm as having improved productivity.

In assessing profitability and productivity, we took into account any exogenous factors that might have accounted for changes we observed, including shifts in world factor and product prices, labor strikes, government mandated wage increases, and recessions in product markets.

Table 3.10 Summary of Outcomes

Enterprise	Methodology used[a]	Profitability improved?	Productivity improved?
Successful			
Manila Terminal	1	Yes	Yes
Mumias Sugar	2	Yes	Yes
Hino-Pak	1,2	Yes	Yes
Domestic Appliances	1	Yes	Yes
Guyana Sugar Corporation	1	Yes	Yes
SONEG (water)	1	Yes	Yes
SNE (water)	1	Yes	Yes
Shepheard Hotel	1,2	Yes	Yes
Cairo Sheraton	2	Yes	Yes
Nile Hilton	2	Yes	Yes
Sofia Sheraton	1,2	Yes	Yes
Hotel Stadt	1	Yes	Yes
Sri Lanka plantations	1	Yes	Yes
Borderline			
Linmine Guyana	1	Mixed	Yes
Mount Kenya Textiles	1,2	Yes	Mixed
Naga Power Plant	1	Mixed	Yes
State Gold Mining Company	1	No	No
Light Rail (LRTA)	1	No	Mixed
Failures			
Nzoia Sugar	1,2	No	No
Sanata Textile Limited	1	No	No

a. Before and after comparison = 1; cross-sectional comparisons = 2.
Source: Shaikh and Minovi (1994).

Where possible we assessed whether the performance change persists after eliminating the effect of such exogenous variables.

Having made these adjustments, we judged the contract a success in improving performance if both profitability and productivity improved unambiguously. We categorized it as borderline if one measure improved while the other did not and a clear failure if both kinds of measures failed to improve.

As figure 3.5 shows, two-thirds of the contracts (thirteen out of twenty, counting all twenty-two contracts with the Sri Lankan plantations as one case) were successes on both counts. In addition to the Sri Lankan plantations, other successes included five hotels, two utilities (both water), two sugar corporations, a port, an automobile maker, and an appliance manufacturer.

Five firms ranked as borderline, improving for one set of indicators but having mixed results for the other. Three of these approached success. One, the Linmine bauxite mine in Guyana, improved productivity after the contract was signed in 1992, but profitability was mixed, largely because of high expenditures on repairs and rehabilitation the first year. Even so, these expenditures were not inappropriate, since the contract required that management rehabilitate the firm and prepare it for privatization. Another is Naga Power in the Philippines, which saw impressive productivity gains in the first six months but mixed performance on profitability. We also rate it as marginal because the contract period was brief (only nine months). In addition, the contractor refused to bid on a second, longer contract because of labor trouble and resistance to changes specified in the contract by precontract managers who had kept their jobs. A third marginal case, Mount Kenya Textiles, saw rising profits but mixed productivity results. Labor productivity fell because the company increased its labor force by 10 percent to add a fourth shift; when demand slackened, however, the firm yielded to government pressure to avoid layoffs.

Two other borderline cases are closer to failures. The Light Rail Transit Authority of Manila has seldom made profits, largely because of government determination to hold down fares; but on one productivity measure (the ratio of operating revenues to expenses), its performance was comparable to other transit firms in the region. Similarly, although Ghana State Gold Mines did not improve financially, it did show production and productivity gains, albeit lower than those targeted in the contract. Finally, two other contracts, a sugar mill and a textile manufacturer, failed both the productivity and profitability tests.

It is clearly evident, then, that even if we classify all borderline cases as failures, the results from our sample, with two-thirds of the contracts considered successes, still favor management contracts as a tool to improve SOE performance. It is important to understand, therefore, why these contracts improved performance—and why they are so seldom used.

Why Do Management Contracts Improve Performance?

To understand why the management contracts failed or succeeded, we analyzed the same three variables we considered for performance contracts: information, rewards and penalties, and commitment.

Management contracts improved both profitability and productivity in a majority of the cases studied.

Figure 3.5 Implementation of Management Contracts: Summary of Results

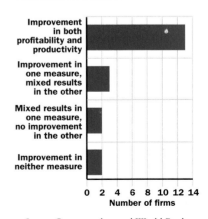

Source: Company data and World Bank estimates.

Information. Competition appears to have played an important role in increasing the availability of information, which, in turn, contributed to the likelihood of success. Of the thirteen contracts that were successful on both counts, ten operate in competitive markets (including the five hotels), while the three that are monopolies (the two water companies and the Manila Terminal) were subject to competitive bidding. The twenty-two Sri Lankan plantations, successes on both counts, were also competitively bid—a factor that may have contributed to their success (see box 3.3). (We reviewed the four auctions in the sample and concluded that they were generally transparent and fair.) In contrast, the two monopolies with borderline performances (Naga Power, a borderline success, and the Light Rail, a borderline failure) were not auctioned.[31] Competition alone does not assure success, however; most of the borderline and failed firms in our sample operate

---

Box 3.3 Sri Lanka's Experience with Management Contracts

THE SRI LANKAN EXPERIENCE WITH CONTRACTS for its twenty-two tea and rubber plantations is still early but already very promising. Eighteen of the twenty-two plantations have improved their financial performance since the contracts were instituted in 1992. This occurred despite a large government mandated wage increase, and losses for the entire group of plantations dropped by 35 percent in the first nine months under contract, compared to the same period the year before. Indeed, if we exclude the wage increase, the plantations were profitable. Moreover, despite a drought that cost the plantations about 15 percent of their output, overall production rose 30 percent from the year before.

Important explanations for the success of the contracts are the extensive use of competition and the structure of rewards. The contracts were auctioned in a fair and transparent process that was favorably reviewed by an independent World Bank consultant. Forty-six Sri Lankan companies (foreigners were excluded) prequalified to bid on the basis of their financial standing and minimum size (40 percent of

the prequalification criteria) and their technical and management skills (60 percent). Eventually, thirty-nine companies submitted 102 bids for twenty-two plantation management contracts. No bidder could win more than one contract, a stipulation that ensured that the winning contractors would compete in terms of the price and quality of the tea they produced. Contracts were awarded on the basis of the bidders' technical proposals for running the plantation (weighted at 50 percent) and the percentage of the profits that would be paid as a success fee plus the size of the lump sum payment that the contractor would charge the government for running the plantation (50 percent). The structure of rewards gives the operators strong incentives to make a profit. Their success fee averages 20 percent of their profits. Moreover, contractors have an added incentive to increase profitability, since they can extend the contract three times (for five years each) if their profits exceed a specified level (3 percent of net assets for the first extension; 7 percent thereafter).

in competitive markets and, in one case (Ghana State Gold Mining), the contract was awarded through an auction as well. Even though competition reveals information, it improves performance only if that information is used to shape rewards and enhance commitment.

Rewards and Penalties. As we have seen for performance contracts, rewards consist of two broad types—money and power—and the withholding or reduction of these constitute the two types of penalties. Theory suggests that performance will improve when rewards and penalties are closely linked to performance. In our sample, this was indeed the case.

As a financial incentive for improvement, success fees directly linked to company performance proved stronger than fixed fees paid regardless of performance. Indeed, fixed fees can be a disincentive, especially if they are set high enough to cover all the contractor's costs, thus eliminating any penalty for poor performance. All the successful contracts used success fees or equity stakes; many did not even include a fixed fee component (figure 3.6). In contrast, all the borderline and failing contracts included fixed fees; some did not even have success fees. Of the four borderline and unsuccessful contracts that included success fees, two based these on production rather than profits, which provides less incentive to control costs or expand revenues. The other two, like most of the successful contracts, included profit-based fees, but other factors reduced the incentive effect. One (Kenya's Nzoia Sugar) combined the success fee with a large fixed fee, ensuring the contractor a good return regardless of performance; the other (the Philippines' Manila Light Rail) was subject to government price controls that prevented the firm from making profits. In contrast, successful contracts required contractors to earn most of their return by improving company performance. For example, compare Nzoia Sugar's large fixed fee with Mumias Sugar, also in Kenya, where the fixed fee covers only the contractor's costs, and the contractor begins to make a return only when the firm becomes profitable. Similarly, performance-linked fees were the rule in all the hotels in our sample. Indeed, our comparison of hotels in Egypt found that the calculation of success fees (and other contract terms, such as replacement reserve and marketing fees) were identical for hotels in the same chain, regardless of whether the hotel was state owned or privately owned.

Rewards and penalties related to power were most evident in the degree to which governments granted contractors autonomy or, con-

Figure 3.6 Contract Effects of Fee Structure, Autonomy, and Duration on Performance

A. The Effects of Fee Structure

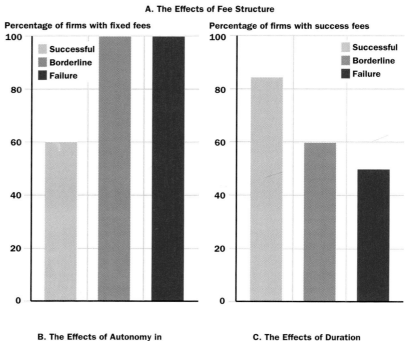

Management contracts were more often successful when they linked fees to performance; when they gave managers autonomy in employment decisions, such as hiring and firing; and when the contract covered more years.

B. The Effects of Autonomy in Employment Decisions

C. The Effects of Duration

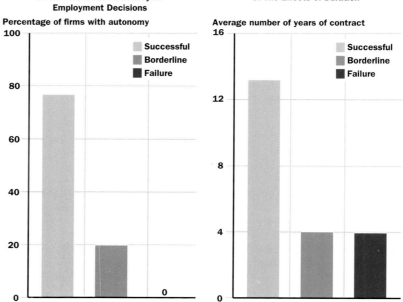

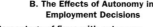

Source: Company data and World Bank estimates.

versely, constrained the contractor's autonomy in ways that raised costs or lowered revenues. The role of power in these contracts differs from that in the performance contracts of the previous section. For public managers, greater autonomy and the removal of constraints on the SOEs made their managerial task easier and may have enhanced their prestige; in a few cases it also affected their ability to get a bonus. For private managers, greater power affected their net earnings under the success fee. In general, the more successful contracts enabled contractors to pursue contract objectives independent of government policy, while the less successful contracts made returns to the contractors dependent on government decisions outside their control. In cases where the contractors were dependent, the government's role in determining outcomes was often not explicitly stated in the contract.

We encountered many examples of this. Manila Light Rail's contract specified a success fee equal to 5 percent of its profits, but the government policy of holding down fares precluded profits in most years. One reason the contractor agreed to this arrangement was that all operating expenses were covered by the government, so although the upside was limited there was little downside. Similarly, the production targets for Ghana's State Gold Mining Company and Kenya's Nzoia Sugar were too high to meet without substantial new investment in the companies— new investments the governments were not prepared to make. In the case of Nzoia Sugar, the contract explicitly confined the contractor to managing the factory, with no authority over finances, supply of cane, or marketing.

Governments intervened in personnel policies more than any other area of decisionmaking. Here, too, enterprise autonomy was closely correlated with improved performance. Most of the successful contracts gave the manager significant autonomy to set wages and to hire and fire, while all but one of the borderline or unsuccessful contracts limited management's authority over labor (figure 3.6B). In one extreme case, the contractor for Domestic Appliances Ltd. in Pakistan was allowed to fire the entire labor force and recruit anew. In other cases, although the contract promised autonomy, the government nonetheless intervened. For example, in 1993 the Sri Lankan plantations had to absorb a government mandated wage increase that was double the average annual increase for the five pervious years. The plantations improved performance despite this increase, perhaps because managers do not expect such large wage increases in the future. Similarly, although Mount Kenya Textile's contract gave contractors the freedom to hire and fire, managers who hired extra workers when demand surged found that the government did not allow the company to lay them off when demand later fell. The added cost contributed to the company's marginal performance.

Price regulation was not an issue for many of these management contracts, because the companies operated in competitive product markets without price controls. As for the monopolies, better performance was closely associated with pricing regulation that gave managers an incentive to increase efficiency. We have already seen with Manila's Light Rail how adverse price regulations can be a disincentive to performance improvements. On the positive side, the prices for the water companies in Guinea and the Central African Republic (SONEG and SNB) were set by competitive auction (the contracts were awarded to the bidder offering the lowest average price for a new water connection).

Commitment. Institutional mechanisms to resolve conflicts and enforce terms seemed not to play a major role in engendering commitment in our sample. None of the contracts specified a domestic third party that could be considered neutral or powerful enough to enforce the contract. In most of the contracts, monitoring was done by the board of directors of the company under contract (which was appointed by the government) or by the holding company that owned the assets, and it used the same indicator as for the success fee. Many of the contracts with foreign managers provide for international arbitration (by the International Chamber of Commerce or ICSID, the International Centre for Settlement of Investment Disputes), and some had provisions for domestic arbitration (for example, Manila's Light Rail could appeal to the court system); but there is no evidence that these channels were ever used. There were only three cases of default (where the contract was canceled or terminated by either party prior to completion) and, judging from these cases, termination was relatively simple and preferred to arbitration.

The absence of effective third-party enforcement suggests that the parties relied on other commitment mechanisms, such as longer contracts, the possibility of contract renewals, a high degree of contractor concern with safeguarding reputation, and costly up-front actions by government; this was indeed the case for the better performing enterprises in our sample. Longer contracts with a greater possibility of renewal motivate improved performance in several ways. Most obviously, contractors have a greater incentive to upgrade an enterprise and invest in other changes (for example, improved marketing or seeking out cheaper suppliers) if they expect to be around to reap the benefits. Longer contracts also give government more information about performance and increase the contractors' concern about maintaining a good reputation, since this will affect prospects for renewal.[32] Thus, other things being equal, a longer contract with greater possibility of renewal reduces the contractor's incentive to run down the assets, fail to serve the market, or otherwise sacrifice the SOE's long-term health for short-run gains, at least until the contract nears its end. Our evidence supports this. As figure 3.6C shows, specified contract periods varied widely, from twenty-five years to nine months, and the more successful contracts were generally longer ones.

Contract duration and renewal possibilities aside, concern about reputation can be instilled by other, perhaps more powerful, factors. This was most obvious in the case of hotels, where large chains such as Sheraton or Hilton were strongly motivated to preserve the quality of their highly visible product. Other large firms with worldwide contracts, such as Booker Tate in sugar (which had fifteen of the twenty-four sugar contracts in our inventory) or Société d'Aménagement Urbain et Rural (SAUR) or Générale des Eaux in water, appeared to be motivated by a similar concern about their international reputation. In our sample, at least, all the contracts with large international contracting firms were successful.

In the successful cases, governments signaled their commitment in many ways: by investing in the costs of finding a contractor and negotiating a contract (in one extreme case preparatory studies and negotiations cost over $300,000 and lasted many months), by paying fees, by making new investments, or by taking politically costly steps such as allowing layoffs or giving partial equity to the contractor.

Strikingly, in most of the less successful contracts, governments did not signal commitment. Instead, a donor government or multilateral lender initiated the contract process and took over costly government responsibilities, such as selecting the contractor and paying most costs, including the contractor's fees (table 3.11). Such arrangements reduce costs and risks to government and, hence, government's incentives to enforce the contract. For the contractor, the need to ascertain government commitment is eroded, since fees are guaranteed by a dependable third party. Moreover, aid agencies often restrict the pool of potential contractors (to firms headquartered in the donor country, for

Table 3.11 The Effects of Selection and Financing on Contract Performance

Enterprise	Selection process	Outside financing
Successful		
Manila Terminal	Bidding	
Mumias Sugar	Negotiated	
Hino-Pak	Negotiated	
Domestic Appliances	Negotiated	
Guyana Sugar Corp.	Negotiated	IBRD/IDA
SONEG	Bidding	IBRD/IDA
SNE	Bidding	
Shepheard Hotel	Negotiated	
Cairo Sheraton	Negotiated	
Nile Hilton	Negotiated	
Sofia Sheraton	Negotiated	
Hotel Stadt	Negotiated	
Sri Lanka plantations	Bidding	IBRD, USAID
Borderline		
Linmine Guyana	Negotiated	IBRD/IDA
Mount Kenya Textiles	Negotiated	Neth.Dev., UNDP
Naga Power Plant	Negotiated	CIDA
State Gold Mining Co.	Bidding	IBRD/IDA, CIDA, UNDP
Light Rail (LRTA)	Negotiated	
Failures		
Nzoia Sugar	Negotiated	AfDB
Sanata Textile Limited	Negotiated	Chinese government

Note: IBRD/IDA: World Bank; USAID: U.S. Agency for International Development; Neth.Dev.: Netherlands Development Agency; UNDP: United Nations Development Program; CIDA: Canadian International Development Agency; AfDB: African Development Bank.
Source: Shaikh and Minovi (1994).

example), thus reducing competition and its attendant advantages. With little at risk and competition limited, a contractor is likely to be less concerned than would otherwise be the case about negotiating a viable contract.

Three of the successful contracts did employ outside financing (the IBRD in all three cases, with additional funding from USAID in the case of the Sri Lankan plantations). Outside funding appeared not to undermine commitment in these cases, because the financing agency did not influence the choice of contractor (two of the three were competitively bid) and did not fund large fixed fees.

Of the six other contracts with outside funding, lack of commitment appears to have been a problem in four. For example, the Canadian aid agency assisted in two contracts by paying the fees of Canadian contractors. One of these contracts, with Ghana Gold Mines (also funded, in part, by the IBRD, IDA, and UNDP), went forward even though a number of government commitments crucial to the rehabilitation of the mines never materialized, partly because the generous fixed portion of the compensation package was not at risk.[33] The other, Naga Power in the Philippines, ended after a nine-month pilot phase when the contractor refused to take on the second phase in the face of labor and management opposition and lack of government backing.

In the case of Mount Kenya Textiles, the contractor (AMSCO) raised its own fees from its shareholders and development agencies, thus lowering the government's risk; but, as we mentioned, the government later curbed AMSCO's freedom to lay off excess workers. Government commitment problems may also have been inherent in the way that the contract was initiated: impetus came not from the government, but from the company's creditors, who feared that they would not be repaid if the firm were liquidated.

One of the most troubled instances of outside financing involved the Chinese government's role in the Sanata Textiles in Guyana. Under the agreement that provided for Chinese financing, the Chinese government picked a Chinese management team, even though it was the Guyanese government that contracted with the management. Communication problems were exacerbated when two interpreters returned to China, leaving the Chinese managers unable to communicate well with the Guyanese managers and workers. Labor problems developed, and there was a massive buildup of spare parts purchased from China, coupled with shortages of other spares.

Outside financing for the Nzoia Sugar contract from the African Development Bank was not the main reason for its commitment problems. Rather, this was a case where the contractor's large returns on a parallel investment program made the incentives in the management contract irrelevant. The contract for Nzoia Sugar was part of the second phase of a larger enterprise rehabilitation project. The contractor for the first phase, ARKEL, successfully argued that the incompetency of Nzoia's management had delayed the first phase of the rehabilitation. Hence the government of Kenya agreed that ARKEL should manage the sugar plant while it also implemented the second phase of investments. In this case the attraction of large returns on the (outside-financed) rehabilitation program led ARKEL to propose the contract to government (which did no studies of the benefits or objectives of a contract); the contract to which ARKEL agreed strictly limited management's control over the company's finances, marketing, and even the supply of cane.

Outside financing did not harm the commitments of the government and the contractor to improve Linmine of Guyana. Rather, in this case outside financing for rehabilitation (from the World Bank) may be keeping alive a firm that cannot be profitable at current bauxite prices. Thus, Linmine was technically bankrupt but was contracted out, because the government wanted to continue to provide bauxite, while the World Bank required a management contract as a condition of its loan to rehabilitate the company.

Strikingly, of the seven contracts that were not fully successful, according to the two measurements of profitability and productivity, only one—Manila's Light Rail—did not involve outside funding of the costs to the contracting parties. In this case, the unusually close relationship between the government then in power and the contractor offers a ready explanation of the evidently poor commitment to improved performance: the contract went to a brother of Imelda Marcos, the influential wife of President Ferdinand Marcos.

Why Are Management Contracts Not More Widely Used?

If the experience of our sample is typical, management contracts can work to improve the performance of SOEs. Yet despite this success, most countries have tried them only a few times and in relatively few sectors. Our survey suggests the following explanations for this:

- *Management contracts work better in some sectors than others.*

They are most often applied to hotels, agriculture, and water for good reasons. Governments find it less costly to monitor and enforce a contract where the supplier has an international reputation to protect, and quality is easily compared, as with hotels; or where the technology is not changing rapidly; or where output is a single, homogeneous product, such as sugar or water. There were some exceptions; for example, we found four management contracts for automobile production. However, these were relatively few probably because contracts are difficult to write and monitor for industries with rapidly changing technology and standards, multiple product lines, and segmented markets. The likelihood that management contracts will be widely and successfully implemented in such industries, especially in developing countries where enforcement capacity is weak, is probably remote.

■ *Management contracts can have lower political costs than privatization, but they also have lower political gains.*

Because management contracts are not as visible as outright sales, they are somewhat less politically costly, but not much. Some special privileges of government officials may be left intact (membership on boards of directors, special rates at hotels under contract, etc.). Commonly, however, management contracts require government actors to pay substantial political costs: they must stop using the SOEs for patronage purposes, they must allow layoffs where appropriate, and frequently they must relinquish management control to foreigners (95 percent of the management contracts in our inventory of 150 went to foreign firms; the one big exception was the Sri Lankan plantations).

At the same time, many of the enterprises suitable for management contracts are also potentially appropriate for privatization, which may offer governments advantages not otherwise available. Many of these contracts are with SOEs in potentially competitive sectors and could, therefore, be sold without establishing extensive regulatory mechanisms if market controls were abolished. Privatization gives the government more ways to win support for reform than a contract, because it raises more revenues and creates the potential to sell discounted shares to the public or to workers (see chapter 4). Finally, transaction costs may be higher with management contracts than with privatization: negotiating and monitoring a successful contract is at least as difficult as privatizing a competitive firm, and the costs are recurrent, since the contract must be periodically monitored and renegotiated; a sale is final.

Management Contract Findings

Management contracts have the potential to improve SOE performance, but they work well only in a limited number of circumstances and sectors. Our sample's experience suggests that, where the situation is right for a management contract, they work best if the following conditions are met:

■ The contract is competitively bid.

- Most of the contractor's returns depend on a success fee based on a composite measure of performance, such as profits, and the contractor has autonomy to take action needed to improve performance, including layoffs.

- Both parties face risks (which are not removed by outside financing), hence each demands that the other take actions to prove commitment. Government can signal commitment by agreeing to a longer contract with the possibility for renewal and by allowing the private manager the autonomy necessary to reap a reasonable return. Contractors show that they are committed to making the contract a success when they put their reputation at stake and agree to base a significant part of their returns on performance.

- Finally, donors can help encourage the use of management contracts where appropriate by financing the search for a contractor and negotiation costs, but should be careful not to dilute the stake of either side in the success of the contract. In particular, they should avoid putting restrictions on competition among contractors or financing large fixed fees that overwhelm the incentive effects of performance-based fees.

Regulatory Contracts: With Private Owners

REGULATORY CONTRACTS, THE THIRD AND FINAL CONTRACT type we discuss in this chapter, define the relationship between a government and the owners of a private, regulated monopoly. These contracts typically arise when the government privatizes a state monopoly; they represent an improvement over continued government ownership when they provide incentives sufficient to persuade the new owner to invest, expand service, and operate the firm efficiently, while protecting consumers from monopoly exploitation.

Devising effective regulatory contracts has become increasingly important as developing countries privatize a growing number of former state monopolies in telecommunications, power, water, railroads, roads, ports, and gas. The value of government sales of firms in these sectors exploded from a mere $431 million in 1988 to nearly $6.5 billion in 1992 (table 3.12). Privatization has been tried for many types of infrastructure monopolies, but most sales have been concentrated in just two

Table 3.12 Value of Recent Infrastructure Privatization in Developing Countries

Subsector	Millions of dollars						Percent of total
	1988	1989	1990	1991	1992	Total[a]	
Telecommunications	325	212	4,036	5,743	1,504	11,820	59.7
Power	106	2,100	20	346	2,726	5,298	26.8
Gas distribution	0	0	0	0	1,906	1,906	9.6
Railroads	0	0	0	110	217	327	1.7
Roads	0	0	250	0	0	250	1.3
Ports	0	0	0	0	7	7	0.04
Water	0	0	0	0	175	175	0.9
Total	431	2,312	4,306	6,199	6,535	19,783	100.0
Telecoms and power as a percentage of total	100	100	94	98	65	87	

a. Numbers may reflect rounding.
Source: Sader (1993) as cited in World Development Report 1994.

sectors—telecommunications (60 percent) and power (27 percent). This rapid growth may be a pragmatic response to the government's inability to meet expanding demand in telecoms and power, in part because of fiscal constraints, or it may reflect a growing sense that private ownership is more efficient than state ownership. It may also be that an increasing number of countries have reached a level of economic development where the private sector is able to mobilize the necessary resources to run these large companies and the government is able credibly to commit not to expropriate them.

To assess the impact of regulatory contracts, we focused on the telecommunications sector (see table 3.13), since it is the sector where developing countries have divested the most. As in the preceding sections, we first evaluate performance before and after the contract, in this case divestiture accompanied by regulation. We then analyze these outcomes according to how the contracts dealt with the now familiar framework of information, rewards and penalties, and commitment. As we shall see, regulatory contracts are most successful when governments do three things. First, they reduce the firm's information advantage by increasing competition (for example, by comparing regional monopolies or by auctioning the right to provide monopoly services). Second, they devise rewards and penalties, primarily in the form of pricing regulations, that induce the firm to operate efficiently and pass some of the savings on to consumers. Finally, they demonstrate their commitment

Table 3.13 Sample of Countries with Private Sector Participation in Telecommunications

Country	Year of regulatory reform[a]	Percent of sector private[b]	Real dollar per capita GNP, 1981	GDP growth rate[c]	Years of waiting time for phone[d]	Teledensity in 1981[e]
Argentina	1990	100	3,442	1.4	4.1	7.7
Chile	1987	100	1,995	4.5	5.7	3.4
Jamaica	1988	100	1,242	1.9	9.0	2.6
Malaysia	1987	25	2,096	6.3	1.6	3.6
Mexico	1990	100	2,510	1.4	4.9	4.4
Philippines	1986	100	669	1.2	14.7	0.9
Venezuela	1991	40	3,647	2.5	2.5	5.6

a. Prior reforms were undertaken in Chile (1978, 1982) and Jamaica (1982); some additional reforms to facilitate partial privatization were undertaken in Malaysia in 1990. With the exception of Malaysia, and the Philippines, where the telecom sector has been privately owned for decades, the year of reform is also the year of privatization.

b. As of 1993.

c. Average real GDP growth rates over the period 1981–92.

d. As of 1987 for Argentina and 1986 for Jamaica; calculated as a ratio of the number of applications on the waiting list to the average number of main lines added over the last three years.

e. Phone lines per 100 people.

Source: Galal and Nauriyal (1995).

with safeguards to protect the producers against opportunistic behavior by future regimes so that owners will make investments necessary to upgrade and extend service. When these requirements are met, privatization with regulation works well; where they are not met, outcomes can be disappointing. The private sector may not invest sufficiently to meet demand or may not expend the necessary effort to improve productivity; and at the same time, it may be able to take advantage of its monopoly position to earn an excessive rate of return.

Assessing the Performance of Regulatory Contracts

To assess the effect of contracts on performance, we compared the performance of telecom sectors before and after regulatory reform in seven countries. Except in the Philippines, where the telecoms company has been privately owned for decades, regulatory reform coincided with privatization. Twenty-nine developing countries shifted some aspects of their telecommunications sector from state to private ownership between 1989 and 1993. However, only seven of these twenty-nine countries have private sector participation in basic telephone service, which is a natural monopoly. We used these seven countries as our sample. Although the sample is small and not random, its diversity in terms of economic development, rate of economic growth, initial telecoms' development, the pace and timing of the regulatory reform, and the extent of divestiture enables us to analyze different aspects of regulatory design under a wide variety of circumstances.

We used the following indicators to assess performance: network growth and labor productivity, rates of return to the producers, and several measures of consumer satisfaction. (Data were insufficient to assess total factor productivity.) Our findings support the notion that private ownership and regulation produce beneficial results to society, but the results vary across countries. Chile, where the results were very positive, and the Philippines, where the results were negative, represent the two extremes.

Expansion and Productivity. First we look at the contribution the contracts may have made to the economy by expanding service and improving productivity. Figure 3.7 shows the change in annual rates of growth of main lines in service, and in labor productivity (as measured by main lines in service divided by the number of employees), before and after reform.

The figure suggests a clear pattern of improvement. Thanks to increased investment, the network expanded dramatically in the postreform period in all countries except Malaysia and the Philippines. Labor productivity also improved significantly in all countries, except Jamaica (where productivity declined) and the Philippines (where productivity showed negligible improvement). The significant investment in five of the seven countries implies private sector confidence that government will not behave opportunistically. At the same time, the large improvements in labor productivity (again in five countries out of seven) suggests that regulatory reforms have been effective in inducing firms to improve efficiency. As we shall see, where expansion and productivity stagnated or declined, as in the Philippines, the regulatory reforms have not adequately resolved the information, rewards and penalties, and commitment problems.

Returns to Capital. Looking next at returns to producers, we find that the average (aftertax) returns on net worth (figure 3.7) improved in all countries, suggesting that assets were more productive under private ownership than they had been under state ownership. (Net worth is used as a denominator because reliable data on revalued assets were not available.) However, returns exhibit a large variance around the mean.

Figure 3.7 Telecommunications Reform: Impact on Network Expansion, Labor Productivity, and Returns

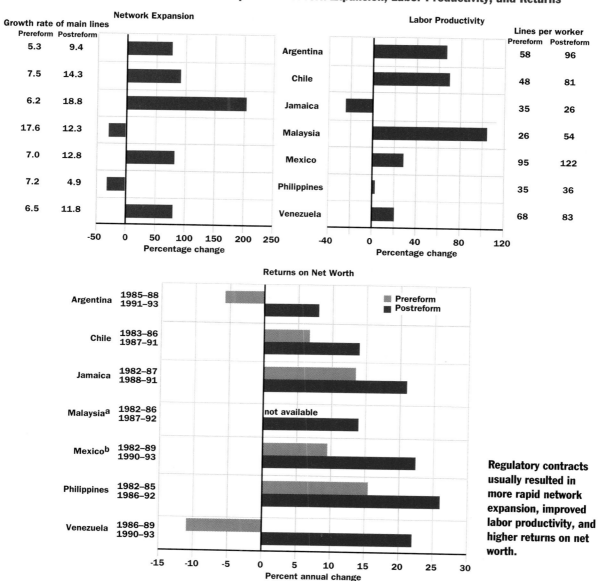

Regulatory contracts usually resulted in more rapid network expansion, improved labor productivity, and higher returns on net worth.

a. Postreform profit before taxes over net worth for 1990 only.

b. Postreform data is an estimate based on World Bank projections of revenues and expenses for TELMEX.

Note: The prereform/postreform periods for which data are reported are: Argentina: 1981–90/1991–92; Chile: 1981–86/1987–92; Jamaica: 1981–87/1988–92; Malaysia: 1981–86/1987–92; Mexico: 1981–89/1990–92; Philippines: 1980–85/1986–92; and Venezuela: 1981–90/1991–93.

Sources: Hill and Abdala (1995); Galal (1994); Spiller and Sampson (1993); World Bank (1993, 1990); Wellenius and others (1994); Esfahani (1994); Clemente (1994); International Telecommunications Union (various years; 1994).

In the postreform period, in the Philippines telecoms monopoly makes the highest rate of return (25.7 percent), while rates of return are lowest in Argentina (7.7 percent) and Chile (13.8 percent). The very high rate of return in the Philippines suggests that the regulatory regime did not succeed in reducing the firm's information advantage and ensuring credible commitment. In contrast, the modest rates of return in Argentina and Chile, combined with their good performance on expansion and productivity, suggest that these countries have successfully resolved their regulatory problems. The remaining countries may have succeeded in resolving some regulatory problems, but not others. As we see in the next section, the extent to which countries resolved these problems is an important factor in the impact of regulatory contracts on consumers.

Effect on Consumers. Consumers undoubtedly benefited from increased service where there was a surge in investment (in Argentina, Chile, Jamaica, Mexico, and Venezuela), as compared with countries where the rate of expansion fell (the Philippines and Malaysia). Not surprisingly, pending demand—the ratio of applications for phone service to phones installed—declined in Argentina and Mexico and increased in the Philippines (table 3.14). But pending demand also increased in Chile, Jamaica, and Venezuela, despite rapid growth in the number of phone lines. This is probably because, as the prospect of actually obtaining a phone improves, more people apply, so that the ratio of applicants to phones initially surges. Thus, the two countries

Table 3.14 Indicators of Quality of Telecommunications Service, before and after Reform

Country	Percentage of unsuccessful calls				Average pending demand (percent)[a]			
	Prereform	Year	Postreform	Years	Prereform	Years	Postreform	Years
Argentina	19	1990	13	1992	32	1981–90	10	1991–92
Chile	—	—	1	1992	33	1981–86	35	1987–92
Jamaica	—	—	—	—	72	1986–87[b]	81	1989–92
Malaysia	—	—	—	—	24	1981–86	7	1987–92
Mexico	11	1988	9	1992	22	1981–89	16	1990–92
Philippines	—	—	18	1992	46	1980–85	79	1986–92
Venezuela	43	1990	37	1992	25	1981–90	35	1991–93

— Not available.

a. Ratio of waiting list to main lines in operation.

b. No information was available for 1981–85.

Source: International Telecommunications Union (1994).

with the highest pending demand (the Philippines with 79 percent and Jamaica with 81 percent) have very different stories to tell: slow system growth in the Philippines; rapid growth in Jamaica.

Besides benefiting from expansion in the system, consumers in all countries for which we had data also benefited from better service, as indicated by improvements in the call completion rate (table 3.14). But levels of quality varied widely; in particular, the sharp contrast between Chile and the Philippines persists: in 1992 only 1 percent of calls were unsuccessful in Chile, while in the Philippines 18 percent of calls failed to go through.[34]

Regulatory Contracts Usually Improved Performance

In sum, our three sets of measures—investment and labor productivity, returns to capital, and the quantity and quality of service—strongly suggest that regulatory contracts generally improved performance in a variety of ways. Reforms spurred investment in expansion in all countries in the sample except the Philippines and Malaysia and led to productivity gains in all but the Philippines and Jamaica. Returns to capital improved in all countries, although the rate of return on net worth was unusually high in the Philippines. Improvements in the quantity and quality of service were seen in all countries with data; however, the Philippines does worse than other countries, which suggests that the owners' unusually high rate of return came at the consumers' expense. To explain this pattern of outcomes, we turn to the now familiar contracting problems of information, rewards and penalties, and commitment.

Resolving Information Problems. As we discussed at the beginning of this chapter, information asymmetry can be ameliorated in a variety of ways. Competition provides the least costly solution. In telecommunications, once a textbook case of a natural monopoly, recent advances in computers, switching devices, fiber optics, and wireless communication have greatly increased the potential for competition. For example, it is now possible for several interconnected suppliers to compete in providing such services as long distance phone calls, cellular phone calls, and a variety of value added services (e.g., data transmission, paging, private circuits). Most countries in our sample took advantage of these advances in technology to inject competition into their regulatory contracts.

Where technology does not permit competitive markets (because of the economies of scale, for example, in laying the cable and wires for local networks), there are other ways to introduce competition. Auctions for the right to provide basic telephone service can extract information, and the threat of competition after the contract is granted can induce the provider to operate efficiently. Contracting with several suppliers in one country (even if each supplier is a regional monopoly) enables the regulator to compare performance across firms. Barring collusion between the firms, such so-called yardstick competition gives the regulator a mechanism to verify information provided by individual firms and to gather information about the impact of common environmental factors (e.g., weather) on relative performance. Finally, governments can discipline firms by threatening to transfer contracts to rival suppliers if the incumbents fail to meet contracted targets.

Table 3.15 shows the extent to which each country in the sample used these mechanisms, as revealed by the market structure of their telecom sectors, the process used to award the franchise, and the use of the threat of competition to discipline incumbent firms. All countries in the sample except Jamaica, which we discuss below, introduced competition in the market for value added services. For basic services, all countries except Argentina ended up essentially with a monopoly. Argentina introduced yardstick competition, splitting the market into two regional monopolies—one in the north and another in the south. Although Chile and the Philippines legally permit entry into the market for basic services, in practice, the dominant firm in each country has a market share of about 95 percent.

Table 3.15 Mechanisms for Revealing Information about Telecommunications

| Country | Market structure | | Bidding/auctions | Contestability |
	Basic services	Value added services	Basic services	Basic services
Argentina	Duopoly[a]	Competitive	Yes	Partial
Chile	Free entry	Competitive	Yes	Full
Jamaica	Monopoly	Monopoly	No	None
Malaysia	Monopoly	Competitive	No	None
Mexico	Monopoly	Competitive	Yes	Partial
Philippines	Free entry[b]	Competitive	No	Partial
Venezuela	Monopoly	Competitive	Yes	Partial

a. Regional monopolies—one confined to operations in the north and the other to the south.
b. There are about sixty telecom service operators, but PLDT, the main operator, controls 94 percent of all telephones.
Source: Galal and Nauriyal (1995).

Four countries awarded contracts through international bidding: Argentina, Chile, Mexico, and Venezuela. Since all received at least two bids from potential suppliers, it is likely that the auctions provided information that limited the ability of the winners to extract information rents. The three other countries in our sample did not use competitive bids to compel firms to reveal information. The costs of not holding an auction are least evident in Malaysia, where the government sold only 25 percent of the telecoms monopoly assets to the private sector and management continued to be dominated by the state bureaucracy. Even so, the lack of an auction, combined with the minority equity sold to the private sector, may explain why Malaysia was one of the few countries where private investment did not increase after the contract. Jamaica negotiated an exclusive concession with Cable & Wireless for basic and value added services for twenty-five years. As for the Philippines, the Philippine Long Distance Telephone Company has operated as a private monopoly for decades. In such a case, even if the initial process of awarding the license involved competitive bidding, technology has since changed so much that the value of that information to the regulator is likely to have evaporated.

Our sample countries also varied in the extent to which they used performance targets as a mechanism to discipline the behavior of firms. On the one hand, Argentina, Chile, Jamaica, Mexico, and Venezuela all included provisions in the operator's license, sector regulation, or sales contract requiring the private operator to meet specific network expansion and service quality targets. Also included was a stipulation that failure to meet these obligations is grounds for the government to revoke the concession and award it to another supplier. In contrast, Malaysia and the Philippines did not explicitly state such a threat in their regulatory framework.

The different ways our sample countries used competition helps explain the relatively high rate of return in the Philippines and Jamaica and the relatively low rates of return in Chile and Argentina. However, rates of return also depend on the pricing regime and the credibility of government commitment. We deal with the pricing regime next.

Price Regulation as a Mechanism for Rewards and Penalties. Price regulation is the most important mechanism that governments have for rewarding or penalizing the owners of private, regulated monopolies such as those in our sample. An ideal price regulating system will provide owners with incentives to invest and improve service and will reward improvements in efficiency, while at the same time passing on the largest possible share of the resulting savings to consumers. In short, ideal price regulation will achieve outcomes very similar to a competitive market. In this section, we briefly describe the strengths and weaknesses of various types of price regulation in telecommunication, then analyze how the use of particular schemes in the countries in our sample influenced outcomes.

Schemes to regulate the price of basic telephone services include rate of return, price caps, and benchmark regulations. Each of these pricing schemes has its own incentive properties, which have been discussed at length elsewhere. Briefly, under rate of return regulation, prices are set so that the firm can recover its costs and make a fair rate of return. This scheme has been criticized on the grounds that it induces a firm to inflate costs, invest excessively, and engage in cross subsidization by shifting costs from services in which it faces competition to those regulated services in which it does not.

Price caps and benchmark regulations both potentially work better than rate of return in motivating producers to reduce their costs and pass some of the savings on to consumers. Under price cap regulation, regulators impose a ceiling, often based on the retail price index, on the average tariff increase for a prespecified basket of services in which the firm has a monopoly. The regulator can periodically change the pricing formula so that improvements in efficiency are passed on to the consumers. In theory, this avoids the problems inherent in rate of return regulation, since firms are protected from inflation and have no incentive to expand their asset base inefficiently; but, to the contrary, they can capture any benefits from improved efficiency that lowers costs below the price ceiling in the period between adjustments in the pricing formula. Benchmark regulation works on a similar principle, except that prices are set according to the costs of a similar firm elsewhere or a hypothetical efficient firm. Again, management has an incentive to improve efficiency, because the firm reaps the benefits until prices are renegotiated. Too frequent downward adjustments in the pricing formula under either system reduce the incentive for the firm to curb costs in order to reap any savings until the next adjustment; they are also costly and cumbersome to administer. Box 3.4 describes how these two forms of regulation operate and some of the advantages and potential problems with each.

Table 3.16 shows the pricing regimes, the frequency of their revisions, the adjustment for inflation, and the parameter for setting prices (explained in box 3.4) for our sample. Only Jamaica and the Philippines

Box 3.4 Price Cap and Benchmark Regulation

PRICE CAP AND BENCHMARK REGULATION ARE useful alternatives to the more common rate of return regulation, because they eliminate incentives for firms to inflate costs, invest excessively, and engage in cross subsidization. This box explains how returns to investors are calculated using these methods and some additional advantages and problems with each.

In price cap regulation (also referred to as RPI minus X regulation, for reasons explained below), the government imposes a ceiling on the average tariff increase for the basket of services in which the firm has a monopoly. For example, the average price increase may be set at the Retail Price Index (RPI) minus a number (X) that the government holds constant for a specified period. With a positive X, this scheme transfers some of the benefits from technological progress and improved productivity to consumers; the extent of the benefits transferred to consumers depends on the size of X. Because X is set independently of the firm's costs, the scheme limits the firm's incentives and opportunity to distort its cost data or shift the costs of competitive services onto its captive monopoly activities. Instead, the firm is motivated to minimize costs and pursue technological innovations, since it will retain any profits that may result from cost cutting during the period between tariff revisions. The main shortcoming of this scheme is that it leaves the determination of the X factor to the regulators, which creates uncertainty that may motivate firms to underinvest. Moreover, if

the regulators also try to influence the firm's rate of return when they are setting X, the scheme may degenerate to rate of return regulation. Among the countries with price caps, only Mexico provides for raising the X factor, from zero until 1996 to 3 percent for 1997–98.[1] Argentina, Venezuela, and Malaysia set X = 0, without provision for a positive X. Unless this is changed, their enterprises' prices will go up with the rate of inflation, and the owners will pocket any cost savings, rather than sharing the benefits of technological improvements with consumers.

In benchmark regulation, tariffs are set to allow the firm a fair rate of return with reference to some yardstick other than to its actual costs. The yardstick can be the costs of a hypothetical efficient firm or the costs of a similar firm. Because the yardstick costs are divorced from the firm's actual costs and because tariffs are only revised every few years, benchmark regulation has similar cost saving properties as those associated with price cap regulation. Moreover, because the scheme explicitly specifies a fair rate of return, it limits the discretion of the regulators and reduces uncertainty. The main shortcoming of this scheme is that disagreements can arise between regulators and the monopoly with respect to the definition of the benchmark.

1. Thereafter, X is to be adjusted on the basis of a review of incremental costs every four years.

opted for rate of return regulation, while the other five countries adopted either price caps or benchmark regulation. Jamaica guarantees the operator net aftertax profits within a band of 17.5 to 20 percent of shareholders' equity and periodic adjustment for inflation. The pricing regime gives little discretion to the regulator, which, as we shall see, has helped demonstrate government commitment, thus giving the owner the confidence to invest. In contrast, the Philippines leaves price determination to the regulator's discretion (within a ceiling, a 12 percent rate

Table 3.16 Price Regulation in Sample Countries

Country	Pricing formula	Frequency of tariff review	Inflation adjustment	Productivity parameter/ rate of return
Argentina	PC	Semiannual	Indexed to US CPI	Partial
Chile	BM	Every five years	Indexed to CPI	Full
Jamaica	ROR	Company request	Indexed to CPI	None
Malaysia	PC	Company request	Indexed to CPI	None
Mexico	PC	Every four years after 1988	Indexed to CPI	Partial
Philippines	ROR	Company request	None	Partial
Venezuela	PC	Quarterly	Fully indexed to WPI until 1996. Partial indexation for 1997–2000.	Partial

Note: BM: benchmark; PC: price caps; ROR: rate of return; CPI: consumer price index; WPI: wholesale price index.

Source: Hill and Abdala (1994); Galal (1994); Spiller and Sampson (1995); World Bank (1993, 1990); Wellenius and others (1994); Esfahani (1994); Clemente (1994).

of return on assets, that the Supreme Court established for all utilities) and is the only country in our sample that does not allow for inflation adjustment. This uncertainty about future profitability has important negative implications for commitment, which we discuss below.

The other five countries adopted one of the two cost savings price regimes: Argentina, Mexico, Venezuela, and Malaysia used price cap regulation, and Chile adopted benchmark regulation. However, some did better in implementing the regulation than others. For example, Chile and Mexico gave firms more incentive to curb costs by reviewing pricing regulations less frequently (five years in Chile and four in Mexico) than in Argentina (semiannual) and Venezuela (quarterly). The countries also vary in how well they motivate the producer to pass savings on to consumers. Mexico provided for passing on efficiency savings by allowing the regulator to set prices below the inflation rate according to an agreed efficiency factor starting in 1997. Argentina, Malaysia, and Venezuela have no such provision. Chile's yardstick pricing scheme motivates firms to operate efficiently by setting tariffs for each regulated service on the basis of the incremental marginal costs of a hypothetical efficient firm. The resulting prices are then adjusted to ensure that the firms can earn a fair rate of return on revalued assets, using the capital asset pricing model (Galal 1994).

Differences in the ways that countries used pricing rewards to motivate firms to minimize costs and make a fair rate of return can be seen most starkly in the contrast between Chile and the Philippines. Earlier we discussed how Chile, one of the best performers on our measures of productivity and service, allocated the franchise to the private sector. Chile used international bidding and included provisions in the benchmark regulation to revoke the license if the firm did not meet agreed targets. It also used benchmark regulation for setting prices, which provided an incentive for the firm not to behave opportunistically. In contrast, the Philippines, one of the worst performers, did not utilize these information-extracting mechanisms. Nor did the Philippine government use rewards to counter the firm's information advantage; it merely put a ceiling on the operator's returns. Of the remaining countries, Argentina and Mexico fall closer to Chile, Jamaica and Venezuela fall closer to the Philippines. The Malaysian experience is still in its infancy in the sense that the private sector only has a minority shareholding and that the regulation is still dominated by bureaucratic control.

Resolving the Commitment Problem

As noted earlier, monopoly owners who fear that the government will expropriate their assets or set prices in ways that preclude a reasonable profit minimize risk by underinvesting. Governments that count on private monopoly owners to make the investments necessary to expand service, particularly in a crucial sector like telecommunications, therefore, have a strong incentive to demonstrate commitment to abide by the contract. Even so, some governments did this much more successfully than others. In this section, we consider how the countries in our sample established their commitment by specifying conflict resolution mechanisms, assigning enforcement of regulation to appropriate agencies, and insulating the regulatory regime from capricious political behavior.

Conflict Resolution Mechanisms. All countries in the sample anticipated conflicts over pricing, entry, and interconnection and devised rules to deal with them. But some stated the rules more clearly than others. Theory suggests that the rules will be more credible, and investors more confident, when the rules are explicit. Although we cannot directly measure this relationship, the evidence from our sample suggests that this is the case. Rules were spelled out most clearly in Chile and Jamaica and were vaguest in Argentina, Malaysia, and Venezuela, with Mexico falling somewhere in between. In the Philippines, conflict resolution procedures were relatively clear, but uncertainty about basic regulations offset this potential advantage.

Chile's regulation defines step-by-step procedures for arbitration and appeals. For example, disputes between the firm and regulator over pricing are resolved through a three-member arbitration committee, with one member selected by each of the two parties and the third by mutual agreement. Disputes over entry are resolved by a government appointed antitrust commission, with possible appeal to the Supreme Court. Disputes over interconnection are subject to binding arbitration. Similarly, in Jamaica, conflicts pertaining to tariff adjustments are subject to binding arbitration. In addition, the operating license explicitly grants the firm the right to appeal any breach of the terms of the agreement on the part of the government to the Supreme Court, whose ruling can be subjected to review by the Judicial Committee of the Privy Council in London. The combination of granting the operator a specific license and the possible appeal outside the country make the regulatory regime credible in Jamaica. Although the courts are known for their independence, embodying the regulation in a law as in Chile would not have worked because in a parliamentary system such as Jamaica's, a new government may overturn laws enacted under a previous government.

In contrast, although firms in Argentina have the right to bring disputes concerning pricing, entry, or interconnection to the attention of the newly established regulatory agency (CNT), the latter's decisions can only be appealed to the national executive (the Minister of Economy). In Malaysia, conflicts are first referred to the regulatory agency; beyond that the procedure is not well defined and often results in ad hoc processes that culminate in decisions by the minister. In Venezuela, disputes over interconnection are resolved through arbitration at the request of either party without further appeal. However, disputes regarding tariffs can only be brought to the attention of the regulatory agency (CONATEL), and it is unclear what recourse the company has beyond that.

In the Philippines, there is an explicit procedure to appeal to the Supreme Court to restrain regulatory discretion and resolve conflicts over tariffs, entry, and interconnections. However, because the regulatory rules themselves are not clearly defined, the process lacks the basis on which to make such appeals. Nowhere is this more apparent than in price regulation, which, as we have seen, just sets a ceiling on the rate of return without explicit provisions for inflation adjustment.

Enforcement. Enforcement is most effective when it is in the hands of a neutral agency with the power to enforce and the capacity to process the necessary information (table 3.17 defines the agencies in our sam-

Table 3.17 Agencies Enforcing Regulations: Their Neutrality, Enforcement Powers, and Skills

Country	Agency(ies)	Neutrality	Enforcement powers	Skills
Argentina	CNT, minister of economy	Lacking	Yes	Moderate
Chile	SUBTEL, antitrust commissions, courts, arbitration	Assured	Yes	Strong
Jamaica	MPU, courts, including commonwealth	Assured	Yes	Moderate
Malaysia	JTM, minister concerned	Lacking	Yes	Moderate
Mexico	SCT	Lacking	Yes	Moderate
Philippines	NTC/DOTC, courts	Lacking	No	Weak
Venezuela	CONATEL, undefined	Lacking	Yes	Moderate

Note: CNT: Comisión Nacional de Telecomunicaciones; SUBTEL: Secretaria de Telecomunicaciones (Ministry); MPU: Minister of Public Utilities; JTM: Jabatan Telekom Malaysia; SCT: Secretaria de Comunicaciones y Transportes; NTC/DOTC: National Telecommunications Commission and Department of Transport and Communications; CONATEL: Consejo Nacional de Telecomunicaciones.
Source: Galal and Nauriyal (1995).

ple in terms of each of these characteristics). Neutrality is assured when the enforcing agencies are independent of the bureaucracy or, where appeal is through the judicial system, the courts are known for their independence. Enforcement power is assumed to exist when the agencies have a clear mandate to request and verify information from the firm. Finally, the skills needed to verify this information are assumed to exist when the agency has the autonomy and financial resources to attract skilled employees or hire consultants when needed.

Only Chile and Jamaica seem to assure the neutrality of their enforcing agencies. In Chile, neutrality is derived from relying on multiple agencies to resolve conflicts (a check on arbitrary behavior by any one agency) and on the courts' reputation for independence. In Jamaica, the right of appeal to the Judicial Committee of the Privy Council in London acts as a deterrent against opportunistic behavior by government (Spiller and Sampson 1993). In all other cases, the regulatory agencies are extensions of the bureaucracy, with the concerned minister having the final say when conflicts arise. The minister may of course attempt to balance the interests of the producers and consumers, but there are no guarantees of such behavior.

All but two of the regulatory agencies in the sample have a clear mandate to request the necessary information from the firms and to enforce the regulation. One exception is the Philippines, where the presence of two agencies with vaguely defined mandates may have undermined their power. Malaysia is another exception: since the company is still largely state owned, the power of enforcement resides in the bureaucracy. Thus, although Malaysia's regulatory agency is modeled after the United Kingdom's telecom regulatory agency and headed by a director general, the minister still approves all tariffs and licensing decisions.[35]

Finally, it appears that the regulatory agencies are generally at a disadvantage compared with the firms they regulate. In large measure, this is because of low civil service salaries, which makes it hard to attract and keep employees with the necessary skills to process the information and negotiate with their better-paid, better-informed, and probably better-motivated counterparts. In Chile, Mexico, and Argentina, these problems were resolved in part by relying on external consultants to prepare proposals, for example, for tariff revisions. Venezuela's regulatory agency was not as successful. It was supposed to finance its operations from licensing and other fees. In reality, however, these resources proved inadequate. This has constrained its capacity to review tariffs quarterly, delaying tariff increases promised to the firm under its pricing regulation for 1993.

Insulating Regulators from Politics. Finally, our sample countries attempted, with varying degrees of success, to insulate their regulatory regimes against arbitrary changes arising from political turnover. Chile and Jamaica seem to have succeeded the most, while the Philippines has been the least successful. Chile resolved this problem by enacting its regulation in a detailed law. The country has a long history of a divided legislature where the executive branch seldom has a majority, which means that laws are difficult to change. Moreover, the judicial system and constitution historically upheld private property rights, for example, against nationalization during the Allende administration in the early 1970s and land expropriation in the 1960s. Both factors seem to have made credible the government commitment not to behave opportunistically.

In Jamaica, the commitment problem was resolved differently. The regulatory regime was incorporated in an explicit license that stipulated a specific rate of return and other terms of operations as well as the conditions under which both parties (firm and regulator) can change the license. To make this agreement binding or costly for the government to renege, it was stipulated that any rulings by the supreme court regarding violations of the terms of the license would be subject to review by the Judicial Committee of the Privy Council in London. This solution was more credible in Jamaica than Chile's approach would have been, because laws can be frequently overturned in Jamaica's parliamentary system, as new administrations enjoy a majority in congress.

The Philippines, on the other hand, illustrates how politics can erode the credibility of regulation. Between 1972 and 1986, power was concentrated in the executive branch, and there were few constraints on administrative discretion. The independence of the judiciary was compromised because the president was empowered to remove any judge. As a result, the Marcos government could not credibly commit that it would adhere to certain policies and not behave opportunistically (Esfahani 1994). After 1986, although the Marcos government had lost power, business allies of the old regime who benefited from the status quo in telecommunications retained enough influence through political institutions (such as Congress) to forestall the introduction of competition or other reforms in the sector.

Mexico, Argentina, Venezuela, and Malaysia were more successful than the Philippines but less successful than Chile and Jamaica in creating credible commitment mechanisms. They regulated by decree or sale contracts, left conflict resolution ill defined, and allowed the concerned minister wide discretion. The greater the chance that presidential decrees and sale contracts can be reversed, the weaker the credibility of a contract's safeguards against opportunistic behavior on the part of successive governments. It has been suggested that reputation and concern for the success of economic reform may mitigate the negative effect of this arrangement, but the long-term effect remains uncertain. For example, Mexico's concern about establishing its reputation as a reformer and its commitment to signing NAFTA, plus the widespread distribution of shares in TELMEX, may have reassured investors that government would sustain the contract, at least in the medium term. However, Venezuela seems to have been able to overcome the adverse effects of dubious commitment on investment by providing companies with relatively large returns, which can be viewed as a premium against the risk of adverse regulatory decisions in the longer term. Logically, one would expect Argentina to have to offer higher returns as well; there, yardstick competition may have helped to minimize rates of return. Malaysia only sold minority shares, and its reputation as a responsible majority partner in other companies may have given it credibility with investors. Malaysia's bureaucratic solution seems to have kept returns at a reasonable level, but investment has declined rather than increased with private involvement.

In sum, the different levels of investment reflect the different degrees of success that governments have had in convincing investors that they are committed to their contracts and that this commitment would be sustained even when the government changed. Chile and Jamaica found the most credible commitment mechanisms, which helps explain the upsurge in investment in these two countries. Chile explicitly provided for conflict resolution and assigned the enforcement of the regulation to multiple agencies, many of which have a reputation for independence. It also encoded the telecoms regulations in a law, which is difficult to change in Chile. Similarly, Jamaica prespecified how conflicts would be resolved and incorporated these covenants in an explicit license that allows disputes to be appealed in London. Mexico, Argentina, and Venezuela did less well but made up for it in other ways, and Malaysia's partial sale of shares was not enough to spur new investment. Finally, commitment to regulation in the Philippines leaves the most to be desired. Although disputes are referred to the court system, the regulatory rules are not stated explicitly, the enforcing agencies do not have clear mandates, and the judiciary is weakened by the influence of the president through the appointment of judges.

Regulatory Contract Findings

Although our sample is small and not random, it includes all developing countries that have recently privatized state monopolies in basic telephone service. Our analysis of the outcomes in these seven countries shows significant expansion of the network and improved productivity in the majority of cases after reform. Although we could not compare this outcome with a counterfactual, one study that did so for Chile and Mexico (among others) attributed substantial gains to the privatization (Galal and others 1994).

Notwithstanding this success, there was a wide range of country outcomes. The variance can be traced to differences in the regulatory contracts. On the one hand, Chile was able to resolve the information and rewards problem (by increasing competition and adopting benchmark pricing) as well as the commitment problem (by embodying the detailed regulation in a law to insulate it from political changes); the result was positive outcomes for producers and consumers. On the other hand, the Philippines failed to resolve all three problems, leading to disappointing performance. The experience of the remaining five countries falls in between. For example, Jamaica resolved the commitment problem but could have done better on competition and pricing, while Venezuela resolved the information and pricing problems but came up short on commitment. In both cases, the new owners invested and expanded service but received relatively high rates of return, at the expense of consumers.

These findings have some lessons for other countries:

- Successful regulatory contracts addressed the information, rewards and penalties, and commitment problems simultaneously. Resolving one problem but not one or both of the others led to underinvestment or excessive rates of return, at the expense of consumers.
- Some differences are due to country characteristics that are not easily changed in the short run, such as courts that are not independent or a legislature that easily overturns laws. But some countries have designed contracts that overcame such constraints.
- Regulatory contracts are tough to design but not impossible; even though compromises were necessary and there were many imperfections in design, important gains were still achieved.

Conclusion

OUR CASE STUDIES SUGGEST THAT MANAGEMENT AND REGUlatory contracts with the private sector do a better job of improving company performance than contracts with public managers. One explanation for this lies in the concept of "residual claimant"; that is, the agent who has claims on whatever residual benefits remain after other claims are met has the greatest incentive to improve performance. Thus, because private owners and, to a somewhat lesser extent, private managers have greater claims on enterprise returns than public managers, they have a much larger stake in the outcome and hence greater incentives to improve performance. Although public managers may be allocated a small share of the returns, by definition they lack the property rights of a private party. Moreover, in our sample at least, public managers were not penalized for poor performance and were seldom rewarded for good results. In contrast, a private investor who purchases an SOE with highly specific assets can claim large returns if performance improves and faces a significant penalty—perhaps even the loss of the investment—if things go wrong. A private manager under contract to the government has less of a stake than a private owner; but the contract can be written to include incentives and penalties that give the private manager a much bigger and more direct interest in improved enterprise performance than public managers typically have. If the private party has a reputation at stake, the incentive effect is even stronger.

A contract with a private party also changes the incentives of government bureaucrats. Such contracts are more prone to scrutiny by the press, public, and politicians than a performance contract with SOE managers. The increased fear of censure arising from this situation gives bureaucrats an incentive to select the contractor carefully, to demand simpler, more easily monitored targets, to monitor results scrupulously, and to enforce the contract. Of course there is a risk that such scrutiny may work against the interests of owners and managers, especially foreign owners and managers, if it fosters opposition to price increases or to layoffs that are reasonable under the contract. Private parties therefore demand evidence that a government is prepared to abide by the contract before they will undertake such risks. Similarly, private contractors, whether managers or owners, are often willing to agree to simple, easily measured standards that are more easily defended against critics; such targets reduce the likelihood of costly disputes or, if a dispute is unavoidable, make it easier to appeal to arbitration or courts when possible. This is a sharp contrast to the preference of public managers, who try to increase the complexity of contract targets in order to improve their chances of a satisfactory rating.

In management and regulatory contracts, some governments used competition, auctions, or yardstick competition to resolve information asymmetries. In theory this could be done with SOE performance contracts (for example, by allowing different teams of public managers to bid); but it was not tried in any of the performance contracts in our sample or indeed by most of the performance contracts we encountered in our search. Similarly, SOE pricing regulation could in theory be designed and implemented as it was for the more successfully regulated privatized monopolies (such as Chile's telecom monopolies); again, this was not done for any of the performance contracts we investigated in detail. These observations suggest that the process of contracting with private actors motivated bureaucrats to use information-revealing mechanisms that they rarely, if ever, apply to SOE managers (who may be fellow bureaucrats). In designing performance contracts for SOEs, then, governments tended to rely on hierarchical approaches rather than markets; in designing management and regulatory contracts, governments more often attempted market solutions. And where market solutions were tried, they produced better outcomes.

Commitment was the Achilles' heel of all three types of contracts, although performance contracts suffered from this the most. As we have seen, commitment problems are compounded when one of the parties is the government because of the obvious difficulties the other party faces in forcing the government to comply. Unlike public managers, private parties have the option of not agreeing to a contract. This forces governments to signal commitment or to offer some sort of bond or risk premium. The availability of outside finance for management contracts undermined this advantage by insuring the private managers' risk. Management contracts with such external financing were therefore generally less effective than management contracts where the two contracting parties were required to manage the risk themselves.

There is a drawback to contracts with private parties, however: the stronger private stake in outcomes may also give private managers and owners stronger incentives to behave opportunistically. Where government's negotiating and monitoring skills are weak, this could lead to exploitation. Safeguards can be designed to reduce the risk of exploitation, and where that was done successfully, the gains from private involvement were significant.

How do management contracts compare with regulatory contracts, that is, with privatization and regulation? Management contracts have been used most often for competitive firms when many contracting problems could have been overcome by opening markets and privatizing, without the need to regulate. When management contracts are used for infrastructure, they do not generate the large, privately financed investments that are possible with privatization (Galal and others 1994). Since management contracts have many of the same problems and costs of regulatory contracts, they thus demand similar effort for smaller returns.

The bottom line of this analysis is that contracting can work for SOE reform but only if incentives are aligned so that government and firm management both strive to achieve greater efficiency. More fundamentally, our surveys have revealed how seldom any of these three types of contracts has been tried, given the many thousands of state-owned enterprises operating in developing countries. This conforms to our earlier conclusion that, although SOE reform can work, many countries are not reforming. Why this is so is the subject of the next chapter.

Notes

1. Caillaud, Guesnerie, Rey, and Tirole (1988), Sappington and Stiglitz (1986), and Besanko and Sappington (1987) survey the literature on regulation under incomplete information. Romer and Rosenthal (1985) survey the political dimension of regulatory research. Baron (1989) provides an overview of the theory.

2. For example, if a private manager does not believe that government will let the contract run its full duration and allow the firm the contracted rate of return, the contractor may run down the assets; or if a private owner believes that the government will regulate away its profits, the buyer of a privatized SOE may under invest.

3. Guarantees of noncommerical risk by a third party, such as a multinational institution, might also serve this purpose (see box 5.3).

4. We define performance contracts as negotiated agreements between government and SOE wherein quantifiable targets are explicitly specified for a given period and performance is measured against the targets at the end of the period. Our definition includes agreements that are not labeled as performance contracts in the country in question.

5. It is not random because we selected contracts from our sample countries, and we included one electricity company from each country to test for industry effects (none was found).

6. Korea Telecoms was created as a separate company only two years before its contract started. Senegal Telecoms was created in the same year that it signed its first contract; we extrapolated backward two years, using data from prereorganization telecom units. We included Senegal Electricity's second contract (starting in 1990), even though it was never signed. The conclusions would not change if that period were omitted. We also took 1987 as the start date for India Oil's contracts, even though it signed a pilot form of contract in 1986 (based on the multiyear French *contrat plan*). The government later switched to a very different sort of contract (closer to the Korean model, using yearly weighted targets). The conclusions would not change if the earlier contract period were included.

7. Performance improvement should not be confused with good performance in some absolute sense. For example, Ghana Water and Sewerage increased TFP by an average of 12.5 percent a year during the three years of contracts for which we have data (1990, 1991, and 1992). Yet this is still a company with almost 50 percent of its water unaccounted for and only about two-thirds of the population served with water.

8. Data were taken from enterprise audited accounts and the contracts and evaluation reports, supplemented by World Bank file data. In addition, a survey of key government and enterprise officials, using a standardized questionnaire and interviews with knowledgeable persons in the country and World Bank, provided further background. See Dyer Cissé (1994) for the sample questionnaire. Although every effort was made to verify the accuracy of the data, in some cases the underlying information systems are weak. However, it seems plausible that errors are not correlated over time and do not greatly affect the trend analysis. Where assets were not revalued by the company, we revalued them, using company figures for depreciation and the GDP deflator for inflation. For total factor productivity, which is calculated as the constant value of production over the constant cost of all production factors, we used company volume data to construct company-specific price indices for each factor and output where available; otherwise we used the relevant country-specific price indices. Return on assets was calculated as sales minus cost of goods sold and depreciation over revalued fixed assets.

9. Its prices are nevertheless about one-third less than those charged to the private sector, but private producers usually have more freedom to change producer prices.

10. The charges are overstated because of exchange rate effects (the comparisons are in deutschemarkes), but Senegal would still rank in the top third of countries even if its rates were half as high.

11. The postcontract return on assets of Philippines Electricity was adversely affected by increases in the cost of imported oil, but this cannot explain its poor performance in constant priced TFP. TFP might have been ad-

versely affected by disruptions caused by the Luzon earthquake, plus devastating typhoons in 1989 and 1990; however, observers knowledgeable about the company regard its performance as consistently weak. Moreover, other disasters (the Mt. Pinatubo eruption and Ormoc flood in 1991) did not prevent the firm from recovering its productivity levels. Senegal Telecoms may have benefited from the fact that it was split off from the postal service in 1986, the first year of the contract. Although we have tried to isolate the telecommunications side prior to this split, that may not always have been possible and could cause the period before the contract to look worse than it otherwise would. (The split itself is not exogenous, even though it is not explicitly part of the contract.)

12. See Jones (1993) for more on the concepts of criterion and criterion values and an excellent review of the issues of performance contracting.

13. Interview with Hafeez Shaikh (1994).

14. In Ghana, government negotiators and monitors in the State Enterprises Commission (SEC) lost power when responsibility for energy contracts was shifted to the sector agencies. Although the shift only affected two SOEs directly (including one of the three in our sample), staff in the SEC believe that the change adversely affected the credibility of all monitoring and negotiating. According to an SEC report, "This situation tends to create considerable uncertainty about who can require performance information from the SOEs. This has affected the ability of the Commission to perform its reporting and evaluation function" (SEC 1991).

15. Interviews with government evaluators and knowledgeable observers also suggest that the managers in our sample negotiated for more and softer targets and were often responsible for changes in the criteria.

16. The targets are for new lines, main lines, and income. Delays in getting information on achievements may also be a reason why government agents agreed to set targets well below the previous year's achievements. Philippines Electricity's targets for return on revalued assets and power generation per employee also fell even after they'd been exceeded.

17. Field interviews.

18. Public profits are private profits adjusted to measure returns to society as a whole and to exclude factors beyond the control of managers (Jones 1981).

19. Data on target achievement were not available for all targets. The differences in achievement of economic targets are offset by the different weights assigned to these targets. If we weight the achievement scores with the weights assigned to economic targets in table 3.3, there is little difference among the groups of TFP performers.

20. The decline in capital spending allowed it to exceed its targets for self-financing and debt service; the combined scores on these two criteria exactly canceled out the company's poor performance on its capital project target.

21. This is partly due to shutdowns of older wells as well as new drilling.

22. In Korea, evaluations of how different departments, divisions, and offices contributed to contract achievements are taken into account in internal promotions (Shirley 1991).

23. The information on reneging in this section and in table 3.5 is from survey responses, field interviews, and company and Bank reports.

24. Standing boards of directors were replaced by executive boards; government representation on the boards was reduced to two members; only board approval of the budget was required when previously the supervising ministry, the Economic Planning Board, and the cabinet also had to approve; responsibility for most personnel decisions was shifted from the supervising ministry to the enterprise; procurement through a centralized office was made voluntary instead of compulsory; all oversight was centered in the contract with one yearly inspection, instead of the extensive system of controls and inspections used previously (in one year before the contracts Korea Power had eight different inspections lasting 108 days); preference was shifted to internal candidates for senior positions (previously over half of all such appointments were from outside the firm); and an explicit merit assessment was introduced (Shirley 1991, 11–12).

25. An opinion survey of 750 employees in all ranks of the SOEs under contract found that 93 percent thought that management had improved, thanks to the performance evaluation system; 55 percent saw substantial improvement; 94 percent of the executive directors said that there had been substantial or significant improvement (Song 1988).

26. A sign of this waning commitment may be the move away from public profitability, as mentioned earlier.

27. The Mexican government distinguishes between such Financial Restructuring Pacts and performance contracts.

28. See statistical appendix for a detailed listing. Some contracts may have been missed or signed since the search was conducted in 1993.

29. The chains were Hyatt, Marriott, Holiday Inn, Intercontinental, and Sheraton.

30. Because contracts for the twenty-two Sri Lankan plantations are very similar, we treated them as a single case study.

31. Light Rail was awarded to a contractor with connections to the then president of the Philippines (the contractor was the brother of Imelda Marcos).

32. Of course, if technology is uncertain or changing rapidly, the contractor may demand to renegotiate the contract after a short period, citing unexpected costs as an explanation. Uncertain technology could allow the contractor to use his or her private information to behave opportunistically and hence reduce the incentive effects of repeated transactions. See Williamson (1976).

33. The government failed to provide all the local currency originally designated for the rehabilitation program. The contractor used 75 percent of the foreign exchange designated for the rehabilitation for "minor" rehabilitation, leaving the "major" rehabilitation underfunded.

34. It was not possible to measure how consumers fared with respect to prices. Compiling comparable data in this area proved to be difficult. Even where it was feasible to distinguish calls by customers and peak from off-peak periods, apportioning fixed costs to different services and exchange rate fluctuations was so complex that it reduced the value and comparability of the data.

35. Tariffs have not changed since 1985, although the company is allowed to adjust them for inflation under the price cap regulation.

CHAPTER 4

The Politics of SOE Reform

WE HAVE SHOWN THAT STATE-OWNED enterprises remain an important obstacle to better economic performance in developing countries, that the benefits of divestiture and other reforms are substantial, but that only a few countries have attempted these reforms and even fewer have succeeded. Clearly, factors other than economic efficiency determine the nature, pace, and extent of SOE reform. The most important of these factors is politics. State-owned enterprise reform can cost a government its support base. Consequently, politicians everywhere carefully weigh any changes in state-owned enterprise policy, naturally preferring policies that benefit their constituencies and help them remain in office over policies that undermine support and may precipitate their removal. While some exceptional leaders may be able to change their support base and mobilize new constituents for reform, most are necessarily responsive to the supporters who put them in office.

What are the political obstacles to reform? In countries that have reformed successfully, how have these obstacles been overcome? How can policymakers in developing countries, as well as institutions providing foreign assistance, decide beforehand whether SOE reforms can succeed? And finally, where conditions for successful reform do not exist, what can be done to bring them about? To address these questions and to make sense of the dynamics of policymaking, we examined the validity of three suppositions regarding successful SOE reform:

- *Reform must be politically desirable—the benefits to the leadership and its constituencies must outweigh the costs.*

- *Reform must be politically feasible—the leadership must be able to enact reform and overcome opposition.*
- *Reform must be credible—promises that the leadership makes to compensate losers and protect investors' property rights must be believable.*

Using objective and usually quantitative indicators to evaluate the evidence from our twelve country case studies, we found that each of these conditions was in fact necessary for successful SOE reform. Countries that reformed successfully satisfied all three at least partially; less successful reformers failed to meet at least one of them.

Our categorization of countries into more successful, mixed, and less successful reformers draws on the analysis in chapter 2. There, we first sorted countries by measures of SOE performance and then showed that good performance was associated with more extensive and sustained reform efforts. Our categorization in this chapter, therefore, reflects both reform efforts and reform outcomes. In chapter 2 we also used 1985 as a midpoint for the analysis because for most countries, except those undergoing the transition from central planning, this was close to the year that reforms started. We continue this practice in the analysis in this chapter.

This analysis is not a judgment about the countries or their governments. Rather, it assesses the obstacles that may prevent even the most effective and selfless leaders from undertaking SOE reform. Nor does the analysis in this section assess a country's actual reform record, which we have already done in previous chapters. Rather, it is an attempt to discover how countries that successfully reformed overcame obstacles that elsewhere stymied reform. In order to achieve this objective, we employ a methodology with three important characteristics. First, our measures of desirability, feasibility, and credibility, and the conclusions that we reach, are transparent and can be checked for accuracy and consistency. Most of our indicators are quantifiable, and six of the eleven are apolitical. Second, we use measures that can be observed independent of and prior to SOE reform attempts. In principle, this allows them to be used for prediction. Finally, we look at every indicator in every country. This marks a break with previous analysis, in which different criteria have been applied to different countries, making generalization difficult.

Nevertheless, the analysis still has limitations. Like all behavioral sciences, the study of political decisionmaking is complex. Variables, such as the intensity of constituent opinion or the qualities of individual leaders can change outcomes, but are difficult to measure and to use in a consistent, generalizable fashion. Political analyses that depend on such variables cannot therefore be easily tested to see if they are true or false, or if they have predictive power. Compared to such analyses, the approach pursued here focuses on variables that can be measured consistently and ex ante. Despite these advantages, however, the analysis, given its present state of development, will not always lead to unambiguous conclusions and predictions. We return to this point in chapter 5.

For reasons of space and clarity of argument, we have limited ourselves in this chapter to presenting selected examples of the ways in which the countries in our case studies met or failed to meet each of the three conditions. Our conclusions are not based on these examples alone but on the finding that the three conditions of reform readiness and the indicators we devised to measure them consistently explain the reform outcomes for our entire sample. For this reason, and because the country case studies are interesting in their own right, we have included material that could not be readily contained in the main text in an appendix to this chapter. Readers who wish to undertake similar analysis of countries not in our sample, as well as those interested in particular countries or conditions, are encouraged to consult the appendix. *As will be seen, our case studies suggest that if the minimum requirements for any one of these three conditions—political desirability, political feasibility, and credibility—are lacking, state-owned enterprise reform is not likely to succeed.*[1]

That all these conditions have to be met suggests the wisdom of avoiding simplistic conclusions. For example, the analysis provides no support for the frequently voiced opinion that SOE reform is more likely in authoritarian regimes than in democratic ones. In our sample, authoritarian governments exhibit both good and bad performance in the SOE sector. Chile under General Augusto Pinochet pursued SOE reforms that helped to lay the foundation for future rapid growth, albeit at great social cost. The Philippines under President Ferdinand Marcos went in the opposite direction, nationalizing private firms and putting up barriers to competition that contributed to economic stagnation and deeper poverty. Nor is there any clear link between democracy and SOE reform. During the period we examine, reform was slow in India, but rapid in the Czech Republic and Poland. In fact, these mixed results are to be expected. While reforms may be more *feasible* in authoritarian regimes, where the leadership need not achieve consensus before acting, the institutions that require consensus-building in democracies increase the *credibility* of the resulting policies, as we discuss below.

Assessing Condition I: Political Desirability

W E BEGIN WITH THE PROPOSITION THAT STATE-OWNED enterprise reform becomes desirable when the political benefits to the leadership and its constituencies outweigh the political costs. We would expect this to happen in two circumstances: either there are changes in the leadership and its constituencies, or there is an economic shock or crisis that alters the calculation of costs and benefits.[2]

The first circumstance arises when groups that benefit from the existing SOE policy and have the power to block reform lose their influence. This can happen because of a change in the regime or because of a shift in the composition of the governing coalition. These shifts lower the political costs of reforming SOEs that benefited the constituencies of earlier regimes.[3] The second circumstance involves shocks such as drought, a decline in foreign aid, or a sudden deterioration in the terms of trade that make it harder for the government to continue subsidizing inefficient SOEs. The size of the economic downturn needed to make reform politically desirable depends on how much the government relies on SOE support.[4] If groups that would lose from SOE reform are not a significant component of the leadership's support base, then the costs of reform to government decision-makers are low, and even a relatively minor economic downturn may be sufficient to make reform desirable to them (as in Korea in 1980). More frequently, however, beneficiaries of the SOE status quo who stand to lose *are* a crucial element of the leadership's support base (as in Egypt, India, and Turkey). In these cases, a crisis must be extremely large before the political benefits of reform outweigh the costs or before the constituencies opposed to reform suspend their resistance. Indeed, there was no instance in our sample where an economic shock alone was large enough to make SOE reform desirable to a government that relied heavily on SOE support.

For these reasons, we rate countries as having satisfied Condition I when they experience one of three circumstances:

- A regime change in which SOE interests are not part of the new leadership support base
- A coalition realignment with a similar effect[5]
- An exogenous shock, provided that the leadership does not depend on the SOE sector for support.

Evidence for these indicators ranges from electoral results to historical information on the role of SOEs in the political life of the country. In most cases, this evidence was available at the time reforms were being considered and could therefore, in principle, have been used to assess the political desirability of SOE reform. The record of the sample countries is summarized in table 4.1. Notes to the table describe the indicators that are used to measure the components of Condition I.

In our sample, the three most successful reformers among the non-transition economies, as well as the three transition economies, at least partially met Condition I; that is, reform was desirable to the leadership and its supporters. None of the countries with the poorer reform records met the condition. The remainder of this section describes the circumstances that made reform desirable in some countries but not in others.

Successful SOE Reformers: Chile, Mexico, and Korea

All three countries with more successful SOE reform records—Chile, Mexico, and the Republic of Korea—met Condition I. Chile and Mexico are described below. Korea, where both the costs and benefits to leaders and their constituents were low, is described in the appendix to this chapter.

Chile exhibited both a regime change and an economic crisis in 1973. There is no dispute that the military ouster of the Allende government and its replacement by the Pinochet regime in 1973 constituted a regime change. Moreover, a significant economic crisis accompanied, and perhaps precipitated, the military takeover. From 1972 to 1973, GDP declined 5.6 percent and real wages dropped 26 percent (Arriagada and Graham 1994).

Significant SOE reform could occur because, as Valenzuela (1978) documents, groups that benefited from the SOE status quo, particularly SOE employees, were not part of the new military government's support base. Although there were obviously no electoral results to document the sources of support of the Pinochet regime, its approach to state-

Table 4.1 Condition I for State-Owned Enterprise Reform: Political Desirability

Country	Period	Regime change or coalition realignment?[a]	Exogenous change?[b]	Are SOE reform losers outside the government support base?[c]
More successful SOE reformers				
Chile	1974–76	Yes	Yes	Yes
	1984–88	No	Yes	Yes
Republic of Korea	1983–90	No	Yes	Yes
Mexico	1982–88	Partial	Yes	Partially
	1988–94	Yes	No	Yes
Mixed SOE reformers				
Philippines	1986–	Yes	No	Partially
Egypt	1980s	No	Yes	No
Ghana	1983–92	Yes	No	Partially
Less successful SOE reformers				
India[d]	1980s	No	No	No
Senegal	1983–88	Yes	No	No
	1988–	No	No	No
Turkey	1983–91	Yes	No	No
	1991–	No	No	No
Transition economies				
China	1975–	Partial	No	Partially
Czech Republic	1989–	Yes	Yes	Partially
Poland	1989–	Yes	Yes	Partially

a. Regime change occurs when the party in power changes. Coalition realignment occurs when the party in power remains the same but the support base of the party shifts. In many cases, electoral data supports the conclusion about coalition realignment.

b. Exogenous events (like a drop in the terms of trade), as reflected in a decline in the growth rate or an increase in budget deficits and unemployment.

c. SOE sector support based on evidence (often electoral) of political allegiance of SOE employees.

Source: See text.

owned enterprises could nevertheless have been anticipated after the coup, but before extensive divestiture began, by analyzing the constituencies that supported and opposed President Allende. Miners, urban wage laborers, and skilled industrial workers, groups that include most SOE employees, were among President Allende's strongest supporters in the 1970 election. Conversely, the middle class and commercial, industrial, and rural elites were his strongest opponents (Valenzuela 1978, tables 13 and 15). Consistent with this pattern of support, the Allende government sharply expanded the number of SOEs, from sixty-eight to several hundred (Hachette and Lüders 1992; Bokil 1990). The

Pinochet regime subsequently privatized all but about thirty state-owned enterprises.[6] It also reformed the remaining SOEs to make them operate as if they were private firms, as discussed in chapter 2.

The evolution of Mexican SOE policy spans two presidential elections—the 1982 vote that brought Miguel de la Madrid to power and the 1988 election that Carlos Salinas won. Throughout this period, Mexico experienced economic crises and a gradual coalition realignment that diminished the SOE sector's importance to the leadership's support base. The pace of SOE reform reflected these economic and political changes.

Economic problems that raised the costs of not reforming were evident throughout President de la Madrid's 1982–88 term. The debt crisis of 1982 triggered a 17.5 percent drop in real manufacturing wages and increased the budget deficit to 15.6 percent of GDP (Kaufman, Bazaresch, and Heredia 1994). These economic events, combined with the coalition realignment that was under way in Mexico (box 4.1), created a political opening for the newly elected president to bring in a group of technocrats (among them Carlos Salinas), reducing the influence of SOEs in the party (the Partido Revolucionario Institucional, or PRI). Economic crisis reinforced the need for reform in 1986, when oil prices plummeted from $25 to $12 a barrel and the deficit rose from 8 to 15 percent of GDP, undoing earlier macroeconomic stabilization efforts.

Crisis preceded the decision to divest more than 600 of the country's nearly 1,200 state-owned enterprises between 1982 and 1988 and to introduce reforms in some of the remaining SOEs. Nonetheless, because SOE interests, particularly unions, continued to be important to the PRI's support base, the reforms the de la Madrid administration undertook were limited in scope. Few of the enterprises privatized were large; government revenues from privatization were highest during his final year in office, at $524 million (Cordón 1993b).

Reforms accelerated under the Salinas presidency following the culmination of the coalition realignment in the 1988 elections, in which many of the opponents of SOE reform supported a new party, the Partido Revolucionario Democrático (box 4.1). Since opponents of SOE reform were not part of President Salinas' winning coalition, the political costs of SOE reform were lower than they had been during the period 1982–88. This made it easier for the Salinas government to divest 200 SOEs between 1988 and 1992, selling off such large firms as TELMEX and the two state airlines. Privatization revenues during the first three years of the Salinas administration totaled $15 billion (Galal and others 1994).

Box 4.1 Indicators of Coalition Realignment—the Mexican Example

DETERMINING WHETHER A COALITION SHIFT has occurred within a single ruling party and assessing if and how such a shift might influence the political desirability of SOE reform require careful analysis of objective indicators. In the case of Mexico, three types of indicators support the view that SOE reform became increasingly politically deisirable under the de la Madrid and Salinas governments: the nature of policy shifts in other sectors of the economy, demographic shifts, and, perhaps most tellingly, electoral data.

Policy shifts in other sectors that are inimical to constituencies that favor the SOE status quo constitute one type of evidence. Many of the policy changes that Carlos Salinas introduced had been advocated by the right wing opposition party Partido de Acción Nacional (PAN). For example, the government imprisoned, on corruption charges, key labor and business beneficiaries of old economic policies (Waterbury 1993). It also repealed long-standing constitutional provisions that denied clergy the right to vote and that denied the Catholic Church the right to hold property or seek redress in the courts. The Salinas administration also supported changes in the constitution permitting private investment in lands formerly held under state regulated communal ownership. These moves changed policies that, together with support for state ownership, had been part of the core ideology of the PRI since the Mexican Revolution (Cordón 1993b).

Demographic changes, in the case of Mexico rural-to-urban migration, are another form of evidence of a coalition shift. The PRI had traditionally counted on strong rural support. In 1982, for example, eight out of ten rural voters opted for the PRI, compared with about half the voters in Mexico City (Molinar 1991). However, the proportion of the Mexican population living in rural areas fell sharply, from more than 40 percent in 1970 to about 26 percent in 1992. Since these new urban residents evidently did not go to work for urban SOEs (the share of SOE employment in total employment was about constant from 1978 to 1988; see statistical appendix, table A.5), the PRI could not expect to court their votes with its long-standing policies, which disproportionately benefited rural areas and the SOE sector. Not surprisingly, then, under President de la Madrid, the PRI began to revise its program to attract support from the growing urban commercial and middle classes, whose interests were not consistent with those of SOE workers.

Electoral and party changes constitute the last and clearest type of evidence of a coalition shift within the PRI. In response to the shift in policies pursued by President de la Madrid, many old-line PRI supporters left the party to support Cuauhtémoc Cárdenas, a son of the first PRI president. Cárdenas created the Partido de Reforma Democrática (PRD) and was its candidate in the presidential elections of 1988. His support base was chiefly composed of peasants and workers—among them many opponents of SOE reform who had previously supported the PRI (Cordón 1993b; Molinar and Weldon 1990).

Taken together with the economic crises documented in this chapter, these three indicators of a proreform coalitional realignment—changes in non-SOE policies inimical to SOE beneficiaries, rural-to-urban migration, and electoral and party shifts—strongly suggest that SOE reform became increasingly desirable to the Mexican leadership under the de la Madrid and Salinas governments.

Mixed SOE Reformers: Egypt, Ghana, and the Philippines

Of the three countries that exhibited mixed success in implementing SOE reforms in the 1980s, Egypt did not meet Condition I according to any of our indicators: there was neither a regime change nor a coalition shift and SOE employees were an important part of the leadership's support base. The other two countries with mixed reform records, Ghana and the Philippines, at least partially met Condition I because they experienced both significant political shifts that reduced the importance of SOE interests and economic crises that increased the costs of delaying reform. Even so, neither government abandoned entirely the use of SOEs as sources of patronage, thus limiting their motivation to reform. Moreover, as we shall see, reform feasibility was problematic in both countries. We discuss Egypt below and Ghana and the Philippines in the chapter appendix.

During the 1980s, Egypt faced increasingly serious economic difficulties: the fiscal deficit averaged about 10 percent of GDP, the highest among countries in our sample, and real per capita GDP growth averaged less than 2 percent per year. These problems, which might have made SOE reform politically desirable, did not for two reasons: first, the state-owned enterprise sector was large and important to the leadership's support base, so downsizing SOEs would have been politically costly; second, foreign aid may have helped to lighten the economic burden of state-owned enterprise subsidies.

It is difficult to use electoral data in Egypt to judge the role of SOEs in the government's support base. We therefore look to less readily quantifiable evidence to assess the political desirability of SOE reform. (For an example of similar methodology in very different circumstances, see the Condition I discussion of Korea in the chapter appendix.) According to Banerji and Sabot (1994), the Egyptian government has long used state-owned enterprises to provide jobs to college graduates to generate elite support. In the 1980s, SOEs accounted for about 14 percent of total employment (statistical appendix, table A.5), while total public sector employment approached 40 percent (Ayubi 1991)—some of the highest percentages in our sample. Ibrahim (1994) reports that by the 1980s, the General Confederation of Labor, a powerful alliance that included most SOE unions, had gained de facto veto power over government policy decisions affecting SOEs. On the other hand, there was no strong constituency in favor of SOE reform in the country.

Although these political obstacles raised the costs of SOE reform, Waterbury (1993) suggests that foreign capital inflows, mostly in the form of grants and highly concessional loans to the government, lowered the cost of maintaining the status quo, reducing the pressure to reform. From 1980 to 1989, partly due to these concessional loans, Egypt's debt increased from $20 billion to $49 billion. Most of these loans were not tied to economic reforms; instead, they were linked to political considerations arising from conflict in the Middle East. During this period, efforts to improve the SOE sector were few and minor. For example, SOEs were reorganized under holding companies, but this produced no fundamental changes in the way the firms operated. Real wages were allowed to decline by 50 percent from 1980–89. Although this decline was associated with a modest increase in profitability of the SOE sector in Egypt, productivity continued to deteriorate (see figures 2.1 and 2.2).

Toward the end of the decade, foreign loans and aid declined sharply, and this picture began to change. Net foreign aid inflows fell from more than 5 percent of GDP in 1980 to zero in 1988 and turned negative in 1989 (figure 4.1). Even so, the political influence of the SOE sector has caused the government to try to adjust without cutting back on support to state firms. While the government reduced the fiscal deficit from around 15 percent in the 1980s to around 5 percent in 1993, devalued its currency by 10 percent, and significantly raised petroleum and electricity prices, only a few small state-owned enterprises were privatized (Ibrahim 1994). By the early 1990s, the government had yet to sell or liquidate a significant number of SOEs or to make a meaningful reduction in the level of redundancy in the SOE work force.

Less Successful SOE Reformers: India, Senegal, and Turkey

None of the less successful reformers in our sample met Condition I. SOE reform was undesirable to significant segments of the support base of the leaders in each of these three countries—India, Senegal, and Turkey. India did not experience a regime change or coalition realignment. Moreover, neither the governing party nor any other major party in India had a support base that favored SOE reform. An economic crisis might have altered this picture, but India did not experience a sharp economic crisis in the 1980s that would have led any of these constituent groups to reverse their opposition to SOE reform. Senegal and Turkey experienced significant changes of government but, as in India, the SOE

Figure 4.1 Net Aid Flows to Egypt

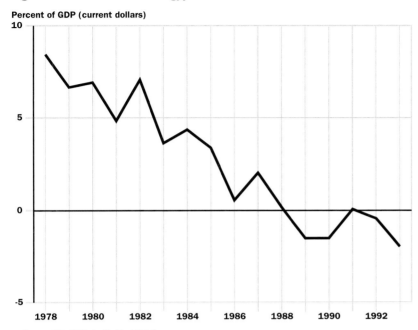

Percent of GDP (current dollars)

Source: World Debt Tables (1994).

High aid flows to Egypt in the early 1980s may have helped offset the high costs of SOEs.

sector remained as important in the support base of the new governments as it was in the old. We illustrate this second situation with a discussion of Senegal. Our assessments of the political desirability of reform in India and Turkey are explained in the chapter appendix.

Senegal, like Mexico, experienced a coalition change and an economic crisis. However, unlike Mexico, Senegal did not meet Condition I because of the continuing political importance of the SOE sector in the new coalition and the sizable amounts of foreign aid that it received. The coalition shift took place in 1980 when, after decades as president and head of the Socialist Party, Léopold Senghor relinquished his posts to Abdou Diouf, who had been prime minister. This shift in leadership took place in the midst of plummeting real GDP and an exploding budget deficit.[7]

Like Mexico's PRI, Ka and van de Walle (1994) observe that Senegal's Socialist Party had both pro- and antireform elements; and, as in the Mexican case, a coalition realignment was signaled when the outgoing president selected a technocratic successor. However, Diouf's ability to mold a technocratic government was initially more constrained than that of President Salinas, since President Diouf had not been popularly elected and was therefore more dependent on the party apparatus for political support. To consolidate his influence, he held multiparty legislative and presidential elections in 1983, which he won with more than 80 percent of the vote. Ka and van de Walle (1994) describe a convincing signal of coalition change when they relate that after the election, the president replaced many of the party old guard with more technically qualified officials.

The election and economic crisis were sufficient to allow the Diouf government to undertake a series of important economic reforms.[8] The role of SOEs in these reforms was relatively modest, however; although twenty-eight of the country's eighty-five SOEs were sold or liquidated by 1991, the largest and costliest remained in state hands. Budget support for all SOEs declined only slightly, from 6.3 percent of government expenditures in 1988–89 to 5 percent in 1990–91 (Ka and van de Walle 1994). As chapter 2 demonstrates, SOE performance in Senegal continued to lag other countries in the sample.

Two of the reasons why these political changes did not result in SOE reforms becoming desirable to the leadership in Senegal could have been observed beforehand. First, in contrast with Mexico, the SOE sector remained a key supporter of the dominant party. President Diouf consistently pursued a policy of co-optation, of bringing competing elements, including the SOE sector, into the political base of the government (Ka and van de Walle 1994); this effectively raised the cost of SOE reform compared with Mexico, making it less likely. Second, substantial foreign aid cushioned Senegal from the full effect of the crisis (figure 4.2). For example, foreign grants-in-aid were sufficient to reduce the 1986–87 budget deficit from 4 percent to 2 percent of GDP (Haggard and Webb 1994). Aid did not relieve Senegal of the necessity to undertake some type of reform; both the policy conditionality that donors placed on Senegal and the depths of its crisis required that broad economic policy reforms be attempted. However, inadequately conditioned aid allowed the government to postpone or moderate politically difficult SOE reforms that might otherwise have been seen as necessary.[9] The sharp fall in net aid flows in the mid-1980s coincided with the initiation of a new reform effort, but the continued importance of those who would lose from SOE reform in the government's support base meant that reform was still not seen as politically desirable.

Figure 4.2 Net Aid Flows to Senegal

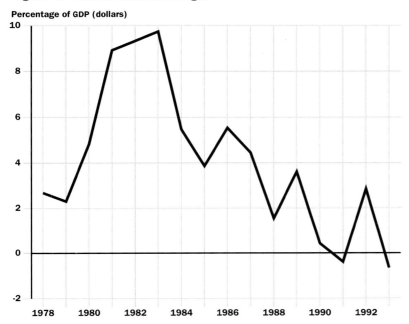

Percentage of GDP (dollars)

Source: World Debt Tables (1994).

In Senegal, significant aid flows through most of the 1980s accompanied lackluster SOE reforms.

Transition Economies: The Czech Republic, Poland, and China

The conditions that make SOE reform politically desirable in transition economies broadly resemble those in the other economies we consider. The influence of proreform groups ebbs and flows with coalition realignments or regime changes; economic shocks provide the same impetus for reform; the presence of opponents of SOE reform in a government's support base similarly arrests reform progress. However, in most transition economies, the SOE sector has embraced nearly the entire industrial work force, creating an imposing force that would usually resist reform. One would therefore not expect SOE reform to have occurred in the transition economies in the absence of radical political shifts and severe economic crises. Both of these occurred in the Czech Republic and Poland; in China, political changes have been much less dramatic in recent years, as have its SOE reforms. However, all three transition countries at least partially meet Condition I. To illustrate, we briefly discuss all three countries.

In the Czech Republic and Poland, the political transition away from the Communist regime constituted a fundamental rejection of totalitarian government and state control of daily life. Because the SOE sector was closely associated with the deposed governments, SOE reform has faced fewer obstacles—even from workers in the sector—than it has in countries that did not experience such a dramatic social and political change. Although we rank all three transition countries as meeting Condition I at least partially, differences in the ways and degree to which SOE reforms became politically desirable help us to understand the different courses that reform has so far taken in these three countries.

Consider the contrast between the Czech Republic and Poland. In the Czech Republic, the primary reform vehicle has been rapid, mass privatization through vouchers (see below, in box 4.4), without preferential considerations for SOE workers. In Poland, ownership changes have proceeded more slowly, and SOE workers have retained a greater stake in the privatized enterprises, even though the budget constraints imposed on Poland's SOEs are at least as hard as those faced by newly privatized and state-owned enterprises in the Czech Republic. These distinctions are explained in part by the differing abilities of SOE workers and management in the two countries to impose costs on leaders inclined toward SOE reform. Unions did not play a significant role in ending Communist rule in the Czech Republic. As a consequence, the unions have not had a strong voice in policymaking and were unable to prevent a form of voucher privatization that gave SOE workers no advantage in the final distribution of SOE ownership rights. In contrast, the Polish trade federation Solidarnosc was instrumental in ending Communist rule and was influential in early transition governments. Even though the political coalition that emerged from Solidarnosc splintered into different parties, the influence of SOE employees has declined only gradually (Milor 1994). SOE workers in Poland, consequently, have been able to claim a greater share of the ownership in privatized enterprises.

China's movement toward SOE reform has been more incremental, and is motivated by coalition changes analogous to those that occurred in some of the nontransition countries that undertook reforms. Following the death of Mao Zedong in 1975, an internecine political conflict began between the "Gang of Four" and Deng Xiaoping from which the latter emerged triumphant in 1978. His victory marked a significant coalition shift. Evidence for this shift is the rise in the number of retired cadres (Communist Party officials) beginning in 1980, as Deng made room for younger technocrats (Manion 1993).[10] The coalition realignment reinforced reforms, such as the expansion of the TVE sector, which operates with a hard budget constraint (box 4.2). However, although supporters of the traditional SOE sector were weakened as a consequence of the coalition realignment, they are still a key constituency of segments

Box 4.2   State Enterprise Reform in China

THE MOST SIGNIFICANT ENTERPRISE REFORMS IN CHINA HAVE involved the Township and Village Enterprises (TVEs) and were essentially an outgrowth of agricultural reforms. Deng Xiaoping took power in the midst of a series of provincial experiments in agricultural decollectivization, which had become acceptable because of continuing agricultural stagnation. By 1981, the government in Beijing formally endorsed this movement and by 1983, most farm households in China had implemented it (Lall 1994). While decollectivization of agriculture was successful in raising farm production, it also significantly increased open unemployment in the rural sector and reduced local government revenue. TVEs were seen by various levels of government as a way to provide alternative employment to newly unemployed peasants who would otherwise have migrated to the cities, as catalysts of rural growth, and as a way to replace lost government revenue. From 1985 to 1990, TVEs grew rapidly, for reasons that we discussed in chapter 2.

Improvements in state enterprises in China have been incremental, however, and of uncertain utility. Beginning in 1978, the government increased the autonomy of state enterprises by giving them greater control over their aftertax profits. To forestall potential opposition from local authorities, who otherwise stood to lose their influence over the use of enterprise funds, the central government granted them supervisory and administrative control over enterprises in their jurisdictions. By the mid-1980s, state enterprises controlled by provincial, county, and municipal authorities accounted for 54 percent of industrial output, while those controlled by the central government accounted for only 20 percent (Lall 1994). Despite this shift, however, massive subsidies have continued. As we saw in chapter 2, the share of SOEs in industrial output declined from 80 percent in 1978 to 50 percent in 1991; but this was due largely to the rise of private enterprises and TVEs rather than to fundamental reforms in the SOE sector itself (Gelb and Singh 1994).

of the Communist Party (Shirk 1993). Moreover, there continues to be only limited acceptance, even among the ruling coalition, of private ownership. Reforms in the SOE sector have therefore been limited to performance contracts, greater autonomy, and other management innovations. These reforms and competitive pressures from TVEs have increased productivity (chapter 2), but a large flow of subsidies to state-owned enterprises continues, and there is little to suggest that the problem of overstaffing has diminished. Because of the coalition realignment and the fact that some supporters of the SOE sector were eased out of the governing coalition, however, China partially meets Condition I.

Assessing Condition II: The Political Feasibility of SOE Reform

WE HAVE SHOWN THAT STATE-OWNED ENTERPRISE REform only succeeds if the leadership or governing coalition considers it desirable. But desirability is only the first step. Reform must also be politically feasible. This requires that the leadership be able to implement reform, first by securing the approval and support of other parts of government whose cooperation is critical to success—legislatures, bureaucracies, and the state or provincial governments that are responsible for formulating policy or carrying out the reform. Even if the leadership's constituencies support reform, making reform desirable, constituencies of these other parts of government may not, creating obstacles for the feasibility of reform. Second, the leadership must be able to withstand opposition to reform. Although reform becomes desirable when reform opponents are no longer important constituents, that does not mean that the leadership can ignore the losers altogether, especially if they are a vocal minority prepared to engage in strikes and protests.

If a reform-minded leadership controls all parts of the government responsible for making and implementing policy, it will, by definition, have no trouble securing their approval and support. This can be determined in several ways. Obviously, reformers in democracies are likely to dominate policymaking when they control a majority of the seats in the legislature and have the power to appoint and remove bureaucrats and state governors. But when the leadership lacks a legislative majority or is unable to control the bureaucracy or state and local governments, and these entities oppose SOE reform, then the process becomes more complex and perhaps slower. Reformers must then attempt to forge a coalition in favor of change, and this is not always possible.[11]

Control of policymaking and policy implementation may not be enough, however, if SOE employees or other groups who stand to lose from SOE reform are so determined in their opposition that they go outside the usual political process and resort to strikes, demonstrations, or other forms of civil disobedience. Such resistance is more likely when opponents are organized and numerous, when they have previously staged strikes to block earlier government policy changes, and when they stand to lose a great deal from SOE reforms. The last situation exists when SOE staffing or wage levels are significantly higher than they would be if the enterprises were divested or otherwise reformed. In some cases, resistance is so costly to the leadership, economically and politically, that reform becomes unfeasible. This risk is greater if employees in strategic sectors, such as telecommunications or electricity, engage in work stoppages.

Leaders can offset resistance through a combination of compensation and compulsion—for example, by offering fired workers severance payments and by banning strikes in strategic industries or otherwise reducing labor union power. However, these actions are also costly, and not only in economic terms.[12] Compulsion, in particular, often exacts high social costs. Moreover, policies implemented through coercion are often not sustainable.

These considerations are especially germane for authoritarian governments. The leadership in an authoritarian regime may have more control over policymaking than the leadership in a nonauthoritarian regime; whether a country has a more or less authoritarian form of government is therefore a strong indicator of feasibility (although not of desirability or credibility). Even so, authoritarian regimes, like democracies, face tradeoffs in overcoming resistance to SOE reforms. While authoritarian regimes are more likely than democracies to ignore or suppress opposition, they also bear social, political, and economic costs from doing so, particularly when opposition is strong and well organized.

How can we predict the extent of opposition to reform? One clue is the extent of overstaffing in state-owned enterprises targeted for reform. If we define overstaffing as the employment of a work force larger than some efficient level, the extent of overstaffing tells us what fraction of

SOE employees would lose their jobs as a result of SOE reform. Estimates of SOE overstaffing have been made for five countries in our sample. Although the estimating methods differ, a rough comparison is nonetheless revealing. Egypt, India, and Turkey, three countries where little progress has been made in SOE reform, exhibit higher levels of overstaffing than Chile and Ghana (table 4.2), which undertook more significant SOE reforms.[13] In general, SOEs comprised a substantially larger fraction of formal sector employment among the poorer countries in our sample, providing one explanation for their lack of success in reforming relative to the richer countries.

The analysis of whether reform was politically feasible for countries in our sample is summarized in table 4.3. Since figures on overstaffing

Table 4.2 Estimates of Overstaffing in State-Owned Enterprises

Country	Year	Sector/state-owned enterprise	Overstaffing (percentage of labor force)	Source	Basis of estimate[a]
Chile	1974	SOEs before 1970	17 (1970)	Hachette (1988)	C
		SOEs nationalized after 1970	24 (1970)	Hachette (1988)	C
Egypt	1973	Manufacturing SOEs[b]	58	El-Issawy (1983)	A
		Trade, hotel, etc., SOEs[b]	52	El-Issawy (1983)	
	1975	Textile SOEs	70–80	Handoussa (1983)	B1
		Delta Spinning and Weaving	93 (in spinning)	Handoussa (1983)	
		Dahkalia Textile Mill	92	Handoussa (1983)	
	1980	Misr Foreign Trade Company	50	Rivlin (1985)	C
		Abu Zamal Pharmaceuticals	55	Rivlin (1985)	
	1990	All nonfinancial SOEs	10	USAID (1990)	
	1991	Steel and cement SOEs	20–80	World Bank (1991a)	
Ghana	1978	State Railways	28	Svejnar and Terrell (1981)	C
	1987	State Transport Corporation	54	Svejnar and Terrell (1981)	
	1989	City Express Bus Service	50–55	Svejnar and Terrell (1981)	
India	1987	Telecommunications	19–80	World Bank data	B2
	1980s	Bombay Port, container section	91	Svejnar and Terrell (1981)	C
	1988	Central SOEs	up to 40	World Bank data	B2
	1990	Steel, chemicals, textiles	more than 33	World Bank data	B2
		Central SOEs	25–33	World Bank data	B2
Turkey	1993	All SOEs	33	World Bank (1993)	C
		TCDD (railways)	40	World Bank (1993)	

a. A: compared to private sector; B1: compared to European firms; B2: compared to Pakistan (1987), Thailand (1988), and Singapore (1987); C: compared to optimal use of existing technology.
b. Administrative staff only.
Source: Banerji and Sabot (1994).

Table 4.3 Condition II for State-Owned Enterprise Reform: Political Feasibility
(prior to 1990)

Country		Could reformers secure approval? Why or why not?		Were compensation packages or compulsion used?
More successful SOE reformers				
Chile	Yes	Military government	Yes	Severance pay, share distribution, labor restrictions
Republic of Korea	Yes	Military government	Yes	Incentives for better performance
Mexico	Yes	PRI majority in legislature	Yes	Share distribution, labor restrictions
Mixed SOE reformers				
Philippines	Partially	Executive lacks legislative majority	No	No compensation program
Egypt	Yes	Executive has a majority in legislature	No	No compensation program
Ghana	No	Military government	Partially	Severance packages offered but eventually discontinued
Less successful SOE reformers				
India	No	No legislative majority in favor of reform	No	No compensation program
Senegal	Yes	Socialist Party majority in legislature	No	No compensation program
Turkey 1983–91	Yes	Motherland Party majority in legislature	Yes	Restrictions on labor activity
1991–	No	Coalition partner resistance after 1990	No	Restrictions removed
Transition economies				
China	Partially	Reformers have incomplete control of party decisionmaking	No	No compensation program for traditional SOE sector
Czech Republic	Yes	Executive has a majority in legislature	Partially	Share distribution program: limited compensation for laid-off workers
Poland	Partially	Resistance from coalition partners	Partially	Packages negotiated firm by firm; limited compensation for laid-off workers

Source: See text.

are not available for all our sample countries, our evaluation of whether resistance outside normal political channels would frustrate reform relies in part on whether plans were in place to entice or oblige workers to comply. Unlike overstaffing data, information on compensation is more difficult to use for predictive purposes but can nevertheless be used to assess past reform efforts and to improve reform design. In individual country discussions, we also consider such information as the past history of strikes in a country and the absolute and relative size of the SOE work force as indicators of the potential for significant opposition. We considered reform politically feasible in countries that show a "yes" in both columns; that is, reformers were able to secure the agreement of all relevant policymaking entities in the state, *and* they were able to overcome resistance from the SOE sector to the policy through some combination of compensation and compulsion. As the table indicates, the three more successful reformers in our sample all fulfilled Condition II, as did, at least partially, all three transition economies.

Successful SOE Reformers

Chile, Mexico, and Korea, the three countries in our sample of non-transition economies that had more successful records of SOE reform, all fulfilled Condition II. It happens that these countries concentrated most or all political authority in the hands of the executive branch. This is not necessary for reform, however, as the Polish and Czech examples amply demonstrate. Because authority in these three countries rested with the executive branch, however, legislatures did not play a significant policymaking role in any of these countries at the time of reform. Consequently, the leadership of all three controlled the state-owned enterprise policymaking apparatus. Gaining consensus among policymaking entities was therefore not a significant constraint on carrying out SOE reforms. In addition, where necessary, these countries were successful in designing policies to overcome resistance from SOE employees and others outside the policy process. The discussion below focuses on how Chile overcame SOE resistance. The Mexican and Korean cases are described in the chapter appendix.

General Pinochet's military government had full control of SOE policymaking (and other types of policymaking) from the time of the 1973 coup. It also avoided and suppressed resistance with both compensation and compulsion, often using harsh measures. As figure 4.3 reveals, SOE reforms resulted in substantial layoffs, suggesting that overstaffing in some SOEs was significant and that resistance to the reform measures could have been severe.[14] Moreover, the demonstrations and strikes that occurred under the Allende government, for whatever reason, were evidence that such forms of opposition could arise in Chile.

The first round of SOE reforms, during the 1970s, centered on the reprivatization of enterprises that had been effectively nationalized during Salvatore Allende's rule.[15] In returning these enterprises to their

Figure 4.3 Chile: Employment Reduction in Selected State-Owned Enterprises

Company (sector: years)

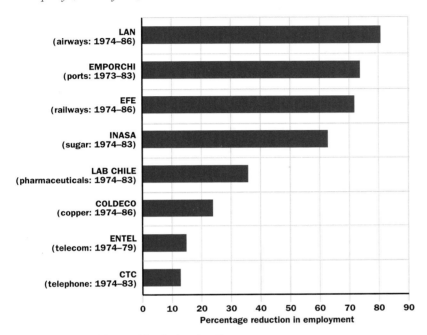

Percentage reduction in employment

Chile sharply reduced employment in some of its state-owned enterprises in the course of reform.

Source: Calculated from Galal and others (1992).

owners, the military regime argued that the Allende government had seized control illegally and that any hiring subsequent to the intervention was also illegal. Thus, workers hired during President Allende's rule who subsequently lost their jobs were not compensated. Also during the first round of reform, other SOEs began to rationalize their work force and pay levels; many of these firms were privatized during the second round of reform in the 1980s. Although the military government overcame resistance to the first round of reforms in part by strictly enforcing new labor laws that severely curtailed union activity and banned strikes, it relied to a limited degree on inducements, as box 4.3 illustrates.

The second round of reform covered two types of enterprises: banks and other firms that the military had privatized during the 1970s but that had gone bankrupt during the 1981–82 economic crisis and were again taken over by the government (due in part to flaws in the design of the 1970s privatization process discussed in box 2.9); and large industrial and utility monopolies, such as electricity and telecommunications, that had been state-owned for decades. The government began to return the renationalized banks and firms to the private sector immediately after the crisis, through a program it termed "popular capitalism" (box 4.3).

Box 4.3 Compensation of Reform Losers in Chilean SOE Reforms

ROUND I. MOST WORKERS WHO WERE LAID OFF IN THE EARLY round of SOE reforms in Chile were not compensated. In the dramatically overstaffed national railway corporation, EFE, for which trucks and coastal maritime transport provided good substitutes in case of strikes, the government laid off 3,000 employees in 1975 and offered only compensation approved by law, which amounted to six months' severance pay or less for employees with less than fifteen years of service (Svejnar and Terrell 1990). However, the government made significant efforts to cushion the reform blow for those in strategic industries. In 1981, the government sought to eliminate the closed shop of the trade unions and the generous work rules of EMPORCHI, the National Ports Authority. Because the ports were a key part of the government's export-oriented economic strategy, avoiding strikes or other job actions in response to these measures was a priority. Port workers were offered amounts averaging $19,000 to accept these changes (Svejnar and Terrell 1990).

Round II. The SOEs that the government reacquired during the 1981–82 crisis were divested through "popular capitalism." Taxpayers were allowed to buy shares in the companies in exchange for a small down payment (approximately equal to a year's expected dividends), with the balance to be paid over fifteen years at 0 percent interest (Martin del Campo and Winkler 1991). Limits on the number of shares that could be purchased by an individual were set according to the amount of taxes paid, on the grounds that tax money had been used to rescue these enterprises during the crisis (Cordón 1993a). In privatizing more traditional, state utility-type SOEs, public employees, including military personnel, and the general public were given the option of purchasing additional shares through various generous financing alternatives that the government made available. One of these was to allow individuals to buy shares with a small down payment, with the remainder to be paid out of company dividends (Martin del Campo and Winkler 1991).

In 1984, the government began to privatize large, monopoly SOEs. Of these, Cordón (1993a) reports that utilities posed a particular challenge to the regime, in part because many Chileans considered government ownership of such firms appropriate. For example, he writes that within the junta itself, the air force expressed substantial reservations about the privatization of telecommunications. In addition, these reforms took place after the considerable social unrest that began during the 1982 economic crisis: demonstrations occurred for the first time under the military government, and armed opposition groups began to operate (Cordón 1993a). The government responded to these difficulties by allowing workers, inhabitants of regions where the SOEs were located, and the general public to acquire shares on favorable terms. These policies defused much of the opposition to the second round of SOE reforms and increased support for the government's policies generally (Cordón 1993a).[16] Box 4.3 provides a brief description of them.

Mixed SOE Reformers

Among the countries that exhibited mixed success in SOE reform, the Philippines could not satisfy the feasibility requirement, and Ghana and Egypt fulfilled it only partially. We leave a description of Egypt's ability to meet Condition II to the chapter appendix. Our discussion here focuses on Ghana, which met Condition I and partly met Condition II, and the Philippines, which fulfilled Condition I but not Condition II because reformers lacked control of the legislature and bureaucracy.

President Rawlings' government controlled policymaking in Ghana through most of the 1980s and into the 1990s. However, it was only in 1985, after the government took steps to defuse opposition, that SOE reforms accelerated. First, as Ninsin (1991) documents, the government strengthened its ability to exercise compulsion by bringing senior army officers into government; it subsequently reorganized the labor unions, reducing the power of the Industrial and Commercial Workers Union, which represented most SOE workers, and detained labor leaders critical of SOE reform. During this period, reform was at least partially feasible.

By 1988, however, reforms became less feasible and the costs of suppressing dissent and compensating losers became too great. As figure 4.4 illustrates, actual SOE layoffs (called "redeployments" in Ghana) dropped below planned layoffs in 1987, and reform eventually stopped alto-

Figure 4.4 Ghana: Planned and Actual Employment Reductions in SOEs

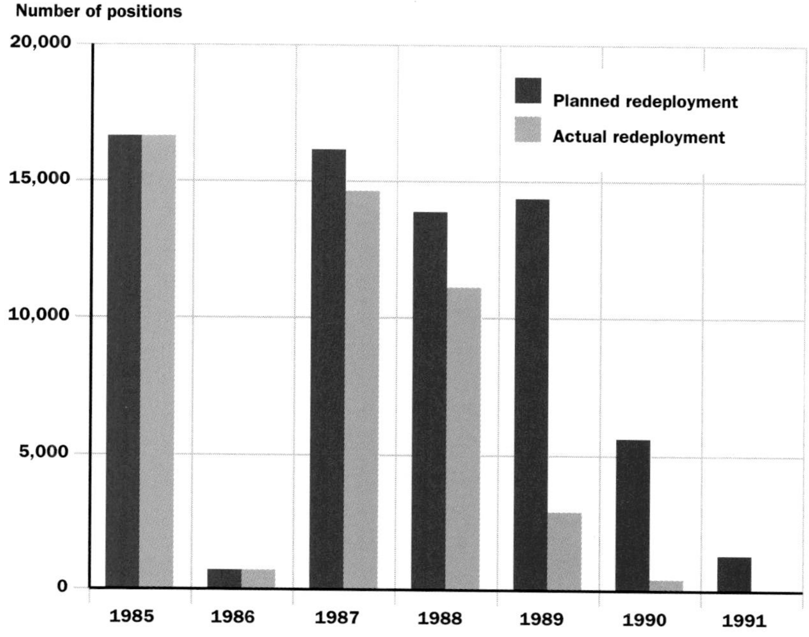

Number of positions

Legend:
- Planned redeployment
- Actual redeployment

By 1988, SOE reforms in Ghana began to slow.

Source: State Enterprises Commission (1991, 1993).

gether. In 1991, severance payments negotiated with unions rose to between three and six months' pay per year of service. Unable to afford such high compensation, the government slowed and eventually abandoned efforts to reduce overstaffing in SOEs. There are two explanations for the upward evolution of severance payments. First, June and July of 1987 were marked by an attempted coup, clashes between trade unions and the government, and student demonstrations (EIU 1987). Second, district elections took place in 1988. Both of these events dissuaded the government from using compulsion and raised the severance payments that the government was willing to pay to redundant workers.

Workers in Ghana had often demonstrated the ability and willingness to strike, which also increased their bargaining power. Ghanaian railway workers struck in 1950, 1961, and 1971. From 1977 to 1981, Ghana lost more than 200,000 worker-days per year to strikes. Although this number dropped to zero in 1982, President Rawlings' first full year in office, it increased to 40,000 in 1983 (Herbst 1991). This indicator of potential opposition, known prior to the onset of SOE reform, could in principle be used as an ex ante indicator that SOE reforms would be less than completely feasible.

In Ghana, the executive controls policymaking, but SOE reform faces a substantial risk of resistance outside policymaking channels. In the Philippines, in contrast, obstacles to the feasibility of reform arose from the executive's partial control of the policymaking and implementing apparatus. Since the end of the Marcos regime and the restoration of democracy in 1986, neither President Aquino nor President Ramos has had control over the legislature, the bureaucracy, or the courts. As in the U.S. system, the Filipino legislature can block policy reforms, and neither post-Marcos president has headed a party with a majority in the legislature. Instead, each has had to rely on an often fragile coalition of several parties to pass initiatives through the legislature. President Aquino headed a coalition made up of more than six parties, but this coalition disintegrated well before the end of her six-year term. President Ramos heads a party that took only 33 of 200 seats in the House and 2 of 24 in the Senate. Although he has since had some success in forging stronger legislative coalitions, opponents of SOE reform in the legislature have been able to slow its pace and reduce its scope. Taken together with the absence of a compensation scheme, this suggests that SOE reform was not politically feasible in the Philippines in the late 1980s and early 1990s.

Less Successful Reformers

All three countries in our sample with poor records of SOE reform did not meet Condition I—that is, the leadership did not consider SOE reform to be politically desirable. Here we note briefly how each country ranked on Condition II (see the chapter appendix for details).

- India did not meet the requirements of Condition II. There was legislative resistance to SOE reform and a high potential for resistance to reform outside political channels.
- Turkey met Condition II during the 1980s but did not meet Condition I—that is, reform was politically feasible but not politically desirable. Accordingly SOE reforms were not implemented. During the 1990s, new leadership that might have favored SOE reform was able to govern only with the support of a

coalition partner opposed to reform, making reform both politically undesirable and politically infeasible.

- Senegal, like Turkey, met Condition II only during the early part of the period. While there was no change of leadership, shifting coalition arrangements and social unrest reduced the power of the leadership so that the political conditions for SOE reform were worse at the end of the period than at the beginning.

Transition Economies

The political feasibility of SOE reform in Central Europe differs from that in the developing-market economies in a fundamental respect. In most of the countries in our sample, SOEs were established after independence from colonial powers, as in Ghana, or as part of an ongoing effort to reaffirm nationalist goals, as in Egypt or India. They were therefore associated with political developments that many citizens, particularly intellectuals, enthusiastically favored. These positive associations increase resistance to SOE reform, making it less feasible. In the Czech Republic and Poland, on the other hand, SOEs are associated with imposed Communist regimes, so despite the very large SOE sector, resistance to reform has been comparatively modest. Therefore, we class the Czech Republic and Poland as meeting Condition II at least partially, despite the unprecedented magnitude of the reforms and the fact that the leadership in these countries did not enjoy parliamentary majorities. China more closely resembles the other countries in our sample. State enterprises were established as part of a movement that had broad support, and there is little indication that the leadership favors significant SOE reform. This means that China only partially meets Condition II. This section summarizes some of the main considerations for each of these countries. Additional analysis of Poland is supplied in the chapter appendix.

Both Polish and Czech leaders had to contend with coalition governments. These can make reform difficult by increasing the chances that opponents of SOE reform will be part of the government. However, as the discussion of political desirability above suggests, the leadership in the Czech Republic has enjoyed firmer control over the policymaking entities and has confronted less organized resistance from SOE workers than the leadership in Poland. The first privatization law was approved in Czechoslovakia in 1991, before the dissolution of the Czechoslovak federation, when the Slovakian representatives in the parliament were almost as numerous as the Czechs.[17] Passage occurred despite the tepid support of Slovakia for privatization (which was widely known at the time and confirmed by the subsequent slowdown of privatization in Slovakia after the dissolution). Subsequently, legislative support in the Czech Republic for SOE reform has only strengthened. Since the 1992 elections, after dissolution, the Civic Democratic Union, led by Vaclav Klaus, has held a significant legislative plurality of 76 out of 200 seats.

In Poland, on the other hand, coalition partners often opposed SOE reform. Securing legislative approval of voucher privatization was therefore easier in the Czech Republic than in Poland. Unable to establish a legislative consensus for Czech-style mass ownership changes, reform-oriented policymakers in Poland have instead imposed hard budget constraints and allowed so-called "spontaneous" privatizations, neither of which requires legislative approval. In Poland, as in most other countries, hard budget constraints can be imposed by finance ministries and central banks without legislative agreement. Similarly, "spontaneous" privatizations, in which SOE assets are transferred to workers after negotiations with supervisory agencies, need not be approved by the legislature. Thus the overall approach to reform in each country has been shaped by what was politically feasible.

The contrasting compensation schemes adopted in the two countries also reflect differences in political feasibility. In the Czech Republic, SOE managers have been able to influence the style of SOE reform (although not the pace of it) in two ways. First, as Milor (1994) notes, some Ministry of Industry officials, who had a voice in approving privatization plans for companies, were themselves former SOE managers and sympathetic to the concerns of SOE managers. Second, plans for individual SOE privatizations were often prepared by enterprise managers (Milor 1994). The government's strategy of universal share distribution (box 4.4) not only increased popular support for privatization, but also overcame the objections of managers. It opened the possibility that the ownership of the divested enterprises would be diffuse, allowing managers to retain control, even if their ownership shares in the company were small.[18] In Poland, on the other hand, not only have SOE employees had greater influence in policy formulation (see political desirability above), they have also had greater legal rights to the state-owned enterprises where they work. Consequently, they have been able to extract a higher level of compensation—typically in the form of ownership rights in the privat-

Box 4.4 Mass Privatization through Vouchers in the Czech Republic

THE VOUCHER PRIVATIZATION PROGRAM IN THE Czech Republic has proven to be an effective way to transfer assets in an economy with limited savings while ensuring popular support and avoiding criticism that privatization is benefiting a few individuals at the expense of many. The program is straightforward: each adult who registers and pays an administrative fee of kr 1,035 (about $35) receives a voucher booklet worth 1,000 investment points. The points can be used to purchase stocks directly or through investment funds, which pool points from many individuals. To address the pricing problem common to initial offerings, shares in the first round of bidding were assigned a point price based on the book value of the firm. If bids for shares at the initial price were equal to or less than the supply of shares, then all bidders were allotted their shares, and any remaining shares were offered in a second round of bidding at a lower price. If demand exceeded supply by more than 25 percent, shares were not distributed but were offered again at a higher price. If the demand exceeded supply by less than 25 percent, shares were distributed, with individuals getting preference over institutional investors.

Privatization Investment Funds (PIFs), which spontaneously emerged, offered to manage vouchers on behalf of recipients by choosing which enterprises to purchase with their points. In 1994, there were about 290 PIFs, with the thirteen largest controlling about 35 percent of all privatized shares (Milor 1994). Of the largest seven PIFs, six are managed by banks, which themselves are objects of the voucher privatization scheme. Most of the PIFs are privately managed and loosely regulated.

The program has been very effective at moving enterprises from the state to the private sector. During the first wave of voucher privatizations in 1992, the state divested itself of 946 companies with a book value of kr 208 billion ($7 billion). Nearly six million people, or about 75 percent of the adult population, became shareholders. The second wave of voucher privatizations began in late 1993, with approximately 861 companies with a book value of about kr 150 billion ($5 billion) slated to be privatized. The popularity of the voucher privatization process can be measured by the fact that about 230,000 more people signed up for the second wave of privatizations than the first.

Source: Gelb and Singh (1994); Sephton (1993); de Keijzer (1993); Klaus (1994); Ceska (1994).

---

ized firm—in exchange for allowing reforms to proceed. (See the chapter appendix for details.)

China also partially meets Condition II, although less fully than the Eastern European countries in our sample; this, together with China's weaker performance on Condition I, helps to explain why China has moved more slowly on SOE reform. While there is evidence of the ability of China's leadership to employ harsh measures to implement reforms in general, the use of these measures still requires consensus among different parts of the government about SOE reforms in particular. For SOE reform in China to be politically feasible, therefore, the reformers would have to control the various organs of the Communist Party, including those at the provincial and city levels, as well as the party's governing bodies at the center. The incomplete coalition re-alignment noted in the discussion of Condition I suggests that this control does not yet prevail. Resistance outside political channels to significant reform of the large SOE sector is also likely to be strong, given the tens of millions of well organized and potentially disruptive state-owned enterprise workers whose jobs or pay levels could be threatened by reform. Under these conditions, it is perhaps not surprising that the government has taken a gradual approach to SOE reform and has avoided the privatization of any major state enterprise.

Assessing Condition III: The Credibility of State-Owned Enterprise Reform

THE THIRD AND FINAL CONDITION FOR SUCCESSFUL STATE-owned enterprise reform is government credibility. The ability of the leadership to minimize resistance and to marshal the support of investors depends in large part on the expectation that government will keep its promises. These promises are of two types: promises to compensate people, particularly SOE workers, who stand to lose from SOE reform; and promises to investors that the government will establish a policy regime conducive to profitable operations and refrain from re-nationalizing or otherwise expropriating privatized assets.

- *Promises to SOE reform losers:* As we have seen in the discussion of political feasibility, SOE workers and managers, and others who stand to lose their jobs or suffer wage cuts due to SOE reform, often seek immediate compensation for their losses. But governments commonly lack the resources to make immediate payments, particularly when, as is frequently the case, they have initiated SOE reform in response to fiscal crisis (Dewatripont and Roland 1993). If governments can credibly promise future compensation, they can overcome this shortage of current resources. However, governments whose promises are not regarded as credible face much higher immediate costs and may be forced to reduce the scope and speed of reform or even to abandon reform altogether. *Thus, the government's ability to credibly promise future compensation to likely losers is crucial to successful reform.*

- *Promises to investors:* The success of SOE reform frequently depends on the willingness of private investors to buy state-owned enterprises and to commit capital to the modernization or expansion of privatized firms. The profitability of these investments depends on a wide array of economic policies, including secure property rights, the tax regime, and the prices that investors are allowed to charge for their output. Because investors cannot easily withdraw the capital that they commit to privatized state-owned enterprises, they must rely on government promises that these policies will remain stable. When they do not regard the promises as credible, they require a steep discount on any state assets that they purchase (or, in the case of regulated monopolies, a high guaranteed rate of return). Significant discounts and high guaranteed rates of return to investors make reform more difficult, because they open the way to allegations that the government is giving away the nation's assets and they reduce the resources available to increase local support for reform. *Thus, the government's ability to commit credibly to future economic policies is crucial to successful reform.*

Three factors, discussed below, increase a government's credibility: its reputation for keeping promises; domestic restraints on policy reversal, such as laws or constitutional restrictions; and international restraints, such as treaties or loan covenants.

- *Reputation.* Reputation allows governments to buy support more cheaply (by promising losers future compensation) and persuades investors to pay a higher price for SOE assets. If governments renege on promises and devalue their reputations, they lose these advantages and face greater costs in the future. Those countries in our sample with the greatest credibility relied heavily on reputation.
- *Domestic restraints on policy reversal.* Domestic restraints that make it harder for governments to renege on prior commitments are of three broad types: (1) constitutional provisions that explicitly make reneging more difficult, such as a stipulation that property rights can only be altered by a two-thirds majority of the legislature; (2) checks and balances that require leadership decisions to be endorsed by an independent judiciary, legislature, or professional bureaucracy regulated by strict internal performance standards; and (3) the design of the SOE reform policies themselves—

in particular, the use of wide share distribution—which reduces the likelihood of reversal by broadly sharing the long-term benefits of reform in ways that create a large proreform constituency, increasing the political costs to governments of reversing policies.[19] Countries such as India and the Philippines, with political systems that make reform both difficult to enact and to overturn, sometimes had problems meeting Condition II. However, they did better on Condition III, suggesting that reforms in countries with political checks and balances are less vulnerable to reversal. Domestic restraints were less important than reputation in establishing credibility in the nontransition countries that meet Condition III, since the executive branch had great discretion in these countries, but have been substantially more important in Poland and the Czech Republic. However, Chile and Korea each took steps after reform to adopt domestic restraints that make the reversal of SOE reforms more difficult and therefore less likely.

- *International restraints.* A country's international commitments can restrain at least two types of SOE reform backsliding. First, governments may restore subsidies or trade protection to state-owned enterprises. They are less likely to do this if their countries belong to trading groups, such as WTO, NAFTA, and the European Union, which explicitly restrict signatories from assisting domestic companies, including state firms, with subsidies and tariff and quota protection.[20] Second, governments may renege on agreements with foreign investors who have purchased SOE assets. They are less likely to do this if the country relies heavily on trade and is therefore vulnerable to the trade sanctions that foreign governments might impose in retaliation.[21] Covenants in loan agreements with multilateral lending institutions can also impede reform reversals.

As we shall see, the greater a government's credibility, the more likely it is to reform its SOEs successfully; moreover, no government that lacked credibility reformed its SOEs successfully. However, governments need not use all three mechanisms to establish credibility. In our sample, reputation achieved through intensive and sustained implementation of macroeconomic adjustment and liberalization programs was key to the credibility of the three successful nontransition reformers; domestic restraints counted for much less. Overall, we find that for countries that satisfied Conditions I and II—that is, where SOE reform was both politically desirable and feasible—satisfying Condition III provided the final necessary ingredient for success. Some of the less successful countries, such as India, seemed to have the attributes necessary to make credible promises. However, this offered them no advantages in SOE reform as they did not satisfy the first two conditions. Box 4.5 describes some of the measures employed to evaluate a country's credibility. In most cases, these measures were available early enough to use as performance predictors; in some instances, the only available measures are contemporaneous with the reform episodes we examine.[22]

The remainder of this section presents several examples of how we applied the indicators in box 4.5 to the countries in our sample to determine which countries satisfy Condition III; that is, which govern-

---

Box 4.5 Measuring Credibility

WE EMPLOY SEVERAL INDICATORS OF THE THREE credibility mechanisms discussed in the text. This box explains how we measured the three aspects of credibility: reputation, domestic restraints, and international restraints.

Measuring Reputation. We measure reputation in two ways: through independently produced country rankings and through our own analysis of whether a country has a history of announcing and following through on reforms.

- *Independent country rankings.* We used the ratings of the International Country Risk Guide (ICRG) of three country characteristics: the rule of law, the risk of expropriation, and the risk of contract repudiation. Because ICRG sells these ratings to foreign investors, their accuracy is subject to a market test. For the nine countries in our sample for which scores were available, the sum of scores for these three indicators averaged 13.5 from 1985 to 1989. In the larger ICRG sample, the same average ranged from 7.6 for Zaire to 21.4 for Singapore to the maximum of 30 for Switzerland. Comparable evaluations by a compet-

ing firm, Business Environment Risk Intelligence (BERI), yielded similar rankings of the sample countries. Although for convenience we take the ICRG measures to represent reputation, they might also be used as an overall measure of country credibility, since domestic and international restraints no doubt affect the ICRG evaluations that countries receive.

- *Policy reform follow-through.* To supplement the ICRG rankings, we analyzed whether or not governments followed through on announced policy reform initiatives other than SOE reform. A government that announces reforms but fails to implement them, or reverses them, tarnishes its overall reputation. In addition, governments that successfully reform in areas other than SOEs signal to supporters and opponents of reform that they are capable of winning reform battles; this encourages supporters and discourages opponents when a government attempts SOE reform. A country is considered to have undertaken broad reform if it implemented a ments had sufficient credibility to make promises about SOE reform believable. Table 4.4 summarizes this discussion.

Successful SOE Reformers

At the time of their SOE reforms, Chile, Mexico, and Korea had strong reputations, based on macroeconomic reforms and performance, and faced significant international restraints, in the form of dependency on external markets and trade treaties. Exports as a percentage of GDP were greater for Chile (32.7 percent of GDP from 1986–90) and Korea (36.2 percent) than for the mixed and less successful reformers, which averaged as a group 21.7 percent and 17.5 percent for the mixed and less successful reformers, respectively. With a 17.1 percent export share,

stabilization program (especially in fiscal and trade policies) around the time that SOE reforms were implemented. (Countries that exhibit a sound macroeconomic environment, as Korea did prior to reform, obviously do not require broad based policy changes to establish the credibility of their SOE reforms.)

Measuring Domestic Restraints. We measure the extent to which domestic restraints increased credibility by asking two questions:

- *Do SOE reforms create constituencies that would oppose reform reversal?* The case studies described in this chapter suggest signals of this, such as the broad distribution of shares in privatized enterprises.
- *Are there domestic institutions that might constrain how much the executive can exercise discretion in decisionmaking, thereby preventing policy reversal?* We use the Polity II data set. This indicates whether countries have elected and effective legislatures and competitively elected executives, and the extent to which executive decisionmaking is con-

strained by a defined set of procedures requiring agreement from other governmental entities (Gurr, Jaggers, and Moore 1989). The score for the executive constraint variable given in the Polity II data set is reported in table 4.4.

Measuring International Restraints. International restraints are evaluated based on whether a country is bound by trade treaty obligations, such as GATT or NAFTA, and the extent to which a country relies on international trade.

- *Trade treaty restraints.* Developing countries are often granted exemptions in such treaties (particularly from GATT), which make the treaty constraints less binding. Our evaluation of the twelve countries takes such exemptions into account.
- *Reliance on international trade.* Trade treaty restraints are only meaningful if the country is heavily enough dependent on foreign trade that threats of retaliation from trade partners are a significant deterrent to reform backsliding. We therefore also consider the fraction of a country's GDP that comes from exports.

Table 4.4 Condition III for State-Owned Enterprise Reform: Credibility

Country	Period	Government reputation	
		Were macro reforms implemented?[a]	Private assessment of firm risk[b]
More successful SOE reformers			
Chile	1972–88	Yes	16.8
Republic of Korea	1983–90	Yes, prior to SOE reform	18.1
Mexico	1982–94	Yes	15.0
Mixed SOE reformers			
Philippines	1986–	Yes	8.9
Egypt	1980s	No	12.0
Ghana	1983–92	Yes	11.6
Less successful SOE reformers			
India	1980s	No	15.4
Senegal	1983–88	Yes	12.8
	1988–	No	
Turkey	1983–91	Yes	14.0
Transition economies			
China		Yes (gradual)	—
Czech Republic		Yes	—
Poland		Yes	—

— Not available.

a. *Yes* means that broad macroeconomic reforms, such as trade liberalization, restoration of fiscal balance, and tax reform, are under way. *No* means that reforms are needed but not undertaken.

b. The ICRG scores (used to determine value associated with private sector assessment of firm risk) are the average of the sum of the ICRG scores over three dimensions described in the text for the years 1985–89 (data for the years 1983–84 were not available). The maximum possible score is 30.

c. Constraints on executive are measured by 1985 Polity II score on a scale of 1 to 7. The Polity II data set does not extend beyond 1986. Executive constraints is scored 1

Domestic restraints on policy reversals		International restraints	
Does reform design discourage reversal?	*Constraints on executive*	*Bound by trade treaty?*	*Exports as a percentage of GDP (1986–90)*
No (1970s)	1	GATT	32.7
Yes (1980s—wide share distribution)			
Yes (performance contracts only)	2	GATT	36.2
Yes (some worker share distribution)	3	NAFTA, GATT	17.1
No	6 or 7	GATT (less binding)[e]	27.5
No	3	GATT (less binding)	20.5
No	1	GATT (less binding)	17.1
No	7	GATT (less binding)	6.9
No	3	GATT (less binding)	25.1
No	5	Prospective EU membership, GATT	20.6
Yes (some decentralization only)	1 or 2[d]	Prospective WTO membership	19.3 (1991)
Yes (wide share distribution)	6 or 7[d]	WTO, prospective EU membership	57.8 (1991–92)
Yes (some management buyouts, employee share participation)	5 or 6[d]	Prospective EU, WTO membership	21.9 (1990–93)

when, for example, constitutional restrictions on executive action are ignored or rule by decree is repeatedly used. The variable is scored 7 when, for example, a legislature initiates much important legislation. Countries lacking political competition, an effective legislature, and an independent judiciary scored lowest; countries with all of these attributes scored highest.

d. Estimated—no Polity II score available after 1986.

e. "Less binding" means a country is exempt from many GATT restrictions on protectionist policies.

Source: OECD (1992); World Tables (1994); see text.

Mexico was an exception among the successful reformers, but was likely to have been constrained by NAFTA negotiations and obligations. The more successful reformers ranked less well in terms of domestic restraints; wide share distribution was an important part of SOE reform only in Chile, and none of the three had significant constitutional or procedural provisions to prevent policy reversals (this has since changed in Chile and Korea). Even so, by scoring well in two of the three sets of indicators, the governments of these countries can be said to have partially met Condition III. We illustrate this with a discussion of Chile; Mexico and Korea are discussed in the chapter appendix.

The credibility of Chile's SOE reforms rested on the strength of the government's reputation gained from broader policy reforms, and the widely recognized fact that opponents of reform had little or no opportunity to slow or reverse the government's policy initiatives. Chile also exhibited an increasing dependence on international markets; exports as a percentage of GDP rose from 15 percent in 1970 to 21 percent in 1974 and more than 30 percent in the 1980s.[23] Both rounds of SOE reform (in the 1970s and 1980s) were closely associated with ambitious macroeconomic programs that included tighter fiscal policies and an easing of trade and financial restrictions. The impact of these reforms on government reputation in Chile can be seen in the improvements in Chile's BERI scores for nationalization risk and contract enforceability. From 1973, right after the coup that brought the military regime to power, to 1982, the sum of Chile's scores on these two kinds of risk rose from 0.6 to 4.9. Chile's credibility in the second round was also high, as indicated by its ICRG score in the 1980s, which is the second highest in the sample.

Policy design and constitutional restrictions on policy reversal contributed little to the credibility of reforms in the 1970s. Both had a greater role in the 1980s, however. We have already described how the Chilean government, as part of the design of SOE reform, promoted mass ownership of shares. Here we note only that mass ownership contributed to both Condition II and Condition III; that is, it assisted the political *feasibility* of reform (Condition II) by building support for implementation, and it strengthened the *credibility* of reform (Condition III) by creating a constituency that would defend the reforms in the future, making it more difficult for any subsequent administration to renationalize privatized firms. Other domestic restraints are described in box 4.6.

Box 4.6 Locking in Reform: Restraints on Executive Discretion in Chile

ESTABLISHING INSTITUTIONAL RESTRAINTS THAT MAKE IT more difficult for successor governments to reverse SOE reforms is one course of action that policymakers can pursue to increase the credibility of reform. Chile's military government took several steps in this direction in 1988 with a plebiscite on an eight-year extension of General Pinochet's rule. Many observers concluded that the government's intent was to guarantee its continued control into the 1990s. This objective produced a constitution that, intentionally or not, had beneficial consequences for reform. The new constitution established an electoral system that increased representation from conservative rural areas and encouraged party fragmentation, thus making it more difficult for strong coalitions to form, and it established an independent central bank. To reduce the likelihood that future governments would revise the constitution itself, the drafters included a provision that any changes in the constitution would require a two-thirds majority of both chambers of the legislature. Although there were important objections to the 1980 referendum and to the kind of democracy it would create, it is nevertheless the case that, on the narrow issue of SOE reform, these constitutional provisions increased the credibility of second-round reforms, thus reducing the risk to investors (Arriagada and Graham 1993).

Mixed SOE Reformers

Of the countries in our sample with mixed success in SOE reform, only the Philippines at least partially met Condition III during the 1980s. The strength of reputation and domestic restraints differed among these countries. None, however, were significantly bound by international restraints; for example, the weight of exports in GDP was lower in each of these three countries than in Chile and Korea, offering fewer opportunities for outside actors to retaliate with sanctions in the event of reneging. The discussion below contrasts Ghana and the Philippines; Egypt, which did not meet Condition III in the 1980s, is discussed in the chapter appendix.

In the 1980s, domestic and international restraints were weak to non-existent in Ghana. Worker demands for immediate compensation (severance pay) meant that compensation plans did not increase future support for the continuity of SOE reforms. Ghana's economic policy reforms in the 1980s included a major currency devaluation, civil service cuts, and a large reduction in the fiscal deficit. These should have boosted the government's reputation, but a low ICRG score of 11.6 indicates that other countervailing factors were at work. One of these was the extent to which the economy had been allowed to deteriorate before the reforms. By 1983, the fiscal deficit was 60 percent of current government expenditures and capital payments, higher than Mexico's worst deficit during the period and four times Korea's deepest deficit.[24]

In addition, some government statements during the 1980s were hostile to private enterprise. This is in sharp contrast to Mexico under President Salinas, where the rhetoric was probusiness and the government actively consulted with business leaders about economic policy decisions. More damaging to Ghana's credibility than these statements were actions that the government took against some businesses. In 1987–88, for example, the government took the principal domestic tobacco company from one set of private owners and gave it to another, changing the name from International Tobacco to Meridian in the process. This episode coincided with the slowing pace of SOE reform in Ghana. Moreover, as Leith and Lofchie (1993) report, in the early years of the Rawlings regime, people's defense committees and workers' defense committees were set up to monitor and arrest business people suspected of "counterrevolutionary" activity. Actions such as these would have severely undermined the credibility of a government with investors.

The Philippines had a strong set of domestic restraints on policy reversal during the period, which explains why it met Condition III, at least partially, despite its weak reputation. The 1986 Constitution contained numerous checks and balances that limited the power of any government entity alone to overturn existing policies. As we noted above, the legislature has been powerful and has not been controlled by the president since the end of the Marcos regime. Once all major players have accepted reforms, they are difficult to reverse and are therefore credible. However, the Philippines had a low ICRG score, perhaps because of the continued threats of coups in the late 1980s and early 1990s. In addition, the Philippines was less consistent than others in the sample in the implementation of sound macro policies, and its external treaty obligations were slight.

Less Successful SOE Reformers

The credibility of Senegalese SOE reforms was low during the 1980s, but Turkey and India at least partially fulfilled Condition III. Although the fraction of GDP from exports was lower for the three less successful SOE reformers than the average for the other developing market economies in our sample, some other credibility indicators, particularly constitutional restraints on policy reversal, were actually stronger for this group. While this may seem surprising, it reinforces the central message of this chapter, that reform cannot succeed until countries fulfill *each* of the three readiness conditions. Credibility alone is not enough. To succeed, reform must also be politically desirable and feasible. The relatively high credibility of India and Turkey suggests that if they were to satisfy Conditions I and II, the prospects for SOE reform would be promising. In this chapter, we illustrate the credibility ratings for the less successful SOE reformers with a discussion of India; Turkey and Senegal are discussed in the chapter appendix.

Compared with other countries with a similar income level, India enjoys a relatively good reputation among investors, despite the absence until recently of a broad macroeconomic reform program. Policy reversals to the detriment of investors have been few, and the country has avoided the broad macroeconomic imbalances that have afflicted, for example, Ghana, Senegal, and Turkey. Moreover, like the Philippines after President Marcos, India has a constitution that imposes significant restraints on the executive branch, making policy reversals less likely. Among the countries in our sample, India ranks highest on the Polity II executive constraints dimension with the maximum score, seven (see table 4.4). On the other hand, international restraints have had only limited impact; India has not fully embraced international trade treaty obligations.

Failure to deliver promised compensation to those who lose in the course of SOE reform may have also hurt the government's credibility. In one textile factory, dismissed workers did not receive promised compensation for four years. Such problems have contributed to sometimes fierce opposition to reform. Mukul (1991) reports on an attempt by the state government of Uttar Pradesh to sell 51 percent of a money-losing cement plant in 1991, which ended in violence that killed forty workers. Although the sales agreement stipulated that all 8,000 employees would be retained, workers feared that at least half would be laid off with a lump sum severance pay they regarded as inadequate. They also objected to selling the firm at book value, although the firm's annual losses averaged $700,000 between 1985 and 1991. Partly as a result of this incident, Mukul concludes, the state government was turned out of office; its successor scuttled the deal.

The Transition Economies

The limited evidence available suggests the transition economies that have successfully reformed their SOEs, such as the Czech Republic, have enjoyed at least as much credibility for SOE reform as any country in our sample, through a combination of sound reputation built on macroeconomic reforms and domestic restraints on policy reversal. This is impressive progress given the exceptional challenges that the transition economies face in building credibility. In their accomplishments, the most successful countries illustrate the effectiveness of moving decisively to establish a sound reputation while at the same time putting in place domestic restraints that make policy reversal more difficult and therefore less likely. China has fewer domestic restraints; the partial credibility it exhibits therefore depends heavily on the reputation derived from macroeconomic reforms and growing exports. We discuss the Czech Republic and Poland below, and China in the chapter appendix.

Both Poland and the Czech Republic have undertaken dramatic macroeconomic reforms as part of their overall efforts at systemic transformation. As in Chile and Mexico, these macroeconomic reforms occurred prior to privatization and could have been observed in advance of SOE reform decisions by investors and those expecting compensation from the government. As the discussion of political feasibility reveals, both countries exhibit domestic restraints on policy reversal. In each country, executive discretion is limited by significant legislative authority over the policymaking process and by electoral processes that make it difficult for single parties to achieve absolute legislative majorities. These constraints have sometimes affected the pace of reform, consistent with the earlier analysis of reform feasibility. Although the continuity of government in the Czech Republic has allowed it to pursue SOE reform consistently, in Poland, political instability has led to occasional temporary reversals, as when Waldemar Pawlak suspended the privatization initiative passed by the previous government.

In addition, SOE reforms have been designed to create constituencies that favor the long-term success of the reformed enterprises. In Poland, this was done through share distributions to SOE employees (or through "spontaneous privatizations" discussed above), thus making them long-term supporters of reform. In the Czech Republic, share distribution was much wider, effectively making the public at large a proreform constituency. Finally, the governments of both countries had a strong desire (since realized with their entry into the World Trade Organization, or WTO) to enter the European Union, the WTO, and NATO, providing an external check on policy backsliding.

Explaining and Predicting Reform Success

THE FRAMEWORK AND EVIDENCE PRESENTED IN THIS CHAPTER offer a basis for analyzing when and where SOE reform can succeed and be sustained. The analysis rests on the premise, set forth at the beginning of the chapter, that countries only implement state-owned enterprise reform successfully when they meet three conditions: first, reform must be politically desirable; second, reform must be politically feasible; and, third, promises crucial to reform (to compensate losers and to protect the property rights of investors) must be credible. Analyzing SOE reform experiences in twelve countries, we found that this was indeed the case: countries that reformed their state-owned enterprises successfully met or partially met all three conditions; countries that did not reform successfully failed to meet at least one condition. Although our sample is small, it is economically and geographically diverse. Moreover, the findings are consistent for more than one reform episode in countries such as Chile, Mexico, and Turkey.

Could reform readiness have been predicted beforehand? Prediction, of course, requires that the indicators be known prior to the reform attempt. The indicators used in table 4.5 have that property. For example, to estimate the desirability of reform, we consider whether there has been a regime change, a coalition shift, or an economic crisis, and we identify the support base of government decisionmakers. To judge reform feasibility, we take into account such characteristics as the constitutional or procedural requirements that make reform more or less feasible, and the distribution of political power among the various entities of government. For credibility, we have relied on such indicators as reputation assessments by investor risk services, the design of the reform,

Table 4.5 Unmet Conditions in Less Than Successful SOE Reformers

Country	Condition I Desirability	Condition II Feasibility	Condition III Credibility
Egypt	●		●
Ghana			●
Philippines		●	
India	●	●	
Senegal 1983–88	●		
1988–	●	●	●
Turkey 1983–91	●		
1991–92	●	●	

● Does not meet the condition.

Condition I: Met if coalition change *or* exogenous crisis *and* SOE reform losers outside government's support base; not met if reform losers in governments' support base.

Condition II: Met if reformers can secure approval *and* design sufficient compensation packages to defuse opposition; not met otherwise.

Condition III: Met if government known for keeping promises, faces domestic international restraints on policy reversal. Note that by OECD standards, in which countries score much higher in ICRG (Switzerland with thirty, for example), and receive scores of seven on constraints on the executive, none of the sample countries would be judged to fully meet Condition III. For the purposes of this table, Chile, Korea, and the Czech Republic were used as benchmarks against which the remaining countries in the sample were compared. In general, countries that did worse on two dimensions and no better than on others were judged not to meet the condition.

and the constraints on executive discretion.[25] All of these are objective characteristics that can be observed independent of reform attempts and often measured with quantitative indicators.

A definitive judgment of the predictive power of this approach must await testing with a larger sample. However, the results in table 4.5 illustrate the promise of the approach taken in this chapter. The table shows that of the twelve countries we examined, countries that failed to meet any one of the conditions were less successful reformers; only those that met all three conditions, at least partially, successfully reformed. Although the analysis does not distinguish the mixed from the less successful reformers, it does identify those countries where reforms were successful.

Table 4.5 also demonstrates the need for more careful analysis of reform readiness. Often analysts assert that the mere fact of a regime change or an economic crisis constitutes a "window of opportunity" for reform, without considering how the observed change influences the credibility and political feasibility of the reforms in question. This overly simple approach would have led analysts to predict, for example, that successful SOE reform was likely during the period we studied in Egypt and Ghana (both of which experienced an economic crisis), and in the Philippines (which experienced an economic crisis *and* a regime change). In fact, as the table shows, consideration of the other components of political desirability (the composition of the government's coalition and its support base), as well as of the feasibility and credibility of SOE reform efforts, would have painted a less optimistic and more accurate picture of the likelihood of reform success in those countries.

Conclusion

ALTHOUGH THIS CHAPTER HAS DOCUMENTED MANY BARRIERS to reform, its message, and indeed the overall message of our findings, is essentially optimistic. All the countries that successfully reformed their state-owned enterprises lacked at the outset one or more of the three conditions we have identified as necessary for reform success. All eventually acquired them and went on to correct the inefficiencies in their state-owned enterprise sectors. Moreover, the successful reformers satisfied these three conditions in different political environments—in the context of significant political liberalization (the Czech Republic and Poland) and in more authoritarian settings (Chile and Korea); in different ways—through extensive distribution of enterprise shares (the Czech Republic and Poland) and through more moderate redistribution (Mexico); and through varying credibility mechanisms—sound macroeconomic policies (Chile and Korea), international trade agreements (Mexico), and domestic restraints on policy reversal (the Czech Republic and Poland). The case studies demonstrate that where reforms are politically desirable, committed leadership can indeed take steps to increase their feasibility and to establish the necessary credibility. How to implement reforms once the three necessary political conditions are in place—and what to do when they are not—is the topic of our final chapter.

Appendix 4.1 The Politics of State-Owned Enterprise Reform: Additional Evidence

THIS APPENDIX PRESENTS EVIDENCE FOR AN assessment of the role of the three conditions for successful state-owned enterprise reform—political desirability, political feasibility, and credibility—that we excluded from chapter 4 for reasons of space and clarity of argument. The appendix will be of particular interest to policymakers and development experts who intend to undertake similar analysis and therefore want further examples of how we evaluated the various ways that countries in our sample met, or failed to meet, each condition. It will also interest readers who want more detail about a specific country in our sample. The appendix follows the organization of chapter 4 without repeating the main arguments of each section. Readers can therefore begin with the chapter and turn to the appendix as their interest dictates.

Assessing Condition I: Political Desirability

The chapter text analyzes in detail the political desirability of reform for two successful reformers, Chile and Mexico, and one mixed, Egypt. It also summarizes the reasons why the three least successful reformers failed to meet Condition I. Here we present additional evidence for our assessment of the political desirability of SOE reform in Korea, a successful reformer; Ghana and the Philippines, mixed reformers; India and Turkey, less successful reformers; and Poland.

Republic of Korea. Korea is unique among the countries in the sample in that both the costs and the benefits to the leadership and their constituencies of SOE reform were low. Dramatic economic and political events, such as those in Chile and Mexico, were therefore not necessary to trigger reform. There was, for ex-

ample, no regime change or coalition realignment during the period of analysis. Instead, slowing per capita GDP growth and increasing SOE losses that might not have been considered serious problems in other countries were sufficient to make SOE reform politically desirable. In 1980, GDP growth, which had averaged about 7 percent in the late 1970s, dropped to −4.5 percent. In 1982, the number of state-owned enterprises losing money increased from two to five, and the aggregate SOE deficit rose. This deficit was small, however, amounting to only 1.5 percent of the central government's total fiscal deficit in 1982 (Song 1988).

Why were a temporary dip in the country's very respectable growth rate and a relatively mild increase in SOE deficits enough to trigger reform? The political motivations for SOE reform are more difficult to identify in Korea than in Chile and Mexico, but there are two likely explanations. First, the Korean government had a strong commitment to fiscal discipline. From 1980 to 1991, Korea's budget deficit averaged 4.5 percent of current government expenditures and capital payments, compared to more than 15 percent for Egypt, Ghana, India, Mexico, the Philippines, Senegal, and Turkey. Rising SOE deficits, however small compared to the government's overall budget deficit, were at odds with this commitment.

Second, SOE reforms had low political costs. The enterprises were being run relatively efficiently and, in contrast with the situation in many other countries, had not been used to generate jobs. Since overstaffing was not an issue, more efficient SOE management did not impose significant costs on workers. Indeed, workers may not have suffered at all. State sector employment as a percentage of total employment in Korea actually rose from 1982 to 1990. The average number of employees per SOE increased from 3,350 in 1983 to 3,420 in 1988; and SOE wages grew, on average, at rates similar to those in the private sector, lagging only from 1982 to 1985. Thus, Korea's unusual experience nonetheless illustrates our paradigm: for reform to be politically desirable, the political benefits must outweigh the political costs. This was the case in Korea, even though both costs and benefits were relatively low.

Ghana. From 1981 to 1983, the government of Ghana pursued neither macroeconomic nor SOE reforms. At that time, opponents of SOE reform were in the government's support base. After 1983, motivated in part by severe economic crisis, the government began to change its base of support and Ghana met Condition I. SOE reforms accelerated during this period. Employment in the 42 largest state firms dropped from 241,000 in 1984 to 83,000 in 1991 (see statistical appendix, table 5). However, toward the end of the 1980s, they once again slowed, a development explained in greater detail in the discussion of Condition II.

By 1983, the policies that the government initially pursued, such as extensive wage and price controls, had further worsened the performance of an economy that had already experienced a decade-long decline in income per capita. Drought, two coup attempts in 1982, and the return in 1983 of 1 million Ghanaians expelled from Nigeria, provided further impetus for a dramatic change in overall economic policies: the government devalued the currency by 1,000 percent, introduced hospital fees, more than doubled water and electricity fees, and eliminated most of the 6,000 price controls (Herbst 1991).

The 1983 economic crisis in Ghana was, arguably, the worst in our sample, and the information it provided the Rawlings government and its constituencies about the real costs and benefits of its economic policies might by itself have been suffi-

cient to motivate the reversal in economic policy that took place. However, there is also evidence that the adjustment policies that the government adopted were consistent with a changing political base of support. The heaviest burden of these policies fell on urban wage earners, including SOE employees, who were among the early supporters of the regime. The political impact on the regime was reduced, however, because the government had a growing military and rural base of support after 1983.[26]

The Philippines. There are a number of circumstances that suggest that SOE reform could have been politically desirable in the Philippines. The country clearly experienced a regime shift with the popular revolt that ousted Ferdinand Marcos and installed Corazon Aquino as president in 1986. Moreover, economic conditions had been rapidly deteriorating. Per capita economic growth in the first half of the 1980s had been negative, inflation had been very high (peaking at an annual rate of about 50 percent in 1984), and the fiscal deficit continued to worsen, hitting about 34 percent of expenditures in 1987. Finally, because state-owned enterprises during the Marcos years were instruments of "crony capitalism"—dispensing favors in exchange for support of the Marcos regime—SOE employees and managers would have been unlikely supporters of the Aquino government.

Consistent with this, the Aquino government tried to move quickly to institute SOE reform. Soon after taking office, President Aquino established an interagency committee on privatization (COP) to oversee the sales of state assets.[27] However, actual progress was slow. By June 1990, the COP had recommended the sale of about one-third of the country's 300 SOEs, but only thirty-nine had actually been offered for sale and thirty-two had been sold (Manasan and Intal 1992). Moreover, as chapter 2 indicates, those state-owned enterprises that were not divested showed continuing poor performance throughout the decade. As in Ghana, the slow pace of reform in the Philippines is likely related to the inability of the Philippines to satisfy Condition II, political feasibility, and also, again as in Ghana, to the tendency of the government to use state-owned enterprises that were not privatized to increase political support.

India. India met none of the prerequisites for Condition I in the 1980s, so it is not suprising that little SOE reform was accomplished. On the contrary, state-owned enterprises employed a fairly constant 8.5 percent of the work force through the 1980s, and the real wages of SOE workers actually rose during the period by approximately 25 percent. India did not exhibit a worsening of the deficit or inflation that would have made it more difficult for the government to continue subsidizing SOE inefficiencies. Inflation remained in single digits for most of the decade, and the fiscal deficit (including the government capital account) did not diverge significantly over the period from an average of 7.5 percent of GDP. Economic growth varied little over the period, as well; real per capita GDP growth never dropped below 1.5 percent per year.

In addition, there was no regime change or coalition shift that would have favored SOE reform–in fact there was no party that had a dominant faction in favor of SOE reform. Ganguly and Ganguly (1982) and Waterbury (1993) report that SOE workers were important supporters of Congress-led governments, which held a majority in the Lok Sabha from 1980 to 1989. Moreover, state control of the economy had been a fundamental tenet of the Congress Party nearly since its beginnings (Waterbury 1993). Because Congress' control of the government was not necessarily assured, particularly in the late 1980s, deviations from its SOE policy, which risked losing this

support base, were unlikely to have been pursued (indeed, the number of seats held by the Congress Party in the Lok Sabha temporarily dropped from 401 in 1985 to 197 after the 1989 elections). There were, therefore, few indications that SOE reform was considered politically desirable in India in the 1980s.[28]

Turkey. The military takeover of the Turkish government in 1980 constituted a regime change that brought to power a government interested in pursuing extensive economic liberalization. The architect of the economic reforms that occurred under the military government, Turgut Özal, retained control of economic policy when civilian government was reintroduced in 1983. He led the Motherland Party (ANAP) to victory in the presidential elections of that year. Although ANAP won again in the general elections of 1987, its support steadily declined (Onis and Webb 1992). It came in third in the municipal elections of 1989 and in 1991 lost control of the national government to a coalition led by the True Path Party (headed at the time by Suleyman Demirel), which was also favorable to market-based economic policies (EIU, 1993). Nonetheless, neither government pursued significant SOE reform, because SOE employees and other SOE supporters were an important constituency for both. Like India and Egypt, Turkey did not meet Condition I; that is, despite regime-changes; reform of SOE was not considered politically desirable to the leadership, for two reasons.

First, state-owned enterprise employees and other SOE supporters were an important constituency for ANAP and the True Path parties. The Özal government did pursue a series of broad economic reforms and passed a law in 1986 that provided a framework for privatization.[29] However, Onis and Webb (1992) conclude that implementing the law could have been politically undesirable, because the SOE sector was part of the government's support base. There was no economic crisis significant enough to push the government to take actions that would have alienated this important constituency in a highly competitive political environment. Even when the government deficit as a percentage of GDP rose from 4.2 percent in 1983 to 10 percent in 1984, the Özal government reduced it to 3.2 percent by 1986 without resorting to SOE reforms. Instead, as in Egypt, measures to contain SOE expenditures were largely limited to allowing real SOE wages to erode over the period 1981–86. Further strong evidence of the importance of SOE employees to the ANAP support base is that in the period leading to the 1989 and 1991 elections, real SOE wages more than doubled.

Second, various sources document that the military opposed SOE reform, although its power declined in the 1980s (EIU 1993). These sources further note that the military has long been regarded as the chief conservator of the economic and social changes that Kemal Attaturk precipitated. Among these was state ownership of much of the industrial sector that began in the 1930s and eventually extended to sectors such as textiles, metal industries, aircraft, electronics, machine tools, and animal foodstuffs. Even today state-owned factories often display a plaque inscribed with a quote from Attaturk: "Every factory is a castle to be defended."[30] Although the military backed the Özal government in other areas of economic reform, it was more difficult for it to allow the reversal of decades-long policies regarding state-owned enterprises (EIU 1993).

Poland. The chapter text notes the difficulties that governments in Poland have had in passing and implementing SOE reform. Some examples of these difficulties are noted here. The government of Hanna Suchocka, which took office in May 1992, succeeded in passing a law on mass privatization in June 1993, gaining parliamentary approval for the first 195 firms to enter the program. However, this success was fleet-

ing; her government fell in October 1993 and was replaced by a coalition of parties in which opponents of SOE reform were influential. An early demonstration of their influence came in 1994, when the new prime minister, Waldemar Pawlak, refused to approve the participation of 100 firms in the mass privatization scheme (EIU 1994–95). Only in 1995 did opposition to the mass privatization of all 400 firms fade. In contrast, by 1993 the mass privatization program in the Czech Republic had transferred nearly 1,000 firms to private ownership and slated 500 others for divestiture (Gelb and Singh 1994).

Assessing Condition II: Political Feasibility

The chapter presents detailed evidence on Chile, Ghana, the Philippines, and the three transition economies. This section of the appendix supplements the chapter with greater detail on the feasibility of reform in two of the good reformers (Korea and Mexico), one mixed (Egypt), all three of the less successful reformers, and Poland.

Mexico. SOE reforms were politically feasible in Mexico because reformers controlled the relevant policymaking entities and had the means to overcome resistance. Although in each case the situation was less clear cut than in Chile, Mexico at least partially met Condition II. The president's office had nearly complete control of the formulation of SOE (and other) policies (Kaufman, Bazdresch, and Heredia 1994). Nevertheless, the opponents of reform in the PRI still exercised influence. Moreover, several state-owned enterprises targeted for reform were strategic enterprises (telecommunications and airlines), where worker resistance to reform could have been very costly.

The Salinas administration offset this potential opposition with a mix of compensation and compulsion. In part to win over potential opponents and to address the concerns of the PRI reform opponents, President Salinas established the National Solidarity Program, PRONASOL. Funded with the proceeds of privatization, the program provided grassroots, project-related assistance, particularly to poor areas where the opposition had gained ground in the 1988 elections (Waterbury 1993).

The administration also used compulsion, in particular by arresting key labor leaders on corruption charges. Subsequently, as Cordón (1993b) concludes, the relative weights of compensation and compulsion that the government used depended on the ability of opponents to disrupt the reforms. For example, when privatizing TELMEX, the government won support of the powerful telephone workers' union by allotting TELMEX employees 4.4 percent of the firm's shares and permitting workers to pay for the shares from future dividends. In contrast, faced with a strike at Aeroméxico airline by employees trying to block privatization, the government declared the company bankrupt, fired most of the workers, then sold the company. Here, too, however, the government offered compensation as necessary to keep the airline running: pilots were not only permitted to keep their jobs, they were offered discount shares in the privatized airline (Cordón 1993b).

Republic of Korea. The Korean executive branch controlled the policymaking entities in the country during the period in which SOE reform was initiated and carried out. Korea also had the capacity to minimize SOE sector resistance to reform with some combination of compensation and compulsion. However, apart from performance contracts, which rewarded managers for achieving various performance goals, neither compensation nor compulsion were needed, because reform was not associated with dramatic retrenchment and opposition to reform was not significant. Korea, therefore, met Condition II because of the absence of opposition,

although it had the capacity to overcome resistance to SOE reforms.

Egypt. Egypt did not meet Condition I in the 1980s (reform was not seen by the leadership as politically desirable); nevertheless, reform in Egypt did seem at least partially feasible. Like most of the countries in the sample, the Egyptian government controlled the policymaking entities in the country. As in Mexico, the president in Egypt directs the dominant political party, which has a large majority in the legislature. However, unlike more successful reformers, who either confronted minimal resistance to reform or had the means to overcome it, a reform-oriented regime in Egypt during the 1980s would have faced strong resistance, making it difficult for the Egyptian government to have mounted the combination of compensation and compulsion necessary to pursue reform successfully.

The potential for resistance to SOE reform was evident from the share of SOE employment in total employment in Egypt, which was several times higher than in Mexico or Korea. And unlike in Chile, where high SOE employment under Allende was a recent (and short-lived) phenomenon, in Egypt this had been the case for decades. Finally, overstaffing seems to be extensive in Egyptian SOEs, suggesting that reforms would require more painful adjustment than in the successful reformers in our sample. Both indicators—the share of SOE employment in total employment and the level of overstaffing—suggest that resistance to SOE reform in Egypt would have been greater than that experienced in the successful reformers.

India. SOE reform does not appear to have been politically feasible in India in the 1980s, because of both opposition in the legislature and the prospect of stiff resistance to policy changes. Moreover, extensive labor unrest suggests that the potential for costly resistance to SOE reform was high (Waterbury 1993). Through the 1980s, India experienced thirty times as many workdays lost, and twenty times as many workers involved in job actions as Mexico, which has one-tenth of the population (ILO various years). This, combined with the high degree of overstaffing in Indian state-owned enterprises and the large absolute number of SOE employees, suggests that, as with Egypt, even if reform had been politically desirable it probably would not have been feasible in the absence of other social and economic changes.

Turkey. The ANAP government of Turgut Özal did not confront problems controlling Turkey's policymaking entities, since ANAP not only held a majority in the legislature, but by 1990 Prime Minister Özal could spend half of government revenues without parliamentary approval. Moreover, prior to 1987, his government benefited from strong rules that inhibited resistance to SOE reforms, such as one banning all strikes (Onis and Webb 1992). Under the Özal government, therefore, Turkey seems to have met Condition II. Since, as is discussed below, Turkey partially met Condition III, its failure to undertake SOE reforms during the 1980s seems to be rooted in its inability to meet Condition I, political desirability.

The coalition that succeeded ANAP in power in 1991, led by the True Path Party, did not meet Condition II, however. This government (led first by Prime Minister Demirel and later, after Demirel became president, by Tansu Ciller) had to contend with the opposition to SOE reforms of its coalition partner, the Social Democratic Populist Party, which advocates greater state intervention in industry (EIU 1993). In addition, the costs of opposing SOE reform have dropped since 1987, when restrictions on labor activity were relaxed. Consequently, although Turkey met Condition II under the Özal government, reform was not politically feasible under the True Path government.

Senegal. After the elections of 1983, when President Diouf consolidated his power, until the 1988 elections, he controlled the policymaking apparatus in the country and confronted little resistance in the form of riots, strikes, or demonstrations. However, relatively little state-owned enterprise reform took place, an outcome that is probably related to the difficulties of developing a compensation package for the large SOE sector in Senegal. Over the period from 1978 to 1991, SOE employment averaged 22 percent of total formal sector employment in the country. It was this obstacle that prevented Senegal from more than partially meeting Condition II prior to 1988.

In 1988, President Diouf's control over the policymaking apparatus weakened, and resistance to reforms dramatically increased; at this point, Senegal could not meet Condition II. In the 1988 elections, the chief opposition party, the Senegalese Democratic Party, drew 25 percent of the vote, up from 14 percent in the 1983 elections. This party that attracted votes from the proreform wing of the Socialist Party, leaving the antireform wing of the party in a stronger position with respect to President Diouf, the party's leader. The president was therefore unable to secure support for more rapid SOE reform.[31] The potential for resistance outside political circles also increased. Ka and van de Walle (1994) report that a wave of civil unrest swept the country beginning in 1987, when schools closed due to student protests. In 1988, SUTELEC, the union of electricity workers, struck the energy parastatal, SENELEC, hospital workers struck for two days a week, and riots took place in Dakar. SOE reforms came almost to a halt after 1988.

Poland. The chapter notes that the costs of compensating opponents of SOE reform are greater in Poland than in the Czech Republic, principally because SOE employees have greater rights to participate in decisionmaking in SOEs. In the waning years of Communist rule, workers and managers of Polish state-owned enterprises enjoyed increasingly strong property rights over the firms, as workers' councils were granted greater authority. In 1981, Polish law defined SOEs as autonomous, self-managed, and self-financing (Milor 1994). Enterprise managers have therefore had the legal leverage to demand firm-by-firm reforms, which are incompatible with mass privatization programs. This influence helps explain why, by October 1993, 852 enterprises had been sold to SOE managers and workers, while only 92 enterprises had been sold in direct sales to buyers or through public offerings (Gelb and Singh 1994).

Assessing Condition III: Credibility

The chapter text presents detailed evidence on the credibility of reform for Chile, Ghana, the Philippines, India, the Czech Republic, and Poland. Here we present the additional evidence for Korea, Mexico, Egypt, Senegal, Turkey, and China.

Republic of Korea. Korean SOE reforms did not require the government to make promises to losers or to investors, since there were few losers and privatization was not the chief SOE reform instrument. Credibility issues were confined to government promises to punish or reward SOE managers according to the terms of their performance contracts. Two characteristics probably helped to convince managers that the government was serious about improving SOE performance and therefore prepared to follow through on these performance contract promises. First, the government had a reputation for fiscal discipline, which SOE mismanagement would have undermined. Second, the government had adopted an export led growth strategy, which SOE inefficiencies would have handicapped.

Mexico. Mexico's SOE reform was at least partially credible. Like Chile, Mexico relied heavily on the reputation gained from comprehensive macroeconomic reforms, although these were not as thorough or systematic as in Chile. However, unlike Chile, in-

ternational restraints seem also to have contributed significantly to the ability of Mexican governments to commit credibly. Domestic restraints were limited to occasional instances of share distribution to SOE employees, particularly in the case of strategic industries like TELMEX (discussed in this chapter under Condition II).

Both the de la Madrid and Salinas governments implemented a broad set of macroeconomic reforms that improved the reputation of the country. These included sharp changes in fiscal policy, from heavy deficits to a balanced budget, trade liberalization, and the lifting of many price controls. According to Cordón (1993b), the Salinas government also improved its reputation by establishing regular channels of communication with representatives of the private sector (Kaufman, Bazdresch, and Heredia 1994). These channels provided the government with a way to announce its future plans to the private sector and to confirm when it had complied with its promises. The measures taken by the Salinas government were reflected in a relatively high average ICRG score over the period, as well as the fact that Mexico's ICRG score rose from twelve in 1986 to seventeen in 1989, when the largest privatizations were undertaken.

International restraints were also important. Mexico's accession to more rigorous GATT requirements in 1986 and the prospect of its accession to NAFTA contributed to government credibility. These provided vehicles for international actors to apply sanctions to Mexico if it reversed reforms that protected the property rights of foreign investors.

Egypt. During the 1980s, the Egyptian government did not satisfy any of the three indicators of credible reform. There were no significant, sustained economic reform initiatives that would have improved Egypt's reputation and signaled the determination or ability of the government to carry out SOE reform. The modest reputation of the Egyptian government during the 1980s is reflected in a low ICRG score of twelve. Moreover, there were few domestic restraints since the president enjoyed considerable authority over the governing political party and the various branches of government. Finally, although Egypt was a GATT signatory, it was bound only to the less restrictive provisions reserved for lower-income countries. Overall, then, Egypt did not meet Condition III, although this situation may be changing with the broader economic reforms introduced in the 1990s.

Senegal. Senegal has a mixed reputation for policy reform, a modest degree of domestic restraint on policy reversals, and the same lack of binding GATT requirements as Ghana and Egypt. Senegal's macroeconomic reforms have included such broad efforts as improved fiscal discipline and currency devaluation, but occasional reversals have undermined the benefits to its reputation that might otherwise have been gained. Its reputation for not expropriating or repudiating contracts, however, is higher than that of the mixed-performing SOE countries, according to the ICRG ratings.

The leadership appears to face few internal restraints, given the dominance of the government and the legislature by the Socialist Party. However, because the party is not monolithic and the authority of the president over the party is partial, the legislature offered some restraint on policy reversal in the 1980s. Gain sharing has not been employed in SOE reform attempts. Overall, therefore, Senegal demonstrates partial ability to meet Condition III.

Turkey. Turkey met Condition III at least partially. On the one hand, in the 1980s, Turkey enacted the series of macroeconomic reforms discussed earlier, it had competitive elections after 1983 for which the Polity II ratings on executive constraints assign it a score of five out of seven, and it took concrete steps to enter the European Union. Its ICRG score of four-

teen out of thirty for the period lies between that of Egypt and those of more successful reformers. In the late 1980s, Turkey continually reaffirmed commitments to the European Union to harmonize its trade policies with those of the European Union by 1995 and took steps to that end. In fact, formalization of Turkish entry into the customs union of the European Union was initiated in 1994, despite Turkey's conflict with Greece concerning Cyprus.

Turkey's credibility was not complete, however. Although the Özal government embarked on significant fiscal, trade, and exchange rate reforms, these were subject to occasional reversals: fiscal goals were missed by a significant margin with the renewal of export subsidies and the reduction of revenues from the value added tax in 1985–86; the country overshot its inflation targets in 1984, when inflation reached 48 percent instead of the targeted 10 percent (Onis and Webb 1992). Nor were domestic restraints complete: the prospect of elections was the only significant constraint on the prime minister in the 1980s. Before 1987, the prime minister had extensive decree powers and substantial discretion over the government budget. The activities of interest groups, such as business and labor associations, were restricted, and political activity by them was forbidden so that there was little oversight of government actions in the political arena.[32]

Strategies to link the interests of reform losers to the long-term success of reform were little developed and sometimes failed. For example, in 1988, the government privatized TELETAS, a maker of telecommunications equipment, in one of the country's first major attempts at privatization through widespread share sales. Shares were sold in small lots through commercial bank branches; the offer was fully subscribed and began trading on the Istanbul stock exchange. Soon afterward, TELETAS' biggest customer, the state-owned telecoms company, sharply cut its investment program—and, by implication, its purchases of TELETAS products. This news, combined with a general decline in the stock market, caused TELETAS' share values to fall by half (Kjellstrom 1990). To avoid a public outcry, the government subsequently bought shares to raise the price, partially reversing privatization. This episode damaged public confidence in the government's ability to follow through on gain sharing promises.

China. The foundations of China's credibility are less compelling than those of the other two transition economies, relying mostly on the reputational effect of China's liberalization program, which has progressed steadily since 1978. In addition, like Korea, China is increasingly dependent on international trade. Exports as a percentage of GNP rose from 9.5 percent in 1985 to 19.3 percent in 1991. Consistent with a strategy of growth through trade, China is seeking entry into the WTO and has changed its initial position on a number of issues (intellectual property rights, for example) in an effort to gain membership.

However, China has also confronted limits on its credibility. There are few domestic restrictions on the ability of Chinese authorities to reverse reforms. The basic legal tenets of a market system, such as corporate and contract laws, are only now being put in place, and there is considerable uncertainty about the applicability and enforceability of the laws that do exist. Legal protections available to investors to avoid contract repudiation or expropriation are unclear and seem to vary unpredictably. This may be one reason for the predominance of ethnic Chinese among foreign investors in China, since, apart from language and cultural ties and geographic proximity, this group enjoys the informal ties that help to protect their property rights in an uncertain legal environment.

Notes

1. This framework for analyzing the conditions under which SOE reform takes place can be applied to most economic reforms. However, details of the analysis will differ from one reform to another. For example, political desirability is calculated in part by weighing constituency interests; the relevant constituencies, and the relevant decisionmakers, often differ from policy to policy. Accordingly, some countries in our sample, such as Ghana and Turkey, undertook significant macroeconomic reforms without substantially altering their SOE policies.

2. If nothing else, a crisis may alter the calculation of costs and benefits simply by changing the information available to decisionmakers about the relative costs of different policy options.

3. Leaders may also be reluctant to privatize when they suspect that political rivals will manipulate the privatization process to their advantage. Among the cases we study, the Philippines may provide one possible example of this (see the appendix to this chapter).

4. It can also depend on the cloudier issue of how central SOEs are to a government's ideology.

5. These political changes make reform more likely but do not assure it. Even when the regime shift is dramatic, as were the shifts to President Corazon Aquino in the Philippines and President Jerry Rawlings in Ghana, the new regime may be torn between the temptation to reform SOEs that exist primarily to satisfy the constituencies of the prior regime and to use SOEs to solidify their own political support (Ghana and the Philippines show evidence of doing both).

6. The Allende government's policies represented a sharp turn toward greater state intervention in the economy, a sharper turn than could be supported by the slight electoral plurality with which President Allende took office—36 percent of the total vote, compared with 35 percent for the candidate of the right and 28 percent for the left-center candidate (Cordón 1993). One possible indicator of the severity of the policy shift is that these and other policies triggered unprecedented strikes by white-collar workers (Cordón 1993). Ironically, the sudden shift to the left created room for more extensive privatization than might otherwise have been the case.

7. Between 1977 and 1982, real GNP declined by an annual average of 5.3 percent. By 1981, the budget deficit had risen to 9.3 percent of GDP (Ka and van de Walle 1994).

8. The current account deficit was cut from 17 percent of GDP in 1983–84 to less than 10 percent in 1988–89. Government expenditures were reduced from 32 percent of the GDP in fiscal 1981–82 to 21 percent in 1989–90 (Ka and van de Walle 1994). The average protection rate declined from 165 percent in 1985 to 98 percent in 1988.

9. Senegal received, on average, more foreign assistance as a percentage of GDP during the 1980s than Egypt but still made greater progress on reforms (limited though they might have been with respect to SOEs). Unlike Senegal, however, Egypt's aid was not conditioned on economic reforms, and Egypt did not experience a regime or coalition shift. Mexico, which did experience both crisis and political change, did not receive signficant amounts of aid relative to its GDP, and its SOE reforms were greater.

10. In 1980, Deng introduced mandatory retirement ages, which forced out large numbers of older officials. This movement was accelerated by retirements of officials who had not reached the statutory retirement age.

11. This is not an unambiguously bad outcome, however, as the discussion below on credibility suggests. Policy reforms produced by governments that require the assent of multiple entities with independently selected membership are more likely to be sustainable or credible than policy reforms that are instituted by a single individual.

12. The greater the inefficiencies that SOE policy incurs, the greater the net gains from reform. These net gains could, in principle, be used to make losers from SOE

reform better off than they were before, raising the likelihood of successful reform. For a number of reasons, it is difficult to use these net gains to reduce opposition. For example, the gains are often realized in the future, after SOE reform losers have acquiesced to the reform. Consequently, reform losers would be required to depend on promises by the country's leadership. As the discussion of credibility in the next section suggests, these promises may not be credible. Other gains may not be available to compensate losers directly. For example, if a more efficient enterprise provides better service at lower prices, the economy and the firm's consumers benefit, but these gains are difficult to apportion to the losers.

13. These estimates may not necessarily mean that redundancy exists in all types of jobs. Usually, most overstaffing occurs in administrative and clerical positions, not in the more technically skilled jobs for which there is sufficient demand in the economy.

14. The numbers in this figure seem to be much higher than the entries for Chile in table 4.2, which were used to substantiate the claim that Chilean overstaffing might have been less than in other countries. However, table 4.2 referred to an average of all firms and the time periods are different between the table and the figure.

15. Strictly speaking, these enterprises were subject to "intervention," a Chilean legal concept in which the government takes over control of a company but not its ownership.

16. The government's policies of wide share distribution were also intended to make the privatizations difficult to reverse by subsequent governments. In this sense, wide share distribution also promoted the credibility of the SOE reforms, as we discuss later.

17. Prior to 1992, the Civic Democratic Party had only thirty-seven seats, only four more than the Movement for Democratic Slovakia, which was not a strong supporter of SOE reforms (EIU 1992; *Europa World Yearbook* 1994).

18. To the extent that this has occurred, the efficiency gains of divestiture may have been reduced.

19. If recipients of these shares subsequently sell them, and ownership becomes concentrated, this advantage is reduced.

20. Enforcement of these provisions is not perfect, since GATT and the European Union restrictions on subsidies are frequently violated. Nonetheless, such provisions raise the cost of maintaining or increasing subsidies to local industries, including SOEs.

21. Although we do not consider this dimension in detail, countries that are heavily dependent on external, particularly private, capital flows are also likely to be more credible, since policy reversals or setbacks can lead to dramatic changes in the direction of those flows.

22. We are only able to use International Country Risk Guide (ICRG) evaluations, for example, from 1985 onward. We do not expect that SOE reforms alone bias these evaluations upward, which would cause these ratings to reflect rather than to predict reform. However, the ratings do seem sensitive, as we would expect, to significant policy reforms across a broad spectrum. Mexico, for example, experienced an increase in its ICRG rating from twelve in 1986 to seventeen in 1989. Nevertheless, even with the reforms undertaken by Chile and Mexico, their ICRG scores were still significantly below Singapore's rating of over twenty-one over the period and Switzerland's top rating of thirty. This suggests that these evaluations are affected by more than sound policies.

23. Chile bound itself to strict GATT requirements as well. (Its own trade reforms in fact exceeded GATT requirements.)

24. Policy reversal was also a concern in Ghana, as later events were to verify. Prior to the 1992 elections, government spending surged to create a fiscal deficit of 4.8 percent of GDP, compared with the surplus of 1.8 percent of GDP that prevailed in 1991.

25. The investor risk guide information is sometimes contemporaneous with reform in our sample, but it can be used as a predictor for all reforms after 1985.

26. Since President Rawlings came to power in a coup, there is no direct evidence dating from before the SOE re-

forms to describe his constituency. The section on feasibility describes government efforts to repress union and student leaders after 1983, however, which is consistent with the notion that he was less dependent on these groups for support. In addition, there is direct evidence for the strength of his rural support base from the 1992 elections, when he received nearly twice as many votes overall as his next closest rival, Albert Adu-Doahen, despite losing to him in most of the major urban-industrial areas of the country (Kwesi 1993; *Daily Graphic* 1992).

27. The SOE sector was never as large in the Philippines as in many of the other countries in the sample. Under President Marcos, the greatest rents seem to have been transferred through government authorized private monopolies. The Aquino government dismantled many of these: it lifted regulations, such as levies on coconut exports and prohibitions on new investment in coconut milling, that protected the coconut milling industry, which was controlled by President Marcos' supporters. It also abolished the Philippine Sugar Marketing Authority, which had the same effect in the sugar industry.

28. The political importance of SOE workers arises not because they constitute the major source of support for the Congress Party (which is in fact heavily rural), but because they are swing votes whose continued support is necessary to maintain the Congress Party in power.

29. Trade was significantly liberalized; for example, the goods on which import licenses were required dropped from 821 in 1983 to 33 in 1989. Tariffs were, in general, reduced (Onis and Webb 1992). A value added tax was introduced, and subsidies were moderated. These reforms followed other stabilization and liberalization measures that President Özal had implemented when he formed a part of the military government.

30. William Willis, Australian Office of Employment, Education, and Training, speech at the World Bank, May 24, 1995.

31. It might also be argued that the 1988 elections triggered a coalition realignment in Senegal so that, after 1988, the country no longer fulfilled Condition I.

32. Since 1987, and particularly in the 1990s, restrictions on political activity have been relaxed, and electoral changes made coalition governments, which do not change policies easily, nearly inevitable (Esfahani 1994). These have increased the restraints on domestic policy reversal and increased the credibility of Turkish government decisions (although they have, as noted in the section on political feasibility, also increased the difficulty of securing SOE reform approval).

How to Spur Reforms and Improve Outcomes

THIS REPORT HAS PRESENTED EVIDENCE THAT RE-ducing the role of bureaucrats in business can bring a country substantial economic gains. Yet, as we have seen, reform has been slow and seldom successful. We conclude by drawing on our findings and other studies to suggest ways that the leaders and policy-makers in developing countries can foster more rapid and successful SOE reform.

State-owned enterprise reform involves a multitude of choices, each leading to a different set of problems and opportunities. The choices made will inevitably vary from country to country, but to lead to the optimum outcome, they must be made in a logical order. It might seem obvious, for example, that countries will not reform until the leader-ship perceives reform as desirable. Yet, perhaps precisely because the economic gains of reform are so impressive, well-intentioned outsiders, including the World Bank, have sometimes attempted to prod devel-oping countries that are not ready for reform into acting. Similarly, de-veloping-country leaders and policymakers, persuaded of the benefits of reforming state-owned enterprises, have sometimes attempted to do so, only to choose an option that meets with failure. How can those who rightly favor reform organize the multitude of choices they face in a way that will increase the likelihood of success?

In thinking about the prerequisites of SOE reform, and the conditions that are necessary for the success of various reform options, we have found it useful to draw a decision tree (figure 5.1). At each juncture we ask a question, the answer to which sends us to another juncture and another question or to a recommended policy course. This chapter traces the main branches of that decision tree, offering checklists that

Figure 5.1 A Decision Tree for State-Owned Enterprise Reform

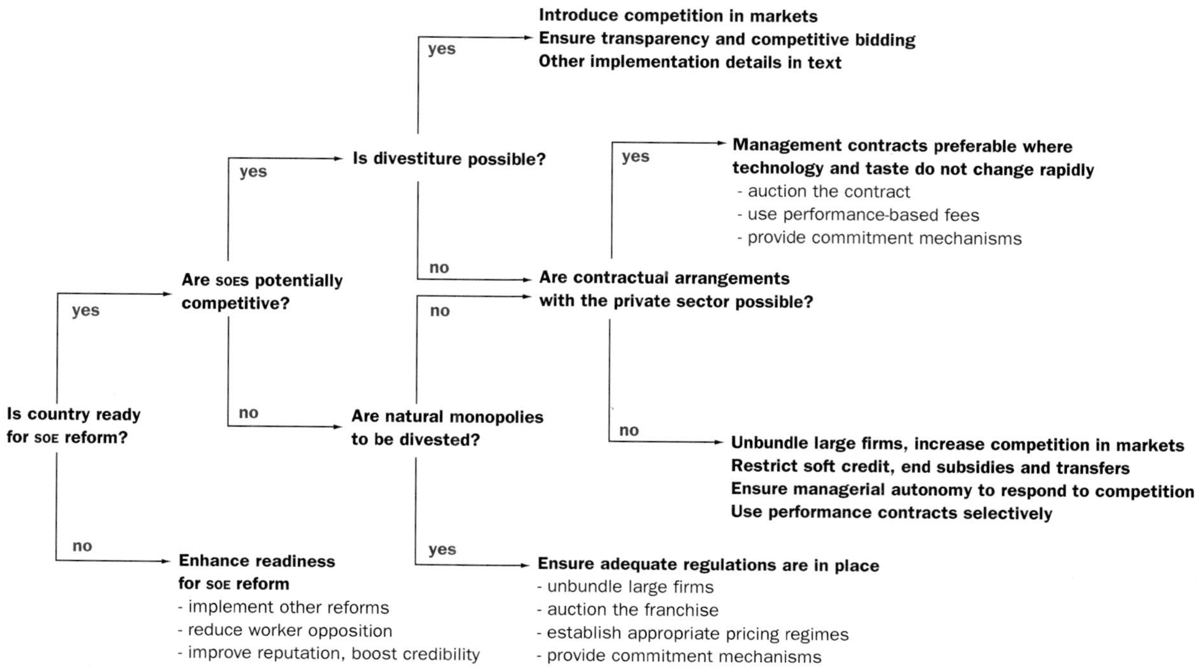

Source: See chapter 5 text.

The decision tree helps to organize the multitude of choices involved in SOE reform. To use it, begin with the first question at left. Each answer leads to another question or a recommended policy course.

advocates of reform can use in devising a strategy for reform in a given country or even for particular enterprises.

The first question: is the country ready for reform or not? Depending on the answer, the next course of action is radically different. If the country is not ready, then SOE reforms should not be pursued, but there are many other things that can be done to lay the groundwork for reform. If the country is ready, then the tree asks policymakers to classify SOEs into two types:

- Those operating in competitive or potentially competitive markets, which includes all manufacturing and most services
- Those operating in natural monopoly markets, where regulation is necessary to prevent enterprises from abusing their market power, which includes some utilities and most infrastructure.

Enterprises in competitive or potentially competitive markets should then be divested, provided that competition is enhanced and arrangements for the sale can be made transparent and open to the possibility of competitive bidding. Enterprises in natural monopoly markets can also be divested, provided again that the sale is transparent and open to competitive bidding *and* that a credible regulatory structure can be put in place.

Even in countries where the leadership is committed to rapid and extensive privatization, at least some SOEs in both types of markets are likely to remain in public hands for a long time, for political if not for economic reasons. For enterprises that are not privatized, the next juncture on the decision tree for policymakers to consider is whether contracts with private management are possible and desirable. In general, we found contracts with private managers to be very successful, but they are not appropriate for all types of enterprises, as we detail below. At the final branch of our decision tree, where neither privatization nor state ownership with private sector management is currently feasible, policymakers can move quickly to strengthen competition, harden SOE budget constraints, and reform financial and institutional arrangements.

In the sections that follow, we provide more guidance on each branch of our tree. First, we detail predictors of whether a country is ready to reform or not and then map out actions for countries that are not ready. To assist policymakers in reform-ready countries, we explore lessons of experience in divestiture, in regulating private monopolies, and in reforming SOEs that cannot be divested. This analysis has important implications for foreign assistance as well as for policymakers that are summarized in box 1 in the overview and discussed in detail in "Implications for Foreign Assistance" at the end of the report.

How to Tell Whether a Country Is Ready to Reform

DETERMINING WHETHER A COUNTRY IS READY TO REFORM IS not easy; many governments that promise reforms turn out to be either unwilling or unable to deliver. Chapter 4 discussed in detail the theoretical and empirical bases for three conditions of reform readiness: reform must be politically desirable to leaders and their constituencies; reform must be politically feasible; and the government must be able to promise credibly to stick to the reform in the future. Drawing on that discussion, we present a brief checklist that helps to distinguish whether or not a country is ready for reform.[1]

Political Desirability

Indications that reform has become politically desirable to the leaders and their constituencies include:

- *A change in regime or coalition.* If the governing regime or coalition changed, there may be a window of opportunity but only if the new governing group does not depend so much on SOEs that its survival would be threatened by reform. In assessing the extent to which a government relies on SOEs, electoral results are especially revealing. How much does the government owe its victory to groups that would support (or at least not oppose) SOE reform (such as the increasingly important urban commercial and middle class in Mexico)? Early actions are another important indicator of whether a new government sees SOE reform as desirable. A new government that rewards supporters with SOE jobs or increases SOE real wages across the board is likely to count on the support of those who benefit from the status quo, while a government that sharply cuts SOE redundancies probably does not.
- *A fiscal or economic crisis.* Even governments that rely on SOEs for support may still reform if a severe crisis makes the status quo unaffordable. Crisis may change the preferences of a government's constituency or persuade a government to build a new constituency that favors reform (as in Ghana or Mexico). How serious does a crisis need to be for change to become desirable? This unavoidably entails subjective judgment; based on past experience, a significant deviation from past trends or sudden worsening of a bad situation (as when Mexico's fiscal deficit doubled to 15 percent of GDP) can persuade a government to take action that may injure some of its own supporters. In some instances, however, even a very severe crisis will not prompt reform: failure to reduce SOE deficits decisively during a fiscal crisis is a strong sign that a country is not ready for SOE reform.

Political Feasibility

Indications that reform is politically feasible include:

- *Control of the policymaking process.* Do the reformers control the legislature, the bureaucracy, the state and local governments, and other relevant bodies that must approve SOE reforms? If the reformers must form coalitions to control these policymaking bodies, who are the constituents of their coalition partners and what is their view of SOE reforms? At varying times partners in intra- or interparty coalitions resisted reform efforts in Mexico, Turkey, Senegal, India and elsewhere.

■ *Ability to overcome resistance to reform.* Even a reform-minded group in complete control of the formal power apparatus may not be able to change policies if informal, ad hoc resistance, often from SOE workers, is sufficiently strong. Thus, another important signal that reforms are feasible is the government's ability to withstand such resistance. Ideally, governments use compensation (by distributing shares to the public or to workers in powerful unions). However, some governments have resorted to compulsion (by limiting strikes, preventing riots, and curbing union powers), sometimes incurring high social costs in the process. No government that reformed successfully used only compulsion, however. For example, Mexico's reformers used compensation, assisting rural communities with funds generated from privatization and distributing shares to TELMEX employees; they also used compulsion, firing striking employees at Aeroméxico and then selling the airline. Because SOE employees often stand to lose the most and are therefore the most outspoken opponents of reform, reform advocates can assess the potential magnitude of opposition by estimating the extent of SOE overstaffing. Whether or not a country has a history of strikes and demonstrations in opposition to economic policy changes provides another clue to the likely strength of opposition, as does the extent to which the military owns SOEs and serves on their boards.

Government Credibility

Signs that the government can credibly commit to upholding its promises in the future include the following:

■ *Reputation.* The ICRG evaluations we reviewed in chapter 4 are one indicator of whether a government is considered a credible reformer. Another is whether a government with a weak reputation is in the process of strengthening its credibility by announcing and then implementing broad economic reforms. Fiscal and trade reforms are particularly useful indicators, since these are difficult reforms closely watched by investors. But over-reliance on macroeconomic policy reforms in judging readiness for SOE reforms can be misleading since the political desirability and feasibility of macroeconomic reforms differ from those for SOE reforms, and countries often do one set of reforms without the other.

■ *Domestic restraints.* Government reform efforts are more credible when there are domestic constraints that raise the cost of reversing the reforms once they are put in place. Does the country have legal restraints, such as a constitutional provision protecting private property? Or institutional curbs on arbitrary action, such as a strong legal system or legislature that can prevent sudden policy reversals by the executive? Has the government created new constituencies that would favor sustained reform, for example, through wide distribution of shares in privatized SOEs? Legal and institutional restraints must be judged carefully, however: on the one hand, they protect reforms already in place; on the other, they may make it difficult to achieve the consensus necessary to get reforms under way. For example, in both Chile (since 1990) and the Philippines, the executive's power is sharply circumscribed by the legislature. In Chile this has helped to safeguard reforms and reassure investors; in the Philippines legislative opposition has slowed enactment of reform.

■ *International restraints.* Is the country adhering to the strictest provisions of GATT, or aspiring to join NAFTA, the European Union, or other agreements that provide an incentive for reform and make it more difficult to reverse reforms once they are in place? Loan covenants with donor governments or multilateral institutions and contracts with multinational firms may also help shore up a government's credibility. International restraints are generally the least compelling of the three signals of credibility; how strong a signal they provide depends on how costly it would be for the government to renege on its international obligation.

Countries that meet all three conditions—that is, countries where reform may be considered politically desirable, feasible, and credible—are ready to reform. Countries that fail to meet any one of the conditions are not. Returning to our decision tree, we consider first how reform advocates could respond in countries that are *not ready* to reform.

What to Do in Countries Not Ready for SOE Reform

FAILED REFORM ATTEMPTS CAN BE VERY COSTLY IN TERMS OF financial, human, and political capital. Money spent to restructure SOEs and pay off their bad debts is wasted if the enterprises fail to improve their performance or, having been privatized, collapse back into the government's arms. More difficult to quantify, but no less important, are the costs in wasted human and political capital. Policymakers who spend months or years designing SOE reform programs when the prerequisites for success are lacking could devote their scarce skills to other issues where success is more likely. Similarly, developing-country leaders and donors that push SOE reforms with a very scant or nonexistent chance of success draw down their political capital without achieving any significant returns.

Are we suggesting that nothing can be done in countries not yet ready to reform their SOEs? Certainly not. Rather, policymakers in these countries can begin laying the groundwork for future SOE reform. Steps include macroeconomic reforms, which help create a constituency for SOE reform, thereby making SOE reform more politically desirable; policies to reduce the opposition to reform by SOE workers and others dependent on the SOE sector, thereby making SOE reform more politically feasible; and improving the government's reputation, particularly with domestic and foreign investors and other potential supporters of reform, thereby enhancing credibility. We discuss each of these steps below. Box 5.1 contains two action checklists—one for countries not ready to reform SOEs and one for those that are ready for reform.

Make SOE Reform More Desirable by Implementing Reforms in Other Areas

In countries that are not ready for SOE reform, policymakers could nonetheless pursue other economic reforms, particularly trade, fiscal and monetary, and other market-oriented reforms, and take limited steps to develop the financial sector. These reforms are not only valuable in their own right, over time they also generate pressures to reduce SOE inefficiencies as discussed below, thus making reform more politically desirable. Different reforms have different constituencies, which explains why countries such as China, Ghana, or Turkey were

Box 5.1 Getting Ready for Reform

IN COUNTRIES *NOT YET READY* TO REFORM SOES, policymakers can lay the foundation for SOE reform to become politically desirable, politically feasible, and credible by taking the following steps:

- Reduce fiscal deficits, which makes the burden of SOE deficits more explicit.
- Ease trade restrictions so that SOE products face import competition.
- Removing barriers to entry such as SOE legal monopolies or competitive advantages bestowed by administrative fiat.
- Begin to reform the financial system by improving supervision and regulation, reducing directed credit, and moving interest rates closer to real rates.
- Eliminate obstacles to private jobs creation, such as subsidies that artificially lower the cost of capital, taxes that raise the cost of labor, or regulatory impediments to hiring and firing.
- Make SOE jobs more demanding by punishing loafing, moonlighting, and corruption.
- Uncouple SOE jobs and social services (health care, housing, etc.) to encourage labor mobility.
- Improve the government's credibility by following through on promised reforms in other sectors and creating legal and other restraints to reversals of reform.

In countries that *are ready* to reform their SOEs, policymakers can maximize the gains with the following measures:

- Open markets and divest potentially competitive SOEs wherever sales can be made transparent and competitive.
- Divest monopolies where an appropriate and credible regulatory framework can be put in

place and sales can be made transparent and competitive. A regulatory framework is more likely to enhance efficiency when it solves the problems of information (by encouraging competition or the threat of competition); rewards (by developing a pricing formula that encourages the owner to increase efficiency yet passes some of the efficiency gains on to consumers); and commitment (by putting in place a neutral, objective mechanism to resolve conflicts, or, where this is not possible, by taking costly action to reassure investors that government is indeed committed).

- Use management contracts for SOEs that cannot be divested and that are in sectors where technology is not changing rapidly and performance is relatively easy to judge (e.g., a single, homogeneous product). These contracts work better when the SOE operates in competitive markets and the contract can be competitively bid; when management is given the freedom to make improvements and rewarded for doing so (e.g., through a success fee) and when government and management take action to show they are committed (e.g., by putting a company's reputation at stake).
- Reform all other SOEs through a comprehensive program to foster competition, while hardening budgets, ending soft credits, and increasing managerial autonomy and accountability. Performance contracts should be part of the package only where they can be designed to convey clear signals for reform, provide rewards for improved performance, and curb government's tendency to renege.

able to implement important macroeconomic or systemic reforms, but were less succesful in reforming their SOEs. Of the three types of measures that countries not yet ready for SOE reform can implement, macroeconomic reform is the most important and the most beneficial.

Indeed, properly implemented, such reform programs not only enhance the political desirability of future SOE reforms, they also help to improve political feasibility and credibility. Steps that governments can take as part of an overall reform program that have particular relevance to SOE reform include:

- *Reducing fiscal deficits.* Fiscal and monetary reforms that bring revenues and expenditures into line also increase pressure for SOE reform by making the burden of SOE deficits explicit, thus fueling demands that they be reduced or eliminated. Such reforms could have priority.
- *Easing trade restrictions.* Liberalized trade restrictions give exporters a stronger position in the economy. Exporters can then become an important constituency for SOE reform, demanding more efficient provision of goods and services that SOEs supply.
- *Removing barriers to entry.* Removing barriers to entry increases the number of voices calling for SOE reform. New entrants who must rely on SOE goods and services, pay taxes to support SOE operations, or compete with subsidized SOE products help enlarge the constituency for reform.
- *Initiating financial sector reform.* Governments that are not ready to reform SOEs may still be prepared to develop their financial system. The first steps toward financial sector reform in these countries could be to improve supervisory and regulatory capacity, to reduce directed credit and direct government control over financial intermediaries, and to move interest rates closer to real positive rates. This makes subsidies to SOEs more explicit and helps reduce the risk that efforts to curb fiscal deficits will spread the problem to the banking system. Privatization of banks and further liberalization is risky before regulatory and SOE reforms are well underway, however. Where both are not present, the bad debts of an unreformed SOE sector and the lack of appropriate supervisory and regulatory reforms can lead to a crisis in the financial system, as happened in Chile in the early 1980s.

Make SOE Reform Feasible by Reducing Employee Opposition

Workers and managers in SOEs stand to lose the most from reform, through layoffs or wage cuts, and are therefore frequently the most vocal and best organized opponents of reform. Even when inflation has eroded SOE wages, as it has in many countries in recent years, many SOE employees cling fiercely to their jobs. This is because they lack alternative employment or because the effort demanded in their SOE jobs is low, and the opportunities for moonlighting or corruption offset the low wages. In transition economies and some developing countries, SOE workers have a further incentive to cling to their jobs, since benefits ranging from housing to recreational opportunities are obtained through the workplace. Governments that are not yet ready to reform SOEs can take several steps to lessen this potential opposition, thereby improving the political feasibility of future SOE reforms. They can:

■ *Eliminate obstacles to private job creation.* The growth of private employment is not only one of the main benefits of an overall reform program, it can also create alternatives for redundant SOE employees who might otherwise oppose SOE reform. Government obstacles to private job creation include policies that artificially lower the cost of capital, such as interest rate subsidies, because they encourage employers to substitute capital for labor, and government impediments to hiring and firing, such as complex regulations and outright bans on layoffs. These have been shown to inhibit private job growth (Banerji and Sabot 1994). Finally, taxes that raise the cost of labor, such as payroll taxes, can be replaced with other taxes that do not discourage job creation. This, too, could be a priority area for action.

■ *Uncouple SOE jobs and social services.* SOE workers who receive a wide array of goods and social services through their jobs are especially fearful of relinquishing them. In most transition economies, for example, state firms have long provided housing, health care, transport, educational assistance, and other benefits not otherwise available. By creating public alternatives to some enterprise benefits, such as health care, bus transport, and education and private alternatives in housing and recreation, governments can begin to uncouple these services from the job. This will give SOE workers greater mobility and reduce their resistance to reforms that may force them to look for work in the private sector.

Improve Reputation and Create Restraints to Boost Credibility

Successful implementation of the reforms described above would go a long way to establish the credibility of any future SOE reform effort with investors and others whose support is necessary. Leaders and policymakers in developing countries can enhance this effect by announcing reform programs in advance and scrupulously adhering to their announced plans. In addition, they can establish domestic restraints, such as constitutional provisions guaranteeing the right to property, to reassure investors that the government will honor its commitments and not expropriate their investments, either directly or through confiscatory regulation. Finally, developing-country governments can enter into trade treaties or multilateral agreements that would raise the cost of reversing future SOE reforms.

For countries not yet ready for SOE reform, these three types of measures constitute a full agenda. Countries that implement it will find themselves on the opposite branch of the decision tree, among the countries that are ready to reform their SOEs.

What to Do in Countries Ready for SOE Reform

HAVING DETERMINED THAT THEIR COUNTRY IS READY FOR SOE reform, how should policymakers proceed? Our findings about the conditions under which SOE reform succeeds suggest that they could next classify SOEs into those in competitive or potentially competitive markets, on the one hand, and those in natural monopoly markets, on the other. Enterprises in competitive or potentially competitive markets can be divested, provided that competition is enhanced and arrangements for the sale can be made transparent and competitive or at least open to the possibility of competitive bidding. Some enterprises in natural monopoly markets can also be divested, provided that the sale is transparent and open to competitive bidding *and* that a credible regulatory structure can be put in place. (These two outcomes correspond to the two outermost branches of our decision tree.) Decisions about which firms belong in which category, and whether or not divestiture is possible, vary by country; they may shift over time, as a country's capacity to divest and regulate improves and as technology increases the potential for competition in sectors once seen as natural monopolies—a trend recently evident in telecoms and electrical power generation. In the remainder of this chapter, we first discuss key questions that policymakers face in deciding when and how to divest. We conclude with advice on what to do with SOEs that remain in government hands.

The potential benefits of divestiture can be lost if the sale is not properly managed. In this section, we first discuss issues that apply to privatization of firms in competitive and noncompetitive markets, examining some of the potential pitfalls of privatization. We then turn to issues that arise primarily when privatizing monopolies; in particular, the need for a credible regulatory structure. We conclude with a discussion of firms that cannot be divested.

How to Divest where Markets Can Be Made Competitive

This report has shown that many SOEs operate in potentially competitive markets but are protected from competition by legal barriers, government subsidies, and privileges. Governments can sell off such enterprises with minimal regulation if they introduce competition by liberalizing trade and price restrictions and by removing barriers to entry. Cutting off access to subsidies, privileges, and soft credit is crucial to making privatization a true economic change and not just a transfer of title. In some cases, ensuring future competition will also require that governments break up large monopolies prior to sale and split potentially competitive activities, such as cellular phones or telephone equipment, from natural monopolies, like local telephone service.

For all types of divestiture, competitive bidding of some form is preferable to a negotiated sale. Competitive bidding not only improves the government's selling price, it also creates pressures for a more transparent process, because competing investors insist on clear rules. The precise form of competitive bidding will depend on the size of the firm. For firms that are very small, open auctions, such as those held in the Czech Republic and Estonia, offer a rapid, simple, and transparent way to divest. For medium and large firms, where potential buyers invest time and resources to determine the firm's value, sealed competitive bids, opened publicly, may be more appropriate, provided that procedures can be put in place to ensure secrecy and fair dealing.

Privatizations can be administratively challenging, and it may be hard to assure transparency in countries with weak legal and bureaucratic institutions. Such problems are compounded if the country is not politically ready to reform. If transparency and competition in the product market or appropriate regulation of monopolies cannot be assured, then privatization must await market, institutional, and legal reforms; otherwise the cost to the economy could be high (box 5.2).

Privatization also needs to be harmonized with financial sector reform. The allocation of credit according to commercial criteria rather than by administrative fiat demands greater autonomy and competition in the banking system. Financial liberalization is extremely risky, however, unless sound regulation and supervision are in place. Another risk to guard against is that privatization does not result in unhealthy ties between banks and the businesses they finance. For example, in the first wave of privatization in Chile in the 1970s, policymakers did not sufficiently scrutinize the buyers of enterprises and their sources of finance or regulate the financial system closely enough (see box 2.10). Some of these buyers purchased banks and used the banks as collateral to purchase other firms in highly leveraged sales. This led to a concentration of ownership, overindebtedness, insider lending, and, during the economic crisis of the early 1980s, the return of some fifty divested banks and their firms to the government.

Assuming that these minimum conditions are in place for divestiture to go ahead, policymakers will still face many questions that have different answers depending on country conditions and, in some instances, on the size and condition of the enterprise being sold. We discuss nine of these questions below, not to impose one-size-fits-all answers, but to raise issues that policymakers will need to consider when planning their strategy.[2]

- ■ *Is it better to begin with small enterprises, or with big enterprises, or to sell SOEs in some sectors before others?* The size of the firm and the nature of the market (potentially competitive versus noncompetitive) are more important than the sector per se in deciding about sequencing. Selling big firms first produces bigger welfare gains: the bigger the firm, the bigger the benefits. In addition, the divestiture of a large enterprise, such as ENTEL in Argentina, signals the seriousness of the reform effort. The proceeds may also help a country weather a debt crisis. Finally, where large firms are privatized in part via wide share distribution, policy reversal becomes costly, thus signaling commitment to reforms. This strategy may be particularly useful where the capacity to handle privatization is high, but the commitment to reform is uncertain. Argentina, for example,

Box 5.2 Privatization Can Have Pitfalls

SOME COUNTRIES HAVE CARRIED OUT RUSHED, poorly planned privatizations, occasionally in response to externally imposed deadlines, that were not sufficiently transparent or competitive. In such cases, the potential benefits of privatization are lost, and the final result may be worse than the situation before divestiture.

Guinea, one of the first countries in Africa to undertake extensive divestiture, privatized or liquidated some 158 SOEs between 1985 and 1992 (Fukui 1992). Unfortunately, the program proceeded without laws to define its scope and identify the implementing agency; transparent procedures for valuation or competitive bidding were lacking; and fiscal and efficiency goals were not well specified. This led to serious problems. Assets were sometimes sold for a small fraction of their value. For example, Huilerie de Kasa, a coconut oil producer, sold for GNF 6 million, when two generators in the plant alone were worth Guinean franc (GNF) 30 million. The SANOYA textile complex sold for ECU 1 million after undergoing an ECU 42 million rehabilitation.

Sale terms were often overly generous, with long payback periods (five to fifteen years with two to five years' grace) at very low interest rates. There was little publicity about impending bidding and very few offers, less than two on average, for most firms (seventeen firms only received one offer). Most damaging of all, however, were the "sweeteners" handed to investors, including domestic monopolies (cement, cigarettes, soft drinks), tax exemptions (a quarry, cigarettes, soft drinks), and import duty exemptions (most of the firms). Although the costs of the monopolies and tax exemptions are difficult to determine, the duty exemptions alone were estimated to have cost the government GNF 1.5 billion ($2.5 million) by 1989. Despite the generous sales terms and operating privileges, by 1991 only four of the privatized companies were profitable, and most of the new owners had yet to pay fully for their firms. This has raised the possibility that these enterprises will revert to government ownership in worse condition than when they were sold.

Mali's privatizations have also been marked by poor planning and implementation, which has been attributed in part to the government's lack of ownership of a donor-driven privatization program. Initially slow implementation (decrees to authorize and regulate the process were never issued) was followed by rushed, nontransparent valuation and sale or liquidation in an effort to meet donor deadlines. Some potentially salable enterprises were liquidated to meet divestiture timetables in World Bank loan covenants. The emphasis on speed was one reason the government made most sales on installment plans and therefore received little up-front gain. Moreover, payments have generally not been timely.

Some countries thought of as successful privatizers have also had difficulty, particularly in the beginning, suggesting that countries can learn from their mistakes. For example, when Argentina tried to sell the state airline, Aerolíneas Argentinas, the only qualified bidder was the country's only other airline. Rather than cancel the bidding and try again to ensure market competition, the government went ahead with the sale, in part because this was one of its first privatizations and officials were concerned about derailing the entire privatization program. Subsequently, bids were canceled if there was only one bidder, and greater effort was made to avoid sales that would create a private monopoly.

Source: Fukui (1992); Berg (1993); World Bank (1993a, 1994a, 1994b).

began its privatization program in the early 1990s with the airline and the phone company; having thus raised needed funds, retired debt, and shown its commitment to reform, it later moved on to smaller enterprises (and other large firms). Mexico, on the other hand, had success starting small and learning before selling big firms and used wide share distributions in only a few cases. Since either method seems to work, the choice could depend on whether policymakers feel a stronger need to demonstrate commitment and raise capital or to improve their technical ability to handle divestiture.

- *Should government make new investments to expand or improve the enterprise before selling it?* No. New investments prior to privatization are seldom recovered in the purchase price because bureaucrats' ideas of appropriate investment often differ from the ideas of potential buyers. Public investments also send mixed signals about whether the government actually intends to proceed with divestiture.

- *Should the government financially restructure firms before selling them?* Judging from experience, governments need to be prepared to write down some of the typically large SOE debt burden. For example, the governments of Argentina and Venezuela assumed debts of $930 million and $471 million, respectively, prior to sale of their telephone companies. Since it is politically unpalatable to divest an enterprise by paying the buyer to take it over, assumption of debt may be the only feasible way to unload a company whose debt exceeds the sales value of its assets.

- *Should the government lay off workers before selling an enterprise?* Countries as diverse as Argentina, Japan, Mexico, New Zealand, Tunisia, and the United Kingdom have terminated state enterprise employees prior to privatizations. Sometimes governments must do so if an enterprise is to be sold, since investors shy away from highly visible labor disputes. Moreover, governments are usually better able than private investors to alleviate adverse social consequences and thus defuse worker opposition. As we saw in chapter 4, successful privatizers developed programs to inform and involve the work force, to compensate laid off workers, and to encourage worker share ownership in larger sales. In countries that did not prepare workers for massive redundancies, worker opposition was vocal and, in some cases, slowed or halted privatization.

- *How can the social costs of layoffs be reduced?* Severance pay can play an important role in reducing risks faced by workers. In designing severance packages, governments often make the mistake of over-paying some workers to leave and of losing many of the best workers. It would be better to tailor severance packages to the characteristics of different workers, so that no one gets a windfall and able workers who are willing to work hard choose to remain.[3] Retraining, job search assistance, and business start-up allowances are generally not relevant to most developing economies, which lack the necessary preconditions of high administrative capabilities and growing labor demand.

■ *Should a company be sold through public offerings or via bids to a consortium of investors?* Public offerings are politically appealing, since they result in broader share distribution and reduce criticism that the sale was rigged or that the government is transferring assets to a tiny, wealthy elite. Despite these advantages, direct sales accounted for the vast majority of privatizations in developing countries from 1988 to 1993—58 percent by value and 80 percent by the number of transactions (Sader 1994). Direct sales are attractive to developing countries for several reasons. For small to medium firms, direct sale may be simpler and less costly than a public offering. Developing countries tend to reserve public listing for their larger privatizations: the average value of SOEs sold by public offer during 1988–93 was $132 million, more than four times the average value of SOEs sold directly. Direct sale may also be more appropriate for troubled large firms that could benefit from a strong owner and would be an inappropriate risk for government to offer on a fledgling stock market. Direct sale is virtually the only technique used in Sub-Saharan Africa, a reflection, perhaps, of the low value of assets, the underdevelopment of local capital markets, and the widespread use of privatization by liquidating the firm and selling the assets (Sader 1994). In contrast, transition economies, with their need to privatize many large firms, their concerns about equity, and their desire to develop their financial systems, tend to favor public offerings.

■ *How much foreign participation should be allowed?* Foreign participation has much to recommend it. Benefits include new capital for investment, access to overseas markets, and infusions of managerial and technological knowledge. Moreover, foreign participation can foster more competitive bidding, raising the sales price. For some large enterprises in countries with a small private capital base, privatization may not be possible without foreign funds. These factors may explain why, despite lingering nationalistic objections in many countries, foreign investment accounted for one-third of the value of privatizations in developing countries from 1988 to 1993 and for almost 40 percent of the proceeds from sales in telecommunications and energy (Sader 1994). Where opposition is strong and an enterprise is large, governments can sometimes overcome objections by distributing some of the shares widely but selling a minority with management control to foreign investors. In some instances, of course, the political opposition to foreign investment may be so strong that it outweighs the benefits.

■ *Should governments accept debt or only cash in exchange for public assets?* When privatizing, cash is always preferable to debt, since cash reduces the risk to government and prevents the new owners from using their debt to government to exact protection or special privileges. Nevertheless, many governments find themselves with no choice but to accept a buyer's IOU as part of the financing, because the asset being sold is so risky or the capital market so underdeveloped that potential buyers could not otherwise raise the funds. Policymakers can get out of this dilemma in one of two ways. One way is to sell a firm in tranches (passing management control immediately to private, minority shareholders and allowing them time to raise the funds to buy out the government gradually); or the government can enter into a government-private joint venture (private buyers make an equity investment in the enterprise and become the managing partners). The welfare gains from selling minority shares that give private investors management control can be high. Research on two privatized enterprises in Malaysia found that even small private minority shares can yield large economic gains if the private owner has management control (Galal and others 1994).

■ *How should the proceeds from the sale be used?* Privatization proceeds are an exchange of a future income stream for cash; they can be used to retire any obligation that depends on that future income but not to start public projects that will run out of funds once the proceeds are spent. For example, Mexico used some of the proceeds to retire some of its foreign debt. Reducing debt not only increases credibility, it also reduces the fiscal deficit by the amount of the debt service. Another important use is to compensate the losers from reform, for example, by funding severance pay or the distribution of shares to employees and others.

Divest Monopolies Where a Credible Regulatory Framework Can Be Put in Place

Selling monopolies can produce major welfare gains, especially through new investment, as long as the sale is competitive and transparent and a credible regulatory framework can be devised and implemented (Galal and others 1994; Levy and Spiller forthcoming). For example, the divestiture of Chilean telecoms brought estimated welfare gains of $1.3 billion (net present value in 1988 dollars; see Galal and others 1994), largely because of massive investments by the new owners. As a result of this investment, in the first five years after the sale, the annual growth in the total number of lines and the number of phones per 100 people more than quadrupled to 29 percent a year and 13 percent a year, respectively.

To achieve these gains, policymakers and regulators need to design a regulatory contract that improves regulators' information about the firm's costs, induces the firm to operate efficiently while allowing it to make a fair rate of return on its investments, and protects the owners against opportunistic government behavior in the future. In an ideal world, these would be achieved by perfect competition to eliminate the information advantage of the firm; rewards (primarily pricing) designed perfectly to motivate the firm to invest and operate optimally; and government commitment fully assured by anticipating all contingencies and figuring out mechanisms to resolve conflicts. In reality, of course, no contract is perfect. Policymakers must therefore be prepared to assess the tradeoffs between the compromises necessary to put a regulatory contract in place and the advantages that can be gained by pushing ahead with divestiture. Such cost-benefit analysis is an uncertain business, especially since it is only useful when it is done before either the costs or benefits are entirely clear. Even so, it remains the best way we have to think systematically about these tradeoffs. A form of cost-benefit analysis has been devised to assess the welfare effects of privatization after the fact, and work is under way in the World Bank to turn that into a predictive tool. Taking the possibility for compromises into account, policymakers who conclude that divesture and regulation of monopolies suit the needs of their country will want to consider the following in deciding when and how to proceed.

- *Regulatory contracts work better when governments reduce the firm's information advantage.* Competition is the least costly route to improve the information on which the contract is based. It can be increased by splitting off the natural monopoly and regulating access to it (for example, Chile split electricity generation from transmission, organized generation into seven competing firms, and regulated access to the grid); other activities can be horizontally unbundled, allowing yardstick competition. For example, Japan and Argentina split up their railways into regional operators (World Bank 1994d). Argentina split its telecoms monopoly into two regional companies. But even after efforts to increase competition are exhausted, segments of the market will remain monopolies (electricity distribution and transmission and local basic telephone services). To reduce the firm's information advantage in these cases, policymakers could auction the franchise and require that the incumbent meet certain targets or otherwise lose the concession. As we saw in chapter 3, Argentina, Chile, and Mexico followed such procedures in the telecommunications sector and ended up with significant expansion of the network and better services.

- *Rewards (primarily pricing) to the firm are more effective in promoting efficient performance when they rely less on the cost estimates provided by the firm and when they are infrequently revised.* Price regulation can be designed so that firms are induced to invest and operate efficiently, earning a fair rate of return while passing some of the productivity gains to consumers. This can be done in several ways. Chile reduced reliance on the firm's information by using the cost of a hypothetical, efficient firm as a yardstick for pricing. Argentina, Mexico, and Venezuela followed the example of the United Kingdom and set a cap on price increases that was based on the inflation rate minus an adjustment for improvements in efficiency. Chile and Mexico announced that they would wait five and four years, respectively, between price revisions; this motivated the firms to reduce costs because they could retain the benefits in the interim. Where the United Kingdom–style, price cap formula is followed, as in Mexico, it is possible to pass some benefits from efficiency gains to consumers by setting price increases below inflation.

■ *Regulatory contracts induce private firms to invest when the rules are believed to be credible.* When governments were unable to signal that they would uphold their side of the bargain—where, for example, contracts were based on presidential decrees that appeared vulnerable to being overturned or lacked provision for neutral, objective enforcement and conflict resolution—they had to offer higher returns or greater monopoly powers to convince investors that they were indeed committed. Jamaica, for example, gave Cable & Wireless an exclusive concession over all segments of the telecommunications markets and allowed the firm a 17.5 to 20 percent rate of return on net worth. In some cases, it may be too costly to the economy to allow firms to make very high rates of return in order to make up for the lack of credible commitment. This occurs when a country's institutions cannot bond against misbehavior—for example, when the judiciary is not seen as independent and objective, the legislature overturns laws frequently, and a reputation for respecting property rights and rule of law is lacking. In other cases, countries may only need a breathing space while they are building their reputation (especially if the country is undertaking significant reforms—for example, stabilization, trade, foreign investment regulation, financial regulation, and fiscal management—or are in the process of joining important international agreements). In such cases, reform-minded policymakers may find it attractive to seek outside guarantees to strengthen their capacity to commit and to speed up the process of privatization (box 5.3).

What to Do with SOEs That Cannot Be Divested

SOME SOES IN COMPETITIVE AND NONCOMPETITIVE MARKETS cannot be divested, either for political reasons, or because the government is currently unable to divest in a competitive and transparent manner, or because it does not have the administrative capacity to regulate private monopolies. Policymakers have two options in this situation: management contracts—those between the government and private

Box 5.3 Guarantees and Privatization

SOME COUNTRIES THAT ARE READY TO PRIVAT-
ize their infrastructure SOEs are unable to attract buyers at a reasonable rate of return. This happens if potential bidders have reason to worry that the government will renege on an agreed-upon regulatory
contract in ways that will reduce their expected
profit. This risk, termed "regulatory risk," is particularly high when investors question whether future
governments will abide by the present administration's commitments. In such cases, a guarantee by an
outsider (in practice, a donor government or multilateral institution) can reduce investors' regulatory
risk, enabling privatization to proceed.

But outside guarantees may also have unintended
side effects that undermine successful privatization.
Multilateral guarantees of regulatory risk are a relatively recent phenomenon; an empirical assessment
of their effect will not be possible for several years.
Meanwhile, policymakers considering seeking an international guarantee—and the donor governments
and multilateral institutions in a position to offer
one—should carefully consider the following pros
and cons.

Pros: The guarantees might

- *Improve the government's credibility and boost
investor confidence, leading to greater private
capital flows.* For example, the World Bank
guaranteed $240 million of syndicated bank
loans for the Hub Power Project in Pakistan,
and the Export-Import Bank of Japan guaranteed another $120 million. The project is
being built and operated by a private company, and the guarantees are callable only if
the government defaults on specific legal
agreements between it and the company,
causing the company to default on loans from
the commercial banks. Covered events include, for example, a failure of the government's water and power authority to purchase
Hub-generated electricity in accordance with
agreed terms. The guarantees seem to have

given the project access to previously unavailable finance. (Total financing for the 1,292
MW project is about $1.9 billion, 75 percent
debt and 25 percent equity.) Ideally, once the
government has performed in accordance
with guaranteed contractual obligations in
this and a few other projects, investors would
no longer demand such guarantees (unless
they are very inexpensive).

- *Tie the hands of a future administration that
might otherwise violate an agreement entered
into by the existing administration.* Successor
governments may wish to violate a predeces-
sor's commitment for several reasons. The new
government may be less committed to privatization than the old, or it may face an unfore-
seen price shock that makes the agreement less
attractive than before. Whatever the reasons,
donor or multilateral guarantees raise the cost
of reneging, since doing so would have numerous negative spillover effects—not the least of
which may be a halt to further donor and/or
multilateral assistance. By raising the cost of
reneging, guarantees reduce the likelihood that
successor governments will backslide.

Cons: The guarantees might

- *Become too broad.* One advantage of privatization is that it taps the efficiencies generated by
incentives associated with private profitmak-
ing. But if guarantees cover most or all of the
risks, private investors will have little incentive
to run the enterprise better than bureaucrats
did before privatization.

- *Be difficult to price.* The guarantor will want to
charge a fee for the guarantee to cover its costs
(including some of the risk of holding a contingent liability) and to signal investors that their
reduced risk is not without a price. The problem is that there is no clear market for such regulatory risk, and even if there were, guarantees,

(Box continues on the following page.)

Box 5.3 *(continued)*

like other assets, can be mispriced. Also, a fee structure that did not vary according to different levels of coverage or risk or, more generally, a vague guarantee that did not precisely delimit the exposure for the guarantor, the authorities, and private participants might send incorrect signals to financiers. In particular, it might lead them to demand more coverage than was optimal for the country. Although guarantees can lower the rate of return investors demand, they are not free to the consumer, since companies usually pass on the cost of the guarantee in the form of higher prices.

- *Reduce, rather than enhance, credibility.* If other private investors mistakenly take the guarantee as a signal that the country is likely to renege, it could lead to credibility problems in international markets.
- *Delay, rather than speed, privatization.* Since governments cannot credibly commit to servicing a growing supply of guarantees and loans, then to some extent, taking a guarantee displaces a loan. (Indeed, it would be worrisome if this did not occur, as it would suggest that the authorities were taking on contingent

liabilities without any restraint.) If the government believes that the country's ability to generate foreign exchange earnings is limited, and if demands for foreign loans in the country for other projects is high, then the government might be inclined to wait for those to whom guarantees are not necessary, thereby delaying the privatization effort.

In sum, guarantees appear to be useful when a government is committed to reform but the country's history makes it difficult for the government to commit credibly, thus raising the return that investors demand or making it difficult to attract investors at any price. However, guarantees are not without drawbacks and should not be used as a substitute for necessary reforms. Authorities should keep in mind that the first step in attracting domestic or foreign investment should be to improve the underlying economic environment. Perhaps the best general guidance concerning guarantees is that they should only be employed when there are clear advantages beyond merely enabling privatization to proceed. These might be additional investment or investors' acceptance of lower rates of return that result in tangible benefits to the public.

managers—and reforms under public management, such as hard budgets, financial reform, and institutional reform. We first discuss the private management contract option, then reforms under public management.

Use Management Contracts Where Appropriate

Management contracts can improve productivity and profitability, and they are sometimes useful as an intermediate step toward divestiture in countries where there is political opposition to privatization (Kikeri, Nellis, and Shirley 1992). These advantages should not be overestimated, however. In competitive markets, where privatization is relatively straightforward and political opposition can be overcome, outright sale is likely to generate more benefits than management contracts and without the cost of periodically renegotiating. Unlike sales, management contracts do not generate sales revenue for the government and may bring in little or no private investment for the firm. Moreover, although management contracts may be less costly politically than privatization, they do entail political costs: to make a management contract successful, government must stop using the enterprise for political purposes and may have to allow layoffs or the hiring of foreign managers. Finally, even in those instances where privatization is not possible, management contracts are only a useful option for firms in certain types of fields. Policymakers, taking these considerations into account, may nonetheless conclude that management contracts are a useful tool in their country's circumstances. In this event, they will want to consider the following issues in deciding when and how to use them:

- *Management contracts work better (and are found most frequently) in activities with fewer information problems.* Government's information problems are less severe where the enterprises operate in competitive markets or where the contract can be competitively bid. Information problems are also less serious, and management contracts less costly to design and monitor, in sectors where technology is not changing rapidly, so they don't have to be renegotiated frequently. This is also true if the output is a single, homogeneous product (such as water) or a highly visible, easily compared product (such as hotel services), so that performance can be easily judged.

- *Rewards and management's freedom to make changes are important to success.* Management contracts do better when they provide rewards that motivate managers to improve efficiency, such as equity stakes or success fees linked to performance. Many of the successful management contracts in our sample had no or very low fixed fees. Regardless of how well the rewards are designed, however, the contract can only motivate management to improve efficiency if it also provides the opportunity to make the needed changes. Freedom to hire and fire proved an important factor in the successful management contracts we reviewed.

- *Government and management must be able to demonstrate commitment.* Governments can signal their commitment by agreeing to longer contracts and agreeing to explicit conflict resolution mechanisms, including international arbitration. For its part, management can be seen as committed when the contractor has a reputation to worry about (such as large chains in hotels or Booker Tate in agriculture). While outside financing from donors or others may be appropriate to cover some transaction costs, such support should not reduce risks to the point that either party escapes the costly actions needed to signal commitment. Similarly, policymakers must be careful that outside finance does not undermine competition for the contract (by restricting bidders) or lessen management's stake in performance (by funding large fixed fees).

Reform Nondivested SOEs Comprehensively

What about firms in potentially competitive and noncompetitive markets that cannot be divested, but are not suitable for management contracts? For these firms, policymakers may have no choice but to attempt improvements within the existing ownership and management arrangements. Essential specific measures include introducing competition, cutting government subsidies, reforming financial arrangements to eliminate soft credits, and holding managers responsible for results while giving them the freedom to make necessary changes. The performance of SOEs that are not divested can be improved through these actions, but, as we saw in chapter 2, getting the details right is tough, because each reform relies on the successful implementation of others. Policymakers designing a package of reforms for firms that cannot be privatized will want to keep in mind the following:

■ *Foster competition to create incentives for improved performance.* State-owned enterprise managers will be more motivated to exert the effort needed to improve performance if pushed by competition. Governments should therefore reduce trade protection and ease barriers to entry. Chile provides a prime example. In 1974, the government eliminated all quantitative restrictions on imports, introduced a 10 percent tariff rate on all imports, and allowed entry into all markets. This subjected state and private firms in the tradable sector to immediate competition. (The Czech Republic and Poland are also examples of this.)

■ *Require competitive SOEs to follow the same rules as private firms in their commercial activities.* This means abolishing special tax breaks, preferences under procurement, and exemptions from anticompetitive restrictions or the like and subjecting SOEs to private commercial law on an equal footing with their private competitors.

■ *End subsidies and transfers.* Fostering competition is fundamental to improving the performance of SOEs in potentially competitive markets. But competition can only be effective if government transfers and subsidies are eliminated. Drawing on government subsidies, transport SOEs in Ghana and Senegal and textile SOEs in Egypt survived and even expanded despite the losses they incurred in a competitive market.

■ *Restrict access to soft credit.* Cutting subsidies and transfers only results in hard budgets if access to soft credit is also restricted. SOEs in countries as diverse as China, Egypt, and Ghana, faced with mounting competition and reductions in government subsidies, turned to bank credit instead. Where such firms then fail to improve their performance, the buildup of bad debt may undermine the entire financial system and hurt otherwise sound firms that find it increasingly difficult to obtain credit.

■ *Give managers the autonomy to respond to competition and hold them accountable for results.* If an SOE sets its output prices in competitive markets, is cut off from subsidies, must borrow at market terms, and cannot run up arrears to its suppliers, then the situation is ripe for management to take actions that raise efficiency. This will not happen, however, if managers do not have the freedom to act—to lay off workers, seek lower cost suppliers, end unprofitable activities, and pursue new markets. In addition, managers must have incentives to act, including the knowledge that they are accountable for results (see below). Lacking autonomy and incentives, managers may respond to increased competition and a harder budget in ways that hurt the enterprise, such as cutting spending on maintenance, marketing, and even supplies.

■ *Use performance contracts with public managers selectively.* Performance contracts can, in theory, hold SOE managers accountable to better performance standards. But our findings suggest that they should be used only when they can be designed to convey clear signals for reform, provide rewards for improved performance, and curb governments' tendency to renege. Signing a formal agreement without these factors may do more harm than good. Writing a contract with a few targets aimed at improving efficiency is a simple act in theory; in practice it is quite complex to overcome the by now familiar problems of contracting information, rewards and penalties, and commitment. Competition could be used to reveal information, by inviting SOE managers to bid to supply a service for example, but, aside from the notable exception of China, this has seldom happened. Similarly, the contract could provide rewards, such as greater autonomy and bonuses, that are large enough to make managers want to share information and achieve the targets. But the effectiveness of government rewards is often undermined because governments appoint and remove SOE managers for reasons unrelated to performance. For example, Egypt and India each have more than 5,000 SOE managers who are political appointees (Waterbury 1993). Another requirement for performance contracts to work is that the government negotiators have the motivation, skills, and power to extract and understand information about what the firm can (and did) accomplish and set targets accordingly. This will be hard to achieve where civil service pay is low and responsibilities are often shifted around for political reasons, a common situation in developing countries. Korea was able to get unpaid volunteers from the private sector to serve on ad hoc task forces by appealing to their civic mindedness; that may not work in all countries, however.

Performance contracts are especially vulnerable to commitment problems. Management and regulatory contracts benefit from a built-in screening process—a private party that doubts the government will uphold its side of the bargain can refuse to sign. Public managers, on the other hand, have no choice but to participate. Involvement of third parties, such as donors, private monitors, or the press, may help enhance government's commitment. In Korea, for example, the Korean Development Institute and private evaluators helped to increase the effectiveness of performance contracts; but, in the final analysis, these contracts will only succeed if the government is willing to take costly actions to tie its own hands. These may include settling arrears, increasing autonomy, firing managers who do not perform, and giving monitors more pay and power. Moreover, even if a government does all these things, the contract may be hard to sustain if the political circumstances change. Private parties have an incentive to negotiate some insulation from future political reversals, something that public managers are not in a position to do. *This implies that performance contracts should be used sparingly and only where the right conditions can be created, especially since they may do harm as well as good.*

Conclusion

W E HAVE SHOWN IN THIS BOOK THAT BUREAUCRATS STILL run important segments of the economies in developing countries and that large SOE sectors can be a significant impediment to economic growth. Yet reform is possible and offers potentially large benefits, including increased availability of resources for health, education, and other social spending; more goods and services of better quality at lower prices; and improved fiscal stability—all of which make it easier for economies to grow and for people to improve the quality of their lives. Reforming SOEs isn't easy, of course, and reforms often entail political costs. Indeed, we found that political obstacles are an important reason why state-owned enterprise reform has made so little headway in the last decade. We hope that the evidence and analysis presented in this book, together with the road map for successful reform, will give political leaders, policymakers, and the broader development community a clearer picture of the very substantial benefits that could result from state-owned enterprise reform and, just as important, a better understanding of how the many obstacles to successful reform can be overcome.

Notes

1. An attempt was made to use objective, quantifiable indicators wherever possible; see chapter 4 for details.

2. This note draws on Kikeri, Nellis, and Shirley (1992).

3. Research is currently under way in the World Bank to develop tools that will help governments make these calculations.

Implications for Foreign Assistance

VIRTUALLY ALL SOE REFORM PROGRAMS PLANNED and under way in developing countries are supported by foreign assistance. Although much of this support is highly beneficial, our evidence suggests that assistance can sometimes do harm as well as good. Aid intended to promote SOE reform can be counterproductive in several situations. First, ill-timed financial assistance to unready countries may undermine the pressure to reform. As we have seen in at least two of our sample countries, Egypt and Senegal, foreign assistance that helped ease the fiscal crisis may have made it easier to preserve the SOE status quo. Second, formalistic SOE reform in the absence of real change may cause a deterioration in SOE performance. Formalistic reforms are those that appear to be real but do not result in meaningful improvements in practice. For example, we have seen how signing a performance contract without changing incentives may have allowed managers to set multiple soft targets at odds with improved performance. Third, we have shown how governments that ended overt SOE subsidies to meet aid conditions sometimes then expanded covert subsidies and bank credits, which are harder to identify and curb and which spread SOE problems to the financial system. Fourth, we have also shown how countries that rushed to implement poorly planned and designed privatization to meet requirements set by foreign assistance agreements struck bad bargains. And finally, although this is hard to document, support for formalistic reforms that don't show results tarnishes the reputation of external assistance and undermines the credibility of reform. *This suggests that foreign assistance follow a different course of action in countries that are ready to reform from those that are not. Specifically, assistance with SOE reform is more likely to achieve its goals in countries that satisfy the three* *conditions for* SOE *reform success: reform is politically desirable for the leader-ship; reform is politically feasible; and reform promises are credible.*

Of course, foreign assistance already distinguishes committed from uncommitted countries. We are recommending that this be done systematically, using the indicators of readiness detailed in chapter 5.

Given the uncertain nature of predictions, many countries will be hard to categorize as ready or unready. In these cases, *up-front actions can distinguish countries where* SOE *reform is politically desirable and feasible and governments are credible, from those where they are not.* A good indicator of whether SOE reform is politically desirable to a new regime is when a government lays off redundant workers. Layoffs are also a sign that reform is feasible, since they demonstrate that a government is able to overcome resistance, for example, by designing severance packages to win over opponents. Another action that evidences both desirability and feasibility is the liquidation or sale of a large enterprise. Credibility is harder to test with a few up-front actions, since a government builds up believability by consistently fulfilling its promises over time. However, such measures as the International Country Risk guide or domestic polls of investor confidence can signal that credibility may be weak. In such cases foreign assistance could help governments enhance their credibility by supporting them in enacting domestic restraints on reform reversal (such as renationalization) or in the use of wide share distribution programs to give beneficiaries a stake in the future of reforms.

Foreign assistance can help governments of unready countries lay the groundwork for SOE *reform by assisting reform in other economic areas.* As we have seen in chapter 5, this leaves a large agenda of action for external support, including the reduction of fiscal deficits and trade restrictions, the removal of barriers to entry, the implementation of initial financial sector reforms, the introduction of measures to enhance private job creation, and the uncoupling of SOE jobs from social services. External aid could also help lay the groundwork for reform by providing information on the costs of not reforming and the net benefits from reform and by helping familiarize countries with experiences elsewhere.

External assistance could help reform-ready governments attract private investors. A government that is just beginning to establish a reputation for being reform-minded may find it hard to attract private buyers for large, asset-specific investments in regulated monopolies. In countries that meet the first two conditions, guarantees by international agencies could be explored as a way to attract initial private investments while the government is establishing its credibility. Guarantees have pros and cons (see box 5.3) and should be approached cautiously.

Finally, design of foreign assistance needs to allow for the possibility that readiness for SOE reform was overestimated or that circumstances have deteriorated. As we document in chapters 2 and 3, SOE reform components are interrelated: promised actions in one area can be undermined by backsliding in another. Examples of backsliding in our sample include reinstituting measures to protect SOEs from competition, such as import levies and nontariff barriers (Turkey); the write-off, or government assumption, of SOE debts without measures to improve SOE financial management or to address the underlying cause of over-indebtedness (in Egypt, the Philippines, and Senegal); arrears in payments by public agencies to SOEs for goods and services rendered (as with the electricity companies in Senegal and India); and refusal to increase the prices of monopoly SOEs or privatized firms in line with agreed pricing formulae (the Ghana and Senegal electricity companies).

In sum, by clearly distinguishing between assistance to reform-ready and unready countries, foreign aid can reduce the risk of perverse effects and improve the credence of SOE reform measures; it can also help reform-minded governments build their reputation. If assistance for SOE reform is provided only selectively, recipients will have greater credibility with investors and potential supporters. Assistance for SOE reform that goes only to governments that meet the three readiness conditions would look different in volume and kind and so convey a positive signal about the country's likely future actions. In essence, countries that agreed to meet strict conditions for SOE reform assistance would be taking external constraints similar to those involved with an important international treaty—and would be seen as doing so.

Statistical Appendix

THIS NOTE EXPLAINS THE GENERAL METHODOLOGI-cal conventions employed in assembling the data reported in the following tables. The note also explains the limitations of the data, which were compiled from more than one source, with different definitions and coverage.

Definition and Methodology

State-Owned Enterprises. SOEs are defined here as government owned or controlled economic entities that generate the bulk of their revenue from selling goods and services. This definition limits the SOE set to commercial activities in which the government is able to control management decisions by virtue of its ownership stake alone. However, it still encompasses enterprises directly operated by a government department and those in which the government holds a majority of the shares, directly or indirectly, through its SOEs. It also encompasses enterprises in which the state holds a minority of the shares if the distribution of the remaining shares would leave the government with effective control.

The data did not always fit this definition. In fact, not only do countries vary as to what they consider an SOE, but such variations exist even within the same country over time. In exceptional cases, governments include in their SOE set activities that do not have a commercial character—for example, agricultural research institutes. However, they more frequently omit activities that are clearly SOEs. The most frequent omissions occur when governments define SOEs narrowly—for example, by excluding SOEs of a particular legal form (e.g., departmental enterprises), SOEs owned by local governments (typically utilities), or SOEs that are considered less important in terms of size or need for fiscal resources. Accordingly, data on SOEs tend, on average, to underestimate their relative importance in economic activity.

In compiling the data, an attempt has been made to correct for any omissions of SOEs. However, that attempt was not always successful. Cases in which insufficient information compelled us to deviate from our definition are noted in the country-specific notes. Finally, unless specifically noted otherwise, the data cover only federal nonfinancial SOEs.

SOE Value Added. Data availability dictated the use of two procedures to estimate the SOE contribution to economic activity. SOE value added is estimated as the sales revenue minus the cost of intermediate inputs, or as the sum of operating surplus (balance) and wage payments. SOE value added is then reported as a proportion of gross domestic product (GDP) at market prices. In recognition of the fact that the size of the agricultural sector varies substantially across countries, although the presence of SOEs in this sector is rarely large, SOE contribution to nonagricultural GDP is also reported.

SOE Investment. Unless otherwise noted, investment in SOEs refers to their fixed capital formation reported as a share of both gross domestic investment and GDP at market prices.

SOE Share in Employment. The figures here are not directly comparable. For many countries, they refer to the share of full-time SOE employees in total formal sector employment only. At times, they refer to all SOEs, including financial SOEs. This is especially true for most of the African countries, for which we placed heavy reliance on African Development Indicators as our source.

SOE Savings-Investment Gap. SOE savings (or current account balance) are obtained as the sum of net operating and net nonoperating revenues. Unless otherwise noted, net operating revenue (or operating surplus or balance) refers to gross operating profits, or operating revenue minus the costs of intermediate inputs, wages, factor rentals, and depreciation. The sum of operating surplus and net nonoperating revenue is SOE savings (or current account balance). In turn, the SOE savings-investment balance is obtained as SOE savings minus SOE net capital expenditure.

Excluded from SOE savings are all transfers, which include such items on the revenue side as subsidies and such items on the expenditure side as dividends. The reason for excluding these transfers is twofold: they are not part of SOE revenues or costs, and their inclusion would cloud the very measure being captured, namely, the resources they require from the economy.

Net Government Transfers to SOEs. These are defined as the difference between all financial flows from the government to SOEs (including government loans, equity, and subsidies) and all flows from SOEs to the government (including dividends and taxes). Our measure differs from the one reported by Nair and Filippides (1989) because we treat taxes paid by SOEs as a transfer of financial resources from the SOEs to the government. The data are reported as a percentage of GDP at market prices.

SOE Share of Domestic Credit. Domestic credit to SOEs is reported as their share of both gross domestic credit and GDP. Unlike Nair and Filippides (1989), we define gross domestic credit in the economy as the sum of gross credit outstanding of the financial system to the private sector, and the SOE sector, and also to the government (i.e., not net credit to the government). This facilitates a more consistent cross-country comparison and eliminates distortions and negative ratios that may otherwise arise if government deposits with the central bank exceed central bank credit to the government.

SOE Share of External Debt. These data refer to the total external borrowing of SOEs and include all debt outstanding and disbursed. They generally do not include debt that may have been assumed or incurred by the government on behalf of SOEs. Since these numbers are reported in U.S. dollars, we report them as a share of total external debt as well as a share of GDP at market prices in U.S. dollars.

Averages by Income and Regional Classification. For each indicator defined above, both unweighted and weighted averages are reported for developing economies classified into three broad regional groups (Latin America and the Caribbean, Africa, and Asia) and by per capita according to the World Bank 1992 gross national product (GNP) classification (low-income, $675 or less; middle-income, $676–$8,355). All weighted averages are obtained using GDP at market prices in U.S. dollars as weights. The group averages reported here are based on a subset of economies in each table for which there was a sufficiently long time series for each indicator. Three-year moving average estimates were used to extrapolate the desired value for those remaining years for which observations were missing. Although these estimates were used to generate the period and group averages reported in each table, they are not reported in the respective country time series. Any country-specific exceptions to this rule are noted in the corresponding country notes.

Finally, value added and investment shares for state-owned enterprises in industrial economies (per capita GNP of more than $8,355) are also reported. However, as there were not sufficiently long time series for enough industrial economies, estimates are not extrapolated for this group. Instead, group averages are reported for four dispersed years spanning 1978–88. Lack of data made impossible a comprehensive comparison between the SOE sectors in industrial and developing economies. Nevertheless, the measures of SOE value added and investment that are reported here provide a partial gauge for comparing the size of public enterprise sectors in these economies and in developing economies.

Data Sources

NUMEROUS COUNTRY-SPECIFIC SOURCES WERE CONSULTED, and these are referenced in the Technical Notes immediately following the tables. Other main sources of data were:

- World Bank country and sector reports, World Bank *Economic and Social Database* (BESD), *World Debt Tables, World Tables,* and *African Development Indicators* (ADI).
- International Monetary Fund Recent Economic Developments (country reports) and *International Financial Statistics*
- Floyd, Gray, and Short (1984)
- Nair and Fillipides (1989)
- Centre européen de l'entreprise publique reviews—*Statistics of Public Enterprises in the EEC*
- United Nations—*Yearbook of National Accounts Statistics*
- OECD—*National Accounts Statistics.*

Table A.1 Share of State-Owned Enterprises in Economic Activity, 1978–91

(percentage share in GDP)

Group and economy[a]	1978	1979	1980	1981	1982	1983	1984
Group							
All economies							
40 Developing economies							
Weighted average[b]	9.1	9.8	10.6	10.0	10.2	10.8	11.1
Unweighted average	10.1	10.2	11.0	10.5	10.5	10.5	10.8
8 Industrial economies							
Weighted average	...	4.3	...	...	4.5	...	...
Unweighted average	...	7.7	...	...	8.5	...	...
Developing economies by income							
15 Low-income economies							
Weighted average	11.3	11.8	12.1	12.4	12.8	12.6	12.7
Unweighted average	14.0	14.1	14.7	13.8	13.4	12.7	12.9
25 Middle-income economies							
Weighted average	8.3	9.1	9.9	9.0	9.2	10.0	10.3
Unweighted average	7.8	7.9	8.7	8.5	8.8	9.2	9.5
Developing economies by region							
18 Latin America and the Caribbean							
Weighted average	7.5	8.7	9.5	8.6	8.7	9.5	9.8
Unweighted average	8.5	8.9	9.9	8.8	9.1	8.9	9.6
14 Africa							
Weighted average	18.6	18.3	18.2	18.0	18.5	19.0	19.5
Unweighted average	14.0	13.7	14.1	14.3	14.0	14.1	13.7
8 Asia							
Weighted average	8.8	9.0	9.6	9.7	10.0	9.9	10.3
Unweighted average	6.9	7.3	7.7	7.6	7.8	7.8	8.3
Economy							
1. Algeria[c]	...	...	66.7	71.8	70.5	72.2	70.6
2. Argentina	6.4	4.6	4.9	5.7	3.6	3.9	4.1
3. Austria[c]	6.5	6.6	...	...	...	...	...
4. Bangladesh[c,d]	...	...	...	2.1	2.6	3.2	2.1
5. Belgium[d]	2.5	2.5	...	...	...	2.6	2.7
6. Bolivia[d]	...	...	14.9	11.9	15.3	8.8	10.0
7. Botswana[c]	7.3	7.3	3.2	4.5	6.6	5.7	4.7
8. Brazil[e]	5.8	7.7	6.0	3.7	3.9	2.9	3.9
9. Burundi	...	...	...	...	...	...	5.4
10. Cameroon	...	...	...	...	...	...	...
11. Central African Rep.	...	...	...	...	3.5	4.4	4.3
12. Chile	11.0	12.7	13.5	9.5	13.3	16.2	15.5
13. Colombia	3.9	4.0	...	7.2	7.3	7.9	8.5
14. Comoros[c]	...	...	...	...	...	...	5.6
15. Congo[c,d]	...	...	11.0	10.5	9.9	9.8	9.8
16. Costa Rica	5.0	4.9	4.8	4.6	6.2	9.3	9.9
17. Côte d'Ivoire[c]	...	10.5	...	...	...	...	...
18. Denmark[c]	...	...	...	...	...	...	...
19. Dominica	2.1	-2.0	1.8	4.8	5.8	5.5	3.4
20. Dominican Rep.[e]	2.2	1.7	1.1	1.9	2.5	2.8	3.2
21. Ecuador	...	...	...	...	...	8.3	9.1
22. Egypt, Arab Rep. of[e]	...	...	...	...	38.9	...	...
23. El Salvador[d]	...	...	...	...	...	3.0	2.6
24. France	9.3	9.1	...	...	11.3	...	...
25. Gambia, The[d]	...	...	...	...	...	...	...
26. Germany[c]	8.3	8.4	...	...	6.4	6.5	6.5
27. Ghana[c]	...	...	...	...	...	...	4.6
28. Greece[c]	...	5.3	...	...	...	...	...

1985	1986	1987	1988	1989	1990	1991	1978–85	1986–91	1978–91
11.7	11.4	11.5	11.0	10.8	10.8	10.2	10.4	11.0	10.7
11.3	11.4	11.3	10.9	11.4	11.4	10.7	10.6	11.2	10.9
4.6	...	...	6.0	...	...	...	...	...	4.9
8.3	...	...	6.6	...	...	...	...	...	7.8
13.8	14.2	13.5	13.0	13.3	13.5	13.0	12.4	13.4	12.9
13.8	14.1	14.2	13.8	15.1	14.5	13.6	13.7	14.2	13.9
10.7	10.1	10.6	10.1	9.9	9.8	9.3	9.6	10.0	9.7
9.8	9.7	9.6	9.2	9.2	9.6	9.0	8.8	9.4	9.0
10.1	9.2	9.9	9.3	9.1	9.1	8.4	9.0	9.2	9.1
10.0	10.4	10.6	9.7	10.2	10.3	9.8	9.2	10.2	9.6
19.8	19.1	18.3	17.6	17.6	17.7	17.3	18.7	17.9	18.4
14.0	13.8	13.6	13.7	14.4	14.3	13.3	14.0	13.9	13.9
11.6	12.1	11.6	11.2	11.2	11.3	10.7	9.9	11.4	10.5
9.4	9.4	8.7	8.7	8.8	8.8	8.5	7.9	8.8	8.3
68.3	63.4	65.2	59.9	45.9	...	...	69.9	57.6	64.6
4.7	5.6	6.2	6.0	4.9	3.5	2.2	4.7	4.7	4.7
...	...	...	13.9	...	...	...	6.5	13.9	9.0
2.9	3.2	2.5	2.7	3.1	3.3	3.4	2.5	3.0	2.7
2.8	2.8	2.8	2.8	...	...	...	2.6	2.8	2.7
15.3	15.6	11.4	12.5	14.7	14.4	...	13.0	13.7	13.3
6.2	5.6	7.0	6.8	4.5	5.4	6.0	5.7	5.9	5.8
6.1	7.7	9.1	9.1	8.1	7.7	9.7	5.0	8.6	6.5
...	5.0	7.9	...	...	9.0	...	5.4	7.3	6.8
18.0	...	18.0	...	...	18.0	...	18.0	18.0	18.0
4.9	3.7	3.9	4.0	...	...	...	4.1	3.9	4.0
17.0	15.5	14.6	14.5	12.7	12.0	8.0	13.6	12.9	13.3
8.9	...	...	5.6	6.4	7.2	...	6.9	6.7	6.8
...	...	...	11.1	...	...	12.8	5.6	11.9	9.8
10.7	17.7	15.0	16.0	16.2	...	...	10.4	16.1	12.8
8.6	8.7	7.7	8.8	7.5	8.0	8.2	6.7	8.2	7.3
...	...	...	...	...	...	...	10.5	...	10.5
...	...	...	5.1	...	...	...	...	5.1	5.1
5.0	6.3	5.6	4.3	3.2	4.7	4.5	3.3	4.8	3.9
0.6	...	...	...	...	...	...	2.0	...	2.0
8.6	10.3	10.6	11.1	10.9	9.8	10.5	8.6	10.5	9.5
...	...	27.2	...	...	...	32.8	37.1	30.0	34.1
2.3	1.6	1.7	1.7	...	...	...	2.4	1.6	2.1
12.9			10.0	...	...	...	10.7	10.0	10.5
3.9	3.1	3.9	4.1	4.2	...	...	3.9	3.8	3.8
6.4				...	...	...	7.1	...	7.1
5.5	10.6	11.9	8.3	8.0	6.9	4.6	5.8	8.4	6.9
...	14.2	12.5	10.4	8.9	...	...	5.3	11.5	10.3

Table A.1 *(continued)*

Group and economy[a]	1978	1979	1980	1981	1982	1983	1984
29. Grenada[d]	...	...	...	...	...	...	...
30. Guatemala	0.8	1.0	1.0	0.9	1.2	1.4	1.3
31. Guinea[c]	...	...	...	25.0	...	...	...
32. Guyana[c]	44.6	46.7	48.2	37.5	31.7	24.6	32.4
33. Honduras[c]	...	...	4.0	4.3	4.7	5.2	4.9
34. India[c]	...	...	9.1	10.3	11.6	11.7	11.2
35. Indonesia	13.8	15.2	17.7	16.3	14.9	13.6	15.0
36. Italy[c]	6.6	...	...	...	6.8	...	...
37. Jamaica[c,d]	...	...	...	...	...	...	21.0
38. Kenya	...	...	...	...	...	...	8.0
39. Korea, Rep. of [c]	...	...	10.4	...	8.8	9.0	9.8
40. Madagascar[d]	...	...	...	...	...	...	2.3
41. Malawi[d]	...	...	9.5	6.3	7.1	6.8	6.0
42. Malaysia[c]	...	...	...	...	...	...	...
43. Mali[d]	15.4	13.2	12.1	...	...	...	...
44. Mauritania	...	...	...	...	...	25.0	...
45. Mauritius [c]	2.0	2.0	2.0	2.3	2.2	2.2	2.0
46. Mexico[c]	6.9	7.5	10.3	10.2	13.7	17.2	16.0
47. Morocco[e]	...	...	20.0	20.0	19.7	9.1	11.8
48. Nepal	2.5	...	...	...	...	...	...
49. Niger[d]	...	...	...	...	4.5	4.4	4.8
50. Nigeria[c]	...	...	...	...	...	13.6	13.9
51. Pakistan[c,e]	8.0	...	...	...	...	...	...
52. Panama[c]	5.3	5.9	7.5	8.0	7.1	8.2	8.3
53. Paraguay	...	3.1	3.1	2.8	4.3	4.4	3.4
54. Peru	5.9	6.7	7.8	6.5	8.1	10.6	10.5
55. Philippines[c]	0.9	1.1	1.6	1.7	1.3	1.7	1.7
56. Portugal[c]	...	...	...	...	...	22.9	25.8
57. Rwanda[c]	...	...	...	...	...	...	...
58. Senegal	...	...	8.4	8.0	9.1	8.9	10.3
59. Sierra Leone[c]	...	19.6	24.8	20.2	15.3	...	...
60. South Africa[c]	14.3	13.8	12.9	12.6	12.7	14.4	15.2
61. Spain[c]	...	4.0	...	...	...	...	...
62. Sri Lanka[c]	...	...	...	...	...	...	...
63. Sudan[c,e]	...	...	...	...	...	...	...
64. Taiwan (China)	5.6	6.4	6.2	6.8	8.2	8.4	8.6
65. Tanzania	10.5	8.1	10.8	12.5	12.6	11.5	10.4
66. Thailand[e]	...	...	...	...	...	...	...
67. Togo	...	...	11.8	...	...	...	...
68. Trinidad and Tobago[d]	...	...	...	...	...	...	...
69. Tunisia[c]	25.4	25.4		32.1	30.6	31.1	31.2
70. Turkey[c]	5.2	5.2	5.5	5.4	5.6	5.1	7.3
71. Uruguay	3.5	3.0	5.5	5.1	3.4	3.0	4.4
72. United Kingdom	6.1	5.6	6.2	6.4	6.6	6.4	5.2
73. United States[c]	...	...	1.2	1.3	1.3	1.3	1.4
74. Venezuela[c]	19.2	24.1	26.9	25.5	21.9	20.5	24.8
75. Zaire	...	...	...	...	...	22.8	...
76. Zambia[c]	...	...	...	35.0	26.8	30.9	31.5

a. Only a subset of economies within each classification was used in deriving averages. Forty developing economies refer to the low- and middle-income economies listed below. Eight industrial economies include Belgium, France, Germany, Greece, Italy, Portugal, United Kingdom, and United States. Fifteen low-income economies include Bangladesh, Bolivia, Central African Republic, Egypt, Ghana, Guyana, India, Indonesia, Kenya, Malawi, Pakistan, the Philippines, Senegal, Tanzania, and Zambia. Twenty-five middle-income economies include Argentina, Botswana, Brazil, Chile, Colombia, Congo, Costa Rica, Dominica, Ecuador, El Salvador, Guatemala, Honduras, Korea, Mauritius, Mexico, Morocco, Panama, Paraguay, Peru, South Africa, Taiwan (China), Tunisia, Turkey, Uruguay, and Venezuela. Latin America and the Caribbean averages exclude Dominican Republic, Jamaica, and Trinidad and Tobago. Africa averages include Botswana, Central African Republic, Congo, Egypt, Ghana, Kenya, Malawi, Mauritius, Morocco, Senegal, South Africa, Tanzania, Tunisia,

1985	1986	1987	1988	1989	1990	1991	1978–85	1986–91	1978–91
...	18.9	16.7	20.9	19.1	20.8	19.9	...	19.4	19.4
1.5	1.8	1.9	1.6	1.9	2.5	...	1.1	2.0	1.5
...	8.6	...	...	...	8.7	...	25.0	8.7	14.1
30.7	43.1	56.8	45.0	50.1	40.8	...	37.0	46.9	41.2
5.3	5.3	5.6	5.3	5.1	6.3	...	4.6	5.5	5.0
12.6	13.8	14.1	13.5	13.8	14.1	13.6	10.8	13.8	12.1
16.4	16.9	14.2	13.6	13.0	...	...	15.4	14.1	14.8
...	...	...	5.6	...	...	...	6.7	5.6	6.3
...	...	...	...	...	...	...	21.0	...	21.0
12.0	11.7	11.7	10.9	11.4	11.7	...	10.0	11.5	10.6
10.4	10.4	...	...	...	10.2		9.6	10.3	9.9
...	...	...	...	...	...	...	2.3	...	2.3
4.9	3.9	4.1	...	...	...	...	7.0	4.1	5.8
...	17.0	...	...	...	...	...	...	17.0	17.0
...	...	...	...	...	...	...	13.6	...	13.6
...	...	...	...	...	...	...	25.0	...	25.0
2.0	1.8	1.8	...	...	...	...	2.1	1.8	2.0
13.9	12.0	13.3	10.8	10.4	11.3	8.4	12.0	11.0	11.6
15.4	...	20.0	...	...	15.0	...	18.6	17.2	18.0
2.0	...	...	...	...	...	...	2.3	...	2.3
5.3	5.8	4.6	4.7	...	...	5.5	4.8	5.2	5.0
12.9	14.8	...	...	...	...	...	13.5	14.8	13.8
11.5	...	...	11.6	...	...	...	9.4	11.4	10.3
7.7	7.8	7.0	8.7	9.0	9.1	8.6	7.3	8.4	7.7
6.4	5.9	4.4	4.0	3.1	4.8	2.6	3.8	4.1	4.0
11.9	8.0	5.7	3.4	4.1	5.4	5.0	8.5	5.3	7.1
1.8	2.0	1.9	2.6	3.0	...	...	1.5	2.4	1.9
17.8	14.6	13.9	14.2	...	...	...	22.2	14.2	18.2
...	...	...	...	10.0	...	...	...	10.0	10.0
9.6	6.1	5.8	6.3	6.7	...	...	8.9	6.2	7.7
...	...	...	...	...	...	...	20.0	...	20.0
15.2	16.0	15.3	14.7	13.3	...	...	13.9	14.7	14.2
...	...	...	...	...	...	...	4.0	...	4.0
...	...	10.4	10.3	...	...	...	...	10.4	10.4
...	47.5	50.0	...	...	...	...	48.2	48.2	48.2
8.7	7.5	6.1	6.2	6.2	5.6	5.6	7.4	6.2	6.9
10.3	8.5	12.1	13.1	13.4	20.0		10.8	13.7	12.1
...	...	...	5.4	...	...	...	...	5.4	5.4
...	...	...	...	14.4	10.5	10.5	11.8	11.8	11.8
...	5.9	8.4	10.3	10.2	10.5	...	...	9.1	9.1
31.4	30.2	...	...	...	...	...	29.8	30.7	30.2
10.7	9.8	9.8	9.1	9.5	9.4	7.2	6.3	9.1	7.5
4.1	6.0	4.5	5.1	4.1	6.0	7.0	4.0	5.4	4.6
4.4	4.4	3.4	3.0	3.3	2.1	1.9	5.9	3.0	4.6
1.4	1.4	0.6	...	...	...	...	1.3	1.0	1.2
22.0	17.1	19.0	17.7	26.7	31.1	26.5	23.1	23.0	23.1
...	...	...	...	...	...	...	22.8	...	22.8
35.0	...	23.9	29.4	40.0	32.8	21.8	31.7	29.8	30.9

and Zambia. Asia averages include Bangladesh, India, Indonesia, Korea, Pakistan, Philippines, Taiwan (China), and Turkey. Excluding all industrial economies, Egypt, Pakistan, and Sudan, three-year moving average estimates were used, in case of missing observations, to complete our time series.

b. Weighted averages were obtained using GDP in current U.S. dollars as weights.

c. See specific country note.

d. Selected major state-owned enterprises only.

e. Financial state-owned enterprises are included.

Table A.2 Share of State-Owned Enterprises in Nonagricultural Economic Activity, 1978–91

(percentage share in nonagricultural GDP)

Group and economy[a]	1978	1979	1980	1981	1982	1983	1984
Group							
All economies							
40 Developing economies							
Weighted average[b]	11.3	11.9	12.6	11.9	12.3	13.0	13.3
Unweighted average	12.6	12.6	13.5	12.9	13.1	12.9	13.2
8 Industrial economies							
Weighted average	...	4.5	...	...	4.7	...	...
Unweighted average	...	8.2	...	...	9.1	...	...
Developing economies by income							
15 Low-income economies							
Weighted average	16.2	16.5	16.8	17.0	17.7	17.6	17.4
Unweighted average	18.5	18.5	19.3	17.9	17.8	16.7	17.1
25 Middle-income economies							
Weighted average	9.3	10.2	11.0	10.0	10.1	10.9	11.4
Unweighted average	9.1	9.1	10.0	9.9	10.2	10.6	10.8
Developing economies by region							
18 Latin America and the Caribbean							
Weighted average	8.2	9.5	10.4	9.3	9.5	10.4	10.8
Unweighted average	10.1	10.3	11.7	10.4	10.9	10.7	11.5
14 Africa							
Weighted average	22.2	21.5	21.2	21.3	22.1	22.3	22.9
Unweighted average	17.5	16.9	17.5	17.6	17.4	17.2	16.7
8 Asia							
Weighted average	12.6	12.5	13.2	13.3	13.7	13.5	13.8
Unweighted average	9.7	10.1	10.5	10.2	10.4	10.3	10.8
Economy							
1. Algeria[c]	...	...	71.0	76.3	75.0	76.8	74.2
2. Argentina	6.9	5.0	5.2	6.1	4.0	4.3	4.5
3. Austria[c]	6.8	6.9	...	...	...	...	...
4. Bangladesh[c,d]	...	...	...	3.5	4.3	5.3	3.6
5. Belgium[d]	2.5	2.5	...	...	...	2.7	2.8
6. Bolivia[d]	...	...	18.2	14.3	19.3	12.1	15.4
7. Botswana[c]	9.2	8.6	3.6	5.1	7.5	6.3	5.1
8. Brazil[e]	6.4	8.5	6.6	4.0	4.3	3.3	4.4
9. Burundi	...	...	...	...	...	...	11.9
10. Cameroon	...	...	...	...	...	...	...
11. Central African Rep.	...	...	...	...	5.8	7.1	7.1
12. Chile	11.9	13.7	14.6	10.1	14.1	17.2	16.7
13. Colombia	5.1	5.1	...	8.9	8.9	9.7	10.3
14. Comoros[c]	...	...	...	...	...	...	8.2
15. Congo[c,d]	...	...	12.3	11.4	10.5	10.5	10.5
16. Costa Rica	6.3	6.0	5.8	6.0	8.2	11.9	12.6
17. Côte d'Ivoire[c]	...	14.4	...	...	...	...	...
18. Denmark[c]	...	...	...	...	...	...	...
19. Dominica	4.0	-3.9	3.5	9.2	11.1	10.5	6.4
20. Dominican Rep.[e]	2.7	2.1	1.4	2.3	3.0	3.4	3.9
21. Ecuador	...	...	...	...	...	9.5	10.5
22. Egypt, Arab Rep. of [c]	...	...	...	...	51.1	...	...
23. El Salvador[d]	...	...	3.2	2.4	3.9	3.9	3.2
24. France	9.8	9.6	...	...	11.9	...	...
25. Gambia, The[d]	...	...	...	...	...	...	...
26. Germany[c]	8.5	8.6	...	...	6.6	6.7	6.6
27. Ghana[c]	...	...	...	...	...	...	7.7
28. Greece[c]	...	6.2	...	...	...	...	...

1985	1986	1987	1988	1989	1990	1991	1978–85	1986–91	1978–91
14.2	13.9	13.8	13.1	12.8	12.8	12.0	12.6	13.1	12.8
13.9	14.0	14.0	13.4	13.9	14.1	13.0	13.1	13.7	13.4
4.8	...	...	6.2	...	...	...	...	...	5.0
8.9	...	...	7.0	...	...	...	...	...	8.3
18.8	19.3	18.2	17.8	17.9	18.1	17.3	17.2	18.1	17.6
18.3	18.6	18.8	18.3	19.7	19.5	17.6	18.0	18.7	18.3
11.9	11.3	11.8	11.1	10.8	10.8	10.3	10.6	11.0	10.8
11.3	11.3	11.1	10.5	10.4	10.9	10.3	10.1	10.7	10.4
11.1	10.3	10.8	10.1	9.9	9.9	9.3	9.9	10.1	10.0
12.2	12.7	13.0	11.8	12.2	12.8	11.5	11.0	12.3	11.6
23.7	22.5	21.6	20.4	20.6	20.5	20.1	22.1	20.9	21.6
17.0	16.6	16.7	16.7	17.6	17.4	16.2	17.2	16.9	17.1
15.5	15.9	15.2	14.7	14.4	14.4	13.3	13.5	14.6	14.0
12.2	12.2	11.3	11.3	11.3	11.2	10.7	10.5	11.3	10.9
71.8	66.3	66.5	63.7	48.8	...	...	74.2	61.3	69.0
5.1	6.1	6.7	6.6	5.4	3.8	2.4	5.1	5.2	5.1
...	...	...	14.3	...	...	...	6.9	14.3	9.3
5.0	5.3	4.2	4.4	4.9	5.3	5.4	4.3	4.9	4.6
2.8	2.8	2.9	2.9	...	...	...	2.7	2.8	2.7
24.3	23.2	16.7	18.6	21.9	21.5	...	17.3	20.4	18.7
6.5	5.9	7.3	7.0	4.7	5.6	6.3	6.5	6.1	6.4
6.8	8.5	10.0	10.0	8.7	8.5	11.0	5.5	9.5	7.2
...	10.5	15.9	...	...	16.8	...	11.9	14.4	13.8
22.4	...	24.3	...	...	23.8	...	22.4	24.1	23.5
7.8	6.0	6.5	6.8	...	...	...	6.9	6.4	6.7
17.8	16.1	14.7	14.5	12.6	12.1	8.1	14.5	13.0	13.9
10.7	...	...	6.7	7.6	8.6	...	8.4	7.6	8.2
...	...	...	17.5	...	...	21.6	8.2	19.6	15.8
11.5	19.9	16.9	18.3	18.4	...	...	11.4	18.6	14.5
10.7	11.0	9.4	10.7	9.0	9.5	9.7	8.4	9.9	9.1
...	...	...	...	...	...	...	14.4	...	14.4
...	...	...	5.4	...	...	...	...	5.4	5.4
9.4	11.9	10.6	8.1	6.0	9.0	8.6	6.3	9.0	7.5
0.7	...	...	...	...	...	...	2.5	...	2.5
9.9	12.1	12.5	13.0	12.7	11.3	12.2	10.0	12.3	11.5
...	...	35.3	...	...	...	42.6	51.1	39.0	43.0
2.8	1.9	2.0	1.9	...	...	...	3.2	1.9	2.8
13.4	...	...	10.3	...	...	...	11.2	10.3	11.0
5.2	4.5	5.6	5.5	5.7	...	...	5.2	5.3	5.3
6.5	...	...	...	...	...	...	7.2	...	7.2
9.0	15.2	17.7	13.0	12.6	9.9	6.8	9.3	12.5	10.7
...	16.6	14.5	12.1	10.4	...	...	6.2	13.4	12.0

Table A.2 *(continued)*

Group and economy[a]	1978	1979	1980	1981	1982	1983	1984
29. Grenada[d]	...	...	...	...	...	...	...
30. Guatemala	1.1	1.4	1.4	1.3	1.8	2.0	1.9
31. Guinea[c]	...	...	...	...	...	...	...
32. Guyana[c]	55.9	58.3	60.8	46.1	39.7	30.7	40.9
33. Honduras[c]	...	...	5.1	5.4	5.9	6.5	6.1
34. India[c]	...	...	13.9	15.4	16.9	17.3	16.3
35. Indonesia	19.2	20.9	23.3	21.3	19.6	17.6	19.4
36. Italy[c]	7.1	...	...	...	7.1	...	...
37. Jamaica[c,d]	...	...	...	...	...	...	22.3
38. Kenya	...	...	...	...	...	...	8.1
39. Korea, Rep. of [c]	...	...	12.2	...	10.3	10.4	11.3
40. Madagascar[d]	...	...	...	...	...	...	3.5
41. Malawi[d]			14.3	9.3	10.7	10.3	9.1
42. Malaysia[c]	...	...	...	...	...	...	...
43. Mali[d]	34.0	24.0	26.4	...	...	...	...
44. Mauritania	...	...	...	...	...	33.9	...
45. Mauritius[c]	2.4	2.3	2.2	2.6	2.6	2.5	2.3
46. Mexico[c]	7.7	8.2	11.2	11.1	14.8	18.7	17.5
47. Morocco[e]	...	...	23.5	24.2	22.1	19.1	19.9
48. Nepal	6.1	...	...	...	...	...	...
49. Niger[d]	...	...	...	...	7.7	7.8	9.4
50. Nigeria[c]	...	...	...	...	...	17.0	17.4
51. Pakistan[c,e]	...	...	12.8	...	14.1	13.5	14.9
52. Panama[c]	6.0	6.6	8.3	8.8	7.8	9.0	9.2
53. Paraguay		4.5	4.3	3.9	5.8	6.0	4.7
54. Peru	6.8	7.6	8.6	7.4	9.2	12.0	11.9
55. Philippines[c]	1.3	1.5	2.1	2.3	1.7	2.2	2.3
56. Portugal[c]	...	...	...	...	...	24.9	28.1
57. Rwanda[c]	...	...	...	...	...	...	...
58. Senegal	...	...	...	9.7	10.6	11.1	12.9
59. Sierra Leone[e]	...	30.6	37.9	35.3	26.9	...	...
60. South Africa[c]	15.4	14.7	13.5	13.5	13.5	15.1	16.0
61. Spain[c]	...	4.0	...	...	...	...	...
62. Sri Lanka[c]	...	...	...	...	...	...	...
63. Sudan[c,e]	...	...	...	...	...	...	...
64. Taiwan (China)	6.7	7.6	7.2	7.9	9.5	9.8	9.7
65. Tanzania	17.1	13.7	17.8	19.8	21.3	19.6	17.4
66. Thailand[c]	...	...	...	...	...	...	...
67. Togo	...	...	14.8	...	...	...	...
68. Trinidad and Tobago[d]	...	...	...	...	...	...	...
69. Tunisia[c]	29.9	29.4		37.2	35.2	35.4	36.2
70. Turkey[c]	6.8	6.6	7.0	6.8	7.0	6.2	9.0
71. Uruguay	6.2	5.8	6.3	6.5	6.7	6.6	5.3
72. United Kingdom	1.4	1.3	1.3	1.3	1.3	1.3	1.4
73. United States[c]	4.1	3.6	6.2	5.8	3.8	3.4	5.1
74. Venezuela[c]	20.2	25.4	28.3	26.8	23.1	21.7	26.1
75. Zaire	...	...	...	...	...	27.4	...
76. Zambia[c]	...	...	...	40.0	31.7	35.0	35.8

a. Only a subset of economies within each classification was used in deriving averages. Forty developing economies refer to the low- and middle-income economies listed below. Eight industrial economies include Belgium, France, Germany, Greece, Italy, Portugal, United Kingdom, and United States. Fifteen low-income economies include Bangladesh, Bolivia, Central African Republic, Egypt, Ghana, Guyana, India, Indonesia, Kenya, Malawi, Pakistan, Philippines, Senegal, Tanzania, and Zambia. Twenty-five middle-income economies include Argentina, Botswana, Brazil, Chile, Colombia, Congo, Costa Rica, Dominica, Ecuador, El Salvador, Guatemala, Honduras, Korea, Mauritius, Mexico, Morocco, Panama, Paraguay, Peru, South Africa, Taiwan (China), Tunisia, Turkey, Uruguay, and Venezuela. Latin America and the Caribbean averages exclude Dominican Republic, Jamaica, and Trinidad and Tobago. Africa averages include Botswana, Central African Republic, Congo, Egypt, Ghana, Kenya, Malawi, Mauritius, Morocco, Senegal, South Africa, Tanzania, Tunisia, and Zambia. Asia

1985	1986	1987	1988	1989	1990	1991	1978–85	1986–91	1978–91
...	22.3	20.2	24.9	22.4	23.9	22.6	...	22.7	22.7
2.2	2.6	2.6	2.2	2.6	3.4	...	1.6	2.7	2.0
...	12.3	...	...	...	11.5	...	...	11.9	11.9
39.6	54.9	73.6	58.1	61.3	58.9	...	46.5	61.4	52.2
6.4	6.5	6.9	6.4	6.1	7.6	...	5.9	6.7	6.3
17.9	19.2	19.5	19.0	18.9	...	...	16.3	19.2	17.4
21.3	22.3	18.5	17.9	17.0	...	...	20.3	18.9	19.9
...	...	...	5.8	...	...	...	7.1	5.8	6.7
...	...	...	...	...	...	...	22.3	...	22.3
12.2	11.9	11.9	11.0	11.6	12.0	...	10.1	11.7	11.3
11.9	11.7	...	...	...	11.2	...	11.2	11.5	11.3
...	...	...	...	...	...	...	3.5	...	3.5
7.3	5.8	6.1	...	...	...	...	10.2	5.9	9.1
...	21.0	...	...	...	...	...	...	21.0	21.0
...	...	...	...	...	...	...	28.1	...	28.1
...	...	...	...	...	...	...	33.9	...	33.9
2.2	2.0	2.1	...	...	...	...	2.4	2.0	2.3
15.3	13.2	14.5	11.7	11.2	12.1	9.0	13.1	12.0	12.6
17.7		24.6	...	...	17.8	...	21.1	21.2	21.1
4.3	...	...	...	...	...	...	5.2	...	5.2
8.2	8.9	6.8	7.4	...	...	8.5	8.3	7.9	8.1
16.1	18.5	...	...	...	...	...	16.8	18.5	17.2
16.4	16.5	...	...	...	16.0	...	14.3	16.3	14.9
8.5	8.6	7.8	9.7	10.1	10.1	9.7	8.0	9.3	8.6
9.0	8.1	6.0	5.7	4.4	6.6	3.5	5.5	5.7	5.6
13.2	8.9	6.4	3.9	4.8	6.6	6.2	9.6	6.1	8.1
2.4	2.6	2.5	3.4	3.9	...	...	2.0	3.1	2.3
19.4	15.8	15.0	15.1	...	...	...	24.1	15.3	19.7
...	...	...	...	14.5	...	...	...	14.5	14.5
11.3	7.3	6.0	6.4	7.0	...	...	11.1	6.7	9.1
...	...	...	...	...	...	...	32.7	...	32.7
16.0	16.8	16.2	15.6	14.1	...	...	14.7	15.7	15.0
...	...	...	...	...	...	...	4.0	...	4.0
...	...	13.6	13.5	...	...	...	...	...	...
66.3	72.4	76.5	...	...	...	...	71.7	74.4	71.7
9.8	8.4	6.7	6.8	6.8	6.0	6.0	8.5	6.8	7.8
18.2	15.7	21.5	24.0	24.7	33.2	...	18.1	23.8	20.3
...	...	...	6.2	...	...	...	...	6.2	6.2
...	...	...	...	21.2	15.3	15.4	14.8	17.3	16.6
...	6.1	8.6	10.6	10.3	10.5	...	...	9.2	9.2
37.0	34.8	...	...	...	...	...	34.3	34.8	34.4
13.0	11.8	11.7	10.8	11.2	11.2	8.5	7.8	10.9	9.1
4.5	4.5	3.4	3.0	3.3	2.1	2.0	6.0	3.1	4.7
1.5	1.4	0.6	...	...	...	...	1.3	1.0	1.3
4.8	6.8	5.2	5.9	4.6	6.7	7.5	4.6	6.1	5.2
23.4	18.3	20.3	19.0	27.9	32.8	28.1	24.4	24.4	24.4
...	...	...	...	...	...	...	27.4	...	27.4
39.0	...	26.0	31.7	43.7	35.8	24.0	36.3	32.2	34.3

averages include Bangladesh, India, Indonesia, Korea, Pakistan, Philippines, Taiwan (China), and Turkey. Excluding all industrial economies, Egypt, Pakistan, and Sudan, three-year moving average estimates were used, in case of missing observations, to complete our time series.

b. Weighted averages were obtained using GDP in current U.S. dollars as weights.

c. See specific country note.

d. Selected major state-owned enterprises only.

e. Financial state-owned enterprises are included.

Table A.3 Share of State-Owned Enterprise Investment in Gross Domestic Investment, 1978–91

(percentage)

Group and economy[a]	1978	1979	1980	1981	1982	1983	1984
Group							
All economies							
55 Developing economies							
Weighted average[b]	24.8	27.3	26.4	27.6	29.5	28.2	25.9
Unweighted average	22.6	22.4	22.5	22.6	23.7	23.5	21.8
10 Industrial economies							
Weighted average	8.8	...	...	...	8.9	...	...
Unweighted average	12.6	...	...	...	15.7	...	...
Developing economies by income							
18 Low-income economies							
Weighted average	31.2	34.5	32.3	32.9	35.7	33.2	33.2
Unweighted average	31.8	30.9	32.8	30.8	30.2	29.0	26.1
37 Middle-income economies							
Weighted average	22.4	24.8	24.2	25.7	27.1	26.1	22.9
Unweighted average	18.1	18.3	17.5	18.6	20.6	20.9	19.6
Developing economies by region							
27 Latin America and the Caribbean							
Weighted average	22.2	25.1	22.8	25.7	26.1	27.6	22.2
Unweighted average	17.5	16.8	15.9	16.8	18.3	19.6	17.7
15 Africa							
Weighted average	30.0	30.5	29.8	26.4	26.2	26.6	28.2
Unweighted average	30.3	30.3	30.9	29.3	28.4	28.2	26.2
13 Asia							
Weighted average	26.7	29.2	30.3	31.1	35.3	29.3	29.7
Unweighted average	24.1	25.0	26.5	26.9	29.5	26.1	25.1
Economy							
1. Algeria[c]	75.6	79.8	69.5	56.4	51.0	42.0	36.8
2. Argentina	14.0	11.0	10.4	11.3	10.6	11.6	11.9
3. Australia[c,e]	15.7	17.1	15.7	16.6	22.0	19.3	17.2
4. Austria	6.6	5.7	...	...	...	...	...
5. Bangladesh[c]	...	...	...	6.7	3.3	5.4	1.8
6. Barbados[d]	10.3	9.7	9.4	7.3	7.6	12.2	14.6
7. Belgium[c,d]	8.6	8.9	...	...	...	11.4	10.2
8. Belize	...	31.1	7.9	12.1	24.9	16.1	8.1
9. Benin[d]	...	...	...	...	...	...	...
10. Bolivia[d]	29.9	23.9	24.3	20.8	34.7	34.4	32.5
11. Botswana[c]	9.1	6.6	6.4	11.6	14.1	23.0	26.9
12. Brazil[e]	21.0	34.0	25.0	28.0	28.0	26.0	24.0
13. Burundi	43.3	36.8	42.7	31.4	34.8	31.2	36.1
14. Central African Rep.	...	...	...	...	...	...	...
15. Chile	15.7	10.7	12.4	11.9	23.9	29.6	28.6
16. Colombia	...	...	10.9	10.3	12.0	22.7	21.2
17. Comoros	...	...	...	...	...	22.1	11.7
18. Congo[c]	...	...	...	...	...	39.8	...
19. Costa Rica	19.6	20.6	17.3	20.1	14.2	14.2	11.6
20. Côte d'Ivoire[e]	...	...	7.7	6.5	23.2	23.9	30.6
21. Denmark[c]	...	...	...	...	...	...	...
22. Dominica[c]	10.7	7.3	3.9	14.0	9.7	1.0	2.0
23. Dominican Rep.[e]	12.9	9.1	9.3	12.2	10.2	8.6	10.8
24. Ecuador[c]	12.6	13.5	12.7	14.1	10.6	13.8	14.0
25. Egypt, Arab Rep. of[c]	47.8	...	...	51.4	55.9	53.0	56.1
26. El Salvador[d]	13.6	18.2	20.8	17.6	26.1	22.7	8.3
27. Fiji[e]	20.9	28.2	28.0	27.6	33.7	38.0	22.6
28. France[c]	13.8	13.3	...	...	16.3		

1985	1986	1987	1988	1989	1990	1991	1978–85	1986–91	1978–91
25.3	23.8	21.3	20.2	20.3	19.3	17.9	26.9	20.5	24.1
21.2	20.9	19.7	18.8	18.9	18.7	18.4	22.5	19.2	21.1
6.8	...	...	6.2	...	...	...	...	...	7.7
13.5	...	...	11.1	...	...	...	...	...	13.2
33.1	34.7	30.8	29.7	30.9	29.9	30.0	33.3	31.0	32.3
26.5	29.2	29.2	26.4	26.9	23.9	27.3	29.8	27.2	28.6
21.8	19.0	17.3	16.5	16.5	15.8	14.3	24.4	16.6	21.0
18.7	16.8	15.0	15.0	14.9	16.1	14.0	19.0	15.3	17.4
20.8	18.6	16.0	15.8	15.5	15.5	12.1	24.1	15.6	20.4
15.9	16.6	14.5	14.3	13.9	15.2	12.6	17.3	14.5	16.1
33.3	33.6	29.8	22.3	25.6	23.0	24.2	28.9	26.4	27.8
28.3	27.0	25.8	23.6	24.2	20.6	25.5	29.0	24.5	27.1
28.3	26.9	24.6	24.4	24.4	22.7	22.8	30.0	24.3	27.6
24.2	22.6	23.2	22.4	23.0	23.6	22.2	25.9	22.8	24.6
32.2	28.1	...	...	...	...	...	55.4	30.7	44.8
10.0	9.2	10.4	9.1	10.3	7.1	4.8	11.4	8.5	10.1
17.8	17.9	13.8	11.6	13.9	15.1	15.8	17.7	14.7	16.4
...	...	...	...	...	...	...	6.2	...	6.2
36.7	44.5	30.2	27.3	23.0	28.2	25.8	10.8	29.8	21.2
13.0	12.5	8.5	6.2	4.4	6.3	8.3	10.5	7.7	9.3
10.2	8.4	6.8	5.8	...	...	...	9.9	7.0	8.8
11.0	16.1	16.2	14.2	10.1	13.8	11.7	15.9	13.7	14.9
51.9	11.7	14.8	15.9	23.3	13.4	...	51.9	15.8	21.8
14.3	23.2	31.7	28.5	26.3	24.7	...	26.9	26.9	26.9
43.6	9.5	18.4	28.6	20.8	...	...	17.7	20.6	18.9
24.0	18.0	17.0	18.0	13.0	14.0	11.0	26.3	15.2	21.5
42.6	44.9	46.3	39.6	39.6	33.7	...	37.4	40.3	38.6
...	17.0	...	...	...	...	...	...	17.0	17.0
30.6	32.2	21.9	19.4	12.8	9.4	...	20.4	19.1	19.9
19.8	15.4	11.6	12.0	12.7	9.7	10.4	16.2	12.0	14.1
15.2	15.8	...	...	...	...	...	16.3	15.8	16.2
...	...	...	...	...	...	...	39.8	...	39.8
8.6	9.2	8.3	8.4	7.6	8.3	8.7	15.8	8.4	12.6
22.0	28.0	18.4	15.9	23.6	20.6	19.5	23.9	21.0	22.7
...	...	...	13.5	...	...	...	...	13.5	13.5
2.3	4.5	6.8	8.0	2.8	18.7	1.4	6.4	7.0	6.6
16.6	9.7	9.9	11.9	12.2	9.4	...	11.2	10.6	11.0
10.3	15.0	13.6	11.0	15.1	11.1	14.7	12.7	13.4	13.0
68.5	79.3	79.6	54.5	59.4	51.9	...	55.0	63.3	58.5
6.2	6.8	4.1	6.9	11.3	7.3	9.6	16.7	7.7	12.8
15.9	12.6	22.6	33.6	38.8	50.7	33.4	26.9	32.0	29.0
17.5	...	...	11.6	...	...	...	15.2	11.6	14.5

Table A.3 *(continued)*

Group and economy[a]	1978	1979	1980	1981	1982	1983	1984
29. Gambia, The[d]	42.4	40.4	17.4	22.9	...	...	...
30. Germany[c]	10.8	9.3	...	...	12.8	11.8	12.0
31. Ghana[c,d]	...	...	27.6	26.2	28.7	17.4	8.2
32. Greece[c]	7.8	8.6	...	17.5	20.1	19.6	22.5
33. Grenada[d]	7.6	3.4	3.7	7.7	...	...	...
34. Guatemala	10.1	12.1	15.8	20.6	20.9	20.0	12.2
35. Guyana[c]	42.2	34.4	26.2	24.4	23.9	27.1	23.0
36. Haiti[d]	15.4	10.5	8.3	10.2	8.3	16.9	18.2
37. Honduras[c]	12.1	11.3	12.9	24.5	39.9	47.4	41.5
38. India[c]	33.7	...	41.1	44.6	45.0	43.0	45.4
39. Indonesia	22.5	12.6	11.1	11.7	26.8	16.0	10.6
40. Italy[c]	11.1	...	...	...	11.7	12.9	12.6
41. Ireland[c]	...	10.5	...	...	...	...	...
42. Jamaica[d]	29.2	22.2	20.9	23.0	27.7	15.1	35.6
43. Japan[c,e]	12.0	11.1	10.6	10.7	10.4	10.3	9.4
44. Kenya	17.3	17.3	24.6	24.0	26.1	24.0	22.7
45. Korea, Rep. of [c]	...	...	27.6	30.7	47.6	19.0	20.7
46. Malawi[d]	21.2	...	49.6	34.9	12.2	6.1	7.3
47. Malaysia[c]	6.9	7.4	9.9	11.6	17.1	23.3	29.2
48. Mali[d]	7.6	9.3	8.1	...	...	...	...
49. Mauritania	37.2	37.2	49.2	58.1	...	...	28.1
50. Mauritius	14.4	14.4	...	...	...	...	7.2
51. Mexico[c]	34.9	27.0	26.9	31.4	28.7	23.5	22.3
52. Morocco[d]	...	...	22.0	22.0	21.0	24.0	27.0
53. Myanmar[e]	55.4	57.2	48.2	51.9	61.3	55.0	55.2
54. Namibia[c,d]	...	...	13.2	21.0	24.2	21.4	15.3
55. Nepal	42.7	40.8	35.0	29.1	...	31.7	27.7
56. Netherlands[c,d]	10.4	7.8	...	...	...	...	...
57. Niger[d]	...	...	...	...	...	10.6	...
58. Nigeria[c]	...	...	...	...	...	20.0	10.6
59. Norway[c,e]	13.3	11.9	18.8	23.5	18.6	26.9	20.4
60. Pakistan	...	52.8	35.5	31.6	29.8	31.9	30.4
61. Panama[c]	32.9	20.9	13.4	10.9	15.1	13.8	16.1
62. Papua New Guinea[e]	...	...	...	8.5	6.2	6.7	7.7
63. Paraguay	6.5	8.7	6.4	5.5	15.4	26.2	23.7
64. Peru	10.9	9.2	9.2	9.9	14.8	21.1	21.7
65. Philippines[c]	17.5	18.1	18.4	23.1	16.6	11.0	14.3
66. Portugal	...	...	...	...	...	...	...
67. Senegal	...	...	...	...	40.5	80.1	33.7
68. Sierra Leone[e]	...	19.6	...	...	1.4	1.2	1.1
69. South Africa	23.2	24.8	25.8	19.8	17.7	17.9	18.4
70. Spain	...	11.4	...	...	...	...	...
71. Sri Lanka[c]	24.1	19.8	36.2	35.9	36.2	...	...
72. St. Kitts and Nevis	...	...	24.1	35.1	3.6	2.0	2.3
73. St. Lucia	6.4	7.9	3.9	4.3	...	...	...
74. St. Vincent and the Grenadines[d]	6.8	14.8	41.3	9.5	10.8	13.2	7.2
75. Sweden[c]	24.5	21.6	22.6	25.4	26.3	...	...
76. Taiwan (China)	28.2	23.8	27.8	36.2	35.5	31.3	29.5
77. Tanzania[c]	31.2	25.1	26.3	21.7	28.9	21.0	19.4
78. Thailand	13.2	19.1	17.7	15.4	16.1	14.0	14.7
79. Togo[d]	...	...	...	...	...	...	...
80. Trinidad and Tobago[d]	...	...	...	...	...	...	...
81. Tunisia	44.5	43.5	33.8	35.8	39.7	37.7	38.6
82. Turkey[c]	...	...	48.4	43.7	38.5	40.5	41.2
83. United Kingdom[c,e]	15.0	14.4	17.5	18.0	16.8	16.1	13.2

1985	1986	1987	1988	1989	1990	1991	1978–85	1986–91	1978–91
...	...	...	...	...	...	...	30.8	...	30.8
13.1	...	...	...	...	...	...	11.6	...	11.6
20.4	25.2	21.6	16.9	26.4	0.6	59.2	22.9	25.0	23.8
22.6	20.7	20.8	17.8	19.1	...	...	16.9	19.6	17.9
...	5.8	8.0	9.0	7.0	4.1	2.7	5.6	6.1	5.9
8.7	8.5	5.3	5.6	7.5	12.1	...	15.1	7.8	12.3
20.8	35.2	43.3	38.6	40.2	37.4	...	27.7	38.9	32.0
13.4	12.5	13.3	10.2	9.9	8.2	4.4	12.7	9.8	11.4
27.6	19.4	10.0	8.6	8.5	16.6	...	27.2	12.6	21.6
43.6	43.7	36.0	37.7	40.0	...	...	42.5	39.0	41.0
6.2	6.4	4.0	9.6	8.8	14.1	18.7	14.7	10.3	12.8
12.7	12.6	13.5	12.6	...	...	...	12.2	12.9	12.5
...	...	...	...	...	...	...	10.5	...	10.5
35.1	25.5	20.8	28.9	11.4	19.7	...	26.1	21.3	24.2
7.2	6.7	6.2	5.4	4.8	4.7	4.9	10.2	5.5	8.2
18.8	22.2	18.5	17.3	20.8	25.0	...	21.8	20.8	21.4
18.4	15.6	...	...	...	8.9	...	26.2	15.3	21.5
4.9	10.5	8.0	12.3	10.2	...	...	21.0	10.3	16.5
29.0	20.9	17.0	14.5	15.7	12.1	14.4	16.8	15.8	16.4
...	...	...	...	...	...	...	8.3	...	8.3
19.1	24.7	30.0	25.8	5.6	10.8	18.8	37.6	19.3	29.8
...	...	...	...	...	...	...	12.0	...	12.0
19.8	18.2	16.2	14.3	13.0	12.2	12.0	26.8	14.3	21.5
23.0	17.0	18.0	18.0	22.0	18.0	...	22.8	18.7	21.1
49.4	51.7	48.2	26.8	27.0	19.4	11.9	54.2	30.8	44.2
15.9	14.1	13.0	11.5	8.8	8.2	9.0	18.5	10.8	15.2
40.4	49.0	60.5	...	...	...	...	35.3	53.3	43.0
...	...	...	6.0	...	...	...	9.1	6.0	8.1
33.5	14.5	...	...	...	...	...	22.1	14.5	19.5
14.0	15.1	...	...	...	...	...	14.9	15.1	14.9
23.0	29.5	28.8	27.8	29.7	16.0	29.0	19.6	26.8	22.7
29.9	30.2	31.4	28.7	29.6	26.3	25.6	35.8	28.6	32.7
13.5	13.4	10.1	12.0	6.7	5.6	5.4	17.1	8.9	13.6
10.4	8.6	8.5	7.7	5.3	6.1	...	7.7	7.1	7.4
20.4	16.0	15.3	18.1	7.1	6.1	1.4	14.1	10.7	12.6
18.1	10.6	8.1	8.0	7.8	6.8	4.7	14.4	7.7	11.5
12.5	5.7	6.8	6.3	7.7	11.6	2.2	16.5	6.7	12.3
20.6	16.8	14.2	14.8	...	...	...	20.6	15.3	16.6
49.5	30.5	20.9	18.6	21.5	...	...	46.0	22.0	35.7
...	...	...	...	...	...	...	5.8	...	5.8
20.7	18.4	15.6	12.9	15.2	16.1	...	21.0	15.5	18.7
12.1	...	...	8.6	...	...	...	11.7	8.6	10.7
...	36.8	29.7	26.2	22.8	19.1	18.5	31.1	25.5	28.7
5.0	5.2	10.2	5.4	4.9	1.8	...	12.0	5.5	9.0
...	10.1	6.5	14.4	17.5	20.8	14.1	5.6	13.9	10.6
18.1	32.3	23.3	16.3	7.7	12.7	12.6	15.2	17.5	16.2
11.4	11.9	11.2	9.7	8.8	8.8	10.0	22.0	10.1	16.0
24.0	19.2	19.1	16.4	17.0	...	...	29.5	17.7	24.5
23.4	26.8	27.2	33.8	44.0	24.9	23.2	24.6	30.0	26.9
14.6	13.6	16.2	11.2	13.8	12.9	13.3	15.6	13.5	14.7
7.0	6.2	17.2	8.5	10.5	14.6	...	7.0	11.4	10.7
...	10.4	17.9	14.8	21.7	17.2	...	...	16.4	16.4
33.7	35.8	34.0	28.2	26.8	27.2	30.5	38.4	30.4	35.0
38.8	31.1	31.5	31.6	29.0	35.1	33.3	38.6	31.9	35.7
9.7	8.5	6.0	4.8	5.1	4.7	4.2	15.1	5.6	11.0

Table A.3 *(continued)*

Group and economy[a]	1978	1979	1980	1981	1982	1983	1984
84. United States[c,e]	4.0	3.6	4.1	3.8	3.9	3.7	3.0
85. Uruguay	15.9	13.3	13.3	15.8	12.5	10.8	16.5
86. Venezuela[c]	24.4	28.5	39.9	40.9	49.0	70.2	39.2
87. Zaire	...	...	39.9	34.5	11.6	19.1	24.1
88. Zambia[c]	...	61.2	54.8	49.6	50.0	58.8	57.2

a. Only a subset of economies within each classification was used in deriving averages. Fifty-five developing economies refer to the low- and middle-income economies listed below. Ten industrial economies include Australia, Belgium, France, Greece, Italy, Japan, Norway, Sweden, United Kingdom, and United States. Eighteen low-income economies include Bolivia, Burundi, Egypt, Ghana, Guyana, Haiti, India, Indonesia, Kenya, Malawi, Mauritana, Nepal, Pakistan, Philippines, Senegal, Sri Lanka, Tanzania, and Zaire. Thirty-seven middle-income economies include Argentina, Barbados, Belize, Botswana, Brazil, Chile, Colombia, Congo, Côte d'Ivoire, Dominica, Dominican Republic, Ecuador, El Salvador, Fiji, Grenada, Guatemala, Honduras, Jamaica, Korea, Malaysia, Mexico, Morocco, Namibia, Panama, Papua New Guinea, Paraguay, Peru, South Africa, St. Kitts and Nevis, St. Lucia, St. Vincent and the Grenadines, Taiwan (China), Thailand, Tunisia, Turkey, Uruguay, and Venezuela. Latin America and the Caribbean averages exclude Trinidad and Tobago. Africa average

1985	1986	1987	1988	1989	1990	1991	1978–85	1986–91	1978–91
3.3	3.6	3.7	3.7	3.6	3.7	4.2	3.7	3.7	3.7
14.7	20.1	9.8	13.0	10.5	16.9	17.5	14.1	14.7	14.3
33.6	43.4	32.3	30.3	76.5	89.3	49.8	40.7	53.6	46.3
18.2	18.7	17.6	20.5	...	...	...	26.3	19.0	23.2
...	...	...	...	...	...	...	55.3	...	55.3

includes only Botwsana, Côte d'Ivoire, Egypt, Ghana, Kenya, Malawi, Mauritania, Morocco, Namibia, Senegal, South Africa, Tanzania, Tunisia, and Zaire. Asia average includes Fiji, India, Indonesia, Korea, Malaysia, Nepal, Pakistan, Papua New Guinea, Philippines, Sri Lanka, Taiwan (China), Thailand, and Turkey. Except for industrial economies, three-year moving average estimates were used, in case of missing observations, to complete our time series.

b. Weighted averages were obtained using GDP in current U.S. dollars as weights.

c. See specific country note.

d. Selected major state-owned enterprises only.

e. Financial state-owned enterprises are included.

Table A.4 State-Owned Enterprise Investment as a Proportion of Gross Domestic Product, 1978–91

(percentage)

Group and economy[a]	1978	1979	1980	1981	1982	1983	1984
Group							
All economies							
55 Developing economies							
Weighted average[b]	6.1	6.7	6.2	6.6	6.9	5.6	5.3
Unweighted average	5.0	5.0	5.4	5.3	5.4	4.7	4.4
10 Industrial economies							
Weighted average	2.2	...	...	...	1.9	...	...
Unweighted average	2.9	...	...	...	3.3	...	...
Developing economies by income							
18 Low-income economies							
Weighted average	7.2	7.1	6.6	7.1	7.9	7.0	6.9
Unweighted average	6.2	6.0	7.0	6.7	6.2	5.5	5.0
37 Middle-income economies							
Weighted average	5.6	6.6	6.0	6.4	6.5	5.0	4.6
Unweighted average	4.5	4.6	4.6	4.6	5.0	4.4	4.1
Developing economies by region							
27 Latin America and the Caribbean							
Weighted average	5.0	6.1	5.5	6.3	6.0	4.5	3.9
Unweighted average	4.1	4.0	4.0	3.9	4.1	3.5	3.3
15 Africa							
Weighted average	6.7	6.9	7.0	6.7	6.8	6.5	6.7
Unweighted average	5.8	5.8	6.7	6.7	6.3	5.6	5.2
13 Asia							
Weighted average	7.3	7.5	6.8	7.1	8.2	6.6	6.6
Unweighted average	6.0	6.3	6.6	6.6	7.2	6.3	5.7
Economy							
1. Algeria[c]	36.7	31.3	23.5	18.6	17.5	14.4	12.3
2. Argentina	3.8	2.8	2.6	2.6	2.3	2.4	2.4
3. Australia[c,e]	3.9	4.1	4.0	4.5	4.9	4.5	4.1
4. Austria	1.7	1.5	...	...	...	...	...
5. Bangladesh[c]	...	...	...	1.1	0.5	0.7	0.2
6. Barbados[d]	2.4	2.2	2.2	2.0	1.7	2.4	2.4
7. Belgium[c,d]	1.9	1.9	...	...	...	1.8	1.7
8. Belize	8.1	8.3	1.9	3.2	5.2	3.3	1.9
9. Benin[d]	...	...	...	...	...	...	...
10. Bolivia[d]	7.2	4.8	3.6	2.9	4.8	3.0	2.4
11. Botswana[c]	2.4	1.9	2.0	4.1	4.8	6.4	6.5
12. Brazil[e]	4.5	7.8	5.7	6.4	6.0	4.7	4.1
13. Burundi	6.1	5.5	5.9	4.3	5.3	6.0	6.4
14. Central African Rep.	...	...	...	...	...	...	...
15. Chile	2.8	1.9	2.6	2.7	2.7	2.9	3.9
16. Colombia	...	...	2.1	2.1	2.5	4.5	4.0
17. Comoros	...	...	...	...	...	6.4	5.3
18. Congo[c]	...	...	...	...	...	15.3	...
19. Costa Rica	4.6	5.2	4.6	5.8	3.5	3.4	2.7
20. Côte d'Ivoire[e]	...	...	2.0	1.7	5.4	4.4	3.4
21. Denmark[c]	...	...	...	...	...	...	...
22. Dominica[c]	2.1	2.1	1.9	4.5	2.7	0.3	0.7
23. Dominican Rep.[e]	3.0	2.3	2.3	2.9	2.0	1.8	2.3
24. Ecuador[c]	3.6	3.4	3.3	3.3	2.7	2.4	2.4
25. Egypt, Arab Rep. of [c]	...	...	...	15.5	16.1	14.6	15.0
26. El Salvador[d]	3.2	3.3	2.8	2.5	3.5	2.7	1.0
27. Fiji[e]	4.5	6.5	7.1	7.3	7.9	8.0	3.9
28. France[c]	3.2	3.1	...	...	3.6	...	...

1985	1986	1987	1988	1989	1990	1991	1978–85	1986–91	1978–91
5.2	4.9	4.7	4.6	4.4	4.2	4.0	6.1	4.5	5.4
4.3	4.0	4.2	4.0	3.9	4.1	4.1	4.9	4.1	4.6
1.5	...	...	1.4	...	...	...	...	...	1.8
2.9	...	...	2.6	...	...	...	...	...	2.9
7.0	7.1	6.7	6.3	6.7	6.6	6.9	7.1	6.7	6.9
5.1	5.4	6.2	5.3	5.9	5.7	5.9	6.0	5.7	5.9
4.4	3.9	3.9	3.8	3.6	3.3	3.2	5.6	3.6	4.8
3.9	3.3	3.2	3.3	3.0	3.3	3.2	4.5	3.2	3.9
3.7	3.5	3.4	3.5	3.0	2.7	2.2	5.1	3.1	4.2
3.1	3.3	3.3	3.2	2.9	3.3	2.8	3.8	3.1	3.5
7.4	6.2	6.4	4.7	5.3	4.8	5.1	6.8	5.4	6.2
5.3	4.5	5.2	4.6	4.9	4.4	5.3	5.9	4.8	5.5
6.3	6.1	5.7	5.6	5.8	5.7	5.8	7.0	5.8	6.5
5.5	4.9	5.1	4.9	5.1	5.5	5.2	6.3	5.1	5.8
10.5	9.8	...	...	...	...	...	20.6	10.4	16.2
1.8	1.6	2.0	1.7	1.6	1.0	0.7	2.6	1.4	2.1
4.5	4.3	3.3	3.0	3.5	3.2	3.0	4.3	3.4	3.9
...	...	...	...	...	...	...	1.6	...	1.6
4.7	5.5	3.8	3.3	2.8	3.4	2.7	1.4	3.6	2.6
2.0	2.0	1.4	1.1	0.8	1.1	1.8	2.2	1.4	1.8
1.5	1.3	1.1	1.0	...	...	...	1.8	1.1	1.5
2.4	3.3	3.6	3.6	3.1	3.9	3.7	4.3	3.5	3.9
4.6	1.6	1.9	2.0	2.6	1.7	...	4.6	2.0	2.4
1.5	1.8	3.5	3.4	3.2	3.1	...	3.8	3.1	3.5
11.5	1.6	3.6	5.7	4.3	6.1	10.7	5.0	5.3	5.1
4.1	3.4	3.8	4.1	3.2	3.0	2.1	5.4	3.3	4.5
6.1	6.3	9.7	6.0	6.7	6.2	...	5.7	6.9	6.2
...	2.1	...	...	...	...	...	...	2.1	2.1
4.2	4.7	3.7	3.3	2.6	1.9	...	3.0	3.1	3.0
3.8	2.8	2.3	2.6	2.5	1.8	1.6	2.9	2.3	2.6
4.5	3.7	...	...	...	...	...	5.4	3.7	5.0
...	...	...	...	...	...	...	15.3	...	15.3
2.4	2.3	2.3	2.1	2.0	2.3	2.1	4.0	2.2	3.2
2.8	3.1	2.2	2.3	2.0	1.9	...	3.1	2.3	2.8
...	...	...	2.4	...	...	...	...	2.4	2.4
0.7	1.0	1.6	2.4	1.2	7.2	0.5	1.9	2.3	2.1
3.4	1.9	2.8	3.5	3.4	2.1	...	2.5	2.8	2.6
1.9	3.1	3.1	2.4	3.1	2.0	3.2	2.9	2.8	2.8
16.3	14.3	19.2	12.7	13.0	10.6	...	15.5	13.7	14.7
0.7	0.9	0.5	0.9	1.7	0.9	1.3	2.5	1.0	1.8
2.9	1.8	3.5	4.7	5.2	9.2	4.6	6.0	4.8	5.5
3.3	...	...	2.5	...	...	...	3.3	2.5	3.1

Table A.4 *(continued)*

Group and economy[a]	1978	1979	1980	1981	1982	1983	1984
29. Gambia, The[d]	13.4	11.0	4.6	5.6	...	...	...
30. Germany[c]	2.3	2.2	...	...	2.5	2.4	2.4
31. Ghana[c,d]	...	...	1.6	1.2	1.0	0.7	0.6
32. Greece[c]	2.2	2.6	...	4.4	4.2	4.3	4.4
33. Grenada[d]	0.6	0.5	0.8	2.6	8.3	5.2	4.3
34. Guatemala	2.2	2.3	2.5	3.5	3.0	2.2	1.4
35. Guyana[c]	8.1	8.4	7.8	7.2	6.0	5.8	6.3
36. Haiti[d]	2.6	2.0	1.4	1.9	1.4	2.8	2.9
37. Honduras[c]	3.2	3.0	3.2	5.2	5.6	6.6	7.2
38. India[c]	...	...	7.9	8.8	9.0	8.3	8.9
39. Indonesia	5.4	3.4	2.7	3.5	7.4	4.6	2.8
40. Italy[c]	2.7	...	...	...	...	2.7	2.8
41. Ireland[c]	3.4	...	...	...	...	...	...
42. Jamaica[d]	4.4	4.3	3.3	4.7	5.8	3.4	8.2
43. Japan[c,e]	3.7	3.6	3.4	3.3	3.1	2.9	2.6
44. Kenya	4.3	4.0	5.7	5.6	5.0	4.3	4.1
45. Korea, Rep. of[c]	...	...	8.9	8.6	13.5	5.6	6.0
46. Malawi[d]	6.5	...	12.3	6.1	2.6	1.4	0.9
47. Malaysia[c]	...	...	...	4.1	6.4	8.8	9.8
48. Mali[d]	1.3	3.2	1.4	...	...	...	...
49. Mauritania	3.6	5.6	15.4	21.7	...	...	6.7
50. Mauritius	4.4	4.5	...	...	...	...	1.5
51. Mexico[c]	5.7	6.4	6.7	8.3	6.6	4.1	4.0
52. Morocco[d]	...	...	4.1	5.9	5.7	6.1	6.4
53. Myanmar[e]	10.1	12.8	10.3	11.9	13.6	9.9	8.3
54. Namibia[c,d]	...	...	2.3	2.5	2.8	2.2	1.4
55. Nepal	7.8	6.5	6.4	5.1	...	6.2	5.2
56. Netherlands[c,d]	2.3	1.7	...	...	...	...	...
57. Niger[d]	...	...	...	...	...	1.4	...
58. Nigeria[c]	...	...	...	...	...	3.2	1.2
59. Norway[c,e]	3.8	3.3	5.2	6.0	4.9	6.6	5.2
60. Pakistan	...	9.4	6.6	5.9	5.7	6.0	5.5
61. Panama[c]	7.6	5.1	3.3	3.0	4.2	2.9	2.9
62. Papua New Guinea[e]	...	...	...	2.3	2.0	2.0	1.8
63. Paraguay	...	2.5	2.0	1.7	3.9	5.6	5.4
64. Peru	2.1	2.0	2.7	3.4	5.0	5.1	4.5
65. Philippines[c]	4.4	5.0	5.0	6.4	4.6	3.3	3.5
66. Portugal	...	...	...	...	...	...	...
67. Senegal	...	...	...	...	4.9	10.4	4.1
68. Sierra Leone[e]	...	2.6	...	...	0.2	0.2	0.1
69. South Africa	6.1	6.5	6.8	5.5	4.9	4.8	4.5
70. Spain	...	2.5	...	...	...	...	...
71. Sri Lanka[c]	4.8	5.0	11.4	9.8	10.7	...	...
72. St. Kitts and Nevis	...	...	7.5	4.9	1.3	0.8	0.7
73. St. Lucia	4.0	4.0	2.1	2.5	1.3	1.3	1.0
74. St. Vincent and the Grenadines[d]	1.6	5.2	16.3	3.2	3.3	4.1	1.8
75. Sweden[c]	4.3	4.3	4.8	4.6	4.6	...	...
76. Taiwan (China)	8.0	7.8	9.4	10.8	8.9	7.3	6.5
77. Tanzania[c]	7.9	6.5	6.0	5.0	6.6	3.1	3.3
78. Thailand	3.7	5.2	4.7	4.1	3.7	3.6	3.7
79. Togo[d]	...	...	...	...	...	...	...
80. Trinidad and Tobago[d]	...	...	...	...	...	...	...
81. Tunisia	13.8	13.3	9.6	11.1	13.5	12.0	11.9
82. Turkey[c]	...	...	10.6	9.6	7.9	7.9	8.0
83. United Kingdom[c,e]	2.9	2.9	3.0	2.7	2.6	2.7	2.3

1985	1986	1987	1988	1989	1990	1991	1978–85	1986–91	1978–91
...	...	...	...	...	...	...	8.6	...	8.6
2.6	...	...	...	...	...	...	2.4	...	2.4
2.0	2.4	2.9	2.4	4.1	0.1	9.4	1.2	3.6	2.2
4.8	4.1	3.7	3.4	4.0	...	...	3.8	3.8	3.8
1.7	2.3	2.8	3.1	2.6	1.5	1.0	3.0	2.2	2.7
1.0	0.9	0.7	0.8	1.0	1.6	...	2.3	1.0	1.7
6.2	11.9	13.5	8.1	13.4	18.9	...	7.0	13.2	9.6
1.9	1.4	1.7	1.3	1.2	0.9	0.5	2.1	1.2	1.7
4.7	2.6	1.6	1.7	1.5	3.5	...	4.8	2.2	3.7
9.0	9.3	7.8	7.9	8.5	...	...	8.6	8.3	8.5
1.7	1.8	1.3	3.0	3.0	5.0	6.6	3.9	3.5	3.7
2.9	2.9	2.6	2.8	2.7	...	...	2.8	2.8	2.8
...	...	...	...	...	...	...	3.4	...	3.4
8.9	4.8	4.9	6.5	2.4	4.1	...	5.4	4.5	5.0
2.0	1.9	1.8	1.7	1.5	1.5	1.6	3.1	1.7	2.5
3.4	4.4	3.6	3.5	4.0	5.1	4.2	4.6	4.1	4.4
5.2	4.3	...	...	...	3.3	...	8.4	4.5	6.7
0.9	1.3	1.2	2.3	2.1	...	...	4.7	1.8	3.5
8.0	5.4	3.9	3.8	4.6	3.9	5.2	5.5	4.5	5.1
...	...	...	...	...	...	...	1.9	...	1.9
4.7	5.3	6.1	4.2	0.8	1.4	2.1	9.7	3.3	7.0
...	...	...	...	...	...	...	3.5	...	3.5
3.8	3.5	3.0	2.8	2.4	2.3	2.3	5.7	2.7	4.4
5.1	4.0	4.1	4.2	5.2	5.2	...	5.5	4.6	5.1
7.7	6.6	5.6	3.4	2.5	2.6	1.9	10.6	3.8	7.6
1.2	0.9	1.0	0.6	0.4	0.4	0.3	2.2	0.6	1.5
9.3	10.3	13.2	...	...	...	...	6.6	11.5	8.7
...	...	...	1.3	...	...	...	2.0	1.3	1.8
4.3	1.5	...	...	...	...	...	2.8	1.5	2.4
1.3	2.2	...	...	...	...	...	1.9	2.2	2.0
5.6	8.7	8.1	7.5	7.2	3.3	5.5	5.1	6.7	5.8
5.5	5.7	6.0	5.2	5.6	5.0	4.8	6.5	5.4	6.0
2.3	2.3	1.8	1.1	0.5	0.5	0.9	3.9	1.2	2.7
1.9	1.8	1.6	1.8	1.4	1.5	...	2.1	1.6	1.9
4.5	4.0	3.8	4.4	1.7	1.4	0.4	3.5	2.6	3.1
3.3	2.3	1.8	2.0	1.5	1.1	0.7	3.5	1.6	2.7
2.2	1.0	1.1	1.1	1.6	2.5	1.8	4.3	1.5	3.1
4.3	3.8	3.9	4.4	...	...	...	4.3	4.0	4.1
5.7	3.6	2.6	2.4	2.7	...	...	6.5	2.7	4.9
...	...	...	...	...	...	...	0.8	...	0.8
4.8	3.7	3.0	2.6	3.2	3.2	3.0	5.5	3.1	4.5
2.3	...	...	2.0	...	...	...	2.4	2.0	2.3
...	8.5	6.8	5.8	4.8	4.1	4.2	8.8	5.7	7.5
1.6	1.4	3.5	3.1	0.8	0.9	...	3.4	1.9	2.7
2.5	3.0	2.1	4.8	7.4	7.3	6.1	2.4	5.1	3.5
4.5	9.3	7.0	4.5	2.1	3.2	3.6	5.0	4.9	5.0
2.2	2.1	2.1	1.9	1.9	1.9	1.8	4.1	2.0	3.0
4.6	3.4	3.9	3.8	3.8	...	...	7.9	3.8	6.1
4.2	6.0	9.7	12.3	16.7	13.0	10.9	5.3	11.4	7.9
3.5	3.0	3.9	3.2	4.3	4.9	5.2	4.0	4.1	4.0
2.0	1.4	3.5	1.7	2.2	...	...	2.0	2.2	2.1
...	2.3	3.6	2.5	4.1	3.0	...	...	3.1	2.3
9.0	8.6	6.9	5.5	5.6	6.2	6.8	11.8	6.6	9.5
8.1	7.6	8.0	7.6	6.6	8.1	6.3	8.9	7.4	8.3
1.7	1.4	1.1	1.0	1.1	0.9	0.7	2.6	1.0	1.9

Table A.4 *(continued)*

Group and economy[a]	1978	1979	1980	1981	1982	1983	1984
84. United States[c,e]	0.9	0.8	0.8	0.8	0.7	0.7	0.6
85. Uruguay	3.6	3.2	3.2	3.4	2.5	1.5	2.0
86. Venezuela[c]	10.7	9.5	10.5	10.0	13.6	8.6	6.9
87. Zaire	...	...	3.5	3.3	1.1	1.9	2.6
88. Zambia[c]	...	8.6	10.0	8.7	8.6	8.6	7.2

a. Only a subset of economies within each classification was used in deriving averages. Fifty-five developing economies refer to the low- and middle-income economies listed below. Ten industrial economies include Australia, Belgium, France, Greece, Italy, Japan, Norway, Sweden, United Kingdom, and United States. Eighteen low-income economies include Bolivia, Burundi, Egypt, Ghana, Guyana, Haiti, India, Indonesia, Kenya, Malawi, Mauritana, Nepal, Pakistan, Philippines, Senegal, Sri Lanka, Tanzania, and Zaire. Thirty-seven middle-income economies include Argentina, Barbados, Belize, Botswana, Brazil, Chile, Colombia, Congo, Côte d'Ivoire, Dominican Republic, Ecuador, El Salvador, Fiji, Grenada, Guatemala, Honduras, Jamaica, Korea, Malaysia, Mexico, Morocco, Namibia, Panama, Papua New Guinea, Paraguay, Peru, South Africa, St. Kitts and Nevis, St. Lucia, St. Vincent and the Grenadines, Taiwan (China), Thailand, Tunisia, Turkey, Uruguay, and Venezuela. Latin America and the Caribbean averages exclude Trinidad and Tobago. Africa average

1985	1986	1987	1988	1989	1990	1991	1978–85	1986–91	1978–91
0.7	0.7	0.7	0.7	0.7	0.6	0.6	0.7	0.7	0.7
1.7	2.2	1.4	1.7	1.2	1.9	2.2	2.6	1.8	2.3
6.2	9.1	7.9	8.5	9.7	9.1	9.3	9.5	8.9	9.3
2.0	2.4	2.4	3.0	...	...	...	2.5	2.7	2.6
...	...	...	...	...	...	...	8.6	...	8.6

includes Burundi, Côte d'Ivoire, Egypt, Ghana, Kenya, Malawi, Mauritania, Morocco, Namibia, Senegal, South Africa, Tanzania, Tunisia, and Zaire. Asia average includes Fiji, India, Indonesia, Korea, Malaysia, Nepal, Pakistan, Papua New Guinea, Philippines, Sri Lanka, Taiwan (China), Thailand, and Turkey. Except for industrial economies, three-year moving average estimates were used, in case of missing observations, to complete our time series.

    b. Weighted averages were obtained using GDP in current U.S. dollars as weights.

    c. See specific country note.

    d. Selected major state-owned enterprises only.

    e. Financial state-owned enterprises are included.

Table A.5 Share of State-Owned Enterprises in Employment, 1978–91

(percentage)

Group and economy[a]	1978	1979	1980	1981	1982	1983	1984
Group							
All economies							
21 Developing economies							
Weighted average[b]	4.8	4.7	4.7	4.6	4.9	5.1	5.1
Unweighted average	9.8	9.9	10.0	9.7	10.0	10.5	11.1
Developing economies by income							
10 Low-income economies							
Weighted average	8.3	8.3	8.4	8.4	8.5	8.9	9.0
Unweighted average	14.8	14.6	15.3	14.8	14.1	14.9	15.3
11 Middle-income economies							
Weighted average	3.1	3.1	2.9	2.9	3.0	3.0	3.2
Unweighted average	5.3	5.6	5.2	5.1	6.3	6.6	7.2
Developing economies by region							
6 Latin America and the Caribbean							
Weighted average	4.5	4.3	3.9	3.9	4.0	4.5	4.6
Unweighted average	3.0	2.9	2.8	2.8	2.7	2.8	2.8
9 Africa							
Weighted average	14.8	15.4	14.6	14.6	16.6	16.9	17.3
Unweighted average	19.1	19.3	19.5	18.9	19.6	20.7	21.9
6 Asia							
Weighted average	4.6	4.5	4.8	4.8	5.0	5.2	5.1
Unweighted average	2.8	2.8	2.9	2.9	2.9	3.0	3.1
Economy							
1. Algeria[d,c]	...	8.0	8.1	7.9	8.5	8.3	7.9
2. Argentina	3.6	3.4	3.1	2.9	2.8	2.9	2.9
3. Benin[c]	27.1	27.2	25.6	25.5	23.4	25.2	26.0
4. Bolivia[d]	...	...	3.1	3.1	3.0	3.3	3.2
5. Botswana	...	...	...	...	...	...	...
6. Brazil[e]	...	1.1	1.4	...	...	1.2	...
7. Burundi[e,f]	...	...	35.0	...	26.9	27.9	...
8. Cameroon[f]	...	...	...	...	...	...	...
9. Chile[d]	...	3.8	3.7	...	2.8	2.8	...
10. Colombia	1.9	2.0	2.0	2.0	1.9	2.0	2.0
11. Congo[c,d]	...	...	...	...	...	...	...
12. Côte d'Ivoire[e,f]	...	...	7.7	6.4	23.2	22.9	26.1
13. Egypt, Arab Rep. of	...	...	...	...	13.6	13.6	13.6
14. Gabon	...	...	...	...	...	...	...
15. Gambia, The[f]	...	...	...	...	...	...	...
16. Ghana[f]	...	...	...	28.9	21.0	...	27.6
17. Grenada	...	...	...	29.9	...	...	...
18. Guinea[f]	...	...	68.8	67.9	67.3	...	75.0
19. India[c]	7.7	7.8	8.0	8.1	8.4	8.5	8.6
20. Indonesia	...	...	...	...	...	...	...
21. Kenya	...	...	...	8.5	9.2	9.0	8.5
22. Korea, Rep. of[c]	1.6	1.6	1.6	1.6	1.5	1.6	1.8
23. Madagascar	...	...	...	...	...	5.1	2.1
24. Malawi[c]	...	...	11.2	10.1	11.4	11.9	11.9
25. Mali[f]	...	18.6	17.4	...	...	...	...
26. Mauritius[f]	...	...	...	...	...	...	7.2
27. Mexico[c]	3.5	3.5	3.3	3.5	3.6	3.7	3.8
28. Namibia	...	...	...	...	...	...	...
29. Peru	...	...	1.7	1.8	1.9	2.1	2.2
30. Philippines	0.7	0.7	0.8	0.9	0.9	0.8	0.8
31. Senegal[c,f]	...	...	...	23.3	23.6	23.4	22.1

1985	1986	1987	1988	1989	1990	1991	1978–85	1986–91	1978–91
5.3	5.4	5.2	4.9	4.7	4.4	4.1	4.9	4.8	4.8
10.3	10.2	10.5	10.8	11.0	10.8	11.0	10.2	10.7	10.4
9.1	9.2	8.9	8.8	8.8	8.7	8.9	8.6	8.9	8.7
14.7	14.3	14.8	15.7	16.3	16.0	16.6	14.8	15.6	15.2
3.1	3.0	3.0	2.8	2.6	2.5	2.4	3.0	2.7	2.9
6.4	6.4	6.6	6.3	6.1	6.0	5.9	6.0	6.2	6.1
4.3	4.5	4.4	4.3	3.5	3.7	3.7	4.3	4.0	4.1
2.7	2.7	2.5	2.3	2.2	2.2	2.0	2.8	2.3	2.6
16.3	16.5	16.4	16.9	17.4	17.1	18.3	15.8	17.1	16.4
20.2	19.9	20.8	21.7	22.2	21.7	22.5	19.9	21.5	20.6
5.3	5.3	5.2	4.8	4.5	4.3	3.9	4.9	4.7	4.8
3.1	3.1	3.0	2.9	2.9	2.9	2.8	2.9	2.9	2.9
7.9	7.3	7.4	7.2	7.3	7.0	7.0	8.1	7.2	7.7
2.8	2.7	2.7	2.6	2.6	2.5	1.6	3.1	2.5	2.8
...	...	...	...	...	...	...	25.7	...	25.7
3.1	3.1	2.3	1.8	1.9	1.9	...	3.1	2.1	2.7
7.6	6.2	5.8	6.6	6.0	5.7	5.3	7.6	5.9	6.2
1.2	...	...	...	...	...	...	1.2	...	1.2
...	28.1	33.0	35.7	31.4	...	...	30.4	32.5	31.3
10.4	...	10.0	...	...	...	...	10.4	10.0	10.2
...	2.4	...	...	1.1	...	...	3.3	1.1	2.8
1.9	1.8	...	...	...	...	...	1.9	1.9	1.9
21.8	18.9	...	...	...	...	...	21.8	18.9	20.4
18.8	20.4	...	...	...	...	...	15.8	20.8	18.0
14.7	14.2	13.7	13.7	13.5	13.2	13.5	13.7	13.6	13.7
...	...	...	25.5	24.7	25.1	24.3	...	24.9	24.9
...	...	...	25.0	...	...	...	...	25.0	25.0
...	27.8	27.4	33.3	44.9	38.0	45.1	26.7	36.1	30.7
...	...	...	...	...	...	...	29.9	...	29.9
...	...	...	...	...	...	...	68.0	...	68.0
8.6	8.7	8.6	8.5	8.5	8.3	...	8.2	8.5	8.3
...	...	1.1	...	0.9	1.2	...	...	1.0	1.0
7.7	8.2	7.6	8.1	8.1	8.1	...	8.7	8.0	8.4
1.9	1.9	...	...	...	1.9	...	1.6	1.9	1.8
1.8	...	...	...	...	...	...	3.0	...	3.0
12.0	12.0	...	...	...	...	...	11.4	12.0	11.5
...	...	...	...	...	...	...	18.0	...	18.0
6.0	...	...	...	...	...	...	6.6	...	6.6
3.8	3.7	3.7	3.6	3.3	3.0	...	3.6	3.4	3.5
...	...	...	2.7	...	...	...	...	2.7	2.7
2.3	2.4	2.5	2.4	2.7	2.7	...	2.0	2.5	2.2
0.7	0.7	0.7	0.7	0.7	1.2	0.5	0.8	0.8	0.8
21.2	19.4	20.9	21.7	19.0	...	...	23.0	20.3	21.9

Table A.5 *(continued)*

Group and economy[a]	1978	1979	1980	1981	1982	1983	1984
32. Seychelles	...	...	...	...	25.1	27.5	30.6
33. Sierra Leone[f]	...	...	...	...	17.1	...	...
34. Sri Lanka[c,e]	...	...	...	...	...	...	...
35. Taiwan (China)	2.2	2.2	2.3	2.4	2.4	2.3	2.2
36. Tanzania	22.0	22.7	23.2	23.0	22.8	22.1	25.4
37. Thailand[e]	...	...	...	...	...	...	1.0
38. Togo[f]	...	...	...	...	...	24.0	...
39. Trinidad and Tobago[d]	...	...	...	6.0	5.9	6.5	6.3
40. Tunisia	...	...	...	...	...	18.5	...
41. Turkey	...	...	3.6	3.4	3.4	3.7	4.2
42. Zaire[f]	...	...	...	...	...	...	...
43. Zambia[f]	...	...	43.4	37.0	34.1	34.4	...

a. Only a subset of countries within each classification was used for deriving averages. Ten low-income economies include Bolivia, Burundi, Egypt, Ghana, India, Kenya, Malawi, Philippines, Senegal, and Tanzania. Eleven middle-income economies include Chile, Colombia, Côte d'Ivoire, Jamaica, Korea, Mexico, Peru, Seychelles, Thailand, Turkey, and Taiwan (China). Latin America and the Caribbean regional average includes only Bolivia, Chile, Colombia, Jamaica, Mexico, and Peru. Africa regional average includes Burundi, Côte d'Ivoire, Egypt, Ghana, Kenya, Malawi, Senegal, Seychelles, and Tanzania. Asia regional average includes only India, Korea, Philippines, Taiwan (China), Thailand, and Turkey. Three-year moving average estimates were used to complete of missing values, when deriving averages.

1985	1986	1987	1988	1989	1990	1991	1978–85	1986–91	1978–91
28.7	28.3	29.4	29.0	27.2	25.8	26.4	27.5	27.7	27.6
...	...	...	...	...	...	...	17.1	...	17.1
14.4	...	...	...	...	14.0	13.2	14.4	13.6	13.9
2.2	2.1	2.0	1.9	1.9	...	...	2.2	2.0	2.1
17.2	21.0	21.8	21.6	23.1	23.7	...	22.3	22.3	22.3
1.0	1.0	1.0	0.9	0.9	0.9	0.8	1.0	0.9	1.0
...	...	...	...	...	...	...	24.0	...	24.0
7.5	...	...	...	...	...	...	6.4	...	6.4
...	...	...	...	...	...	...	18.5	...	18.5
4.1	4.1	4.1	3.5	3.3	3.2	3.3	3.7	3.6	3.6
...	10.0	...	...	...	...	...	...	10.0	10.0
...	...	...	...	...	...	...	37.2	...	37.2

b. Weighted averages were obtained using GDP in current U.S. dollars as weights.
c. See specific country note.
d. Selected major state-owned enterprises only.
e. Financial state-owned enterprises are included.
f. Numbers are proportion of formal sector employment.

Table A.6 State-Owned Enterprise Overall Balances before Transfers as a Proportion of Gross Domestic Product, 1978–91

(percentage)

Group and economy[a]	1978	1979	1980	1981	1982	1983	1984
Group							
All economies							
46 Developing economies							
Weighted average[b]	-2.6	-3.4	-2.3	-1.6	-3.5	-2.0	-0.9
Unweighted average	-2.7	-2.6	-2.6	-2.6	-3.1	-2.3	-1.4
Developing economies by income							
17 Low-income economies							
Weighted average	-2.8	-2.4	-2.0	-2.8	-3.8	-2.5	-2.2
Unweighted average	-2.3	-2.4	-2.3	-1.9	-2.7	-2.2	-1.1
29 Middle-income economies							
Weighted average	-2.5	-3.7	-2.4	-1.2	-3.4	-1.7	-0.3
Unweighted average	-2.9	-2.7	-2.7	-3.0	-3.3	-2.3	-1.6
Developing economies by region							
21 Latin America and the Caribbean							
Weighted average	-1.5	-2.9	-1.3	-0.3	-2.6	-1.4	0.4
Unweighted average	-1.9	-2.2	-1.7	-2.2	-1.8	-1.7	-0.7
15 Africa							
Weighted average	-1.5	-2.1	-1.8	-2.1	-3.0	-2.2	-2.1
Unweighted average	-2.8	-3.0	-3.5	-3.0	-4.3	-3.1	-2.4
10 Asia							
Weighted average	-4.4	-4.2	-3.8	-3.8	-4.9	-2.7	-2.3
Unweighted average	-4.4	-4.0	-4.2	-4.1	-4.5	-3.1	-2.9
Economy							
1. Argentina	-2.1	-2.5	-3.0	-1.8	-2.9	-11.1	-6.0
2. Bangladesh[c]	...	...	...	-1.6	-0.2	0.2	-0.2
3. Barbados[d]	-2.8	-2.7	-2.7	-3.3	-2.6	-2.6	-2.0
4. Belize[c]	-9.4	-8.7	-2.2	-3.6	-7.1	-5.2	-3.0
5. Benin[d]	...	...	...	...	...	-1.5	...
6. Bolivia[c,d]	2.8	3.8	6.9	8.0	6.9	2.8	0.2
7. Botswana[c]	-0.6	-0.6	-4.5	-3.5	-5.7	-6.0	-14.0
8. Brazil [c,e]	-5.1	-11.0	-9.2	-5.6	-6.8	-4.6	-2.4
9. Burundi	...	...	...	...	...	...	0.4
10. Cameroon[c]	...	...	...	...	-2.2	-2.2	-1.2
11. Central African Rep.[c]	...	...	...	...	-2.6	-1.0	-0.7
12. Chile	4.3	7.3	7.2	2.9	5.8	8.8	7.5
13. Colombia	...	...	0.7	-2.1	-1.6	-2.7	-1.7
14. Congo[c]	...	...	...	-1.5	-3.5	-3.4	-2.9
15. Costa Rica	-2.6	-3.8	-4.3	-7.0	-5.1	0.3	2.1
16. Côte d'Ivoire[c]	-8.4	-8.4	...	...	-1.9	-4.1	-4.8
17. Dominica	-2.7	-7.3	-7.1	-7.2	-4.0	-1.3	-1.0
18. Dominican Rep.[e]	-2.9	-2.8	-3.4	-4.6	-2.6	-1.7	-1.3
19. Ecuador[c]	-2.6	-1.3	-2.4	-2.1	-1.6	0.1	0.4
20. Egypt, Arab Rep. of	...	...	...	...	...	...	-3.4
21. El Salvador[d]	-1.6	-2.1	-1.7	-2.1	-1.6	-1.1	0.3
22. Gambia, The[c]	...	...	...	-4.8	-8.7	-9.0	2.3
23. Ghana[c]	...	...	-0.2	-0.9	-3.3	-0.3	-0.4
24. Guatemala[c]	-1.9	-1.9	-2.2	-3.2	-2.3	-1.5	-0.8
25. Guyana[c]	4.4	4.5	-0.6	-16.6	-19.3	-21.9	-12.0
26. Haiti[c,d]	...	...	-0.5	-0.6	0.6	-0.5	-0.1
27. Honduras[c]	-2.2	-1.9	-4.2	-4.0	-5.1	-5.3	-5.9
28. India[c]	...	...	...	-3.4	-2.7	-1.9	-1.8
29. Indonesia[c]	-4.3	-1.5	-1.3	-2.6	-7.0	-3.9	-1.9
30. Jamaica[c]	-3.6	-3.4	-3.2	-7.0	-6.2	-5.3	-4.3

1985	1986	1987	1988	1989	1990	1991	1978–85	1986–91	1978–91
-0.3	-0.9	-0.4	0.6	0.3	0.6	0.1	-2.1	0.1	-1.2
-0.4	-1.0	-0.8	-1.0	-0.9	-0.4	-0.8	-2.2	-0.8	-1.6
-1.3	-2.9	-1.8	-1.4	-1.9	-2.3	-2.1	-2.5	-2.1	-2.3
-0.1	-1.6	-1.8	-1.6	-2.0	-1.4	-1.7	-1.9	-1.7	-1.8
0.2	0.0	0.2	1.4	1.1	1.7	0.8	-0.4	2.8	0.9
-0.6	-0.6	-0.2	-0.6	-0.2	0.1	-0.3	-2.3	-0.3	-1.4
0.8	0.2	0.8	2.0	1.9	3.1	2.8	-1.1	1.8	0.1
0.8	0.9	0.5	0.4	0.7	1.1	1.5	-1.4	0.8	-0.5
0.0	-2.1	-2.1	-3.0	-1.8	-2.0	-2.5	-1.8	-2.3	-2.0
-1.7	-2.8	-2.2	-2.9	-3.2	-2.3	-3.2	-3.0	-2.8	-2.9
-1.5	-2.1	-1.5	-0.6	-1.2	-1.8	-2.6	-3.4	-1.6	-2.7
-2.0	-2.5	-1.9	-1.4	-1.9	-2.6	-3.4	-3.6	-2.3	-3.1
-4.9	-3.1	-4.9	-3.5	-1.9	-0.7	-1.3	-4.3	-2.6	-3.5
-4.1	-4.5	-3.6	-2.9	-2.6	-2.6	-1.8	-1.0	-3.0	-1.9
-1.2	-2.1	-2.2	-2.5	-2.0	-1.6	-2.7	-2.5	-2.2	-2.4
-0.6	-1.7	-1.9	-0.4	-1.4	-2.5	-1.3	-5.0	-1.5	-3.5
...	...	...	...	...	...	...	-1.5	...	-1.5
15.0	8.9	2.1	6.8	7.3	8.0	...	5.8	6.8	6.2
-0.3	-2.3	-2.6	-4.1	-3.3	-4.5	-10.0	-4.4	-4.5	-4.4
-2.4	-0.5	0.1	3.5	1.4	2.5	2.9	-5.9	1.7	-2.7
...	...	...	...	...	...	...	0.4	...	0.4
...	...	...	...	...	...	...	-1.9	...	-1.9
-2.0	-3.3	-4.7	-2.5	...	...	...	-1.6	-3.5	-2.4
9.4	7.8	9.4	11.0	9.9	...	...	6.7	9.8	8.0
-0.8	2.7	0.0	-0.2	0.9	2.2	1.8	-1.2	1.2	-0.2
-2.6	...	...	...	...	...	...	-2.8	...	-2.8
0.9	2.3	1.4	3.0	1.8	2.0	2.6	-2.4	2.2	-0.5
-5.0	...	...	...	...	...	...	-5.4	...	-5.4
0.9	2.5	1.0	-1.5	-1.3	-6.6	-0.3	-3.7	-1.0	-2.6
-5.5	...	...	...	...	...	...	-3.1	...	-3.1
-0.4	-1.0	-2.2	-2.2	-1.0	-0.1	-0.7	-1.2	-1.2	-1.2
0.2	-3.7	-2.8	-5.5	-1.4	...	...	-2.1	-3.3	-2.6
0.3	-0.6	0.0	-0.3	-1.2	-0.1	-0.7	-1.2	-0.5	-0.9
-2.6	-3.2	...	...	...	...	...	-5.5	-2.2	-4.1
0.1	0.9	-0.6	-0.1	-2.0	2.4	...	-0.9	0.1	-0.5
-0.1	0.0	0.3	0.0	-0.2	-0.2	...	-1.7	0.0	-1.0
1.5	...	...	...	...	...	...	-7.5	...	-7.5
0.7	0.5	...	...	...	...	...	-0.1	0.5	0.0
-2.5	-1.6	0.4	0.1	-0.6	-1.4	...	-3.9	-0.6	-2.5
-2.0	-3.4	-3.0	-1.9	-2.5	-2.6	-1.7	-2.5	-2.5	-2.5
-1.3	-1.3	2.7	0.4	-0.8	-3.0	-3.8	-3.0	-1.0	-2.1
-1.7	1.4	1.2	-5.4	-1.5	-2.6	...	-4.4	-1.4	-3.2

Table A.6 *(continued)*

Group and economy[a]	1978	1979	1980	1981	1982	1983	1984
31. Kenya	...	...	...	...	...	...	-4.0
32. Korea, Rep. of	...	...	-4.6	-3.1	-9.9	-0.7	-0.8
33. Malawi[c,d]	...	...	-12.0	-5.4	-1.1	0.0	0.5
34. Malaysia[c]	...	...	...	-0.2	-1.0	-2.6	-3.5
35. Mali[c]	-2.7	...	...	-2.7	-1.8	-0.9	-1.9
36. Mauritania[c]	...	...	-0.3	0.2	-1.5	-0.6	...
37. Mauritius[c]	...	...	-2.9	-4.3	-3.5	-3.5	-1.8
38. Mexico[c]	...	...	...	...	-0.3	4.0	3.6
39. Morocco[c]	...	...	-4.9	-6.0	-4.6	-4.9	-3.7
40. Myanmar	-1.6	-6.4	-6.4	-3.9	-5.2	-5.0	-2.1
41. Namibia[c]	...	...	...	-5.4	-5.5	-3.8	-2.1
42. Nepal[c]	-7.5	...	-7.3	...	...	-6.0	-5.6
43. Niger[c]	...	...	...	-0.9	-2.1	-1.3	-0.9
44. Nigeria[c]	...	...	...	...	...	0.7	2.3
45. Panama[c]	-7.8	-5.2	-2.1	-1.4	-3.2	-1.3	0.1
46. Paraguay	...	-1.1	-0.8	-0.5	-3.1	-4.5	-5.0
47. Peru	0.8	2.7	1.7	0.3	0.0	1.6	2.3
48. Philippines	...	...	-4.2	-5.3	-5.0	-6.3	-8.6
49. Rwanda[c]	...	...	...	...	0.2	0.3	1.0
50. Senegal	...	...	...	...	-3.3	-9.0	-2.9
51. Seychelles[e]	...	-7.3	-9.3	-9.0	-17.5	-9.8	-13.9
52. Sierra Leone[c]	...	...	...	0.6	-1.0	-1.7	-0.3
53. St. Kitts and Nevis	...	...	-10.3	-8.9	4.1	-6.6	-1.1
54. St. Vincent and the Grenadines[d]	-1.8	-6.7	-17.4	-4.9	-5.1	-5.3	-1.9
55. Taiwan (China)[c]	-4.7	-3.8	-5.5	-6.6	-3.7	-1.7	-0.5
56. Tanzania	...	...	...	-2.7	-3.6	1.1	1.1
57. Thailand	...	-4.3	-4.4	-2.6	-2.0	-0.8	-1.3
58. Togo	...	...	...	...	0.1	0.1	0.1
59. Trinidad and Tobago[d]	...	...	...	...	...	...	...
60. Turkey	...	...	-10.6	-9.1	-6.6	-6.9	-4.8
61. Uruguay	0.0	-0.1	2.3	1.8	0.9	1.4	2.4
62. Venezuela[c]	4.4	10.5	12.0	10.8	3.4	6.7	12.9
63. Zaire[c]	...	...	4.7	4.8	-2.8	0.6	3.6
64. Zambia[c]	...	...	1.0	-3.5	-2.2	4.6	7.1

a. Only a subset of countries within each classification was used for deriving averages. Seventeen low-income economies include Bangladesh, Bolivia, Central African Republic, Egypt, the Gambia, Ghana, India, Indonesia, Malawi, Mali, Nepal, Niger, Philippines, Rwanda, Senegal, Tanzania, and Zaire. Twenty-nine middle-income economies include Argentina, Barbados, Belize, Botswana, Brazil, Chile, Colombia, Costa Rica, Dominica, Ecuador, El Salvador, Guatemala, Honduras, Jamaica, Korea, Malaysia, Mexico, Morocco, Namibia, Panama, Paraguay, Peru, St. Kitts and Nevis, Seychelles, Taiwan (China), Thailand, Turkey, Uruguay, and Venezuela. Latin America and the Caribbean averages exclude Dominican Republic, Guyana, Haiti, St. Vincent and the Grenadines, and Trinidad and Tobago. Africa average excludes Benin, Burundi, Congo, Côte d'Ivoire, Kenya, Mauritania, Mauritius, Nigeria, Sierra Leone, Togo, and

1985	1986	1987	1988	1989	1990	1991	1978–85	1986–91	1978–91
...	...	...	...	...	...	...	-4.0	...	-4.0
-0.7	0.4	0.4	2.1	0.6	1.3	-0.9	-3.8	0.7	-1.9
-0.2	-2.5	-1.0	...	...	...	...	-3.5	-1.5	-2.6
-0.7	-1.2	0.3	0.4	0.6	0.8	-1.0	-1.3	0.0	-0.8
-1.6	-0.7	...	...	...	...	...	-1.9	-1.1	-1.6
...	...	...	...	...	...	...	-0.6	...	-0.6
...	...	...	...	...	...	...	-3.2	...	-3.2
2.9	0.8	3.4	2.4	2.1	3.3	3.1	2.3	2.5	2.4
-3.9	-2.1	...	...	...	...	...	-4.8	-2.9	-4.0
-1.6	-0.6	...	...	...	...	...	-4.0	-1.1	-2.8
-1.8	-1.4	-1.2	-0.8	-0.5	-0.3	0.1	-4.3	-0.7	-2.7
-9.1	-9.9	...	...	...	...	...	-6.9	-9.0	-7.8
0.3	0.0	-0.5	-0.2	...	...	...	-1.1	-0.2	-0.8
...	1.0	...	...	...	...	...	1.5	1.0	1.3
0.3	0.8	1.0	1.4	2.6	3.3	3.3	-2.6	2.1	-0.6
-3.7	-2.5	-2.1	-3.7	-1.6	0.6	0.8	-2.4	-1.4	-2.0
5.8	2.4	1.2	-2.5	-0.3	2.6	2.6	1.9	1.0	1.5
-0.6	-5.0	-2.4	1.0	-1.5	...	...	-5.0	-1.6	-3.5
1.0	1.0	1.0	...	...	...	...	0.5	1.0	0.7
-2.9	1.3	-1.5	...	...	...	...	-4.9	-0.6	-3.0
-20.3	-24.3	-9.0	-14.6	...	...	...	-11.9	-15.3	-13.4
1.4	...	...	...	...	...	...	-0.2	...	-0.2
-4.0	-1.9	-1.9	-1.3	-2.1	-0.2	0.5	-5.0	-1.2	-3.3
-2.8	-6.1	-3.3	-1.7	1.1	-0.9	-1.2	-5.8	-2.0	-4.1
1.6	1.7	0.0	0.1	-0.2	-2.3	-2.7	-3.1	-0.6	-2.0
3.2	-4.0	-8.2	-11.6	-16.2	-7.6	...	-1.0	-9.9	-4.8
-0.2	0.5	-0.3	0.7	0.0	-0.9	-1.5	-2.4	-0.3	-1.5
...	...	...	...	0.0	...	...	0.1	0.0	0.1
...	-1.8	-1.2	1.2	1.4	3.8	...	...	0.7	0.7
-2.8	-2.3	-4.6	-4.5	-3.8	-7.0	-10.6	-7.4	-5.5	-6.6
2.5	3.7	3.1	3.4	2.9	4.1	4.7	1.4	3.7	2.4
11.1	2.7	7.2	5.3	12.2	17.3	13.4	9.0	9.7	9.3
4.9	1.7	...	...	...	...	...	2.7	2.9	2.8
...	...	...	...	...	...	...	1.4	...	1.4

Zambia. Asia averages excludes Myanmar. Three-year moving average estimates were used to complete our time series, in case of missing values, when deriving averages.

b. Weighted averages were obtained using GDP in current U.S. dollars as weights.

c. See specific country note.

d. Selected major state-owned enterprises only.

e. Financial state-owned enterprises are included.

Table A.7 Net Financial Flows from Government to State-Owned Enterprises as a Proportion of Gross Domestic Product, 1978–91

(percentage)

Group and economy[a]	1978	1979	1980	1981	1982	1983	1984
Group							
All economies							
37 Developing economies							
Weighted average[b]	-0.5	-1.2	-1.4	-1.1	0.1	-0.7	-0.3
Unweighted average	0.3	0.1	0.2	-0.1	0.5	0.3	0.2
Developing economies by income							
12 Low-income economies							
Weighted average	0.4	0.7	0.6	-0.1	1.7	0.5	1.0
Unweighted average	1.3	1.4	1.8	0.8	1.5	1.4	0.9
25 Middle-income economies							
Weighted average	-0.8	-1.8	-2.0	-1.4	-0.3	-1.1	-0.7
Unweighted average	-0.3	-0.5	-0.5	-0.6	0.0	-0.3	-0.1
Developing economies by region							
18 Latin America and the Caribbean							
Weighted average	-1.6	-3.0	-3.1	-2.1	-0.8	-1.8	-1.7
Unweighted average	-0.8	-1.3	-1.5	-0.9	-0.4	-0.7	-1.0
12 Africa							
Weighted average	1.1	1.5	1.8	0.2	1.3	2.6	2.3
Unweighted average	0.8	1.1	1.5	0.0	0.6	1.2	1.1
7 Asia							
Weighted average	1.1	1.3	1.1	0.7	1.6	0.6	1.4
Unweighted average	2.1	2.1	2.5	1.6	2.4	1.5	2.0
Economy							
1. Algeria[c]	24.0	21.4	20.1	17.1	14.0	14.7	12.2
2. Argentina	1.3	0.6	1.5	1.6	1.9	7.0	3.0
3. Barbados[d]	3.2	3.0	2.8	3.3	2.9	1.9	1.5
4. Belize	...	...	...	...	...	...	1.5
5. Benin[d]	...	2.9	0.7	-0.5	-0.6	0.4	...
6. Bolivia[c,d]	-4.1	-2.5	-4.6	-4.4	-4.2	-2.2	-2.4
7. Botswana[c]	...	...	-5.6	-8.1	-9.8	-10.6	-7.1
8. Brazil[c,e]	0.4	-1.3	-0.5	...	...	...	...
9. Burkina Faso	...	...	...	...	...	...	...
10. Burundi[c]	...	2.0	1.3	1.4	1.8	0.3	...
11. Cameroon	...	...	...	...	...	1.1	2.0
12. Central African Rep.	...	...	...	0.3	-0.1	1.1	1.2
13. Chile	-3.9	-7.8	-7.2	-5.0	-7.0	-8.8	-8.3
14. Colombia	...	...	-1.8	-0.6	-0.1	0.4	0.5
15. Congo	...	...	...	0.8	1.6	0.9	...
16. Costa Rica	-1.2	-1.5	-0.4	-0.7	-0.8	-1.7	-2.1
17. Côte d'Ivoire	...	...	2.5	...	...	...	0.6
18. Dominica	0.3	-0.2	1.3	-0.1	0.0	-0.2	-0.1
19. Dominican Rep.[e]	0.9	3.1	1.7	1.3	0.5	0.5	0.6
20. Ecuador[c]	0.2	0.5	0.6	2.0	1.9	0.2	0.2
21. Egypt, Arab Rep. of	...	...	...	...	...	...	-0.1
22. El Salvador[d]	0.7	0.6	0.7	0.4	0.3	0.2	-0.4
23. Gambia, The[d]	...	...	...	...	...	...	...
24. Ghana[d]	...	...	0.5	0.6	0.6	0.1	0.2
25. Guatemala[d]	1.8	2.2	2.2	3.3	2.0	1.2	0.5
26. Guinea[c]	-13.1	4.0	...	-4.2	3.9	6.3	3.6
27. Guinea-Bissau	...	...	...	...	...	0.8	-0.9
28. Guyana[c]	-4.0	-5.2	-3.5	-1.7	-2.6	-0.8	-2.0
29. Haiti[c,d]	...	...	...	-1.0	-0.9	-1.0	-0.8
30. Honduras[c]	...	...	0.0	0.0	0.0	0.0	0.0

1985	1986	1987	1988	1989	1990	1991	1978–85	1986–91	1978–91
-0.6	-0.6	-0.7	-0.9	-1.2	-1.6	-1.8	-0.7	-1.1	-0.9
0.0	-0.3	-0.7	-0.7	-1.0	-1.3	-1.2	0.2	-0.9	-0.3
0.5	0.3	0.0	-0.2	-0.2	-0.7	-0.3	0.7	-0.2	0.3
0.9	0.5	0.2	0.2	0.5	0.2	-0.1	1.3	0.3	0.8
-1.0	-0.9	-1.0	-1.1	-1.5	-1.9	-2.2	-1.1	-1.4	-1.3
-0.4	-0.7	-1.2	-1.2	-1.7	-2.0	-1.8	-0.3	-1.4	-0.8
-1.8	-1.7	-1.7	-1.8	-2.4	-3.2	-3.7	-2.0	-2.4	-2.2
-1.2	-2.0	-1.9	-2.0	-2.4	-2.9	-2.8	-1.0	-2.4	-1.6
1.6	1.8	1.1	1.5	1.1	1.1	1.6	1.6	1.4	1.5
0.9	1.5	0.2	0.4	0.2	0.0	0.2	0.9	0.4	0.7
0.8	0.5	0.3	0.0	0.0	0.0	0.0	1.1	0.1	0.7
1.6	1.0	0.7	0.7	0.8	0.5	0.5	2.0	0.7	1.4
9.3	...	...	...	...	...	...	16.6	...	16.6
3.0	2.3	3.2	...	...	...	...	2.5	2.7	2.5
1.5	1.8	1.4	1.6	0.9	1.3	1.9	2.5	1.5	2.1
4.8	3.9	3.0	0.6	-0.9	-1.5	-1.2	3.2	0.6	1.3
...	...	...	...	...	...	...	0.6		0.6
-2.9	-11.2	-6.6	-8.1	-8.0	-9.0	-8.4	-3.4	-8.5	-5.6
-12.5	-8.1	-7.6	-13.0	-18.5	-15.4	-13.8	-8.6	-12.7	-10.4
...	-0.6	0.8	0.2	-1.2	-1.8	-2.4	1.4	-0.8	0.4
...	...	-0.5	-0.4	...	...	...	...	-0.5	-0.5
...	...	1.6	2.0	3.8	3.4	-1.0	1.3	2.1	1.6
1.4	2.2	0.2	...	...	...	...	1.5	1.2	1.4
...	...	...	...	...	...	...	0.6	...	0.6
-8.4	-8.2	-9.1	-10.7	-10.7	...	...	-7.1	-9.9	-8.3
0.7	-0.3	-0.5	-0.7	-1.1	-1.5	-1.8	-0.3	-1.0	-0.6
...	...	...	...	...	...	...	1.1	...	1.1
-2.2	-2.0	-2.1	-1.9	-1.9	-1.4	-1.3	-1.3	-1.8	-1.5
5.2	...	...	...	...	...	...	2.8		2.8
0.3	0.4	0.7	1.5	-0.1	1.6	...	0.2	0.9	0.5
3.5	...	...	...	...	...	...	1.5	...	1.5
0.7	0.1	0.4	0.3	0.4	0.0	-0.2	0.8	0.2	0.5
-5.0	2.4	-0.2	0.6	-1.2	-0.5	...	-2.6	0.2	-0.6
-0.4	0.2	0.2	0.2	0.0	0.5	0.9	0.3	0.3	0.3
0.3	4.8	7.4	0.3	1.4	2.9	...	0.3	3.4	2.9
0.2	0.5	0.6	0.3	0.4	...	...	0.4	0.4	0.4
0.7	0.1	-0.1	0.3	0.4	-0.2	...	1.7	0.1	1.0
...	...	...	...	...	...	...	0.1	...	0.1
-0.3	...	...	...	...	...	...	-0.1	...	-0.1
-0.6	...	...	...	...	...	...	-2.6	...	-2.6
-0.9	...	...	...	...	...	...	-0.9	...	-0.9
0.0	0.0	0.0	0.0	0.0	0.0	...	0.0	0.0	0.0

Table A.7 *(continued)*

Group and economy[a]	1978	1979	1980	1981	1982	1983	1984
31. India[c]	...	...	...	-0.4	0.9	0.1	0.8
32. Indonesia	...	...	...	...	...	...	6.0
33. Kenya	2.1	0.6	2.3	1.4	0.6	0.5	1.1
34. Korea, Rep. of[c]	...	...	0.3	1.0	0.8	0.6	0.5
35. Madagascar	...	...	-0.8	-1.2	-0.7	...	...
36. Malawi[d]	...	...	6.1	3.8	3.1	1.0	0.4
37. Malaysia[c]	...	...	...	3.3	3.7	2.9	3.3
38. Mali[d]	...	...	...	...	...	...	...
39. Mauritania	...	...	...	...	...	1.3	...
40. Mauritius[c]	...	...	...	...	2.5	2.4	1.1
41. Mexico[c]	...	...	...	...	-2.2	-4.2	-3.1
42. Morocco[d]	0.1	1.6	0.6	-0.6	0.9	0.6	0.1
43. Myanmar[c]	-2.0	-2.8	-3.6	-4.0	-4.7	-3.9	-3.8
44. Namibia[d]	...	...	...	...	...	...	...
45. Nepal	...	-0.8	-1.3	0.4	1.2	1.3	-0.3
46. Niger[d]	...	...	0.3	0.2	0.1	-0.3	...
47. Nigeria[d]	...	...	...	...	-7.5	-4.9	-6.2
48. Panama[c]	2.5	3.8	2.7	1.2	0.2	0.2	-0.2
49. Paraguay	...	0.3	0.2	0.2	1.5	1.1	0.6
50. Peru	-2.1	-3.2	-3.6	-3.1	-4.0	-3.9	-4.4
51. Philippines[c]	...	...	0.9	0.8	5.9	2.3	2.2
52. Rwanda[c]	...	-0.2	-0.3	...	...	...	0.2
53. São Tome and Principe[d]	...	...	-19.0	...	...	-3.8	-7.4
54. Senegal	...	...	...	0.7	3.1	6.9	2.3
55. Seychelles[e]	...	4.5	2.4	-1.6	0.4	0.5	3.5
56. Sierra Leone[e]	-0.7	-0.2	-0.2	0.0	0.3	1.7	...
57. Sri Lanka[c]	8.8	7.9	12.9	5.5	4.9	4.8	4.4
58. St. Vincent and the Grenadines[d]	...	...	...	...	...	...	0.1
59. Tanzania[c]	0.1	-0.3	1.1	1.4	0.4	0.8	-1.3
60. Thailand	...	0.4	0.4	0.4	0.2	0.1	-0.2
61. Togo[c]	...	...	...	...	...	...	...
62. Trinidad and Tobago[c]	-0.5	-0.2	-0.4	9.3	13.4	11.9	11.2
63. Tunisia	...	...	...	0.4	3.8	10.2	10.4
64. Turkey[c]	...	...	4.4	3.3	3.0	1.0	6.4
65. Uruguay	-0.5	-1.0	-2.2	-2.8	-2.4	-2.2	-1.7
66. Venezuela[c]	-7.8	-12.1	-13.1	-19.3	-11.5	-10.0	-12.9
67. Zaire	...	...	...	-2.9	-1.0	-2.1	-2.9
68. Zambia	...	...	0.8	-0.1	1.8	-2.9	-3.6

a. Only a subset of countries within each classification was used for deriving averages. Twelve low-income economies include Bolivia, Burundi, Ghana, India, Kenya, Malawi, Nepal, Philippines, Rwanda, Senegal, Sierra Leone, and Sri Lanka. Twenty-five middle-income economies include Barbados, Botswana, Brazil, Chile, Colombia, Costa Rica, Dominica, Ecuador, El Salvador, Guatemala, Honduras, Korea, Mauritius, Mexico, Morocco, Panama, Paraguay, Peru, Seychelles, Thailand, Trinidad and Tobago, Tunisia, Turkey, Uruguay, and Venezuela. Latin America and Caribbean regional average excludes Argentina, Belize, Dominican Republic, Guyana, Haiti, and St. Vincent and the Grenadines. Africa regional average includes only Botswana, Burundi, Ghana, Kenya, Malawi, Mauritius, Morocco, Rwanda, Senegal, Seychelles, Sierra Leone, and Tunisia. Asia regional averages exclude Malaysia and Myanmar. Three-year moving average estimates were used to complete our time series, in case of missing values, when deriving averages.

1985	1986	1987	1988	1989	1990	1991	1978–85	1986–91	1978–91
0.2	0.2	-0.2	-0.4	-0.8	-1.2	...	0.3	-0.5	-0.1
3.0	1.1	2.1	1.0	0.6	-0.2	2.1	4.5	1.1	2.0
1.5	-0.2	-0.2	0.0	0.0	0.4	...	1.3	0.0	0.7
0.4	-0.3	0.4	-0.9	-0.8	-0.1	-0.1	0.6	-0.3	0.2
...	...	...	...	...	...	...	-0.9	...	-0.9
0.7	0.7	0.6	1.1	1.0	...	...	3.0	0.8	2.1
2.7	...	...	...	...	...	...	3.2	...	3.2
...	-1.0	-0.6	...	...	...	...	...	-0.8	-0.8
...	...	...	...	...	...	...	1.3		1.3
1.0	-0.8	-0.9	-0.6	0.6	-1.0	...	2.0	-0.5	0.9
-2.4	-0.7	-4.2	-2.4	-2.1	-3.1	-3.2	-3.0	-2.6	-2.8
-0.3	0.2	-0.1	0.1	0.2	-0.1	1.2	0.4	0.2	0.3
-3.6	-3.2	...	...	...	...	...	-3.6	-3.4	-3.5
...	3.5	5.2	1.7	1.0	1.0	...		2.5	2.5
1.2	-1.5	...	...	...	...	...	0.1	-0.5	-0.1
...	...	...	...	...	...	...	0.1	...	0.1
-5.3	...	...	...	...	...	...	-6.0	...	-6.0
-0.4	-0.5	-0.3	-1.3	-0.8	-1.6	-1.5	1.2	-1.0	0.3
0.6	0.0	-0.1	0.2	0.1	0.0	-0.1	0.6	0.0	0.4
-6.3	-4.3	-2.4	-1.7	-0.9	-3.1	-3.0	-3.8	-2.6	-3.3
1.4	1.2	1.6	1.0	3.2	...	...	2.2	1.8	2.0
0.3	0.6	0.5	0.2	0.4	0.4	-0.1	0.1	0.3	0.2
...	...	...	-4.0	-4.9	-0.8	-1.3	-8.2	-3.1	-6.0
2.4	8.3	2.9	...	...	...	...	3.0	5.0	3.8
8.3	7.3	-0.7	0.4	1.6	-0.3	2.3	2.5	1.8	2.2
0.2	0.3	-0.1	0.1	-0.2	...	...	0.2	0.0	0.1
4.7	4.5	2.4	2.2	1.5	1.2	1.3	6.7	2.2	4.8
1.5	3.1	0.2	1.0	0.7	-0.1	-0.1	0.8	0.8	0.8
-2.3	...	...	...	...	...	...	0.0	...	0.0
-0.3	-0.3	-0.2	-0.2	-0.3	-0.3	-0.5	0.2	-0.3	0.0
...	...	3.6	2.1	-0.8	...	...	...	1.6	1.6
10.0	-1.2	-1.8	-1.6	-2.2	-3.1	...	6.8	-2.0	3.0
8.0	6.8	6.3	9.3	...	...	...	5.4	7.6	6.4
3.7	3.4	1.2	3.3	3.3	2.7	1.7	3.6	2.6	3.2
-2.8	-3.6	-3.1	-3.3	-3.0	-3.6	-4.0	-1.9	-3.4	-2.6
-11.6	-6.8	-8.2	-9.3	-13.7	-17.0	-16.4	-12.3	-11.9	-12.1
...	...	...	...	...	...	...	-2.2	...	-2.2
...	-3.1	...	...	...	...	...	-0.8	-3.1	-1.2

b. Weighted averages were obtained using GDP in current U.S. dollars as weights.

c. See specific country note.

d. Selected major state-owned enterprises only.

e. Financial state-owned enterprises are included.

Table A.8 Share of State-Owned Enterprises in Gross Domestic Credit, 1978–91

(percentage)

Group and economy[a]	1978	1979	1980	1981	1982	1983	1984
Group							
All economies							
36 Developing economies							
Weighted average[b]	5.7	6.2	5.9	6.7	7.7	10.9	12.5
Unweighted average	10.3	9.9	11.9	12.1	12.1	12.3	12.6
Developing economies by income							
16 Low-income economies							
Weighted average	13.6	13.7	14.1	14.8	14.0	13.6	14.9
Unweighted average	15.9	15.1	18.9	17.5	16.4	15.4	15.4
20 Middle-income economies							
Weighted average	4.3	4.8	4.5	5.5	6.7	10.3	12.0
Unweighted average	5.7	5.7	6.4	7.8	8.7	9.9	10.3
Developing economies by region							
18 Latin America and the Caribbean							
Weighted average	4.3	5.0	4.6	5.6	6.8	10.8	12.6
Unweighted average	6.1	6.1	6.8	7.8	8.2	9.3	9.3
10 Africa							
Weighted average	14.2	14.1	14.7	17.1	15.7	15.2	17.7
Unweighted average	14.1	13.0	16.5	16.2	17.4	13.8	16.5
8 Asia							
Weighted average	9.3	10.0	10.4	11.3	10.7	10.4	10.4
Unweighted average	14.8	14.6	17.8	16.9	14.5	17.2	15.0
Economy							
1. Antigua and Barbuda	2.3	4.6	4.0	2.1	4.3	1.9	0.5
2. Bangladesh	23.0	22.7	23.5	22.7	21.9	25.9	20.4
3. Bhutan	...	...	...	...	...	46.4	26.2
4. Botswana	4.5	0.3	1.6	3.3	5.3	8.3	7.7
5. Brazil	6.4	8.6	8.3	10.0	10.8	19.7	22.3
6. Burundi	14.0	10.8	11.8	6.7	8.2	7.6	16.6
7. Cape Verde	19.1	16.6	46.8	37.4	43.1	34.8	37.9
8. Chile	2.3	1.0	1.2	1.1	1.3	1.1	1.2
9. Colombia	1.0	0.5	0.4	0.7	0.5	0.5	1.3
10. Djibouti	...	...	...	...	...	...	1.8
11. Dominica	1.9	5.8	2.7	7.9	3.9	2.3	5.9
12. Dominican Rep.	8.3	7.5	8.8	14.0	17.5	19.9	19.7
13. Ecuador	...	0.0	0.0	0.2	0.0	0.0	0.0
14. Egypt	...	...	22.4	23.9	18.8	21.6	22.5
15. El Salvador	...	...	...	...	5.2	5.1	4.6
16. Ghana	16.4	21.0	19.6	20.8	29.0	4.0	8.4
17. Grenada	...	...	1.5	1.8	6.9	5.9	4.6
18. Guyana	14.2	15.3	15.5	20.5	12.2	17.0	13.5
19. Haiti	17.1	19.0	21.5	19.3	15.6	13.2	13.0
20. Jamaica	5.9	4.8	6.3	6.7	6.6	5.6	5.0
21. Kenya	1.4	1.4	2.0	1.6	2.0	4.3	5.2
22. Liberia	...	...	14.0	10.7	11.3	10.4	11.0
23. Maldives	...	...	...	...	...	12.0	15.0
24. Mexico	2.7	2.4	2.6	3.6	5.4	8.8	10.2
25. Nepal	...	...	...	9.6	10.8	10.3	7.7
26. Philippines	8.8	8.9	8.6	8.8	9.5	7.5	9.3
27. Solomon Islands	...	...	...	...	...	6.7	14.1
28. St. Kitts and Nevis	...	12.6	25.9	29.5	26.9	27.8	24.8
29. St. Lucia	...	3.2	1.1	2.6	2.0	1.0	1.1
30. St. Vincent and the Grenadines	7.4	12.2	13.0	4.2	21.9	22.5	24.5
31. Sudan	32.2	31.4	32.6	33.5	33.1	23.8	24.8

1985	1986	1987	1988	1989	1990	1991	1978–85	1986–91	1978–91
14.1	11.0	14.3	12.5	12.7	12.5	10.5	8.7	12.2	10.2
13.2	11.2	9.9	10.4	10.5	9.8	9.2	11.8	10.2	11.1
17.5	16.6	16.0	13.8	14.3	13.4	12.4	14.5	14.4	14.5
15.5	13.2	12.4	14.3	14.5	13.7	12.7	16.3	13.5	15.1
13.5	9.8	13.9	12.2	12.4	12.4	10.2	7.7	11.8	9.5
11.4	9.6	7.9	7.3	7.2	6.7	6.3	8.2	7.5	7.9
14.0	10.1	14.8	13.2	13.3	13.4	11.1	8.0	12.6	10.0
10.1	6.8	6.2	6.4	6.3	6.5	5.9	8.0	6.4	7.3
21.2	20.8	20.0	17.4	18.8	16.7	15.3	16.2	18.2	17.1
19.2	18.5	15.5	16.5	17.8	15.4	15.0	15.8	16.4	16.1
10.7	8.6	8.4	9.5	9.5	9.7	12.4	10.4	9.7	10.1
12.8	12.1	11.2	11.8	10.8	10.4	9.2	15.4	10.9	13.5
1.5	2.0	2.6	1.7	1.6	1.1	0.8	2.7	1.6	2.2
19.4	20.1	16.7	15.8	15.9	15.0	15.2	22.4	16.4	19.9
13.2	10.3	12.6	21.4	12.4	19.6	17.3	28.6	15.6	19.9
11.3	12.5	7.9	7.0	10.4	7.5	5.8	5.3	8.5	6.7
26.7	15.3	23.2	21.8	20.1	21.7	21.2	14.1	20.5	16.9
17.4	17.8	17.8	20.8	21.3	20.6	34.3	11.7	22.1	16.1
32.5	28.3	23.3	40.1	37.1	34.4	32.7	33.5	32.7	33.2
1.6	1.9	2.1	1.0	1.4	4.1	2.8	1.3	2.2	1.7
1.3	1.0	6.3	6.1	4.5	7.1	1.3	0.8	4.4	2.3
1.6	1.3	1.2	1.6	0.6	1.5	1.4	1.7	1.3	1.4
4.5	1.5	0.6	3.2	3.6	6.2	7.4	4.4	3.7	4.1
19.2	13.4	16.5	16.1	13.7	11.2	14.3	14.4	14.2	14.3
0.0	0.0	0.0	0.0	0.0	0.0	0.0	0.0	0.0	0.0
22.8	21.6	21.1	20.8	21.0	21.4	21.9	22.0	21.3	21.7
4.2	4.1	4.5	3.7	2.8	0.1	0.0	4.8	2.5	3.4
20.4	15.9	9.3	3.8	15.0	9.9	11.3	17.5	10.9	14.6
3.9	3.5	3.6	3.6	4.0	3.6	2.9	4.1	3.5	3.8
15.5	5.1	4.3	4.1	3.2	2.9	1.2	15.5	3.5	10.3
18.2	6.7	6.3	8.1	7.4	7.3	7.6	17.1	7.2	12.9
7.0	1.6	3.0	2.6	3.4	2.4	1.3	6.0	2.4	4.4
5.2	4.2	6.9	...	...	...	...	2.9	5.6	3.4
8.4	8.6	5.5	5.6	4.5	...	4.5	11.0	5.7	8.6
17.4	17.2	19.0	23.8	31.7	23.4	20.1	14.8	22.5	20.0
8.1	8.4	8.4	5.8	5.6	2.9	1.0	5.5	5.4	5.4
8.2	8.8	8.7	7.5	5.3	5.8	3.1	9.3	6.6	7.8
11.6	8.8	8.4	7.6	7.2	7.4	7.2	9.1	7.8	8.6
2.3	1.1	1.3	5.5	5.2	7.2	4.6	7.7	4.2	5.4
26.4	26.7	1.3	3.4	6.3	9.8	8.2	24.8	9.3	17.7
0.9	0.6	0.7	0.6	1.7	2.2	1.6	1.7	1.2	1.5
25.2	12.2	10.8	10.8	8.7	8.9	8.0	16.3	9.9	13.6
35.8	36.9	36.7	36.9	40.1	33.1	15.9	30.9	33.3	31.9

Table A.8 *(continued)*

Group and economy[a]	1978	1979	1980	1981	1982	1983	1984
32. Thailand	...	...	1.7	1.7	1.4	2.1	2.0
33. Trinidad and Tobago	...	...	1.2	4.9	5.7	7.1	8.0
34. Uruguay	...	...	...	...	4.4	8.5	7.5
35. Vanuatu	1.3	1.2	1.4	1.2	1.1	1.8	0.7
36. Venezuela	1.1	1.1	1.0	0.9	1.1	1.2	0.6
37. Western Samoa	12.3	22.8	24.8	27.6	26.1	26.8	25.1
38. Zaire	0.6	0.4	0.1	0.5	0.8	0.2	0.4
39. Zimbabwe	...	14.6	14.0	23.7	22.1	23.1	30.0

a. Only a subset of countries within each classification was used for deriving averages. Sixteen low-income economies include Bangladesh, Bhutan, Burundi, Cape Verde, Egypt, Ghana, Guyana, Haiti, Kenya, Liberia, Maldives, Nepal, Philippines, Solomon Islands, Sudan, and Zaire. Twenty middle-income economies include Botswana, Brazil, Chile, Colombia, Dominica, Dominican Republic, Ecuador, El Salvador, Grenada, Jamaica, Mexico, St. Kitts and Nevis, St. Lucia, St. Vincent and the Grenadines, Thailand, Trinidad and Tobago, Uruguay, Venezuela, Western Samoa, and Zimbabwe. Latin America and the

1985	1986	1987	1988	1989	1990	1991	1978–85	1986–91	1978–91
1.9	1.9	1.6	1.4	1.2	1.1	2.4	1.8	1.6	1.7
10.1	9.9	10.5	13.2	11.6	9.2	8.1	6.2	10.4	8.3
7.7	9.8	9.1	11.1	13.4	15.1	15.4	7.0	12.3	10.2
0.8	2.2	1.8	0.4	0.5	0.2	0.2	1.2	0.9	1.1
0.7	0.8	0.5	0.3	2.0	2.0	4.7	1.0	1.7	1.3
28.3	28.3	21.3	11.7	7.7	3.7	3.3	24.2	12.7	19.3
0.2	0.3	0.2	0.5	0.7	1.3	2.1	0.4	0.8	0.6
38.2	38.8	26.0	23.0	22.9	16.2	17.0	23.7	24.0	23.8

Caribbean regional averages exclude Antigua and Barbuda. Africa regional average excludes Djibouti. Asia regional average excludes Vanuatu. Three-year moving average estimates were used to complete our time series, in case of missing values, when deriving averages.

b. Weighted averages were obtained using GDP in current U.S. dollars as weights.

Table A.9 Gross Domestic Credit to State-Owned Enterprises as a Proportion of Gross Domestic Product, 1978–91

(percentage)

Group and economy[a]	1978	1979	1980	1981	1982	1983	1984
Group							
All economies							
37 Developing economies							
Weighted average[b]	1.5	1.5	1.5	1.8	2.0	2.6	2.8
Unweighted average	3.9	3.9	4.4	5.4	5.4	6.0	5.9
Developing economies by income							
17 Low-income economies							
Weighted average	7.2	7.5	7.6	9.0	8.1	9.3	10.1
Unweighted average	5.7	5.9	6.5	7.6	6.8	7.8	7.8
20 Middle-income economies							
Weighted average	0.5	0.4	0.5	0.7	0.9	1.3	1.4
Unweighted average	2.3	2.2	2.6	3.4	4.3	4.5	4.4
Developing economies by region							
18 Latin America and the Caribbean							
Weighted average	0.4	0.4	0.4	0.6	0.9	1.3	1.4
Unweighted average	2.9	3.0	3.5	4.5	5.2	6.7	6.0
11 Africa							
Weighted average	8.4	8.9	8.9	11.8	10.4	11.8	13.8
Unweighted average	5.0	4.8	5.4	6.5	6.5	5.6	6.4
8 Asia							
Weighted average	3.3	3.4	3.4	3.4	3.2	3.5	3.2
Unweighted average	4.5	4.6	5.0	5.8	4.4	5.1	5.2
Economy							
1. Antigua and Barbuda	1.5	2.6	2.1	1.1	2.3	1.1	0.3
2. Bangladesh	...	...	...	...	...	7.9	6.7
3. Bhutan	...	...	...	...	...	3.2	2.0
4. Botswana	0.9	0.0	0.2	0.6	0.9	1.3	1.3
5. Brazil	0.0	0.0	0.0	0.0	0.0	0.0	0.0
6. Burundi	2.0	1.9	2.0	1.5	1.8	1.8	3.7
7. Cape Verde	5.2	5.0	13.7	15.0	16.7	13.5	15.5
8. Chile	1.1	0.5	0.6	0.7	1.2	1.0	1.4
9. Colombia	0.2	0.1	0.1	0.1	0.1	0.7	0.4
10. Djibouti	0.9	0.9	0.9	0.9	0.9	0.9	1.0
11. Dominica	0.9	3.3	1.4	4.9	2.5	1.6	3.7
12. Dominican Rep.	2.8	2.5	2.9	4.9	6.6	8.3	7.2
13. Ecuador	...	0.0	0.0	0.0	0.0	0.0	0.0
14. Egypt	...	...	20.1	25.9	20.6	24.5	26.2
15. El Salvador	...	...	...	...	3.2	2.8	2.6
16. Ghana	5.3	5.8	4.6	4.7	7.0	0.7	1.6
17. Grenada	...	...	0.9	1.1	4.9	3.9	2.7
18. Guyana	9.6	13.0	15.2	23.5	21.2	41.8	33.2
19. Haiti	7.2	7.5	8.2	8.5	7.0	6.3	5.7
20. Jamaica	2.8	3.0	4.1	5.2	5.6	5.3	4.1
21. Kenya	0.4	0.4	0.6	0.5	0.8	1.4	1.7
22. Liberia	3.7	3.8	3.9	3.4	4.2	4.7	4.9
23. Maldives	...	...	...	13.9	4.2	12.2	16.7
24. Mexico	0.8	0.7	0.8	1.2	2.3	3.2	3.4
25. Nepal	3.1	3.2	3.3	3.5	2.8	3.2	2.4
26. Philippines	...	...	...	...	...	4.4	4.1
27. Sierra Leone	...	...	...	0.3	0.2	0.2	0.1
28. Solomon Islands	...	...	4.6	4.6	3.8	1.8	2.9
29. St. Kitts and Nevis	...	7.5	16.4	21.6	22.5	27.5	24.4
30. St. Lucia	...	1.9	0.7	1.7	1.3	0.7	0.7

1985	1986	1987	1988	1989	1990	1991	1978–85	1986–91	1978–91
2.9	2.9	2.6	1.9	1.8	1.8	1.6	2.1	2.1	2.1
6.4	5.0	4.0	4.0	4.2	3.9	3.4	5.2	4.1	4.7
11.3	10.5	9.8	8.3	8.8	9.5	8.7	8.8	9.2	9.0
8.6	6.5	5.8	6.2	6.5	5.9	5.1	7.1	6.0	6.6
1.3	1.3	1.1	0.8	0.8	0.6	0.6	0.9	0.9	0.9
4.6	3.7	2.4	2.2	2.2	2.2	2.0	3.5	2.4	3.1
1.3	1.2	1.1	0.7	0.7	0.6	0.4	0.8	0.8	0.8
6.6	3.9	2.5	2.7	2.6	2.4	1.9	4.8	2.7	3.9
15.5	14.4	13.9	12.2	13.1	14.6	13.8	11.2	13.7	12.2
7.1	6.8	6.1	6.3	6.5	6.3	6.0	5.9	6.4	6.1
3.4	2.8	2.4	2.1	2.1	2.0	2.4	3.4	2.3	2.9
5.2	4.8	4.3	3.8	4.7	3.9	3.5	5.0	4.2	4.6
0.9	1.2	1.6	1.0	1.0	0.7	0.5	1.5	1.0	1.3
6.5	6.6	5.4	5.2	5.6	5.2	5.0	7.2	5.5	6.5
1.1	0.7	0.4	0.8	0.6	1.1	1.2	2.3	0.8	1.6
1.4	1.4	0.8	0.7	1.0	0.9	0.9	0.8	1.0	0.9
0.0	0.0	0.0	0.0	0.0	0.0	0.0	0.0	0.0	0.0
3.9	4.0	4.2	5.1	5.0	5.0	3.8	2.3	4.5	3.3
15.2	13.0	10.7	18.0	17.1	16.4	16.6	12.5	15.3	13.7
2.0	2.2	2.2	0.9	1.1	3.3	2.1	1.1	1.9	1.4
0.3	1.5	1.5	1.5	1.0	1.6	0.3	0.3	1.2	0.7
0.9	0.8	0.7	0.9	0.3	0.8	0.6	0.9	0.7	0.8
2.7	0.8	0.3	1.5	1.9	4.0	5.0	2.6	2.3	2.5
5.8	4.7	5.5	4.5	3.4	2.4	2.7	5.1	3.9	4.6
0.0	0.0	0.0	0.0	0.0	0.0	0.0	0.0	0.0	0.0
27.0	26.5	25.8	25.0	26.4	30.1	29.3	23.7	27.2	25.2
2.3	1.8	1.9	1.4	1.1	0.0	0.0	2.8	1.0	2.1
4.8	4.0	2.7	0.8	2.9	1.6	2.1	4.3	2.3	3.5
2.4	2.2	2.4	2.4	2.9	2.3	1.9	2.4	2.4	2.4
43.0	14.9	10.2	13.3	9.4	7.7	2.5	25.1	9.7	18.5
4.9	2.6	2.6	3.6	3.3	0.0	0.0	6.9	2.0	4.8
5.0	1.1	1.7	1.5	1.9	1.1	0.5	4.4	1.3	3.1
1.7	1.5	2.7	2.2	1.6	1.6	1.7	1.0	1.9	1.4
4.3	4.9	3.4	...	...	...	...	4.1	4.1	4.1
18.1	17.0	16.7	14.7	23.4	16.1	13.9	12.0	17.0	14.1
2.9	3.6	3.0	1.7	1.9	1.0	0.4	1.9	1.9	1.9
2.9	3.3	3.1	2.8	2.1	2.2	1.3	3.1	2.5	2.8
4.5	2.9	2.6	2.3	2.2	2.4	2.1	4.3	2.4	3.5
0.1	0.2	0.1	0.1	0.1	0.0	0.1	0.2	0.1	0.2
0.7	0.3	0.4	1.6	1.6	2.3	1.7	3.4	1.3	2.5
27.9	22.8	0.8	2.5	5.1	8.4	6.9	20.4	7.8	15.0
0.5	0.3	0.4	0.3	1.1	1.4	1.0	1.1	0.7	0.9

Table A.9 *(continued)*

Group and economy[a]	1978	1979	1980	1981	1982	1983	1984
31. St. Vincent and the Grenadines	3.9	6.8	7.3	2.3	13.4	13.9	15.9
32. Sudan	7.9	8.7	9.5	10.7	11.3	4.9	4.9
33. Thailand	0.8	0.8	0.8	0.8	0.8	1.3	1.3
34. Trinidad and Tobago	...	...	0.3	1.4	1.8	2.7	3.1
35. Uruguay	...	...	...	...	...	0.0	0.0
36. Venezuela	0.3	0.3	0.3	0.3	0.3	0.4	0.2
37. Western Samoa	2.7	5.3	6.5	9.7	9.8	6.8	5.6
38. Zaire	0.1	0.0	0.0	0.1	0.2	0.1	0.1
39. Zimbabwe	...	4.9	5.0	8.8	8.1	8.5	9.9

a. Only a subset of countries within each classification was used for deriving averages. Seventeen low-income economies include Bangladesh, Bhutan, Burundi, Cape Verde, Egypt, Ghana, Guyana, Haiti, Kenya, Liberia, Maldives, Nepal, Philippines, Sierra Leone, Solomon Islands, Sudan, and Zaire. Twenty middle-income economies include Botswana, Brazil, Chile, Colombia, Dominica, Dominican Republic, Ecuador, El Salvador, Grenada, Jamaica, Mexico, St. Kitts and Nevis, St. Lucia, St. Vincent and the Grenadines, Thailand, Trinidad and Tobago, Uruguay, Venezuela, Western Samoa, and Zimbabwe. Latin

1985	1986	1987	1988	1989	1990	1991	1978–85	1986–91	1978–91
14.8	6.4	5.9	5.8	5.0	4.6	4.4	9.8	5.4	7.9
7.5	7.6	8.0	6.2	5.2	3.5	1.4	8.2	5.3	6.9
1.3	1.3	1.2	1.0	0.9	0.9	2.0	1.0	1.2	1.1
4.2	5.0	6.1	8.0	6.8	4.7	4.6	2.0	5.8	3.6
0.0	0.0	0.0	0.0	0.0	0.0	0.0	0.0	0.0	0.0
0.2	0.3	0.2	0.1	0.6	0.6	1.4	0.3	0.5	0.4
6.1	5.9	4.8	2.1	1.3	0.8	0.7	6.6	2.6	4.9
0.1	0.1	0.0	0.1	0.1	...	...	0.1	0.2	0.1
12.3	11.8	9.1	7.4	7.7	5.8	6.0	8.0	8.0	8.0

America and the Caribbean regional averages exclude Antigua and Barbuda. Africa regional average excludes Djibouti. Asia regional average excludes Vanuatu. Three-year moving average estimates were used to complete our time series, in case of missing values, when deriving averages.

b. Weighted averages were obtained using GDP in current U.S. dollars as weights.

Table A.10 Share of State-Owned Enterprises in Total External Debt, 1978–91

(percentage)

Group and economy[a]	1978	1979	1980	1981	1982	1983	1984
Group							
All economies							
74 Developing economies							
Weighted average[b]	16.9	17.7	17.9	17.9	17.4	16.6	15.6
Unweighted average	14.4	14.3	15.0	15.4	15.2	15.4	14.5
Developing economies by income							
32 Low-income economies							
Weighted average	12.9	12.3	11.3	10.8	10.1	9.5	9.0
Unweighted average	12.7	12.0	12.5	12.0	11.3	11.5	10.8
42 Middle-income economies							
Weighted average	18.5	19.6	20.4	20.5	20.3	19.7	18.3
Unweighted average	15.6	16.1	16.9	17.9	18.1	18.4	17.3
Developing economies by region							
27 Latin America and the Caribbean							
Weighted average	21.5	23.6	23.9	23.2	22.3	21.2	19.6
Unweighted average	18.5	19.1	18.8	19.5	19.1	19.1	17.3
34 Africa							
Weighted average	16.4	14.7	14.0	13.4	15.9	16.4	14.1
Unweighted average	13.3	12.8	14.0	13.9	13.8	14.1	13.4
13 Asia							
Weighted average	10.9	10.7	10.9	11.4	11.0	11.1	11.2
Unweighted average	8.4	8.3	9.7	10.6	10.7	11.1	11.8
Economy							
1. Algeria	59.7	64.1	66.9	66.8	65.4	62.3	64.4
2. Argentina	16.4	21.0	13.0	12.5	8.4	6.7	6.9
3. Bangladesh	0.7	0.6	0.6	0.5	0.5	0.5	0.4
4. Barbados	1.2	0.7	1.0	2.7	4.3	11.3	7.4
5. Belize	3.4	13.6	15.8	31.0	35.2	32.6	24.5
6. Benin	11.5	16.6	37.3	32.8	35.5	31.9	30.3
7. Bolivia	29.7	27.8	26.0	24.9	20.1	19.4	13.4
8. Botswana	1.1	2.1	2.3	9.1	10.7	8.0	9.3
9. Brazil	28.4	30.5	31.9	30.9	31.5	32.7	31.0
10. Burkina Faso	7.2	4.7	8.5	7.5	8.0	8.0	8.8
11. Burundi	0.0	2.5	1.8	1.0	1.0	0.6	0.5
12. Cameroon	38.2	36.6	38.3	39.6	38.5	32.1	28.6
13. Cape Verde	0.0	0.0	0.0	0.0	44.2	50.2	52.3
14. Central African Rep.	46.4	30.5	27.8	24.2	12.2	18.4	16.7
15. Chile	17.9	20.7	18.1	15.6	13.9	16.2	15.6
16. Colombia	15.7	16.6	17.3	17.1	16.7	19.1	21.8
17. Comoros	0.4	0.3	0.5	0.0	0.0	1.7	2.6
18. Congo	7.5	7.4	7.1	5.8	6.6	6.2	8.0
19. Costa Rica	18.8	19.9	19.8	19.5	19.4	17.3	12.7
20. Côte d'Ivoire	26.2	24.6	26.0	24.1	19.8	16.1	15.7
21. Dominica	5.1	3.3	2.4	5.7	11.1	10.2	7.0
22. Dominican Rep.	18.9	15.6	12.2	16.3	15.2	16.6	13.6
23. Ecuador	10.9	14.2	13.3	13.9	13.4	12.9	11.8
24. Egypt	9.2	12.9	14.5	14.2	14.6	14.1	14.3
25. El Salvador	13.4	11.0	11.9	13.4	11.1	9.5	8.0
26. Ethiopia	9.5	10.1	10.0	12.8	14.0	12.8	11.7
27. Fiji	9.6	10.7	19.1	23.3	25.5	28.4	32.5
28. Gabon	10.6	11.5	14.4	14.2	14.5	12.3	9.6
29. Gambia, The	7.6	1.2	4.2	8.2	6.4	9.8	10.2
30. Ghana	7.6	8.2	10.3	13.5	14.0	15.7	14.4
31. Grenada	7.7	6.8	9.6	10.2	6.7	6.0	7.3
32. Guatemala	9.7	9.9	12.6	13.7	16.9	22.1	19.6

1985	1986	1987	1988	1989	1990	1991	1978–85	1986–91	1978–91
15.6	16.2	16.3	15.2	12.2	11.8	11.6	16.9	13.9	15.6
14.0	13.6	13.3	12.9	11.9	10.7	9.8	14.8	12.0	13.6
9.7	9.9	10.5	10.2	10.3	10.3	9.4	10.7	10.1	10.4
9.8	9.5	9.2	8.8	8.2	6.9	6.2	11.6	8.1	10.1
18.3	19.1	19.0	17.3	13.0	12.3	12.3	19.4	15.5	17.8
17.2	16.8	16.4	16.0	14.7	13.6	12.5	17.2	15.0	16.3
20.0	20.3	19.8	17.1	10.9	10.7	11.2	21.9	15.0	19.0
16.9	15.8	15.3	15.0	13.6	12.7	11.9	18.5	14.0	16.6
12.8	14.0	13.7	12.7	11.3	10.2	10.2	14.7	12.0	13.6
12.2	12.2	11.6	10.9	10.1	8.4	7.5	13.4	10.1	12.0
11.6	12.2	13.3	13.8	13.8	13.3	12.3	11.1	13.1	12.0
12.3	12.9	13.5	13.8	13.2	12.3	11.2	10.4	12.8	11.4
56.2	46.3	36.5	36.1	31.8	27.3	25.3	63.2	33.9	50.6
9.4	8.1	8.1	4.4	5.3	8.0	10.2	11.8	7.3	9.9
0.3	0.3	0.6	0.2	0.2	0.2	0.4	0.5	0.3	0.4
13.9	13.5	12.1	11.3	7.7	7.0	5.3	5.3	9.5	7.1
21.9	14.0	11.3	11.3	15.9	15.4	8.7	22.2	12.8	18.2
28.5	28.1	28.4	28.9	27.9	10.5	5.0	28.1	21.5	25.2
11.7	11.0	9.9	10.1	9.5	11.0	11.5	21.6	10.5	16.9
20.6	29.0	30.3	27.6	25.6	22.2	21.5	7.9	26.0	15.7
31.4	35.2	32.1	27.5	11.1	11.0	12.1	31.0	21.5	26.9
8.7	8.8	7.7	6.6	5.3	5.1	4.1	7.7	6.3	7.1
0.3	0.4	0.3	0.3	0.4	0.3	0.2	1.0	0.3	0.7
23.9	24.1	21.7	21.6	17.7	10.9	8.7	34.5	17.4	27.2
41.3	34.6	31.2	23.5	21.5	19.5	17.5	23.5	24.6	24.0
11.4	12.3	13.1	13.4	11.9	11.9	6.3	23.5	11.5	18.3
13.7	12.9	11.4	10.2	8.4	8.2	7.7	16.5	9.8	13.6
22.7	24.0	31.5	32.1	30.8	29.3	28.8	18.4	29.4	23.1
4.7	7.3	8.5	11.4	12.6	2.3	3.1	1.3	7.5	4.0
8.3	7.4	6.8	5.8	5.1	4.5	3.0	7.1	5.4	6.4
12.8	11.3	11.7	13.0	12.5	10.4	10.8	17.5	11.6	15.0
13.2	11.3	9.8	7.9	5.7	4.8	3.4	20.7	7.1	14.9
5.3	4.8	4.4	3.3	3.2	2.9	2.1	6.3	3.5	5.1
14.4	10.3	7.7	7.4	7.0	7.4	7.6	15.3	7.9	12.2
9.5	9.2	11.5	10.5	7.3	6.5	6.2	12.5	8.5	10.8
13.9	15.0	16.2	15.3	14.7	15.1	22.6	13.5	16.5	14.8
5.9	6.3	6.2	6.3	5.8	5.1	6.0	10.5	6.0	8.6
16.7	18.2	16.4	16.5	16.2	13.8	11.3	12.2	15.4	13.6
32.9	35.1	34.8	33.3	30.7	29.3	25.8	22.7	31.5	26.5
7.1	7.2	7.0	6.8	5.5	4.8	4.8	11.8	6.0	9.3
9.1	8.9	6.1	4.2	1.5	1.4	0.2	7.1	3.7	5.6
10.5	9.8	8.6	8.0	7.9	6.2	5.2	11.8	7.6	10.0
8.8	9.1	9.7	8.7	7.2	6.6	4.9	7.9	7.7	7.8
13.8	15.0	15.7	17.0	17.0	17.7	17.9	14.8	16.7	15.6

Table A.10 *(continued)*

Group and economy[a]	1978	1979	1980	1981	1982	1983	1984
33. Guinea	0.9	0.7	1.4	1.0	2.1	1.9	2.6
34. Guinea-Bissau	1.0	0.7	4.2	2.2	3.1	3.4	2.7
35. Guyana	19.3	18.6	18.2	15.0	11.5	9.1	6.2
36. Haiti	16.8	13.6	12.9	9.4	9.7	9.0	8.0
37. Honduras	11.8	11.0	12.0	10.5	12.5	12.8	13.8
38. India	12.0	11.7	10.6	10.4	9.5	9.4	9.4
39. Indonesia	11.4	9.7	8.5	8.6	7.9	6.9	5.3
40. Jamaica	14.3	14.9	11.7	10.1	7.2	5.3	7.2
41. Kenya	20.8	22.9	19.7	16.9	17.1	15.8	13.3
42. Korea, Rep. of	11.1	12.4	11.8	12.1	12.5	12.6	12.9
43. Liberia	15.0	12.1	12.1	10.8	8.6	8.2	8.3
44. Madagascar	17.6	22.0	24.0	24.1	22.2	23.4	23.5
45. Malawi	10.3	11.7	14.0	16.1	15.5	13.2	10.0
46. Malaysia	9.7	10.7	17.6	17.0	15.3	12.8	16.4
47. Mali	6.2	6.4	3.4	3.7	2.5	2.2	2.1
48. Mauritania	12.0	10.2	9.7	7.8	10.0	15.5	19.4
49. Mauritius	3.9	4.0	2.8	3.8	3.1	2.8	2.3
50. Mexico	23.5	27.4	28.0	26.4	25.4	25.7	20.3
51. Morocco	23.0	25.6	24.1	22.6	19.0	17.8	16.2
52. Nepal	...	...	...	...	...	0.1	0.6
53. Nicaragua	13.5	13.4	13.3	8.1	7.7	6.6	5.3
54. Niger	3.8	3.9	8.9	12.3	16.8	13.0	11.4
55. Nigeria	9.5	5.8	5.4	5.1	12.2	14.8	11.1
56. Pakistan	3.9	3.5	4.0	6.0	5.2	4.6	4.6
57. Panama	30.8	25.3	17.8	14.1	12.6	13.1	12.9
58. Papua New Guinea	0.0	0.0	0.0	0.0	1.6	2.4	2.5
59. Paraguay	29.5	32.2	24.9	23.9	24.0	31.0	34.5
60. Peru	15.8	17.3	19.0	19.2	19.7	15.7	17.1
61. Philippines	18.1	17.5	17.8	16.2	14.7	13.2	15.6
62. Senegal	12.5	12.4	10.9	12.3	8.9	8.3	7.6
63. Seychelles	...	...	...	3.4	6.3	7.7	6.2
64. Sierra Leone	11.2	11.2	10.2	8.8	8.8	8.8	8.2
65. Somalia	3.5	2.6	2.6	3.0	2.0	1.1	0.8
66. Sri Lanka	4.6	3.3	3.7	4.2	7.8	12.3	12.3
67. St. Lucia	44.3	50.6	50.9	48.5	45.5	42.6	40.6
68. St. Vincent and the Grenadines	68.1	64.9	62.5	67.0	68.6	65.7	62.9
69. Sudan	4.7	4.1	3.5	3.3	2.6	2.2	1.6
70. Swaziland	0.8	10.4	19.7	23.3	20.8	22.8	20.1
71. Tanzania	6.2	8.2	9.8	10.8	10.6	9.0	8.1
72. Thailand	19.1	18.3	21.2	26.8	27.1	29.8	29.9
73. Togo	2.5	1.7	5.5	6.3	5.0	4.7	3.6
74. Trinidad and Tobago	10.0	7.2	18.5	27.5	29.7	27.8	23.4
75. Tunisia	23.9	22.7	28.6	30.5	30.5	31.8	30.4
76. Turkey	6.5	7.0	8.0	9.6	10.8	12.0	11.0
77. Uganda	2.6	4.7	3.8	4.6	3.8	2.7	2.5
78. Uruguay	13.8	16.3	14.3	16.0	15.7	14.7	10.9
79. Venezuela	5.7	4.3	13.1	11.3	9.2	9.6	8.1
80. Zaire	38.3	36.1	31.9	25.6	24.1	23.1	18.7
81. Zambia	29.2	25.5	20.0	17.0	17.6	19.1	18.3
82. Zimbabwe	12.7	5.1	3.7	2.6	12.9	24.1	26.7

a. Only a subset of countries within each classification was used for deriving averages. Thirty-two low-income economies include Bangladesh, Benin, Bolivia, Burundi, Cape Verde, Central African Republic, Comoros, Egypt, the Gambia, Ghana, Guinea, Guinea-Bissau, Guyana, Haiti, India, Indonesia, Kenya, Malawi, Mali, Mauritania, Nepal, Niger, Pakistan, Philippines, Senegal, Sierra Leone, Sri Lanka, Tanzania, Togo, Uganda, Zaire, and Zambia. Forty-two middle-income economies include Argentina, Barbados, Belize, Botswana, Brazil, Cameroon, Chile, Colombia, Congo, Costa Rica, Côte d'Ivoire, Dominica, Dominican Rep., Ecuador, El Salvador, Fiji, Gabon, Grenada, Guatemala, Honduras, Jamaica, Korea, Malaysia, Mauritius, Mexico, Morocco, Nigeria,

1985	1986	1987	1988	1989	1990	1991	1978–85	1986–91	1978–91
2.4	2.0	1.1	0.9	0.5	0.3	0.3	1.6	0.8	1.3
1.7	1.6	1.5	0.8	0.1	0.1	0.1	2.4	0.7	1.7
4.9	4.0	5.4	6.0	5.4	3.3	1.9	12.8	4.3	9.2
6.4	5.8	5.6	4.6	4.4	3.3	3.4	10.7	4.5	8.1
13.3	14.3	14.9	15.2	13.2	11.6	8.8	12.2	13.0	12.5
11.4	11.9	13.0	13.1	14.3	14.9	14.2	10.5	13.6	11.8
4.1	2.7	1.5	0.8	0.5	0.2	0.0	7.8	0.9	4.9
7.0	7.2	7.0	7.5	8.3	8.2	7.4	9.7	7.6	8.8
11.6	11.3	14.1	14.1	13.3	14.0	13.0	17.3	13.3	15.6
12.7	12.9	13.7	14.2	14.2	13.4	12.8	12.2	13.6	12.8
7.2	7.0	6.8	6.8	7.0	7.0	6.8	10.3	6.9	8.8
17.3	16.4	16.0	14.4	14.3	11.6	7.6	21.8	13.4	18.2
6.7	5.3	4.2	4.3	3.8	4.2	3.7	12.2	4.3	8.8
19.0	19.8	19.8	20.5	17.9	13.8	12.9	14.8	17.5	15.9
1.4	1.3	1.2	0.9	0.5	0.5	0.5	3.5	0.8	2.3
19.1	20.6	20.6	20.2	19.0	16.9	13.8	13.0	18.5	15.3
3.3	3.7	3.9	6.0	16.9	18.5	21.0	3.2	11.7	6.9
17.6	9.8	9.6	9.0	8.9	8.8	9.1	24.3	9.2	17.8
14.1	13.6	12.6	10.7	8.3	7.5	6.5	20.3	9.9	15.8
3.0	3.3	5.1	8.4	10.8	8.8	6.8	1.2	7.2	5.2
4.1	3.7	2.3	2.4	2.0	1.9	1.9	9.0	2.4	6.2
9.6	7.8	6.3	5.5	3.9	2.8	2.7	10.0	4.8	7.8
10.3	12.6	11.6	9.6	8.9	8.0	5.5	9.3	9.4	9.3
5.0	5.2	4.3	3.6	3.4	3.5	2.9	4.6	3.8	4.3
13.3	13.4	14.0	13.3	12.3	11.6	11.1	17.5	12.6	15.4
3.8	4.8	7.4	7.5	8.3	12.7	12.0	1.3	8.8	4.5
34.8	30.0	30.5	29.5	30.1	27.0	33.8	29.3	30.1	29.7
17.0	17.6	17.2	16.8	15.8	15.1	14.9	17.6	16.2	17.0
16.8	17.3	18.6	18.4	17.5	15.7	13.4	16.2	16.8	16.5
7.0	6.9	6.7	7.1	6.4	5.3	4.7	10.0	6.2	8.3
7.2	7.6	6.7	8.3	7.8	8.0	10.4	6.2	8.1	7.2
6.9	7.2	5.4	4.6	4.1	3.4	3.0	9.3	4.6	7.3
0.7	0.7	0.8	0.8	0.8	0.8	0.7	2.0	0.8	1.5
12.5	10.5	8.6	7.2	5.3	4.9	3.8	7.6	6.7	7.2
32.2	27.9	19.2	28.5	35.8	37.2	36.9	44.4	30.9	38.6
66.7	65.1	55.6	52.2	45.8	40.6	34.1	65.8	48.9	58.5
1.4	1.4	1.2	1.0	0.9	0.7	0.7	2.9	1.0	2.1
18.9	16.4	16.7	16.1	14.7	11.6	5.3	17.1	13.5	15.6
7.8	8.3	6.6	5.9	4.6	4.7	3.6	8.8	5.6	7.4
28.3	31.4	34.2	36.0	31.4	27.6	26.7	25.1	31.2	27.7
4.9	5.2	4.6	4.6	4.6	4.0	4.2	4.3	4.5	4.4
30.6	29.4	35.0	34.1	26.3	16.7	10.4	21.8	25.3	23.3
27.6	27.0	25.5	24.5	20.8	18.7	17.4	28.2	22.3	25.7
10.7	12.9	14.3	15.5	16.6	15.8	13.4	9.5	14.8	11.7
2.7	3.7	4.0	3.7	3.6	3.3	3.0	3.4	3.6	3.5
10.5	9.2	7.8	6.5	3.9	3.2	2.8	14.0	5.5	10.4
7.7	7.0	6.7	7.8	8.2	10.2	7.9	8.6	8.0	8.3
16.9	16.3	15.7	14.9	13.4	13.4	13.6	26.8	14.6	21.6
17.5	18.1	16.2	15.6	13.7	13.9	12.7	20.5	15.0	18.2
24.3	23.4	20.4	18.1	14.8	11.9	9.7	14.0	16.4	15.0

Panama, Papua New Guinea, Paraguay, Peru, Seychelles, St. Lucia, St. Vincent and the Grenadines, Swaziland, Thailand, Trinidad and Tobago, Tunisia, Turkey, Uruguay, Venezuela, and Zimbabwe. Latin America and the Caribbean regional averages exclude Nicaragua, and the Africa regional average excludes Algeria, Burkina Faso, Chad, Djibouti, Ethiopia, Lesotho, Liberia, Madagascar, Somalia, and Sudan. Three-year moving average estimates were used to complete our time series, in case of missing values, when deriving averages.

b. Weighted averages were obtained using GDP in current U.S. dollars as weights.

Table A.11 External Debt of State-Owned Enterprises as a Proportion of Gross Domestic Product, 1978–91

(percentage)

Group and economy[a]	1978	1979	1980	1981	1982	1983	1984
Group							
All economies							
74 Developing economies							
Weighted average[b]	5.4	5.6	5.7	5.9	7.0	7.4	7.5
Unweighted average	5.9	6.2	6.2	6.6	7.7	8.3	8.3
Developing economies by income							
32 Low-income economies							
Weighted average	4.0	4.0	3.7	3.7	3.9	4.1	4.3
Unweighted average	6.5	6.9	6.8	6.8	8.0	8.6	8.6
42 Middle-income economies							
Weighted average	6.0	6.2	6.4	6.8	8.2	8.9	8.8
Unweighted average	5.5	5.8	5.8	6.5	7.5	8.1	8.1
Developing economies by region							
27 Latin America and the Caribbean							
Weighted average	7.2	7.3	7.3	7.3	9.0	10.0	9.9
Unweighted average	7.2	7.1	6.9	7.4	8.4	8.8	8.7
34 Africa							
Weighted average	6.3	6.5	5.8	7.0	7.9	8.2	7.9
Unweighted average	6.2	6.9	6.8	7.0	8.3	9.1	9.1
13 Asia							
Weighted average	2.8	2.8	3.2	3.4	3.7	4.2	4.4
Unweighted average	2.5	2.8	3.4	3.8	4.5	5.3	5.5
Economy							
1. Algeria	38.1	37.2	30.6	27.1	24.3	21.4	16.7
2. Argentina	4.8	3.9	4.4	3.8	3.5	3.1	3.9
3. Bangladesh	0.2	0.2	0.2	0.1	0.2	0.2	0.1
4. Barbados	0.1	0.2	0.5	1.1	3.8	4.1	4.8
5. Belize	3.3	7.4	10.0	11.0	12.7	13.0	10.1
6. Benin	4.2	12.7	9.9	13.5	16.9	19.7	18.4
7. Bolivia	25.7	24.5	21.9	17.9	20.5	18.9	18.0
8. Botswana	0.5	0.4	1.2	1.5	1.7	2.0	4.4
9. Brazil	8.2	8.6	9.4	9.7	10.8	15.0	15.8
10. Burkina Faso	0.00	0.01	0.01	0.01	0.01	0.01	0.01
11. Burundi	0.3	0.3	0.2	0.2	0.1	0.1	0.1
12. Cameroon	12.3	14.0	13.3	11.7	11.2	10.0	8.1
13. Cape Verde	0.0	0.0	0.0	16.4	27.6	35.4	31.0
14. Central African Rep.	6.8	5.9	5.9	4.1	6.2	6.6	4.8
15. Chile	9.9	8.2	6.8	6.7	11.5	14.2	14.1
16. Colombia	3.6	3.6	3.5	4.0	5.0	6.4	7.1
17. Comoros	...	...	...	...	1.1	2.0	4.6
18. Congo	6.7	6.2	5.2	5.0	5.6	7.7	7.8
19. Costa Rica	9.5	10.4	11.1	24.4	24.2	16.9	13.9
20. Côte d'Ivoire	11.9	13.5	13.8	15.6	16.7	18.0	16.2
21. Dominica	0.7	0.7	1.4	2.4	2.9	3.0	2.8
22. Dominican Rep.	4.4	3.6	4.9	4.8	5.7	5.8	9.0
23. Ecuador	7.4	6.4	7.1	7.4	8.0	8.4	7.7
24. Egypt, Arab Rep. of	12.2	13.0	12.9	15.0	16.3	16.6	16.1
25. El Salvador	3.3	3.1	3.4	3.6	3.9	3.9	2.8
26. Ethiopia	1.6	1.9	2.5	3.7	3.6	3.4	5.3
27. Fiji	1.3	2.6	5.4	7.7	9.6	12.7	11.5
28. Gabon	7.3	8.2	5.0	4.3	3.4	2.6	1.8
29. Gambia, The	0.3	1.5	4.8	5.3	9.5	10.6	12.8
30. Ghana	2.9	3.3	4.3	5.1	5.7	5.8	4.6
31. Grenada	1.9	3.0	2.7	2.7	3.0	4.7	4.3

1985	1986	1987	1988	1989	1990	1991	1978–85	1986–91	1978–91
7.8	8.2	7.9	5.5	4.9	4.5	4.3	6.5	5.9	6.3
9.4	9.5	9.7	8.0	6.9	6.2	5.6	7.3	7.7	7.5
4.8	5.3	5.4	5.0	4.8	4.7	4.6	4.1	5.0	4.5
9.9	9.9	10.4	8.3	6.9	6.3	5.7	7.8	7.9	7.8
9.2	9.6	9.0	5.7	4.9	4.4	4.1	7.6	6.3	7.0
9.1	9.1	9.1	7.8	7.0	6.1	5.6	7.0	7.5	7.2
9.7	9.7	8.9	5.1	4.6	4.3	3.9	8.5	6.1	7.5
9.0	9.0	9.5	8.2	7.4	6.5	5.6	8.0	7.7	7.8
9.3	11.6	13.0	11.2	10.5	9.8	9.0	7.4	10.9	8.9
10.9	10.7	10.8	8.6	7.3	6.6	6.1	8.0	8.3	8.2
5.1	5.6	5.4	4.6	4.0	3.6	3.6	3.7	4.5	4.0
6.6	7.2	7.1	6.0	5.2	4.6	4.4	4.3	5.7	4.9
14.5	13.0	13.4	14.4	14.0	12.6	15.0	26.2	13.7	20.9
4.7	4.0	2.3	2.4	6.8	4.5	3.0	4.0	3.8	3.9
0.1	0.3	0.1	0.1	0.1	0.2	0.1	0.2	0.2	0.2
5.1	5.3	4.5	3.5	2.6	2.1	1.6	2.5	3.3	2.8
7.9	6.0	5.6	7.1	6.1	3.4	3.4	9.4	5.3	7.6
22.0	20.2	21.2	18.3	8.3	3.3	3.3	14.7	12.4	13.7
17.8	14.3	13.7	10.6	10.1	11.0	9.5	20.6	11.5	16.7
8.5	9.3	9.2	5.8	4.2	3.5	3.0	2.5	5.8	3.9
16.7	13.6	11.6	3.9	2.7	2.9	3.8	11.8	6.4	9.5
0.01	0.01	0.01	0.01	0.01	0.00	0.00	0.01	0.01	0.01
0.1	0.2	0.2	0.3	0.3	0.1	0.1	0.2	0.2	0.2
8.7	7.5	7.2	6.5	4.9	4.8	4.4	11.1	5.9	8.9
32.3	25.5	17.7	13.7	11.9	9.8	8.0	17.8	14.5	16.4
6.1	6.2	8.0	7.3	7.5	3.7	4.1	5.8	6.1	5.9
16.0	13.6	10.6	6.8	5.3	4.9	4.0	10.9	7.5	9.5
9.8	13.8	15.0	13.3	12.5	12.3	11.3	5.4	13.0	8.7
8.5	8.7	11.8	12.1	2.0	2.4	0.5	4.0	6.2	5.4
10.3	12.8	10.9	9.5	7.9	5.0	4.6	6.8	8.4	7.5
12.7	12.2	13.5	12.4	9.2	7.2	7.4	15.4	10.3	13.2
15.8	11.6	10.3	7.8	8.0	6.2	5.2	15.2	8.2	12.2
2.5	2.1	1.8	1.6	1.4	1.1	0.9	2.1	1.5	1.8
8.0	5.2	5.7	6.1	4.5	4.7	5.2	5.8	5.2	5.5
6.6	9.5	10.4	7.9	7.4	7.1	7.2	7.4	8.2	7.7
18.3	20.9	22.4	25.0	22.9	25.6	22.5	15.0	23.2	18.6
2.9	2.8	2.8	2.5	2.1	2.3	2.0	3.4	2.4	3.0
7.1	6.9	8.2	8.5	7.0	6.1	6.3	3.6	7.2	5.1
13.6	11.9	13.1	13.0	9.6	7.6	5.9	8.1	10.2	9.0
2.4	3.9	5.1	4.4	3.6	3.2	3.1	4.4	3.9	4.2
10.0	8.1	5.7	1.8	1.6	0.2	0.2	6.9	2.9	5.2
4.9	4.1	5.2	4.6	3.9	3.1	2.6	4.6	3.9	4.3
4.2	4.2	4.1	3.5	2.9	2.5	2.4	3.3	3.3	3.3

Table A.11 *(continued)*

Group and economy[a]	1978	1979	1980	1981	1982	1983	1984
32. Guatemala	1.3	1.9	2.0	2.5	3.9	3.9	3.4
33. Guinea	...	...	...	...	...	...	...
34. Guinea-Bissau	0.3	2.5	2.8	2.8	3.3	3.1	3.0
35. Guyana	21.5	22.3	20.2	17.8	18.1	15.3	14.2
36. Haiti	2.7	2.9	1.9	2.8	3.3	2.8	2.3
37. Honduras	5.3	6.3	6.0	7.5	8.1	9.6	9.1
38. India	1.5	1.3	1.2	1.2	1.4	1.5	2.0
39. Indonesia	3.2	2.9	2.3	1.9	1.8	1.8	1.4
40. Jamaica	8.2	8.2	7.2	6.0	5.1	7.6	10.4
41. Kenya	9.7	8.8	8.0	8.2	8.4	8.3	6.7
42. Korea, Rep. of	4.3	4.2	5.7	5.9	6.3	6.3	5.9
43. Liberia	5.7	6.8	6.6	6.4	6.6	7.9	7.1
44. Madagascar	3.0	5.4	7.3	9.7	12.8	13.7	12.5
45. Malawi	7.2	8.7	10.6	10.1	9.6	7.3	4.9
46. Malaysia	2.7	4.1	4.6	5.6	6.4	9.6	10.6
47. Mali	3.1	1.3	1.7	1.5	1.6	1.9	1.6
48. Mauritania	12.8	10.8	9.3	13.0	23.8	31.9	35.1
49. Mauritius	1.0	0.9	1.6	1.5	1.5	1.2	1.7
50. Mexico	8.9	8.4	7.8	7.9	12.7	12.7	9.5
51. Morocco	12.1	12.9	11.7	13.3	14.5	15.6	15.7
52. Nepal	0.0	0.0	0.0	0.0	0.0	0.1	0.5
53. Nicaragua	9.6	12.9	8.2	7.6	7.8	7.8	6.2
54. Niger	1.3	2.7	4.2	7.9	6.4	6.1	6.3
55. Nigeria	0.5	0.5	0.5	1.8	2.5	2.6	2.3
56. Pakistan	1.6	1.8	2.5	2.0	1.7	1.9	1.9
57. Panama	23.8	16.6	11.8	11.0	12.0	12.9	12.7
58. Papua New Guinea	0.0	0.0	0.0	0.8	1.6	1.9	3.0
59. Paraguay	7.7	5.9	5.0	4.8	7.4	8.7	11.6
60. Peru	13.8	11.3	8.7	6.8	6.8	10.1	10.4
61. Philippines	8.3	8.6	8.7	8.6	8.7	11.5	13.0
62. Senegal	5.1	4.5	6.0	6.0	6.0	6.4	6.6
63. Seychelles	0.0	0.0	2.0	1.5	2.6	2.3	3.4
64. Sierra Leone	4.4	3.8	3.5	4.1	4.1	3.5	3.9
65. Somalia	2.4	2.5	3.3	3.0	1.8	1.5	1.4
66. Sri Lanka	1.7	1.7	1.9	3.9	6.6	6.7	6.3
67. St. Lucia	4.5	5.2	5.6	5.2	5.2	5.1	2.9
68. St. Vincent and the Grenadines	8.4	8.7	12.0	17.8	16.6	17.1	16.2
69. Sudan	1.7	1.9	2.5	2.0	2.0	1.6	1.4
70. Swaziland	3.8	8.0	8.2	6.7	8.4	8.5	7.3
71. Tanzania	3.7	4.5	5.6	5.0	4.5	4.4	5.1
72. Thailand	3.8	5.1	6.9	8.4	10.2	10.5	10.3
73. Togo	1.5	6.3	5.8	5.0	5.5	4.3	5.5
74. Trinidad and Tobago	1.0	2.7	3.7	4.5	4.2	4.2	4.7
75. Tunisia	11.2	13.5	12.3	13.0	14.7	15.2	14.1
76. Turkey	2.0	1.8	3.2	3.6	4.5	4.4	4.7
77. Uganda	...	...	2.5	1.8	1.1	1.1	1.1
78. Uruguay	3.3	2.6	2.6	3.1	4.3	7.1	7.1
79. Venezuela	1.5	5.5	4.8	3.8	3.9	3.8	4.7
80. Zaire	10.5	10.9	8.8	9.8	8.6	9.0	11.4
81. Zambia	23.4	18.1	14.2	15.9	18.2	20.9	24.5
82. Zimbabwe	0.7	0.5	0.4	2.5	6.6	9.4	10.4

a. Only a subset of countries within each classification was used for deriving averages. Thirty-two low-income economies include Bangladesh, Benin, Bolivia, Burundi, Cape Verde, Central African Republic, Comoros, Egypt, the Gambia, Ghana, Guinea, Guinea-Bissau, Guyana, Haiti, India, Indonesia, Kenya, Malawi, Mali, Mauritania, Nepal, Niger, Pakistan, Philippines, Senegal, Sierra Leone, Sri Lanka, Tanzania, Togo, Uganda, Zaire, and Zambia. Forty-two middle-income economies include Argentina, Barbados, Belize, Botswana, Brazil, Cameroon, Chile, Colombia, Congo, Costa Rica, Côte d'Ivoire, Dominica, Dominican Rep., Ecuador, El Salvador, Fiji, Gabon, Grenada, Guatemala, Honduras, Jamaica, Korea, Malaysia, Mauritius, Mexico, Morocco, Nigeria,

1985	1986	1987	1988	1989	1990	1991	1978–85	1986–91	1978–91
4.1	6.0	6.7	5.6	5.5	6.5	5.2	2.9	5.9	4.2
...	0.9	0.9	0.5	0.3	0.2	0.2	...	0.5	0.5
3.0	4.1	2.1	0.3	0.2	0.1	0.1	2.6	1.2	2.0
12.8	17.2	29.2	22.3	16.3	9.6	9.2	17.8	17.3	17.6
2.0	1.8	1.8	1.6	1.1	1.1	0.3	2.6	1.3	2.0
10.7	11.6	12.1	11.0	11.1	10.6	8.3	7.8	10.8	9.1
2.3	2.8	2.8	3.0	3.5	3.3	4.0	1.6	3.3	2.3
1.1	0.8	0.5	0.3	0.1	0.0	0.0	2.1	0.3	1.3
14.5	11.7	11.8	10.8	9.4	8.2	9.2	8.4	10.2	9.2
7.7	9.1	10.2	9.0	9.6	10.5	11.9	8.2	10.0	9.0
6.5	6.1	4.3	2.9	2.1	1.8	1.5	5.6	3.1	4.6
8.0	9.1	10.0	...	...	...	...	6.9	9.6	7.4
14.2	14.4	20.1	21.0	15.9	8.9	10.3	9.8	15.1	12.1
4.8	4.2	4.9	3.9	3.7	3.2	2.0	7.9	3.7	6.1
13.1	16.0	15.4	10.4	6.5	5.5	8.0	7.1	10.3	8.5
1.5	1.2	0.9	0.5	0.5	0.4	0.4	1.8	0.7	1.3
45.3	45.4	45.4	41.1	35.3	29.8	25.3	22.7	37.1	28.9
2.1	1.8	2.7	7.0	7.3	7.8	9.9	1.4	6.1	3.4
5.1	7.5	7.1	5.2	4.1	3.6	2.7	9.1	5.0	7.4
17.5	13.2	11.9	7.9	7.1	5.9	5.4	14.1	8.6	11.8
0.8	1.5	3.1	4.1	3.9	3.5	2.9	0.2	3.1	1.5
8.0	5.3	4.9	6.7	17.6	13.4	7.0	8.5	9.2	8.8
6.5	4.8	4.2	3.0	2.0	2.0	2.0	5.2	3.0	4.2
3.0	6.5	10.9	8.7	8.2	5.4	5.9	1.7	7.6	4.2
2.2	2.0	1.8	1.5	1.6	1.5	1.5	2.0	1.6	1.8
13.0	13.3	14.1	16.4	16.0	15.0	12.0	14.2	14.5	14.3
4.1	5.5	5.5	5.1	8.5	9.6	8.1	1.4	7.1	3.8
17.2	18.0	19.9	17.9	14.7	13.7	11.4	8.5	15.9	11.7
14.1	11.0	10.6	10.3	11.3	12.2	7.9	10.3	10.5	10.4
15.0	17.6	16.4	13.4	10.5	9.2	8.1	10.3	12.5	11.2
6.8	5.8	6.2	5.0	3.7	3.1	2.9	5.9	4.4	5.3
4.4	4.8	5.9	4.7	4.4	5.5	5.9	2.0	5.2	3.4
3.9	3.2	8.4	3.7	3.9	4.1	4.5	3.9	4.6	4.2
1.4	1.5	1.6	1.6	1.5	1.9		2.2	1.6	1.9
6.1	5.4	5.0	3.9	3.6	2.8	2.8	4.4	3.9	4.2
2.7	2.1	4.3	5.8	6.1	6.9	6.6	4.5	5.3	4.9
15.7	13.7	15.3	13.8	12.4	10.2	8.7	14.0	12.4	13.3
1.2	0.9	0.7	1.0	1.0	1.1	1.4	1.8	1.0	1.5
10.8	10.4	8.4	5.6	4.5	1.6	1.2	7.7	5.3	6.7
5.2	6.6	10.1	8.9	9.7	9.4	7.7	4.8	8.7	6.5
14.8	15.2	15.0	11.0	8.9	8.8	8.1	8.8	11.2	9.8
6.4	4.6	4.6	4.1	3.5	3.3	3.1	5.0	3.9	4.5
5.8	13.6	12.8	12.5	8.4	4.7	3.5	3.8	9.3	6.2
15.9	17.1	17.2	13.9	12.8	10.7	10.0	13.8	13.6	13.7
6.3	8.1	9.3	9.5	8.3	6.1	6.0	3.8	7.9	5.6
1.9	1.5	1.6	2.8	2.5	2.9	2.9	1.6	2.4	2.0
7.6	5.2	3.8	2.0	1.7	1.5	1.3	4.7	2.6	3.8
4.0	3.8	5.7	4.7	7.6	5.4	4.2	4.0	5.2	4.5
14.0	13.9	17.0	13.0	14.1	16.5	17.5	10.4	15.3	12.5
37.1	55.6	49.7	25.8	21.5	24.9	21.6	21.6	33.2	26.5
12.5	10.8	9.6	6.2	5.3	4.6	4.2	5.4	6.8	6.0

Panama, Papua New Guinea, Paraguay, Peru, Seychelles, St. Lucia, St. Vincent and the Grenadines, Swaziland, Thailand, Trinidad and Tobago, Tunisia, Turkey, Uruguay, Venezuela, and Zimbabwe. Latin America and the Caribbean regional averages exclude Nicaragua, and the Africa regional average excludes Algeria, Burkina Faso, Chad, Djibouti, Ethiopia, Lesotho, Liberia, Madagascar, Somalia, and Sudan. Three-year moving average estimates were used to complete our time series, in case of missing values, when deriving averages.

b. Weighted averages were obtained using GDP in current U.S. dollars as weights.

Technical Notes

Latin America and the Caribbean

Argentina. Source: World Bank and IMF; Larrain and Selowsky (1991).

Barbados. Major nonfinancial SOEs only. Source: IMF.

Belize. Nonfinancial SOEs since 1980. Source: World Bank and IMF.

Bolivia. Data are for eight major nonfinancial SOEs that in 1990 and 1991 accounted for more than 80 percent of all revenues, value added, and employment generated by the SOE sector; overall balance and net transfers figures for 1978–84 are from Nair and Filippides. Source: World Bank and IMF; Nair and Fillippides (1989).

Brazil. All federal SOEs; overall balance figures for 1981–85 are from Nair and Fillippides. Source: For 1981–85, Larrain and Selowsky (1991); for 1986–91, IMF, Nair and Fillippides (1989); some 1985 data from World Bank sources.

Chile. Employment figures for 1978–86 are from Saez (1992) and refer to selected major SOEs, including Banco del Estado. Source: Budget Office, Ministry of Finance, and World Bank; Larrain and Selowsky (1991); Lüders (1990); and Hachette and Lüders (1993).

Colombia. Source: IMF and World Bank.

Costa Rica. Data refer to the following nonfinancial SOEs: ICE, RECOPE, CODESA, CNP, ICAA, FECOSA, ESPH, JPSSJ (since 1981), FNL, INCOP, JASEMC, JAPQ, and JAPDEVA. Source: IMF.

Dominica. Value added for 1990–91 derived as sum of sectoral disaggregates; investment share reported as proportion of gross fixed capital formation. Source: IMF.

Dominican Republic. All SOEs. Source: World Bank.

Ecuador. Nonfinancial SOEs covered are CEPE, INECEL, ECUATORIANA, ENAC, ENPROVIT, FLOPEC, IETEL, National Railroads, TAME, and TRANSNAVE except in 1981 and 1982, when only CEPE and INECEL are included. Data for 1988–91 include PETROECUADOR, INECEL, ECUATORIANA, ENAC, ENPROVIT, FLOPEC, EMETEL, ENFE, TAME, and TRANSNAVE. Since 1990 eleven smaller nonfinancial SOEs have also been covered. SOE employment numbers are reported as share of urban employment. Overall balance before transfers is estimated as the overall balance after transfers for the ten nonfinancial SOEs identified above minus net transfers to eight major nonfinancial SOEs. Numbers for net transfers are for eight major nonfinancial SOEs only. Source: IMF and World Bank.

El Salvador. Data are for eight major nonfinancial SOEs. Source: IMF and World Bank.

Grenada. Data for 1986–92 cover five major nonfinancial SOEs only: Grenada Electricity Service, Grenada Ports Authority, Water and Sewage Authority, Marketing and National Importing Board, and Grenada Sugar Factory. Data for earlier years cover eleven major nonfinancial SOEs. Source: IMF.

Guatemala. Data cover eleven nonfinancial SOEs: INDECA, GNT, EPN, FEGUA, AVIATECA, EPQ, GUATEL, INDE, PROLAC, ZOLIC, and EMPAGUA. Source: IMF.

Guyana. Data are consolidated from disaggregated accounts of GUYSUCO, GUYMINE, GREC, GLC, and GUYSTAC. Value added for 1986–90 is estimated using wage bill, cost of goods and services, and other expenses based on their average share in operating expenses for 1978–85. Source: IMF.

Haiti. Data are for major SOEs only, including the electric company, water authority, port authority, telecom company, flour mill, and cement company. Figures for overall balance, 1981–86, and net transfers, 1982–86, are from Nair and Fillippides. Source: IMF; Nair and Fillippides (1989).

Honduras. Nonfinancial SOEs include COHDEFOR, ENEE, ENP, SANAA, FNH, INVA, COHBANA, HONDUTEL, BANASUPRO, IHCAFE, and IHMA. Of these, in 1989 HONDUTEL, ENEE, and SANAA accounted for 80 percent of all nonfinancial SOE income and expenditure, 65 percent of the nonfinancial SOE wage bill, and 68 percent of all nonfinancial SOEs' capital formation. Overall balance figures for 1978–79 are from Nair and Fillippides. Source: World Bank and IMF; Nair and Fillippides (1989).

Jamaica. Selected SOEs only. 1984 value added figure is from Nair and Fillippides. SOE overall balances are estimated as operating balance minus capital expenditure. Source: IMF.

Mexico. Figures are for directly controlled nonfinancial SOEs, excluding social security institutes. Source: World Bank; Dirección General de Planeación Hacendaria—*Estadísticas de Finanzas Públicas* 1973–88.

Panama. Data cover major nonfinancial SOEs, including Hydraulic Resources and Electricity Institute (IHRE), National Telecommunications Institute (INTEL), National Water and Sewerage Institute (IDAAU), La Victoria Sugar Corporation, Colón Free Zone, Civil Aviation Authority, Tourism Institute, Bayano Cement Plant, and Port Authority. Value added prior to 1989 is estimated using wage bill, cost of goods and services, and other expenses based on their average share in operating expenses for 1989–91. Source: IMF.

Paraguay. Source: World Bank and IMF.

Peru. Source: World Bank.

St. Kitts and Nevis. Source: IMF.

St. Lucia. Source: IMF.

St. Vincent and the Grenadines. Data cover nine nonfinancial SOEs only. Source: IMF.

Trinidad and Tobago. Value added figures are for major nonfinancial SOEs only. Government transfers to enterprises refer to all state-owned enterprises. Source: World Bank and IMF.

Uruguay. Source: World Bank and IMF.

Venezuela. Nonfinancial SOEs include those in the petroleum and iron ore sectors. Source: World Bank and IMF.

Africa

Algeria. There is a substantial difference between our numbers and those reported in other sources, in that the numbers we report refer to the entire state-owned sector, not just industrial SOEs. Employment numbers are for industrial enterprises only. Figures for net transfers for 1978–85 are from Nair and Fillippides. Source: World Bank and IMF; Nair and Fillipides (1989).

Benin. Selected SOEs only. SOE employment was estimated using the share of civil service employment in SOEs and the share of total civil service employment for 1981–83. Source: World Bank and IMF.

Botswana. Nonfinancial SOEs covered include Botswana Agricultural Marketing Board, Botswana Livestock Development Corporation, Botswana Housing Corporation, Botswana Meat Commission, Botswana Power Corporation, Botswana Telephone Corporation, and Botswana Water Utilities Corporation. Since 1988, Air Botswana and Botswana Railways have also been included. Overall balance figures for 1978–79 are from Nair and Fillippides. Source: Bank of Botswana Annual Report (various annual issues); IMF; Nair and Fillipides (1989).

Burkina Faso. Source: ADI (various issues).

Burundi. Value added numbers are from ADI and other World Bank data. Employment numbers refer to share in formal sector employment; 1982–83 figures are from ADI and 1986–89 from IMF. Source: ADI (various issues); World Bank and IMF.

Cameroon. Employment numbers refer to share in formal sector employment. In 1985, 50 percent of SOE employment was in the agricultural sector. Overall balance numbers are from ADI. Source: ADI (various issues); World Bank.

Cape Verde. Data are for all SOEs. Figures for net transfers are based on government-to-SOE transfers only. Source: IMF.

Central African Republic. Overall balance numbers are from ADI. Source: ADI (various issues); World Bank.

Comoros. Value added figures are for enterprises in the trade sector (SCH, ONICOR, SOCOVIA), tourism (COMOTEL, airport M-H, NSCTA), state-owned utilities (OPT, EEDC), and other (SNI, ECOPOR). Source: World Bank and IMF.

Congo. Among major SOEs are AIC, Hydro-Congo, SNE, SUCO, CIDOLOU/SOCICO, SNDE, and ONPT, which includes the Postal Savings Bank. The sharp increase in SOE contribution to GDP in 1986 is a result of a sharp contraction in GDP rather than an increase in SOE value added. Investment figures are based on the government's investment budget and thus exclude any SOE investment carried out of the budget. Employment numbers are from ADI and refer to share in formal employment. Overall balance numbers are from ADI. Source: ADI (various issues); World Bank and IMF.

Côte d'Ivoire. Value added figure is from Floyd, Gray, and Short. Investment figures are for all SOEs. Overall balance figures for 1978–79 are from Floyd, Gray, and Short; for 1982–86, from ADI. Employment numbers are from ADI (various issues) and refer to share in formal employment.

Source: ADI (various issues); World Bank; Floyd, Gray, and Short (1984).

Egypt. Data cover nonfinancial SOEs, including economic authorities. Value added series are estimated from three data points based on published studies pointing to little change in the contribution of SOEs to economic activity. Investment figures include financial and insurance SOEs, but these represent a very small share of total SOE sector investment. Source: Public Enterprise Information Center, Cairo; World Bank; Handoussa and Potter (1991).

Gabon. Source: ADI (various issues); World Bank.

Gambia, The. Data cover selected major nonfinancial SOEs: Telecom Co., River Transport Co., Atlantic Hotel, Cooperative Union, Gambia Airways, National Trading Co., Port Authority, Gambia Produce Marketing Board, Public Transport Corporation, Utility Corporation, Livestock Marketing Board, and Wing Africa Ltd. Overall balance figures are from ADI. Source: ADI (various issues); World Bank.

Ghana. Value added numbers for 1984–87 are from ADI; for 1988–91, estimated from the average value added share of thirteen core nonfinancial SOEs in total nonfinancial SOEs' value added for 1984–87. All other data except employment refer to thirteen core nonfinancial SOEs: Water and Sewerage Corporation, Electricity Corporation, Volta River Authority, Post and Telecommunications Corporation, Airways Corporation, Supply Commission, State Shipping Corporation, Ports and Harbors Authority, Railways Corporation, National Petroleum Corporation, Ghana Italian Petroleum Co., Ghana Oil Co., and Cocoa Board. Based on 1989 figures, there were close to 300 SOEs; the 14 core nonfinancial SOEs (the above 13 plus the National Procurement Agency) accounted for roughly 60 percent of total SOE employment, 72 percent of sales value, and 67 percent of value added. In 1991, the Cocoa Board accounted for 92 percent of all SOE investment. SOE employment figures for 1981–82 are from ADI. For 1986–91 they are for forty-two nonfinancial SOEs. For 1986 and 1991, they were estimated from the ratio of SOE employment in forty-two nonfinancial SOEs to that in the seventeen nonfinancial SOEs for which figures were available for 1987–90 and 1986–91, respectively. Overall balance numbers for 1980–83 are from ADI. Source: ADI (various issues); World Bank and IMF; State Enterprises Commission; *Ghana Quarterly Digest of Statistics*.

Guinea. The steep decline in the share of SOEs in economic activity from 25 percent in 1981 to about 9 percent in 1986 is apparently explained by an overstatement of the 1981 figure because of grossly overvalued exchange rates in the early 1980s rather than by any significant shrinking of the SOE sector (see Fukui). Net transfer figures for 1978–84 are from Nair and Fillippides. Employment numbers are from ADI and refer to share in formal employment. Source: ADI (various issues); World Bank; Fukui (1992); Nair and Fillippides (1989).

Guinea-Bissau. Source: ADI (various issues); World Bank.

Kenya. Employment figures are nonfinancial SOEs' share of modern sector employment. Overall balance numbers are estimated as operating balance minus capital expenditure. Source: ADI (various issues); World Bank and IMF; Investissement Développement Conseil (1993).

Madagascar. Employment numbers are from ADI and refer to share in formal employment. Source: ADI (various issues); World Bank.

Malawi. Data cover twelve major nonfinancial SOEs: ADMARC, Malawi Railways, ESCOM, Development Corporation, Housing Corporation, Air Malawi, Water Boards for Blantyre and Lilongwe, Malawi Book Service, Wood Industries Corporation, MIDCOR, and Malawi Dairy Industries. 1982–86 SOE employment is estimated based on a 15 percent share of SOE employment in aggregate SOE and private sector employment. SOE overall balances are estimated as operating balance minus capital expenditure. Source: *Malawi Economic Report* (1991); *Malawi Statistical Yearbook* (1987); World Bank.

Mali. Value added data are for twelve major nonfinancial SOEs: SOMIEX, OPAM, SCAER, Air Mali, COMATEX, EDM, ITEMA, PPM, SEPAMA, SEPOM, SMECMA, and SONATAM. Overall balance data are from ADI. Employment numbers are from ADI and refer to share in formal employment. Source: ADI (various issues); World Bank.

Mauritania. Overall balance data are from Nair and Fillippides. Source: ADI (various issues); World Bank and IMF; Nair and Fillippides (1989).

Mauritius. Value added figures are from the national accounts and refer to government enterprises in the manufacturing, construction, transport, and communication sectors. Data for SOE overall balances and net transfers for 1980–84 are from Nair and Fillippides. Employment numbers are from ADI and refer to share in formal employment. Source: *National Accounts of Mauritius* (various years); ADI (various issues); World Bank; Nair and Fillippides (1989).

Morocco. Net transfers data for 1985–90 are for ten major nonfinancial SOEs that account for over 80 percent of SOE investment: OCP (phosphates), ONE (electricity), ONEP (water), ONPT (telecom), ONCF (railways), ONDA (airports), ODEP (ports), RAM (airline), COMANAV (shipping), and BRAM (mining). Figures for SOE operating balances and investment for 1982–85 are for nine major nonfinancial SOEs. Source: ADI (various issues); World Bank.

Namibia. Data cover only nine major nonfinancial SOEs: NBC, NEITH, NFC, SWAWEK, TransNamib, FNDC, NAMCOR, Meat Co., and NHE. Investment share is derived as the sum of investment by state-owned business enterprises and state-owned corporations. SOE overall balances are estimated as operating balance minus capital expenditure. Source: IMF.

Niger. Data are for major nonfinancial SOEs. Of forty-two nonfinancial SOEs, the major ones are OPVN (cereals), NIGELEC (electricity and water), SONICHAR (power generation), RINI (rice processing), SONITEXTIL (textiles), SONIDEP (petroleum), OPT (post and telecom), SONARA (groundnut export), SNC (cement), and Air Niger. Overall balance data are from ADI. Source: ADI (various issues); World Bank and IMF.

Nigeria. Data cover only four major nonfinancial SOEs that accounted for 31 percent of cumulative government investment in the SOE sector. A 1990 World Bank study estimates that the SOE sector contributes 35 percent of GDP and accounts for a 20 percent share of modern sector employment. Excluding the petroleum sector, the SOE sector was estimated to account for about 10 percent of GDP. Investment and overall balance numbers are from ADI. Source: ADI (various issues); World Bank; Swanson and Wolde-Semait (1989).

Rwanda. Data are for sixty-two SOEs, of which thirty-two are wholly government owned, twelve are mixed, with at least 50 percent government ownership, and eighteen have majority private ownership. The value added share of wholly government-owned SOEs only is about 2 to 3 percent of GDP. SOE employment data are given as share of formal employment. Overall balance data are from ADI. For net transfers to SOEs, transfers

from SOEs to government comprise only SOE dividends to the government. Source: ADI (various issues); World Bank and IMF.

São Tome and Principe. Data cover eleven major nonfinancial SOEs, including ROSEMA (brewery), EMAG (printing), EMAE (electric and water authority), ECOMEX, Ecomin-Trading Enterprise, TRANSCOLMAR, TERRESTRE (public transport), CONSTRUCTORA (construction), EMAVE (poultry), and EMSERA (bricks). Source: IMF.

Senegal. Figures for 1987, 1988, and 1989 were estimated based on the share of nonfinancial SOEs in total investment and employment in 1987. SOE employment figures are reported as a share of formal sector employment (civil service plus CUCI estimates). Source: Contrôle Financier (CFP); ADI (various issues); World Bank and IMF.

Seychelles. Data refer to all SOEs. Source: IMF.

Sierra Leone. Data refer to all SOEs. Overall balance and employment numbers that refer to share in formal employment are from ADI. Source: ADI (various issues); World Bank and IMF.

South Africa. Source: South African Statistics (1990); *Quarterly Bulletin,* South African Reserve Bank (1992); IMF.

Sudan. The value added numbers are estimated based on World Bank studies suggesting that the contribution of the SOE sector, 48–50 percent of GDP, remained almost constant throughout the decade. Source: ADI (various issues); World Bank.

Tanzania. The 65 percent spurt in SOE investment for 1989 is attributed to a steep increase in water sector investments from 587 million shillings in 1988 to 34,160 million shillings in 1989. Net transfers figures for 1978–80 are from Nair and Fillippides. For later years, SOE-to-government transfers include dividends from the Bank of Tanzania from 1986–87 onward. This dividend was estimated to be 200 million shillings that year but had not been paid in the past. Source: *Tanzania Economic Survey,* 1988–90; ADI (various issues); World Bank.

Togo. Investment data are for eight major SOEs. Employment numbers are from ADI and refer to share in formal employment. Overall balance numbers are taken from ADI. Data for net transfers are obtained from country sources. Source: ADI (various issues); World Bank and IMF; Ministère de l'industrie et des sociétés d'Etat (1991).

Tunisia. Value added for 1981, 1982, and 1986 is estimated from figures for share of SOE sector in GDP for 1983–85 and value added figures for forty major SOEs for 1981, 1982, and 1986. Investment numbers are from World Bank BESD database. Source: ADI (various issues); World Bank.

Zaire. Figures for value added, overall balance, and employment (which refers to share in formal employment) are from ADI. Figures for net transfers for 1981–84 are from Nair and Fillippides. Overall balance numbers are from ADI. Source: ADI; World Bank; Nair and Fillippides (1989).

Zambia. Value added figures for 1987–91 are estimated based on share of ZIMCO in SOE value added for 1981–84. ZIMCO alone averaged a 14.3 percent share of GDP for 1987–92. 1980–84 figures, overall balances, and net transfers data are from ADI. Source: ADI (various issues); IMF.

Zimbabwe. Data cover twelve major SOEs. Employment numbers are from ADI and refer to share in formal employment. Overall balance numbers are from ADI. Source: ADI (various issues); IMF.

Asia

Bangladesh. Data for 1985–91 are for ten major nonfinancial SOEs. 1981–84 data are for five major nonfinancial SOEs only. SOE overall balances are estimated as operating balance minus capital expenditure. The overall deficit of twenty-five major nonfinancial SOEs excluding railways, post office, and telecom was about 5 percent of GDP for 1986–90. Source: World Bank and IMF.

Fiji. All state-owned corporations; investment numbers are from World Bank BESD database. Source: World Bank.

India. All data except employment figures cover nonfinancial SOEs owned by central, state, and local governments. Employment figures are for central nonfinancial SOEs only, which represented 70 percent of nonfinancial SOEs' value added in 1980–81 and 53 percent in 1989–90. Overall balances and net transfers data are for central nonfinancial SOEs only. Source: *India National Accounts Statistics* (1989, 1992); *Public Enterprise Survey* (various issues); World Bank.

Indonesia. SOE overall balances are estimated as operating balance minus capital expenditure. Source: World Bank and IMF; Indonesian Business Data Center; Premchand and Wijayasuriya (1987).

Korea, Republic of. Source: Economic Planning Board; Korean Development Institute; Economic Statistics Yearbook; Korea Statistical Yearbook; Ministry of Finance and Economy; Shirley (1991).

Malaysia. Value added figure is from Shaikh (1987). Data are for fifty nonfinancial SOEs for 1990, fifty-two to fifty-four nonfinancial SOEs for 1986–89, and thirty-six nonfinancial SOEs for 1980–85. SOE overall balances are estimated as operating balance minus capital expenditure. Data for net transfers for 1981–85 are from Nair and Fillippides. Source: World Bank and IMF; Malaysia *Quarterly Bulletin of Statistics;* Nair and Fillipides (1989); Shaikh (1991b).

Myanmar. Includes financial SOEs. Data for net transfers for 1978–86 are from Nair and Fillippides. Source: IMF; Nair and Fillipides (1989).

Nepal. Employment figures refer to share of nonagricultural employment. SOE overall balances are estimated as operating balance minus capital expenditure. Source: Ministry of Finance: Economic Survey, 1987–88; Performance Review of SOEs in Nepal (1981); IMF.

Pakistan. Value added series are estimated from three data points based on published studies pointing to little change in contribution of SOEs to economic activity. Source: Pakistan Statistical Yearbook (1989); Ministry of Production: Public Sector Industries—Annual Reports (1988–89, 1985–86); World Bank and IMF; Shirley (1989); Shaikh (1991a).

Papua New Guinea. Source: World Bank and IMF.

Philippines. Besides financial SOEs, SOEs in the educational, social, civic, cultural, and research sector are also excluded. Since no data are available for 1985, all figures for 1985 are estimated. Investment figures are for fourteen major nonfinancial government owned corporations (NFGOCs), which in 1989 accounted for 90 percent of total SOE investment. Source: Commission on Audit—*Annual Financial Report on Government Owned and Controlled Corporations* (various years); World Bank and IMF; Manasan and Buenaventura (1986).

Sri Lanka. Data for 1981–85 exclude some smaller nonfinancial SOEs. Value added figures are for thirty state-owned manufacturing enterprises (SMEs), including the three largest—Ceylon Petroleum, National Textiles, and Sri Lanka Cement—which account for 70 percent of all SME output. Investment figures for 1980–81 are from Nair and Fillippides. Employment figures for 1981–90 include government agencies and financial institutions. Prior to 1987, transfers to state-owned corporations include transfers to state-owned institutions, as no disaggregated data are

available. Since 1987, data for net transfers are for eleven monitored state-owned corporations. Capital transfers for 1986 are estimated. Source: Central Bank of Sri Lanka; World Bank and IMF.

Taiwan (China). Overall balance figures are estimated as operating balance minus capital expenditure. Source: Yearbook of Financial Statistics (1991); Taiwan Statistical Databook (1994); Statistical Yearbook (1994).

Thailand. Data for value added are for all SOEs, including financial SOEs. Source: World Bank and IMF; Charoenloet (1989).

Turkey. Data include nonfinancial SOEs that were under privatization schemes. Source: World Bank and IMF.

Western Samoa. Data for 1989–92 cover fifteen SOEs and statutory corporations; data for 1985–89 cover thirty-five SOEs and statutory corporations. Source: IMF.

Industrial Countries

Australia. SOE investment numbers refer to all state-owned corporate and quasi-corporate enterprises, including financial SOEs as defined in the OECD National Accounts Statistics. Source: OECD *National Accounts Statistics.*

Austria. SOE value added and investment numbers for 1978–79 include "nationalized industry," "other state holdings," and "mixed holdings" as reported by Centre Européen de l'entreprise publique (CEEP 1981). Figure for 1988 is an estimate for all (including municipal and provincial) nonfinancial SOEs (CEEP 1990). Source: CEEP (various years).

Belgium. Selected major SOEs only. Value added numbers are for SOEs in transport and communications only. SOE investment numbers are for SOEs in gas and electricity, water, transport, post, telegraph, telecom, radio, and TV only. Generally, SOEs are defined as including financial, housing, public administration, and hospitals. The figures have been adjusted where possible and annotated when not possible. To overcome the problem of missing observations, 1983 value added and investment figures are substituted when deriving respective industrial country averages for 1982. Source: CEEP (various years).

Denmark. SOE value added and investment numbers include regional and municipal SOEs. Source: CEEP (various years).

France. Generally, SOEs are defined as including agricultural, local, and municipal SOEs but excluding housing and financial SOEs. Value added and investment numbers for 1978–79 include financial SOEs. Source: CEEP (various years).

Germany. Refers to preunification Federal Republic of Germany. No postunification numbers were available. SOE value added and investment figures reported here include figures for SOEs in transport, industry, and commerce and exclude SOEs in housing, credit, and insurance. County and local SOEs are included. To overcome the problem of missing observations, a 1985 value added figure is substituted when deriving the industrial economy average for 1988. Source: CEEP (various years).

Greece. Value added numbers for 1986–89 are estimated. No figures are available for 1981–85. SOE investment numbers for 1978–79 and 1986–89 are for all nonfinancial SOEs. 1981–85 figures refer to fifty SOEs under the General Secretariat for Public Enterprise. To overcome the problem of missing observations when deriving averages for industrial economies the 1982 value added figure is estimated as the average of 1979 and 1986, and 1986 value added figures are substituted for 1985. Source: CEEP (various years).

Ireland. Figures include all SOEs, as disaggregation was not available. Source: CEEP (various years).

Italy. Municipal SOEs are included. To overcome the problem of missing observations when deriving industrial economies' averages, the 1985 value added figure is estimated as the average of 1982 and 1988, and 1978 value added and investment figures are substituted for 1979. Source: CEEP (various years).

Japan. SOE investment numbers are for all state-owned corporate and quasi-corporate enterprises, including financial SOEs as defined by OECD *National Accounts Statistics.* Source: OECD *National Accounts Statistics.*

Netherlands. SOE investment numbers are for selected enterprises: Dutch Railways, KLM, PTT, DSM, and Gas Union. Agriculture and public services are not included. Source: CEEP (various years).

Norway. SOE investment numbers are for all state-owned corporate and quasi-corporate enterprises, including financial SOEs as defined by *OECD National Accounts Statistics.* Source: *OECD National Accounts Statistics.*

Portugal. Value added numbers for 1983–84 include financial SOEs. For all other years, both value added and investment numbers are for nonfinancial SOEs. To overcome the problem of missing observations, a 1983 value added figure is substituted when deriving the industrial country average for 1979 and 1982. Source: CEEP (various years).

Spain. Nonfinancial SOEs include industry, transport and communications, energy and mines, and commerce and services. Financial and housing are excluded. Source: CEEP (various years).

Sweden. Numbers refer to all SOEs as defined by the *UN National Accounts Statistics.* Source: *UN National Accounts Statistics.*

United Kingdom. SOE investment numbers are for all state-owned corporate and quasi-corporate enterprises, including financial SOEs as defined by OECD *National Accounts Statistics.* Source: OECD *National Accounts Statistics.*

United States. Value added numbers refer to the "statistical discrepency" in the UN *National Accounts Statistics* and are identified in the footnote as government enterprises. SOE investment numbers are for all state-owned corporate and quasi-corporate enterprises, including financial SOEs as defined by OECD *National Accounts Statistics.* To overcome the problem of missing observations, 1980 and 1987 value added figures are substituted when deriving the industrial country average for 1979 and 1988, respectively. Source: OECD *National Accounts Statistics;* UN *National Accounts Statistics.*

References

Aharoni, Yair. 1986. *The Evolution and Management of State Owned Enterprises.* Cambridge, Mass.: Ballinger.

Arriagada Herrera, Genero, and Carol Graham. 1994. "Chile: Sustaining Adjustment during Democratic Transition." In Haggard, S., and S. Webb. eds., *Voting for Reform: Democracy, Political Liberalization, and Economic Adjustment.* New York: Oxford University Press.

Aspe, Pedro. 1991. "Thoughts on Structural Transformation in Mexico: The Case of Privatization of Public Sector Enterprises." Address given at the World Affairs Council in Los Angeles.

Ayubi, Nazih. 1991. *The State and Public Policies in Egypt since Sadat.* Reading, U.K.: Ithaca Press.

Baer, Herbert, and Cheryl Gray. 1994. "Debt as a Control Device in Transitional Economies: The Experiences of Hungary and Poland." Presentation to a Joint Conference of the World Bank and the Central European University, Privatization Project, Washington, D.C.

Banerji, Arup, and Richard H. Sabot. 1994. "Wage Distortions, Overmanning, and Reform in Developing Country Public Enterprises." Background Paper. Policy Research Department, World Bank, Washington, D.C.

Baron, David. 1988. "Regulation and Legislative Choice." *RAND Journal of Economics* 19 (3):553–68.

Barro, Robert J. 1991. "Economic Growth in a Cross-Section of Countries." *Quarterly Journal of Economics* 106:407–444.

Bates, R. H., and A. O. Krueger. 1993. *Political and Economic Interactions in Economic Policy Reform.* Cambridge, Mass: Blackwell.

Bennett, James T., and Manuel H. Johnson. 1979. "Public versus Private Provision of Collective Goods and Services: Garbage Collection Revisited." *Public Choice.* 34(1):55–63.

Berg, Eliot. 1993. "Privatization in Sub-Saharan Africa: Results, Prospects, and New Approaches." Consultant Report. Development Alternatives Inc., Bethesda, Md.

Besanko, David, and David Sappington. 1987. *Designing Regulatory Policy with Limited Information.* New York: Harwood Academic Publishers.

Bishop, Matthew, and John Kay. 1988. *Does Privatization Work? Lessons from the U.K.* London: London Business School.

Boardman, Anthony E., and Aidan R. Vining. April 1989. "Ownership and Performance in Competitive Environments: A Comparison of the Performance of Private, Mixed, and State-Owned Enterprises." *Journal of Law and Economics* 32:1–33.

Bokil, S. V. 1990. "A Study of Liberalization in the Southern Cone Countries of Latin America: Lessons for India." In Ashok Gunha, ed., *Economic Liberalization, Industrial Structure, and Growth in India.* Delhi: Oxford University Press.

Borcherding, E., W. W. Pommerehne, and F. Schneider. 1982. "Comparing the Efficiency of Private and Public Production: The Evidence from Five Countries." *Zeitschrift für Nationalokonomie.* Supplement 2:127–56.

Boycko, Maxim, Andrei Shleifer, and Robert W. Vishny. 1993. "A Theory of Privatization." Mimeo.

Brada, Josef, and A. E. King. 1993. "Sequencing Measures for the Transformation of Socialist Economies to Capitalism: Is There a J-Curve for Economic Reforms?" In K. Poznanski, ed., *Stabilization and Transformation of the Polish Economy.* Boston: Kluwer Academic Publishers.

Brada, Josef, A. E. King, and Chia Ying Ma. 1993. "Industrial Economics of the Transition: Determinants of Enterprise Efficiency in Czechoslovakia and Hungary." Policy Research Paper EE-RPS. World Bank, Washington, D.C.

Broadman, Harry. 1995. *Meeting the Challenge of Chinese Enterprise Reform.* Discussion Paper 283. Washington, D.C.: World Bank.

Brown, L., M. Einhorn, and I. Vogelsang. 1991. "Toward Improved and Practical Incentive Regulation." *Journal of Regulatory Economics* 3:323–38.

Bruno, M., S. Fischer, E. Helpman, N. Liviatan, and L. Meridor, eds. 1991. *Lessons of Economic Stabilization and Its Aftermath.* Cambridge, Mass.: MIT Press.

Bruno, M., and William Easterly. 1994. "Inflation Crises and Long-Run Growth." Draft. Policy Research Department, Macroeconomic and Growth Division. World Bank, Washington, D.C.

Caillaud, B., R. Guesnerie, P. Rey, and J. Tirole. 1988. "Government Intervention in Production and Incentives Theory: A Review of Recent Contributions." *RAND Journal of Economics* 19 (1):1–26.

Candoy-Sekse, Rebecca. 1988. *Techniques of Privatization of State-Owned Enterprises.* Technical Paper 90, Vol III. Washington, D.C.: World Bank.

Caves, D. W., and L. R. Christensen. 1980. "The Relative Efficiency of Public and Private Firms in a Competitive Environment: The Case of the Canadian Railroads." *Journal of Public Economy* 88:958–76.

CEEP (Centre européen de l'entreprise publique). Various years. *Annales du CEEP.* Bruxelles.

Ceska, Roman. 1993. "Privatization in the Czech Republic." In Andreja Böhm and Marko Simoneti, eds., *Privatization in Central and Eastern Europe.* Ljubljana, Slovenia: Central and Eastern European Privatization Network.

CETESB (Companhia de Technologia de Saneamento Ambiental). 1994. "Acão de CETESB em Cubatão: Situacão em Junho de 1994." São Paulo, Brazil.

Charoenloet, Voravidh. 1989. "The Crisis of State Enterprise in Thailand." *Journal of Contemporary Asia* 19:206–217.

Clemente, Lino. 1994. "Efectividad de la reforma de empresas públicas en Venezuela: La privatización de la Compañía Anónima Nacional Teléfonos de Venezuela, CANTV." Office of Evaluation, Inter-American Development Bank, Washington, D.C.

Cordón, Roberto. 1993a. "The Political Framework of Privatization in Chile." Background Paper. Policy Research Department, World Bank: Washington, D.C. Obtainable from the author at Escuela de Administración, Pontificia Universidad Católica de Chile.

—— 1993b. "The Reform of Mexican Public Enterprises." Background Paper. Policy Research Department, World Bank, Washington, D.C. Obtainable from the author at Escuela de Administración, Pontificia Universidad Católica de Chile.

Dabrowski, J., M. Federowicz, and A. Levitas. 1991. "Polish State Enterprises and the Properties of Performance: Stabilization, Marketization, Privatization." *Politics and Society* 19 (4).

Dabrowski, J., M. Federowicz, and J. Szomburg. 1992. "Privatization of the Polish State-Owned Enterprises." *Economic Transformation* 29. The Gdansk Institute for Market Economies.

Daily Graphic. 1992. "More Election Results Declared." Accra, Ghana.

De Gregorio, José. 1993. "Inflation, Taxation, and Long Run Growth." *Journal of Monetary Economics* 31 (June):271–98.

de Keijzer, J. Th. A. 1993. "Aiming for See-Through Laws." In *Privatisation in Emerging Markets.* London: IFR Publishing.

Dekle, Robert, and Kenneth Sokoloff. 1990. "Patterns of Productivity Growth in South Korean Manufacturing Industries 1963–1979." *Journal of Economic Development* 33:309–327.

Demirgüç-Kunt, Asli, and Ross Levine. 1994. "The Financial System and Public Enterprise Reform: Concepts and Cases." Policy Research Working Paper 1319. World Bank, Washington, D.C.

Dewatripont, M., and G. Roland. 1993. *Design of Reform Packages under Uncertainty.* Discussion Paper 860:1–32. U.K.: Centre for Economic Policy Research.

Dittus, Peter. 1993. "Finance and Corporate Governance in Eastern Europe." Bank for International Settlements, Basle, Switzerland.

Dyer Cissé, Nichola. 1994. "The Impact of Performance Contracts on Public Enterprise Performance." Background paper. Policy Research Department, World Bank, Washington, D.C.

Easterly, William, Carlos Alfredo Rodriguez, and Klaus Schmidt-Hebbel, eds. 1994. *Public Sector Deficits and Macroeconomic Performance.* New York: Oxford University Press.

Easterly, William, and Sergio Rebelo. 1993. "Fiscal Policy and Economic Growth: An Empirical Investigation." *Journal of Monetary Economics* 32 (3):417–58.

Edwards, S., and G. Tabellini. 1991. "The Political Economy of Fiscal Policy and Inflation in Developing Countries: An Empirical Analysis." Policy Research Working Paper 703. World Bank, Washington, D.C.

Einhorn, Michael A., ed. 1990. *Price Caps and Incentive Regulation in Telecommunications.* Boston: Kluwer Academic Publishers.

EIU (Economist Intelligence Unit). 1992. "The Czech Republic Country Profile." London.

——. 1993. "Turkey Country Profile." London.

——. 1994. "Ghana Country Profile." London.

——. 1994–95. "Poland Country Profile." London.

El-Issawy, Ibrahim H. 1983. *Labour Force, Employment, and Unemployment.* Employment Opportunities and Equity in Egypt Papers 4. Geneva: International Labor Office.

Esfahani, Hadi. 1994. "Regulations, Institutions, and Economic Performance: The Political Economy of the Philippines' Telecommunications Sector." Policy Research Working Paper 1294. World Bank, Washington, D.C.

Estrin, Saul, Alan Gelb, and Inderjit Singh. 1993. "Restructuring, Viability, and Privatization: A Comparative Study of Enterprise Adjustment in Transition." Policy Research Paper EE-RPS 31. World Bank, Washington, D.C.

Estrin, Saul, Mark Schaffer, and Inderjit Singh. 1993. "Enterprise Adjustments in Transition Economies: Czechoslovakia, Hungary, and Poland." Policy Research Paper EE-RPS 8. World Bank, Washington, D.C.

Etievent, Alain & Associés. 1993. "Analyse de la SOTRAC." Consultant report commissioned by the World Bank and Coopération française. Grenoble, France.

Europa World Yearbook. 1994. London: Europa Publications.

European Bank for Reconstruction and Development. 1994. *Annual Economic Review.* London: Libra Group Limited.

Fischer, Stanley. 1993. "Role of Macroeconomic Factors in Growth." *Journal of Monetary Economics* 32 (December):485–512.

Floyd, Robert, Clive Gray, and R. P. Short. 1984. *Public Enterprise in Mixed Economies: Some Macroeconomic Aspects.* Washington, D.C.: International Monetary Fund.

Fukui, Ryu. 1992. *Study on the Historical Performance of the Public Enterprise Sector in Guinea.* Tokyo: Japan Economic Research Institute.

Galal, Ahmed. 1991. *Public Enterprise Reform: Lessons from the Past and Issues for the Future.* Discussion Paper 119. Washington, D.C.: World Bank.

———. 1992. "Chile." In Ahmed Galal and others, eds., *Welfare Consequences of Selling Public Enterprises: Case Studies from Chile, Malaysia, Mexico, and the UK.* Washington, D.C.: World Bank.

———. 1994. "Regulation and Commitment in the Development of Telecommunications in Chile." Policy Research Working Paper 1278. World Bank, Washington, D.C.

Galal, Ahmed, Leroy Jones, Pankaj Tandon, and Ingo Vogelsang. 1994. *Welfare Consequences of Selling Public Enterprises: An Empirical Analysis.* New York: Oxford University Press.

Galal, Ahmed, and Bharat Nauriyal. 1995. Forthcoming. "Regulation of Telecom in Developing Countries: Outcomes, Incentives, and Commitment." Policy Research Paper. World Bank, Washington, D.C.

Ganguly, Bengendu, and Mira Ganguly. 1982. *Dimensions of Electoral Behavior*. Calcutta: Pearl Publishers.

Gelb, Alan, Erika Jorgensen, and Inderjit Singh. 1992. "Life after the Polish 'Big Bang': Episodes of Preprivatization Enterprise Behavior." In Ayre Hillman and Branko Milanovic, eds., *The Transition from Socialism in Eastern Europe*. Washington, D.C.: World Bank.

Gelb, Alan, and Inderjit Singh. 1994. "Public Enterprise Reforms in Transitional Economies." Background paper. Policy Research Department, World Bank, Washington, D.C.

Gomulka, Stanislaw. 1994. "The Financial Situation of Polish Enterprise (1992–1993) and Its Impact on Monetary and Fiscal Policies." *The Economics of Transition* 2 (June).

Gora, Marek. 1993. "Industrial Employment Adjustment during Transition: The Case of Polish Industry." Policy Research Paper EE-PB 7. World Bank, Washington, D.C.

Groves, Theodore, Yong-Miao Hong, John McMillan, and Barry Naughton. 1993. "Autonomy and Incentives in Chinese State Enterprises." Discussion Paper 93-16. Department of Economics, University of California, San Diego. Reprinted 1994 in the *Quarterly Journal of Economics* 109 (1):183–209.

Gurr, T., K. Jaggers, and W. Moore. 1989. *Polity II Codebook*. Assembled by ICPSR (Inter-University Consortium for Political and Social Research). Ann Arbor: University of Michigan.

Gylfason, T. 1991. "Endogenous Growth and Inflation." Seminar Papers, 502. Institute for International Economic Studies, University of Stockholm.

Hachette, Dominique. 1988. "Wage and Employment Policies in Chile." Mimeo. Universidad Católica de Chile.

Hachette, Dominique, and Rolf Lüders. 1992. *La privatización en Chile*. Centro internacional para el desarollo económico (CINDE). San Francisco: ICS Press.

Haggard, Stephen, and Steven B. Webb, eds. 1994. *Voting for Reform: Democracy, Political Liberalization, and Economic Adjustment*. New York: Oxford University Press.

Handoussa, Heba A. 1983. *Public Sector Employment and Productivity in the Egyptian Economy.* Employment Opportunities and Equity in Egypt Papers 7. Geneva: International Labour Office.

Handoussa, H., and G. Potter, eds. 1991. *Employment and Structural Adjustment: Egypt in the 1990s.* Cairo: American University in Cairo Press.

Hegstad, Sven Olaf, and Ian Newport. 1987. *Management Contracts: Main Features and Design Issues.* Technical Paper 65. Washington, D.C.: World Bank.

Herbst, Jeffrey. 1991. "Labor in Ghana under Structural Adjustment: The Politics of Acquiescence." In D. Rothchild, ed., *Ghana—The Political Economy of Recovery.* Boulder: Lynne Rienner.

Hettige, Hemamala, Mainul Huq, Sheoli Pargal, and David Wheeler. 1995. "Determinants of Pollution Abatement in Developing Countries: Evidence from South-East Asia." Paper presented at the ACAES session of American Economic Association/Allied Social Science Association meetings, Washington, D.C.

Hill, Alice, and Manuel Abdala. Forthcoming. "Regulation, Institutions, and Commitment: Privatization and Regulation in the Argentine Telecommunications Sector." In Brian Levy and Pablo Spiller, eds., forthcoming, *Regulations, Institutions, and Commitment: Comparative Studies of Telecommunications.* New York: Cambridge University Press.

Hwa, Erh-Cheng. 1992. "Enterprise Reform in China: A Background Note." Draft paper. World Bank Mission, Beijing, China.

Ibrahim, Saad Eddin. 1994. "Governance and Structural Adjustment: The Egyptian Case." Paper presented at the World Bank Governance and Successful Adjustment Conference, Washington, D.C.

ILO (International Labour Organization). Various years. Year Book of Labour Statistics. Geneva.

International Telecommunications Union. 1994. *World Telecommunications Development Report.* Geneva.

———. Various years. *Yearbook of Common Carrier Telecommunications Statistics.* Geneva.

Investissement Développement Conseil. 1993. "Kenya: Study of Subsidies and Other Financial Flows in Favor of Major PEs." Consultant report. Paris.

Jefferson, Gary. 1993. "Are China's Rural Enterprises Outperforming State-Owned Enterprises?" Policy Research Paper CH-RPS 24. World Bank, Washington, D.C.

Jefferson, Gary, and Thomas Rawski. 1992. "A Theory of Economic Reform." Policy Research Paper CH-RPS 15. World Bank, Washington, D.C.

Jefferson, Gary, Thomas Rawski, and Yuxin Zheng. 1992. "Growth, Efficiency, and Convergence in China's State and Collective Industry." *Economic Development and Cultural Changes* 40(2):239–66.

———. 1993. "Innovation and Reform in Chinese Industry: A Preliminary Analysis of Survey Data." Policy Research Paper CH-RPS 16. World Bank, Washington, D.C. Reprinted in *Zhongguo shengchanlubiandong qushi zhi yanjiu* (Studies in the trend of productivity in China). Beijing: Shehui kexue wenxian chubanshe.

Jones, Leroy. 1975. *Public Enterprise and Economic Development: The Korean Case.* Seoul: Korea Development Institute.

———. 1981. "Towards a Performance Evaluation Methodology for Public Enterprises: With Special Reference to Pakistan." Paper presented at the international symposium on Economic Performance of Public Enterprises, Islamabad.

———. 1985. "Public Enterprise for Whom? Perverse Distributional Consequences of Public Operational Decisions." *Economic Development and Cultural Changes* 33 (2):333–47.

———. 1991. *Performance Evaluation for Public Enterprises.* Discussion Paper 122. Washington, D.C.: World Bank.

Jones, L., and E. Mason. 1982. "Role of Economic Factors in Determining the Size and Structure of the Public Enterprise Sector in Less Developed Countries with Mixed Economies." In Leroy Jones, ed., *Public Enterprise in Less Developed Countries.* New York: Cambridge University Press.

Ka, Samba, and Nicolas van de Walle. 1994. "Senegal: Stalled Reform in a Dominant Party System." In S. Haggard and S. Webb, eds., *Voting for Reform: Democracy, Political Liberalization, and Economic Adjustment.* New York: Oxford University Press.

Kaufman, Robert R., Carlos Bazdresch, and Blanca Heredia.1994. "Mexico: Radical Reform in a Dominant Party System." In S. Haggard and S. Webb, eds., *Voting for Reform: Democracy, Political Liberalization, and Economic Adjustment.* New York: Oxford University Press.

Kikeri, Sunita, John Nellis, and Mary Shirley. 1992. *Privatization: The Lessons of Experience.* Washington, D.C.: World Bank.

Kjellstrom, S. B. 1990. "Privatization in Turkey." Policy Research Working Paper 532. World Bank, Washington, D.C.

Klaus, Vaclav. 1993. "Privatization Experience: The Czech Case." In Andreja Böhm and Marko Simoneti, eds., *Privatization in Central and Eastern Europe.* Ljubljana, Slovenia: Central and Eastern European Privatization Network.

Knack, Stephen, and Philip Keefer. Forthcoming. "Institutions and Economic Performance: Cross-Country Tests Using Alternative Institutional Measures." *Economics and Politics.*

Kornai, Jano. 1980. *The Economics of Shortage.* Amsterdam: North Holland.

———. 1990. *The Road to a Free Economy.* New York: W. W. Norton.

Kwesi, Jonah. 1993. "Political Parties, Party Tradition, and the Transition to Multiparty Politics in Ghana, 1991–93." Mimeo. University of Ghana, Legon.

Lall, Rajiv. 1994. Country Economic Memorandum. Report 13399-CHA. World Bank, Washington, D.C.

Larrain, F., and M. Selowsky, eds. 1991. *The Public Sector and the Latin American Crisis.* San Francisco: ICS Press.

Leith, J. Clark, and Michael F. Lofchie. 1993. "The Political Economy of Structural Adjustment in Ghana." In Robert H. Bates and Anne O. Krueger, eds., *Political and Economic Interactions in Economic Policy Reform.* Cambridge, Mass; Oxford, U.K.: Blackwell.

Levy, Brian, and Pablo Spiller, eds. Forthcoming. *Regulations, Institutions, and Commitment: Comparative Studies of Telecommunications.* New York: Cambridge University Press.

López-de-Silanes, F. 1993. "Determinants of Privatization Prices." Mimeo. National Bureau of Economic Research (NBER), Harvard University.

Lüders, Rolf. 1990. "Chile's Massive SOE Divestiture Program, 1975–90: Failures and Successes." Paper presented at the World Bank Conference on Privatization and Ownership Changes in Eastern and Central Europe.

Manasan, Rosario G., and C. Buenaventura. 1986. "A Macroeconomic Overview of Public Enterprises in the Philippines, 1975–84." Staff Paper 86-03. Philippine Institute for Development Studies, Manila.

Manasan, Rosario G., and Ponciano S. Intal, Jr. 1992. "Private Sector-Led Development Strategy and the Role of Government in the Philippines." Prepared for the Senior Policy Forum on the Private

Sector-Led Development Strategy and the Role of Government in Developing Countries, Korea Development Institute, Seoul.

Manion, Melanie. 1993. *Retirement of Revolutionaries in China: Public Policies, Social Norms, Private Interests.* Princeton: Princeton University Press.

Martin del Campo, Antonio, and Donald R. Winkler. 1991. "State-Owned Enterprise Reform in Latin America." Occasional Paper 2. Latin America Technical Department, Public Sector Modernization Division (LATPS). World Bank, Washington, D.C.

Megginson, William, Robert Nash, and Matthias van Randenborgh. 1994. "The Financial and Operating Performance of Newly-Privatized Firms: An International Empirical Analysis." *Journal of Finance* 49 (2):403–452.

Millward, R. 1982. "The Comparative Performance of Public and Private Ownership." In Lord E. Roll, ed., *The Mixed Economy.* New York: Macmillan.

Millward, R., and D. M. Parker. 1983. "Public and Private Enterprise: Comparative Behavior and Relative Efficiency." In R. Millward, D. M. Parker, L. Rosenthal, M. T. Summer, and N. Topman, eds., *Public Sector Economics.* London and New York: Longman.

Milor, Vedat. 1994. "Political Economy of Public Enterprise Reform and Privatization in the Czech Republic and Poland." Background paper. Policy Research Department, World Bank, Washington, D.C.

Molinar Horcasitas, Juan. 1991. *El tiempo de la legitimidad: Elecciones, autoritarismo y democracia en México.* Mexico: Cal y Arena.

Molinar Horcasitas, Juan, and Jeffrey Weldon. 1990. "Elecciones de 1988 en México: Crisis del autoritarismo." *Revista Mexicana de Sociología* 52 (4):229–62.

Morin, Pierre. 1993. "Senegal: Towards the Next Stages in PE Reform and Privatization." West Africa Department, Industry and Energy Division, World Bank, Washington, D.C.

Mukul. 1991. "Workers against Privatization." *Economic and Political Weekly* 1781–5. India.

Nair G., and A. Fillipides. 1989. "How Much Do State-Owned Enterprises Contribute to Public Sector Deficits in Developing Countries—and Why?" Working Paper 45. World Bank, Washington, D.C.

Nellis, John. 1989. "Contract Plans and Public Enterprise Performance." Policy, Planning, and Research Working Paper 118. World Bank, Washington, D.C.

Ninsin, Kwame A. 1991. "The PNDC and the Problem of Legitimacy." In D. Rothchild, ed., *Ghana: The Political Economy of Recovery.* Boulder: Lynne Rienner.

North, Douglass C. 1990. *Institutions, Institutional Change, and Economic Performance.* New York: Cambridge University Press.

OECD (Organization for Economic Cooperation and Development). 1992. *Integration of Developing Countries into the International Trading System.* Paris.

———. Various years. *National Accounts Statistics.* Paris.

Onis, Ziya, and Steven B. Webb. 1992. "Political Economy of Policy Reform in Turkey in the 1980s." Policy Research Working Paper 1059. World Bank, Washington, D.C.

Pargal, Sheoli, and David Wheeler. 1995. "Informal Regulation of Industrial Pollution in Developing Countries: Evidence from Indonesia." Policy Research Working Paper 1416. World Bank, Washington, D.C.

Pinto, B., M. Belka, and S. Krajewski. 1992. "Microeconomics of Transformation in Poland: A Survey of State Enterprise Responses." Staff Working Paper 982. World Bank, Washington, D.C.

———. 1993. "Transforming State Enterprise in Poland: Evidence on Adjustment by Manufacturing Firms." Brookings Papers on Economic Activity 1:213–70.

Polity II dataset—See Gurr, Jaggers, and Moore (1989).

Premchand, A., and P. M. W. Wijaysuriya. 1987. *Indonesia: Financial Performance of State Enterprises, 1982–86.* Fiscal Affairs Department, International Monetary Fund, Washington, D.C.

Privatisation Yearbook. 1992. London: Privatisation International.

Ranganathan, A. 1987. "Public Enterprise Preferences." Consultant report. New Dehli.

Rivlin, Paul. 1985. *The Dynamics of Economic Policy-Making in Egypt.* New York: Praeger.

Romer, Thomas, and Howard Rosenthal. 1987. *Public Regulation: New Perspectives on Institutions and Policies.* MIT Press Series on the Regulation of Economic Activity 14. Cambridge, Mass.: MIT Press.

Rosati, Dariusz. 1993. "The Impact of the Soviet Trade Shock on Output Levels in Central and Eastern European Economies." Paper presented at the conference on Output Declines in Eastern Europe—Prospects for Recovery, International Institute for Applied Systems Analysis (IIASA). Austria.

Ross, S. 1991. "The Economic Theory of Agency: The Principal's Problem." In Robert Kuenne, ed., *Microeconomics: Theoretical and Applied.* International Library of Critical Writings in Economics 2 (11). Aldershot, U.K. and Brookfield, Vt.: Elgar.

Roth, Gabriel. 1987. "The Private Provision of Public Services in Developing Countries." EDI Series in Economic Development. New York: Oxford University Press.

Rothchild, Donald, ed. 1991. *Ghana: The Political Economy of Recovery.* Boulder: Lynne Rienner.

Sachs, Jeffrey D., and Wing Thye Woo. 1994. "Structural Factors in the Economic Reforms of China, Eastern Europe, and the Former Soviet Union." *Economic Policy* 18 (April):101–145.

Sader, Frank. 1993. "Privatization and Foreign Direct Investment in the Developing World, 1988–92." Policy Research Working Paper 1202. World Bank, Washington, D.C.

——. 1994. "Privatization Techniques and Foreign Investment in Developing Countries, 1988–93." World Bank, Washington, D.C.

Saez, Raul E. 1992. "An Overview of Privatization in Chile: The Episodes, the Results, and the Lessons." Consultant report. Contact author at CIEPLAN, Santiago, Chile.

Sappington, David E. M. 1991. "Incentives in Principal-Agent Relationships." *Journal of Economic Perspective* 5 (2):45–66.

Sappington, David E. M., and Joseph E. Stiglitz. 1987. "Privatization, Information, and Incentives." National Bureau of Economic Research (NBER) Working Paper 2196. Harvard University, Cambridge, Mass.

Schaffer, Mark. 1993. "The Enterprise Sector and the Emergence of the Polish Fiscal Crisis, 1990–91." Policy Research Working Paper 1195. World Bank, Washington, D.C.

Schmalensee, R. and R. Willig, eds. 1989. *Handbook of Industrial Organization.* Amsterdam: North-Holland.

Sephton, Graham. 1993. "Dual Markets for Investors." In *Privatization in Emerging Markets.* Washington, D.C.: World Equity/IFC.

Shaikh, A. H. 1991a. "Financing Pakistan's Development through Improved Public Sector Management." In A. Nisam, ed., *Financing Pakistan's Development in the Nineties.* New York: Oxford University Press.

——. 1991b. *Malaysia's Public Enterprises: A Performance Evaluation.* Development Discussion Paper 391. Cambridge, Mass.: Harvard Institute for International Development.

Shaikh, A. H., and M. Minovi. 1994. "Management Contracts: A Review of International Experience." Background Paper. World Bank, Policy Research Department, Washington, D.C.

Sherif, Khaled. 1992. "Egypt's Public Enterprise Experience." Published in Arabic. Cairo: Al-Ahram.

Sherif, Khaled, and Regina Soos. 1993. "Egypt's Liberalization Experience and Its Impact on State-Owned Enterprise Industrial Performance." In Iliya Harik and Dennis Sullivan, eds., *Privatization in the Middle East*. Bloomington, Ind.: Indiana University Press.

Shirk, Susan L. 1993. *The Political Logic of Economic Reform in China*. Berkeley: University of California Press.

Shirley, Mary. 1989. "Evaluating the Performance of Public Enterprises in Pakistan." Policy, Planning, and Research Working Paper 160. World Bank, Washington, D.C.

———. 1991. "Improving Public Enterprise Performance: Lessons from South Korea." *Annales de l'economie publique sociale et coopérative* 62 (1). De Boeck Université, Brussels.

Shirley, Mary, and John Nellis. 1991. *Public Enterprise Reform: The Lessons of Experience*. Washington, D.C.: Economic Development Institute of the World Bank.

Siemens Aktiengesellschaft. 1993. "National Telephone Tariffs: Worldwide Study Including Detailed Comparison." Munich.

Singh, Inderjit, and Gary Jefferson. 1993. "State Enterprises in China: Down from the Commanding Heights." *Transition* 4 (8). World Bank, Washington, D.C.

Singh, Inderjit, Geng Xiao, and Dilip Ratha. 1994. "Nonstate Enterprises as an Engine of Growth: An Analysis of Provincial Industrial Growth in Postreform China." Policy Research Working Paper CH-RPS 20. World Bank, Washington, D.C.

Société Nationale des Télécommunications du Sénégal (SPNATEL). 1989. "Rapport de suivi de l'execution du contrat plan 86–89 entre l'Etat et la SONATEL á la date du 30/06/1989." Dakar, Senegal.

Song, Dae Hee. 1988. "Korea Public Enterprise Performance Evaluation System." *Asian Economic Journal* 106–138.

———. 1993. "The Political Economy of Public Enterprise Reform in Korea." Background paper. Policy Research Department, World Bank, Washington, D.C.

Spiller, Pablo, and Cezley Sampson. 1995. "Regulation, Institutions, and Commitment: The Jamaican Telecommunications Sector." In

Brian Levy and Pablo Spiller, eds., *Regulations, Institutions, and Commitment: Comparative Studies of Telecommunications.* New York: Cambridge University Press.

State Enterprises Commission (SEC). 1991. *1991 SOE Performance Evaluation Report.* Accra, Ghana.

———. 1993. *The SOE Reform Program 1984/1992: Review and Recommendations.* Accra, Ghana.

State Statistical Bureau of the People's Republic of China. Various years. *China Statistical Yearbook.* Beijing: China Statistical Publishing House.

Stiglitz, Joseph E. 1974. "Incentives and Risk Sharing in Sharecropping." *Review of Economic Studies* 41:219–55.

Svejnar, Jan, and Katherine Terrell. 1990. *Labor Redundancy in the Transport Sector: The Case of Chile.* Washington, D.C.: World Bank.

———. 1991. "Reducing Labor Redundancy in State-Owned Enterprises." Policy Research and External Affairs Working Paper 792. World Bank, Washington, D.C.

Swanson, D., and T. Wolde-Semait. 1989. *Africa's Public Enterprise Sector and Evidence of Reforms.* Technical Paper 95. Washington, D.C.: World Bank.

Tandon, Pankaj. 1992. "Mexico." In Galal and others, eds., *Welfare Consequences of Selling Public Enterprises: Case Studies from Chile, Malaysia, Mexico, and the UK.* Washington, D.C.: World Bank.

Trivedi, Prajapati, ed. 1990. *Memorandum of Understanding: An Approach to Improving Public Enterprise Performance.* New Delhi: International Management Publishers.

UNCTAD (United Nations Conference on Trade and Development). 1987. *Handbook of Trade Control Measures of Developing Countries.* New York.

United Nations. Various years. *Yearbook of National Accounts Statistics.* New York.

Valenzuela, Arturo. 1978. *Breakdown of Democratic Regimes: Chile.* Baltimore: Johns Hopkins University Press.

Vickers, J., and G. Yarrow. 1988. *Privatization: An Economic Analysis.* Cambridge, Mass.: MIT Press.

Voravidh, Charoenloet. 1989. "Crisis of State Enterprises in Thailand." *Journal of Contemporary Asia* 19 (2):206–217.

Waterbury, John. 1993. *Exposed to Innumerable Delusions: Public Enterprise and State Power in Egypt, India, Mexico, and Turkey.* New York: Cambridge University Press.

Webster, Leila. 1993. *The Emergence of Private Sector Manufacturing in Poland.* Technical Paper 237. Washington, D.C.: World Bank.

Wellenius, B., and P. Stern, eds. 1994. *Implementing Reforms in the Telecommunications Sector: Lessons from Experience.* Washington, D.C.: World Bank.

Wijnbergen, Sweder van. 1991. "Should Price Reform Proceed Gradually or in a 'Big Bang'?" Working Paper 702. Latin America and the Caribbean Regional Office, World Bank, Washington, D.C.

Williamson, Oliver. 1975. *Markets and Hierarchies.* New York: The Free Press.

——. 1976. "Franchise Bidding for Natural Monopolies—in General and with Respect to CATV." *Bell Journal of Economics* 7 (1):73–104.

World Bank. Various years. *African Development Indicators.* Washington, D.C.

——. 1990. "Mexico." Telecommunications Sector Technical Report 3207. Latin America and the Caribbean regional office, Country Operations Department, Washington, D.C.

——. 1991. *Egypt: Alleviating Poverty during Structural Adjustment.* Country study. Washington, D.C.

——. 1992. "Mexico, Public Enterprise Reform" Loan 3086. Program Performance Audit Report. Operations Evaluations Department (OED). World Bank, Washington, D.C.

——. 1993a. "Africa Telecommunications Policy Study (Phase 1)." Malaysia Country Paper. Industry and Energy Department. Washington, D.C.

——. 1993b. "Regional Study on PE Reform and Privatization in Africa." Africa Technical Department. Washington, D.C.

——. 1993c. "Turkey: State-Owned Enterprise Sector Review," Report 10014 TU, Vol. II. Country Operations Division, Country Department I, Europe and Central Asia Region. Washington, D.C.

——. 1994a. "Performance Audit Report on Public Enterprise Sector Adjustment Project, Mali." Program Pension Audit Report. Operations Evaluation Department (OED). Washington, D.C.

——. 1994b. "World Bank Assistance to Privatization in Developing Countries." OED. Washington, D.C.

——. 1994c. *World Debt Tables.* (Disk.) Baltimore: Johns Hopkins University Press.

——. 1994d. *World Development Report: Infrastructure for Development.* New York: Oxford University Press.

———. 1994e. *World Tables.* (Disk.) Baltimore: Johns Hopkins University Press.

Xiao, Geng. 1991. "What Is Special about China's Enterprises." Policy Research Working Paper CH-RPS 13. World Bank, Washington, D.C.

Index

Africa, 227, 244, 246; African Management Services Company (AMSCO), 136, 147; contracts in, 112, 134–35, 143–44, 147; economic importance of SOEs in, 27, 28, 29, 30, 31

African Development Bank, 147

Aid and assistance, 14, 19, 100, 125, 145, 147, 177, 185, 221, 228, 259, 260, 261; decline in, 178, 184, 186; effect on SOE performance or reform of, 17, 183, 185, 186

Allende, Salvador, 165, 179, 180, 194, 195, 222, 227

Aquino, Corazon, 199, 219, 227

Arbitration, 8, 9, 111, 144, 163, 169. *See also* Dispute resolution and settlement

Argentina, 20, 160; divestiture in, 30, 243, 244, 245; regulatory contracts in, 158, 160, 161–62, 163, 165, 166, 167, 249; telecommunications in, 9, 155, 156

Arrears, 82, 83, 85, 98, 99, 100, 111, 126, 128, 256, 261

Asia, 27, 28, 29, 30, 32, 41, 90, 112. *See also by country name*

Auctions, 110, 140, 157, 158, 169. *See also* Bidding, competitive

Autonomy, managerial, 5, 7, 22, 66, 74, 94, 95, 125, 127, 130, 131, 141, 143, 150, 164, 189, 190, 238, 255, 256

Bangladesh, 1, 38

Banks, 5, 18, 47, 88, 101; privatization of, 5, 88, 89, 92, 99, 101, 195, 239, 243; state-owned, 47, 65, 69, 86, 87, 89, 90, 92, 99, 101, 243, 255

Barriers to entry, 17, 18, 77, 88, 260

Bidding, competitive, 8, 9, 20, 21, 72, 98, 140, 158, 162

Bonuses, 7, 124, 125, 130, 131, 133

Brazil, 41

Burden of state-owned enterprises, 19, 42, 43, 46, 48, 49, 75, 86, 183, 238; contribution to budget, 42, 43. *See also* Savings-investment (S-I) deficit

Capital, 20, 30

Capital markets, 87, 101

Capital transfers, 23, 36, 42, 45, 52, 82, 83, 84, 97, 98, 255

Central Europe, 46, 64, 65, 86. *See also* Eastern Europe

Chile, 3, 4, 9, 38, 39, 57, 84, 88, 97, 101, 177, 214, 215, 217, 228, 239, 254; credibility of government in, 205, 207, 210–11, 224, 228, 236; divestiture in, 69, 70, 73, 80, 92, 93, 103, 243, 248; performance of SOEs in, 58, 60, 61, 63, 64, 77; political desirability of SOE reform in, 11, 179, 218; political feasibility of SOE reform in, 12, 192, 194–97, 221–22; regulatory contracts in, 167, 169, 249

China, 3, 64, 65, 66, 74, 81, 86, 92, 100, 237, 255; credibility of government in, 187, 188–90; divestiture in, 71; performance of SOEs in, 4, 65–66, 73, 75, 76; political desirability of SOE reform in, 214, 224, 226; political feasibility of SOE reform in, 200, 202; performance contracts in, 256

Commitment of government, 6, 7, 8, 9, 19, 21, 24, 36, 108, 109, 111, 113, 128–30, 145–51, 154, 156, 161, 163–68, 171, 204, 224, 235, 238, 241, 243, 245, 250, 251, 253, 254, 256

Compensation: promises of, 12; severance pay, 191, 193, 196, 198, 211–12, 213, 248; to reform losers, 10, 176, 194–95, 197, 199, 201, 203, 204, 214, 215, 221–22, 223, 228, 235, 245

Competition, 3, 4, 8, 9, 23, 55, 67, 76, 80, 85, 87, 95, 248, 249, 256; barriers to or restrictions on, 19, 81, 177, 242, 254–55; foreign, 72, 79–81, 101, 102, 140; introducing or fostering, 5, 9, 21, 22, 39, 65, 72, 77–79, 80, 81, 84, 87, 93, 97–100, 190, 232, 238, 241, 242, 244, 249, 254–55

Competitive bidding. *See* Bidding, competitive

Compulsion, overcoming resistance through, 12, 191, 194, 197, 198, 221, 222, 235

Consumer benefit or satisfaction, 21, 38, 39, 152, 154, 156, 160, 168, 228, 238, 249

Management contracts, 8, 22, 108, 110; components of successful, 8, 148, 149, 150; defined, 6, 134
Managers: incentives, 3, 5, 7, 8, 17, 22, 36, 67, 93, 94, 108, 120, 121, 127, 128, 130, 133, 136, 137, 144, 159, 254, 255; private, 5, 6, 9, 22, 45, 108, 109, 133, 135, 143, 150, 168, 170. *See also* Government and SOEs; Autonomy, managerial
Mao Zedong, 188
Marcos, Ferdinand, 148, 166, 177, 199, 212, 213, 219
Marcos, Imelda, 148, 173
Market failure, 36, 76
Markets, 170; contestability of, 36–38; liberalization of, 69, 80, 81, 84, 97–100, 238; relaxing of barriers to, 238, 254
Mexico, 1, 3, 9, 20, 47, 60, 73, 88, 92, 95, 97, 101, 110, 121, 122, 128, 129, 152, 155, 158, 160–62, 165, 166–67, 215, 217; credibility of government in, 207, 210, 212, 214, 224, 249; divestiture in, 29, 30, 38–39, 69, 80, 245, 247; performance of SOEs in, 4, 7, 58, 60, 61, 63, 64, 77; political desirability of SOE reform in, 11, 179, 181, 182, 185, 186, 218, 227, 234; political feasibility of SOE reform in, 194, 221–22, 223, 235
Monopolies, 35, 36, 38, 40, 50, 80, 81, 84–85, 98, 101; divestiture of, 3, 9, 21, 26, 28, 68, 72, 110, 150, 167, 169, 238, 242, 248; natural, 6, 8, 20–21, 23, 108, 152, 156, 232–33, 241, 249, 250; pricing policies for, 82, 84, 129, 160; splitting off competitive portions of, 69, 80, 157, 242. *See also* Regulatory contracts; Regulatory framework

Nontariff barriers (NTBs), 98, 261

Objectives: conflicting, 36; noncommercial or social, 36, 60, 76, 100
Oil, 1, 41, 58, 76, 99, 103, 122, 124, 136, 171, 172
Overstaffing, 19, 37, 58, 84, 190, 191–93, 194, 196, 198, 218, 222, 228, 235
Ownership, 39, 45–46, 60, 64, 65, 66; private, 6, 36–37, 41, 151–53, 221, 247, 248; public-private joint ventures, 66, 134
Özal, Turgut, 220, 221, 222, 223, 225, 230

Patronage, 149, 229
Pawlak, Waldemar, 214, 221
Performance contracts, 5, 6, 7–8, 17, 22–23, 107, 112–33, 169–70, 171–73, 190, 222, 224, 238, 255–57, 259; defined, 6, 107, 171

Performance evaluation, 172, 173
Personnel policy. *See* Labor; Autonomy, managerial
Peru, 2
Philippines, 3, 9, 76, 95, 98, 101, 122, 126, 127, 141, 147, 152, 153, 155, 156, 158, 159–60, 161–62, 163, 164, 166, 167, 173, 177, 217, 227, 229, 261; credibility of government in, 211–13, 224, 236; electric utilities in, 35, 123, 124, 127, 139; performance of SOEs in, 4, 42, 58, 61, 63, 64, 75, 78; political desirability of SOE reform in, 183, 218, 219–20; political feasibility of SOE reform in, 197, 199, 221, 229
Pinochet, Augusto, 177, 179, 181, 194, 211
Poland, 3, 46, 58, 64, 65, 81, 86, 89, 91, 100, 134, 177, 217, 254; credibility of government in, 205, 214–15, 224; divestiture, 30, 71, 74; performance of SOEs in, 4; political desirability of SOE reform in, 187–88, 221; political feasibility of SOE reform in, 200, 201, 221, 223–24
Policy reversal, 13, 17, 19, 70, 80, 81, 99, 166, 213, 229, 236, 243. *See also* Credibility
Political costs, 10, 12, 16, 23, 129, 145, 149, 175, 178, 181, 205, 218, 219, 253, 257
Pollution, 2, 41
Preferences, purchasing or bidding, 85, 98
Price caps, 159–61, 249
Price controls and regulations, 9, 21, 35, 36, 42, 60, 81, 83, 85, 98, 110, 116, 125, 141, 144, 158, 159–62, 219, 249; deregulation or liberalization of, 58, 60, 65, 77, 80, 97, 98, 99, 100, 219, 224, 242
Private sector growth, 19, 32, 38, 46, 68, 71, 73–75
Privatization, 2, 9, 12, 21, 41. *See also* Divestiture
Productivity, 4, 8, 38–39, 42, 51, 57, 58, 60, 61, 65–66, 70, 75, 86, 101, 109, 123, 130, 131, 136–39, 148, 152, 153, 155, 156, 160, 162, 167, 184, 190, 249, 252; labor, 9, 113, 115, 117–18, 130, 139, 153, 156; total factor (TFP), 7, 57, 61, 66, 76, 101, 102, 113, 115, 118, 126, 153, 171, 172
Profitability, 8; private, 52, 85, 204; public, 42, 58, 123–24, 173, 184, 252

Railroads, 97, 99, 150, 198, 249; in Chile, 84, 103, 196; in the Philippines, 139, 140, 141, 143, 144, 148, 173
Rate of return, 152, 155, 156, 158, 159, 163, 165, 171, 248–51; on assets (ROA), 7, 113, 161; guaranteed, 204; regulation of, 159–60
Rawlings, Jerry, 212, 219

344

The complete backlist of publications from the World Bank is shown in the annual *Index of Publications*, which contains an alphabetical title list and indexes of subjects, authors, and countries and regions. The latest edition is available free of charge from the Distribution Unit, Office of the Publisher, The World Bank, 1818 H Street, N.W., Washington, D.C. 20433, or from Publications, The World Bank, 66, avenue d'Iéna, 75116 Paris, France.